Delicate Pastry

60 Recipes for Step-by-Step Learning

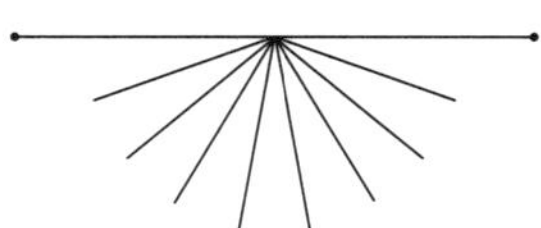

Delicate Pastry

60 Recipes for Step-by-Step Learning

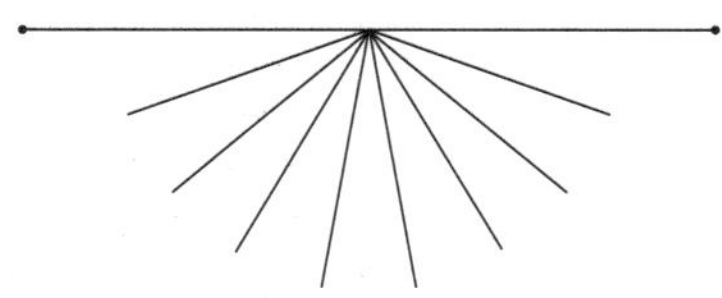

NINA MÉTAYER

PHOTOGRAPHY MATHIEU SALOMÉ
FOOD STYLING SARAH VASSEGHI

GRUB STREET • LONDON

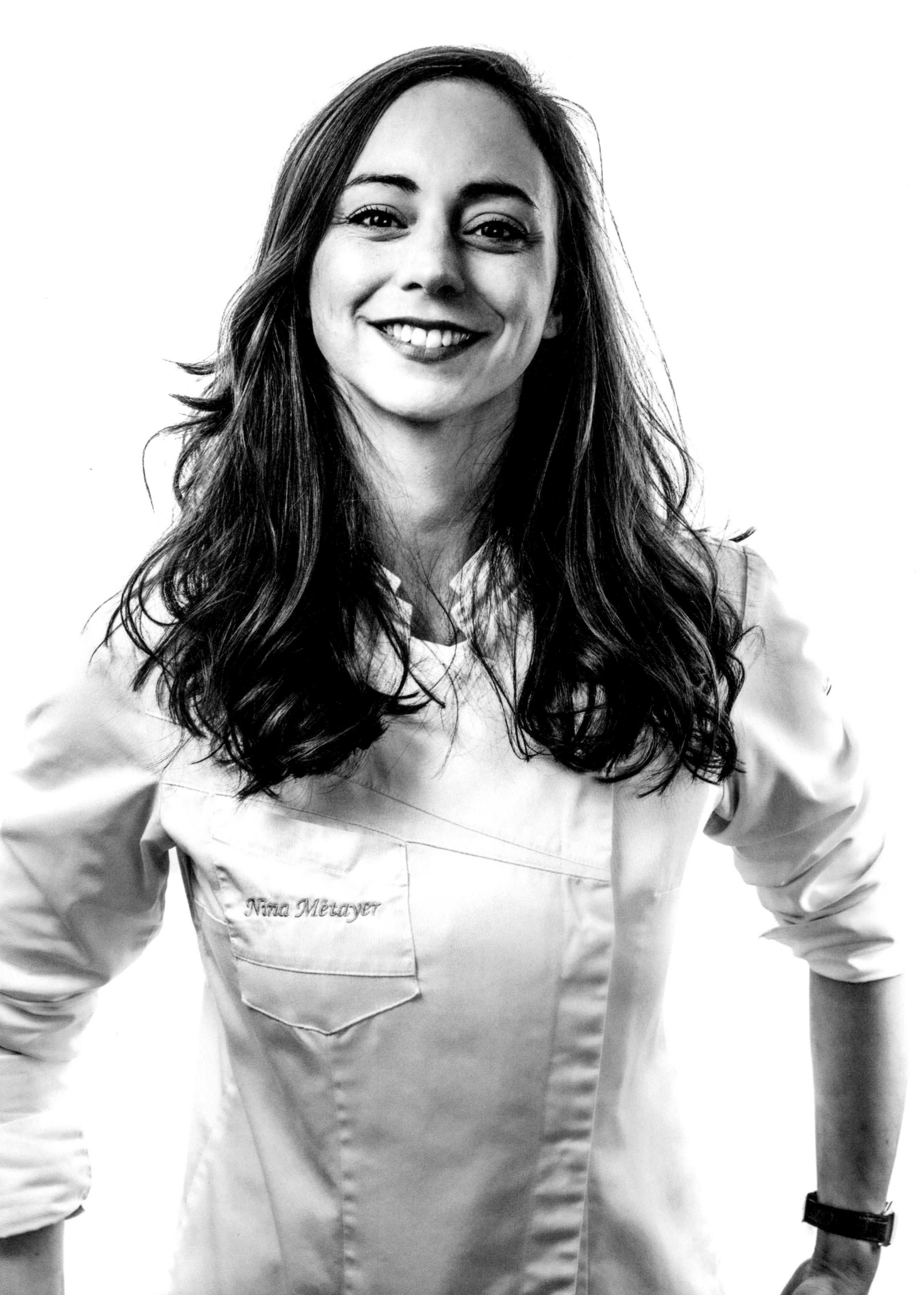
Nina Métayer

Foreword

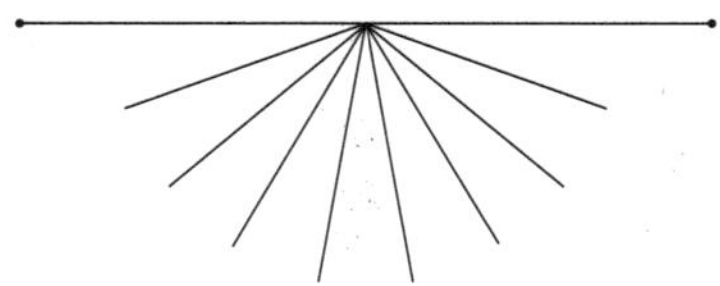

For me, cakes and pastries taste of the joy that comes from togetherness. A beautiful cake is ultimately one that tastes heavenly and is fun to make. This is the common thread running through this book and the recipes I share with you, from breakfast to festive desserts, for all those moments in the day that call for a little indulgence. Like love, cakes and pastries are even more delicious when shared.

This book introduces the basics and shares my recipes for simple and more complex creations. My hope is that it will serve both aspiring bakers with a love of good things and more experienced ones who are keen to take on more ambitious projects.

As some recipes are the unique outcome of my creative process, certain tools may occasionally be specific to them; this is an integral part of my creative vision, especially when it comes to moulds. I'll show you how to create on your own. Above all, feel free. You can choose to reproduce the recipes exactly or let them serve as an inspiration for you. I also recommend allowing your own creativity and sensitivity to guide the way you interpret them. Nothing will give me greater pleasure than discovering your creations on social media.

The precise techniques are there so that you can experience the joy that comes with making things yourself. Seeing them come to life in the sparkling eyes of the recipient is the pleasure you get from devoting your efforts to others.

I look forward to seeing you on my website:

ninametayer.com

I'll be uploading more information, tips, messages and videos
from time to time.

Nina Métayer

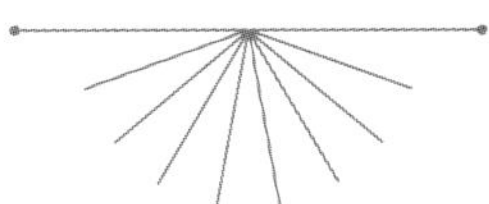

The creative process

While flavour is, naturally, central to a recipe, I always need my creations to have meaning too, either to tell a story or express a commitment, and sometimes both.

I am stirred by the memory of beloved flavours from my childhood, just as Proust was by madeleines. When devising a new dessert, my sensory palette includes the taste of my grandmother's cherry clafoutis, the smell of caramelised fruit in homemade tarts, the flavour of the local butter from my region, the texture of raw pastry, the sensation of melted chocolate, the juiciness of cherries freshly picked from the tree... These formative experiences engage with who I am today to inspire my investigation and contribute to new flavour combinations.

What I share is more than just the story behind flavours; it also involves commitment, feeling and emotion. For Valentine's Day in 2018, for instance, I was inspired by the beauty of a bouquet of roses. In 2019, however, I went against the grain and added a touch of humour by creating a game of marbles. This year, with You + Me, I'm celebrating all forms of love across the gender divide. My galette des rois for Three Kings' Day in 2020 paid tribute to Notre Dame in Paris and was an invitation to renewal.

Creativity means embracing failure

Whether professional or amateur, it's important to release your creative process and allow yourself to take risks. Whenever I set out to create something, I never know whether I'll be able to achieve my goal. It starts off as an often lengthy period of trying out different things and typically failing lots of times. Sometimes you have to give up on an idea altogether and go back to the drawing board. Overcoming a particular obstacle forces me to be even more creative.

This can involve changing the composition of some of the classic recipes that have been taught in schools for generations so that I can stay true to my beliefs regarding the quality and sourcing of ingredients. For example, creating the flaky puff pastry for my Renaissance galette des rois using less refined flours really required a great deal of trial and error. But I kept at it until I perfected a new, very fine texture with a delicately crumbly taste on the palate; what's more, it actually holds its shape better and keeps longer.

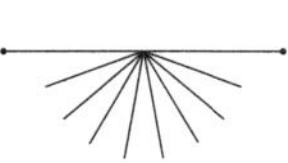

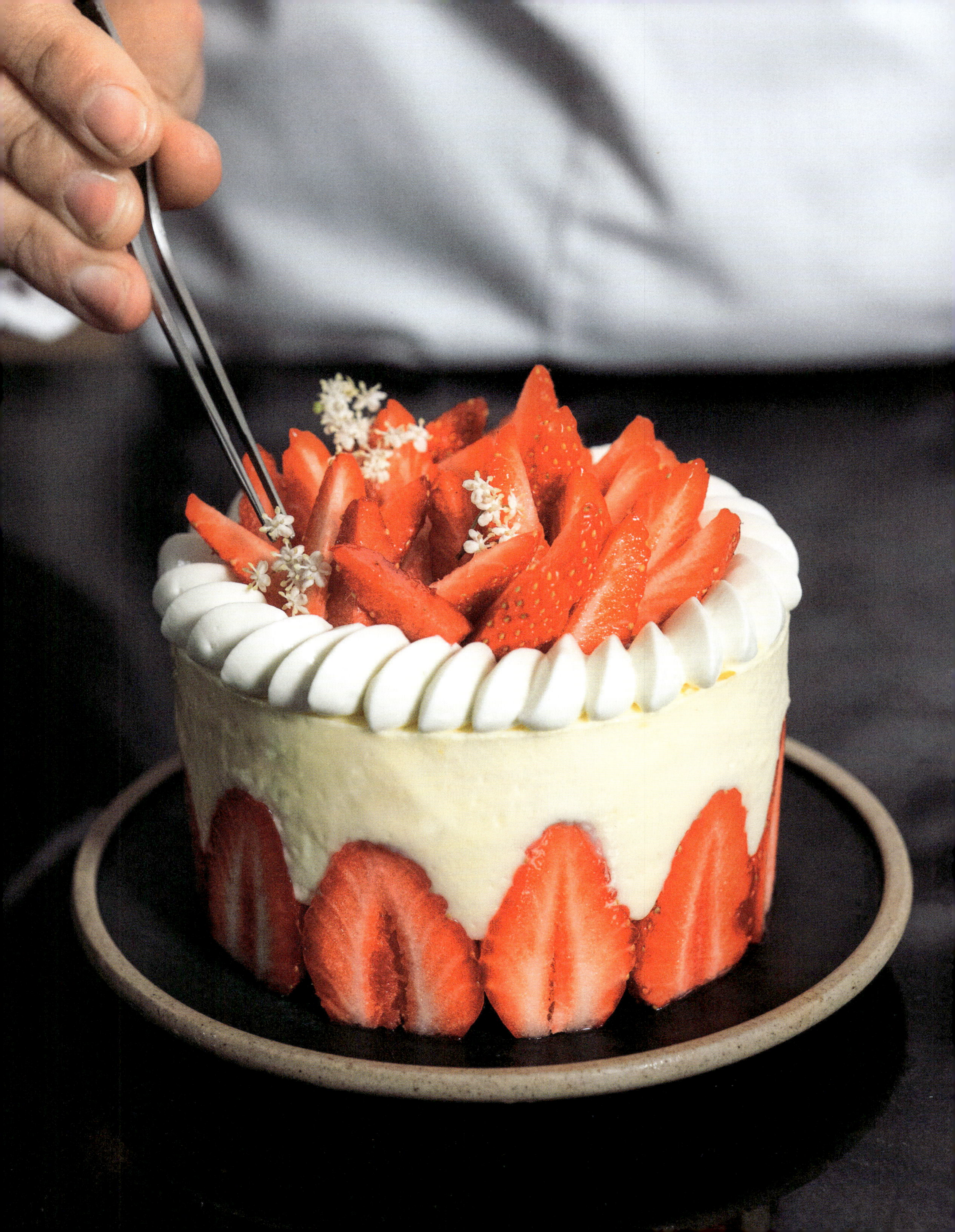

Contents

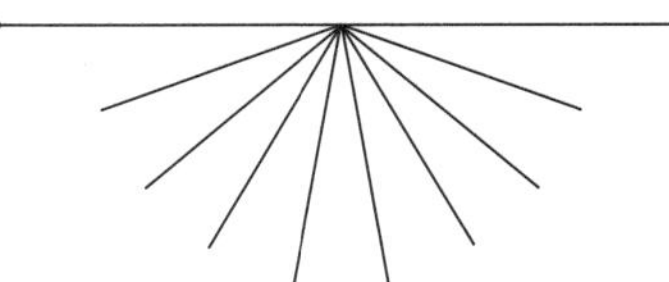

Bread and breakfast pastries

At the start of my particular journey, bread already had special significance for me. I was sixteen and was given the opportunity to go to school in Mexico for a year. On returning to France, my desire to go back there planted the seed of my project. I imagined opening my first bakery and then expanding throughout Latin America. After finishing secondary education, this aim motivated my decision to train as a baker, combining study with work placements.

Where flavour and quality are concerned, my parents were always very demanding, even with the simplest things, like a slice of buttered bread, it was always of the highest quality. Whenever we went on holiday, if they felt that the nearest bakery wasn't up to scratch, they were capable of travelling for miles to find a good artisan baker. This quest for good bread has never left me. I also became a *tourière*, a specialist in leavened and laminated dough and pastry.

I still derive the same pleasure from working with these living materials. Flour, water and salt, and butter for pastries... The quality of the ingredients is essential for the work of an artisan. There is no single recipe for the levain starter I use, just as there isn't for the bread we make with it. Temperature and humidity play their part, as do smell, touch, observation, repeating actions... Between patience and pleasure, learning takes time. You will need to put in a lot of hard work, but being able to share the pleasure of a home-made breakfast with your friends and family is well worth the effort.

Plated desserts

I relished my time working in luxury hotels and leading fine dining establishments, especially with Jean-François Piège, who passed on to me his sense of rigour, his exacting standards and his quest for excellence down to the smallest detail, even for the simplest things. Individual plated desserts offer a great deal of freedom, even if some elements are prepared in advance. It's a pleasure to create a beautiful arrangement on a plate at the last minute, while doing away with the need for storage and providing a delightful end to a good meal. You can give free rein to your creativity by playing with textures, the crispness of a tuile, the freshness of a sorbet, the tanginess of citrus segments and zest, the flavours of young shoots and herbs... When served, their beauty makes them more delectable.

I was inspired by family recipes, such as my dad's Belle-Hélène pears and my mum's spiced Christmas pears, as well as her pear and apple crumble.

Goûter, the French equivalent of afternoon tea, features prominently in my earliest memories of pastries and cakes. They include madeleines I would make after school with my friends and the galette that my grandmother and I would make on Wednesdays. From my childhood years spent in Alsace, I also remember *bredele*, the little Christmas biscuits that we used to cut out in the shape of Christmas trees, stars and little men to give to our teacher, and which we also hung on our Christmas tree.

Sharing and passing on what I can do are the driving forces behind my passion. Today, with my daughters, I'm rediscovering the joy of being and doing things together. Don't hesitate to share these precious, fun and educational times with your children, even the youngest ones. As soon as they can stand on their own two feet, they love to get involved, even if pouring means a bit of spilling at first. Choose simple recipes that are loved by young and old alike and have fun together!

These are the desserts for gatherings, such as Sunday lunches with the family. They are the sensory and emotional memories of shared moments of happiness. A *fraisier* will always be the flavour of my childhood. I'm also particularly fond of the Saint-Honoré I made for my grandfather Philippe's 80th birthday. It was the first big and beautiful cake I'd made for my family, and they still talk about it to this day. I had weighed out the ingredients and made a few of the components before leaving for La Rochelle. I was apprehensive when I got there, but I put lots of love into the cake and the finishing touches, and I was delighted with its success!

Whether in the form of a wedding cake, delicate entremets or an elegant yule log, among others, these desserts make a statement at both traditional celebrations and major events. Their size and beauty deliver on their promise to be both spectacular and excellent. Visuals and flavours come together to leave a lasting impression on palates and minds and create a family memory of indulgence and elegance.

As a pastry chef, I love the idea that I can take part in the special moments of a wedding, when the bride and groom make their entrance at the reception and later cut the cake I made for them, even when I'm not physically present.

This section contains a few recipes that I often use. Their great precision and detail allow you to adapt them at will and give free rein to your imagination. And to unleash your creativity, I've added instructions for making your own silicone moulds.

Some of the recipes and most of the techniques shown are also accompanied by a step-by-step guide containing captioned photographs. The numbers corresponding to the steps are also indicated in brackets on the recipe pages.

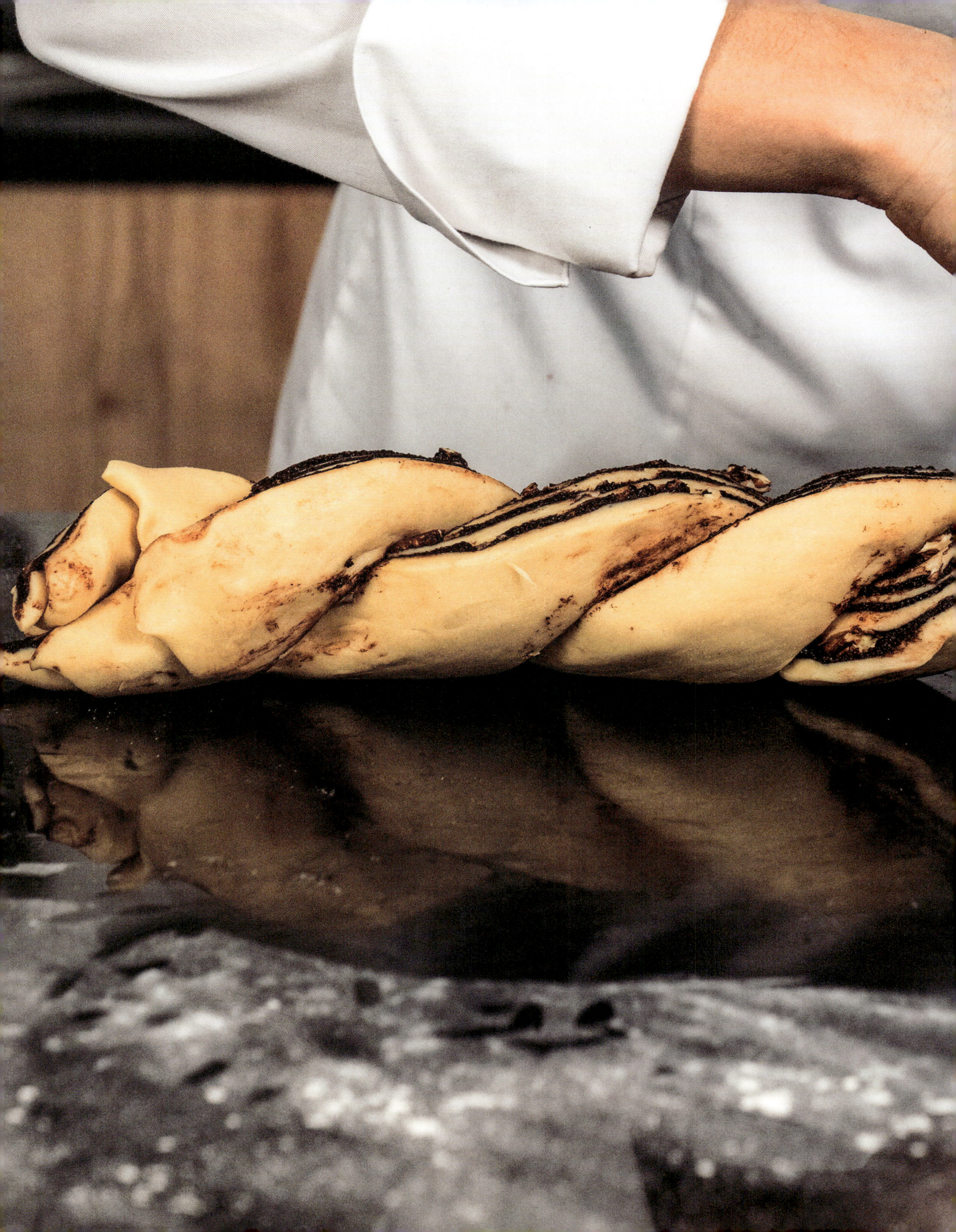

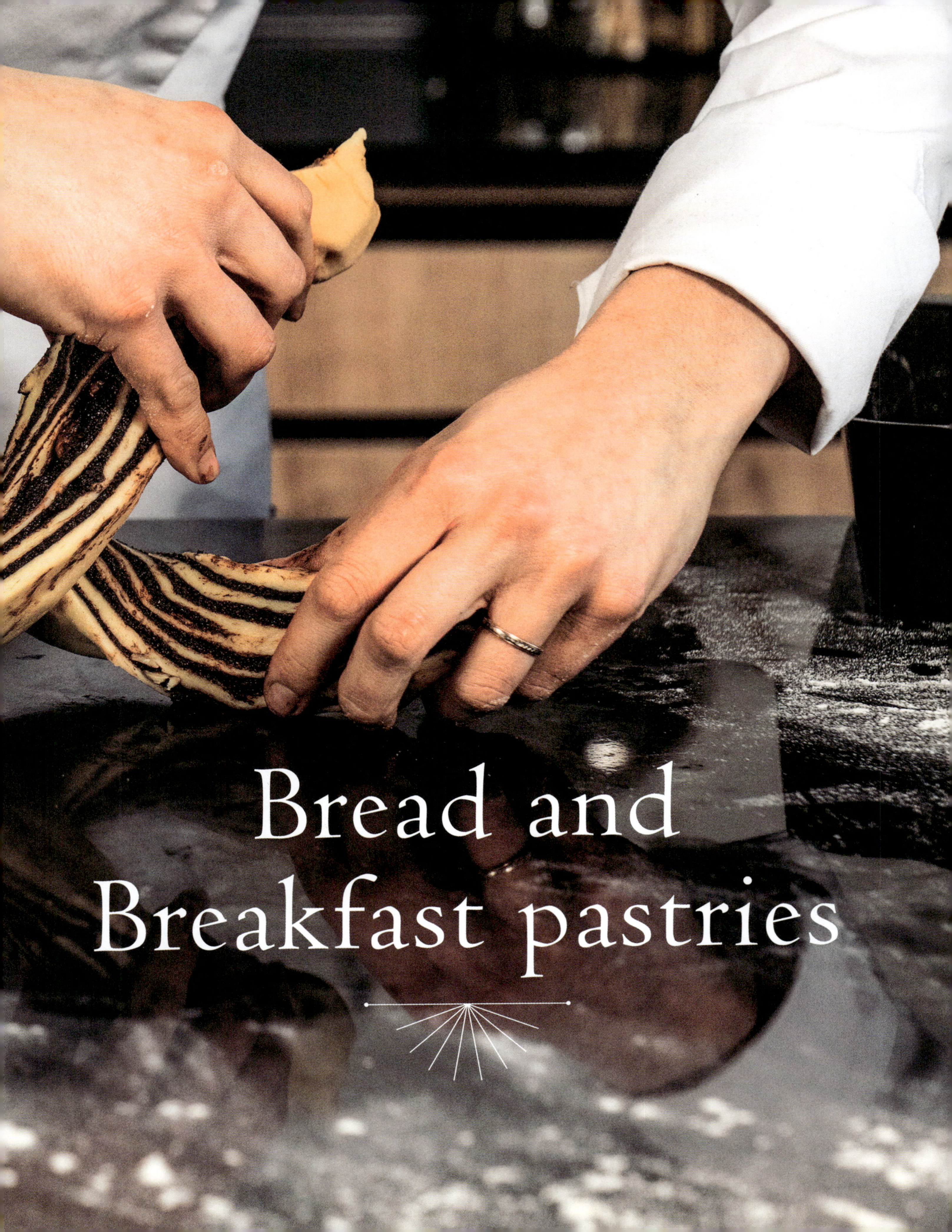
Bread and
Breakfast pastries

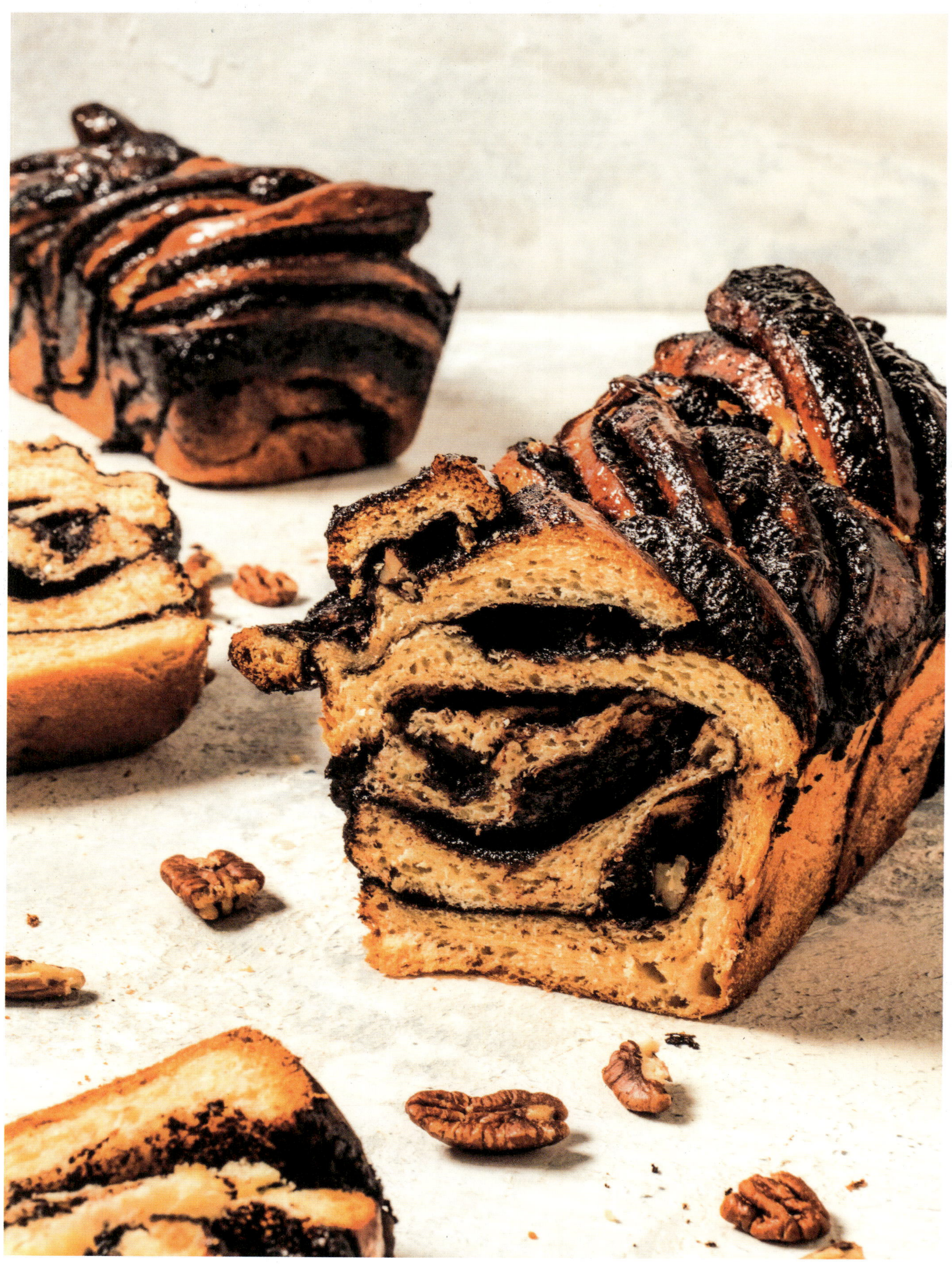

Serves 8	Preparation	Resting	Proving	Baking
	1 hour	12 hours	30 minutes	35 minutes

Pecan babka

Brioche dough

25 g fresh yeast
35 g milk
325 g T45 (soft white) flour
255 g T55 (plain) flour
10 g salt
25 g wildflower honey
300 g eggs
125 g unsalted butter, cold
10 g muscovado sugar
75 g light brown soft sugar

Filling

100 g unsalted butter
125 g light brown soft sugar
40 g cocoa powder
100 g chopped pecan nuts

Egg wash

1 egg
1 pinch of salt

Dissolve the yeast in the milk. In a stand mixer fitted with a dough hook, mix the flour, salt, honey, eggs and milk and yeast mixture for 5 minutes to form a dough. Then knead until the dough pulls away from the sides of the bowl. Add the cold butter in small pieces and both types of sugar. Continue to knead on speed 1 for about 30 minutes, until the dough is very elastic and its gluten structure is well developed. Rest the dough in the fridge for 12 hours.

Roll out the brioche dough to a 4-mm thickness (1).

Soften the butter by bringing it to room temperature. Mix it with the sugar and cocoa (2). Using an angled palette knife, spread this filling over the brioche sheet (3). Sprinkle with chopped pecans. Roll the dough into a log (4). Cut the log in half lengthways (5) and twist both strips together (6). Place the brioche in a loaf tin and prove at about 28°C for 30 minutes.

Make an egg wash by beating the egg with the salt and brush it over the brioche (7). Bake at 160°C for about 35 minutes (8). Turn out the brioche as soon as it comes out of the oven.

'You can add 80 g of milk levain to the brioche dough to make it softer for longer. Take 25 g of the sourdough mother and feed it with 25 g of t55 (plain) flour and 25 g of full-fat milk. Allow the levain to stand for 4 hours at room temperature before making the brioche.'

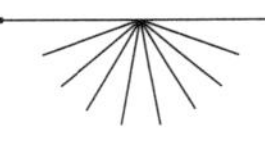

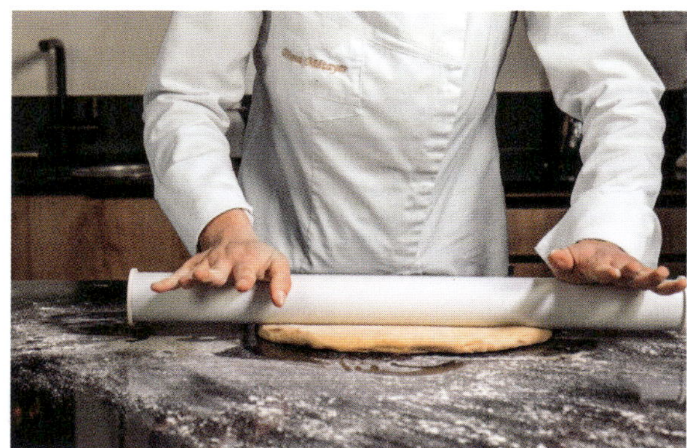

1.

Roll out the brioche dough to a 4-mm thickness.

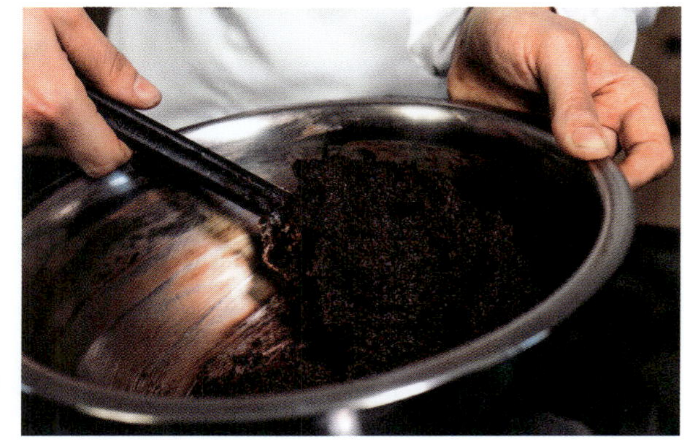

2.

To make the filling: soften the butter and mix it with the sugar and cocoa.

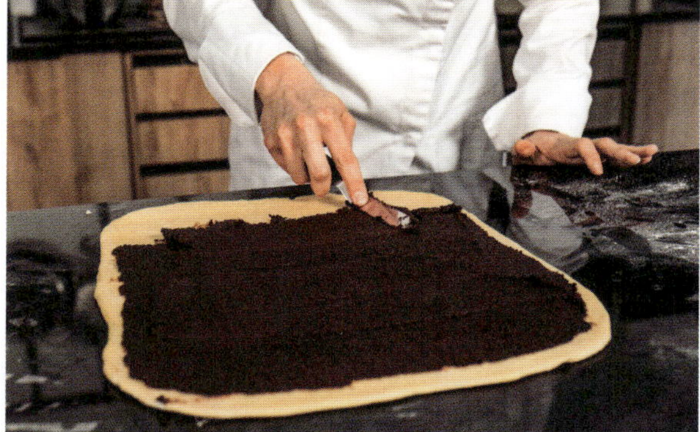

3.

Using an angled palette knife, spread the filling mixture over the brioche sheet.

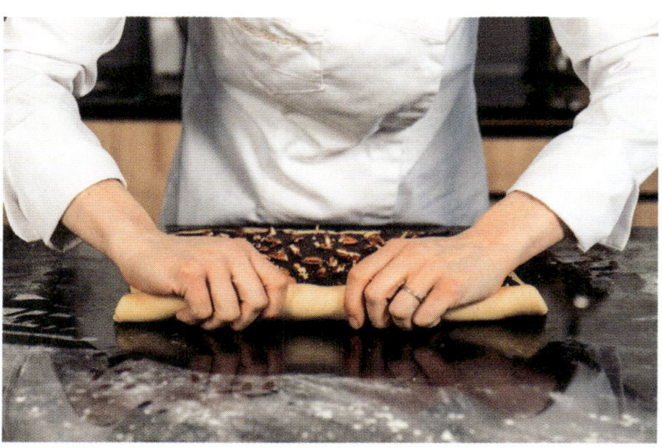

4.

Sprinkle with chopped pecans. Roll the dough into a log.

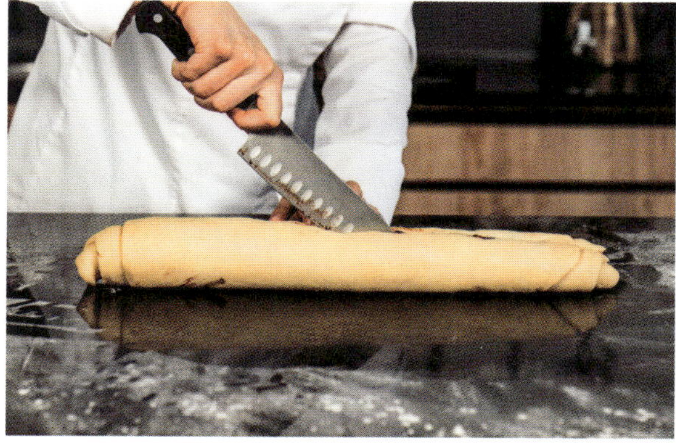

5.

Cut the log in half lengthways.

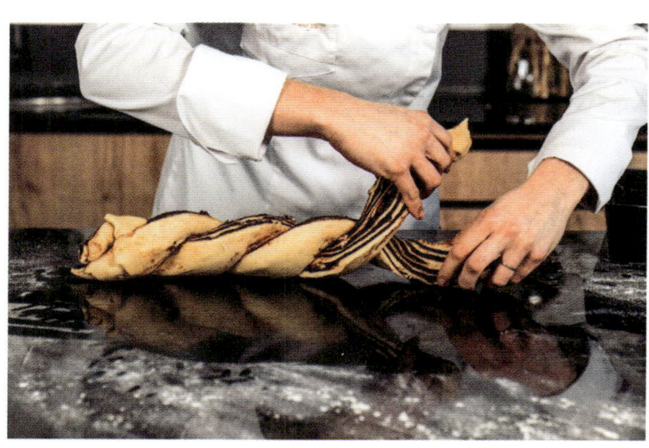

6.

Twist both strips together.

Place in a loaf tin and prove at about 28°C for 30 minutes. Brush with egg wash.
Bake at 160°C for about 35 minutes.

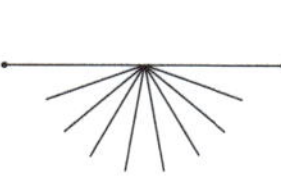

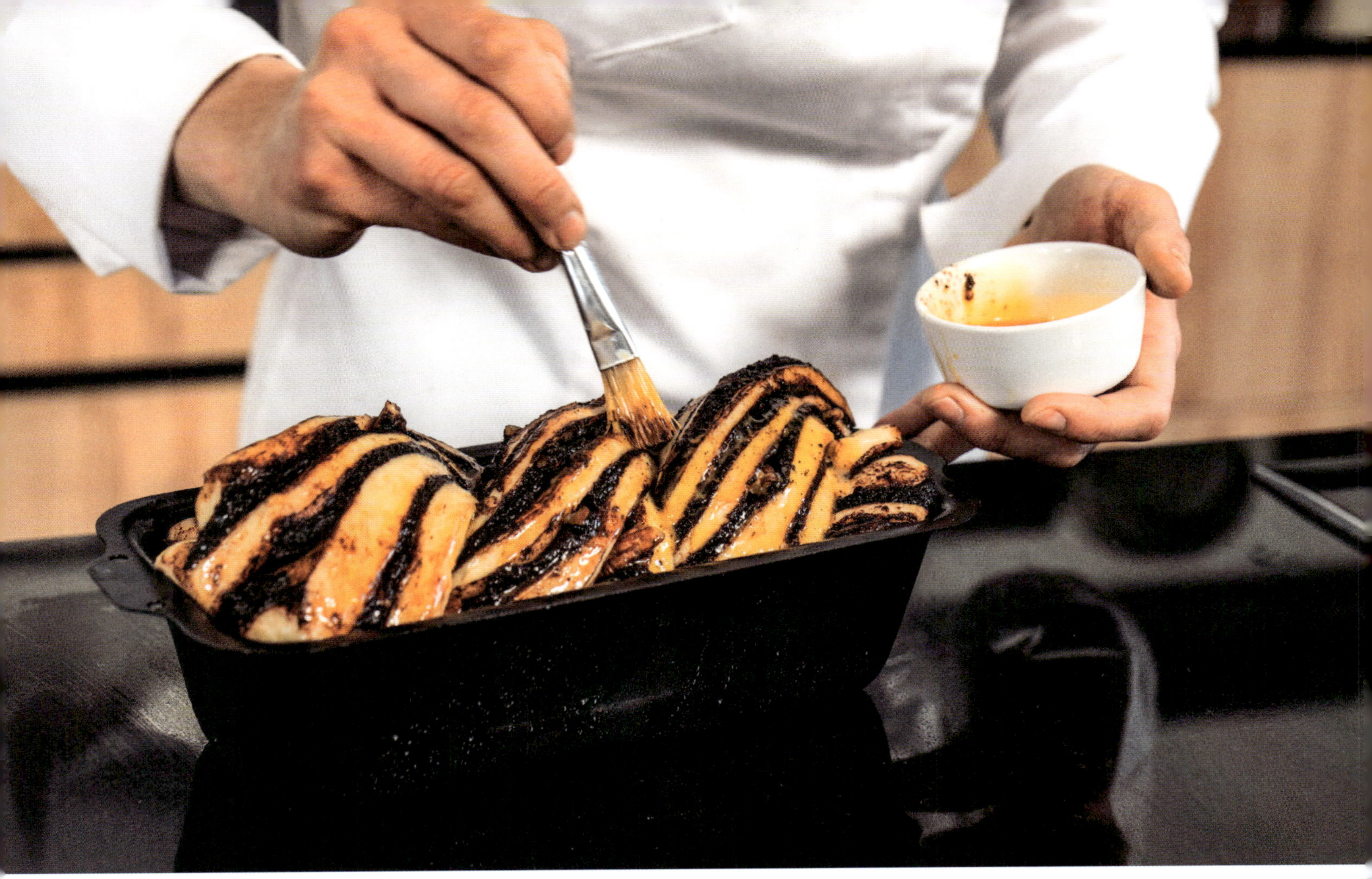

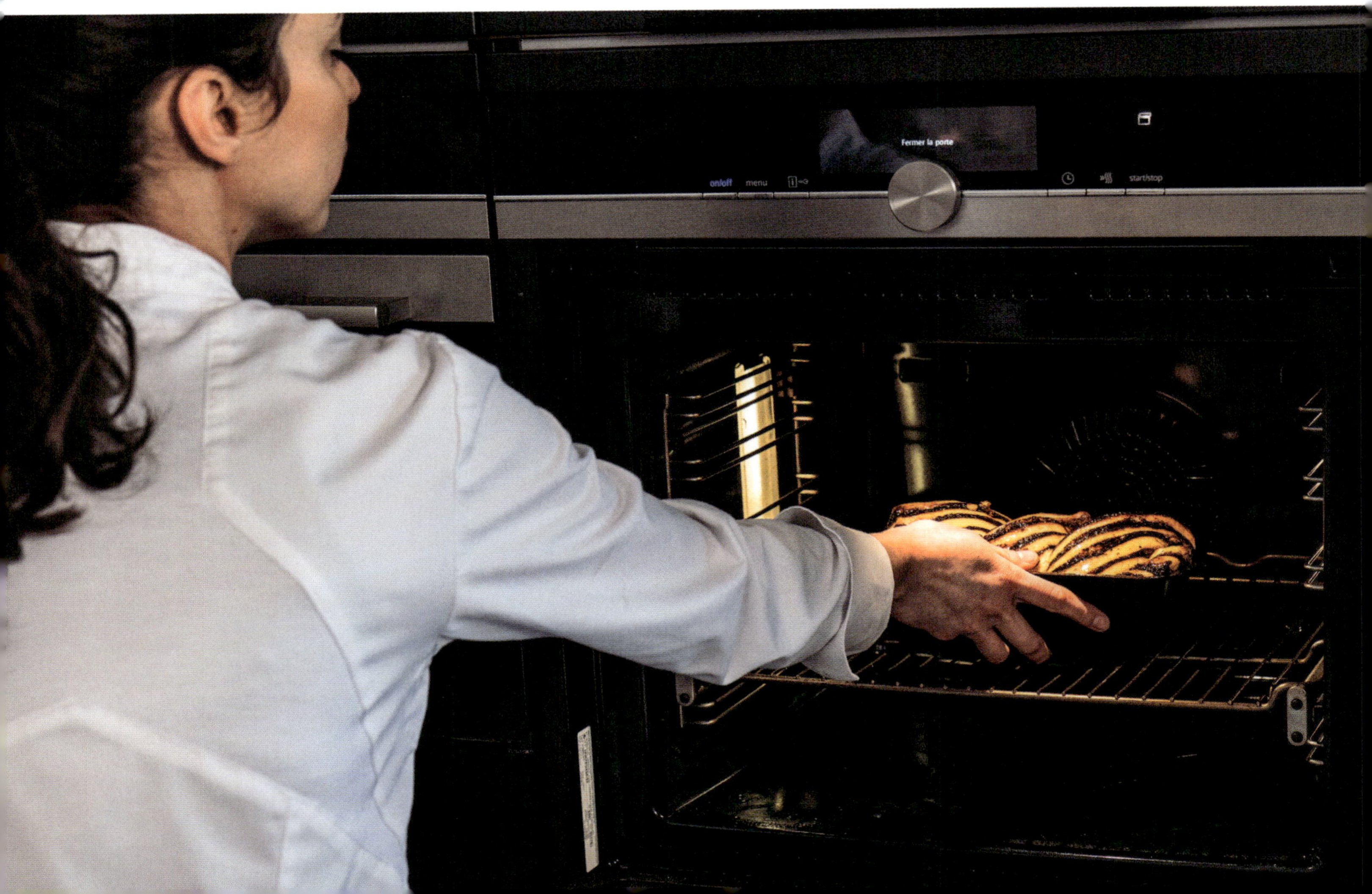

Fermer la porte
on/off   menu   start/stop

Makes 4 x 500-g loaves

Preparation	Resting	Proving	Baking
30 minutes	12 hours	3 hours	1 hour 30 minutes

Praline and hazelnut bread

300 g levain
(see recipe on p. 194)
100 g hazelnuts
500 g T80 (stoneground white) flour
300 g T110 (semi-wholemeal) flour
200 g T150 (wholemeal) flour
700 g water
23 g salt
150 g cocoa nib praline
(see recipe on p. 208)

To make the levain, feed the sourdough mother 6 hours before use. To do this, add 100 g of T80 flour and 100 g of water to 100 g of sourdough mother and allow to ferment for 6 hours at room temperature.

Roast the hazelnuts in the oven at 140°C for 45 minutes and coarsely chop them.

Mix the T110 , T150 and T80 flours with the water, salt and levain (1). Rest the dough for 2 hours, then stretch and fold the dough (2) and allow it to rest for a further 2 hours. Stretch and fold the dough again and then repeat the operation a third time (3).

Add the chopped hazelnuts and the homemade cocoa nib praline. Mix well.

Shape 500-g portions of the dough into balls (4). Prove the loaves for 3 hours at room temperature in large containers, wrapped in a cloth (5).

Preheat the oven to 250°C.

Score the top of each loaf with a box cutter (6).

When the oven is hot, splash the inside with the equivalent of a bowl of water and then add the loaves. Lower the oven temperature to 230°C and bake for 45 minutes.

Transfer to a rack and allow to cool before serving.

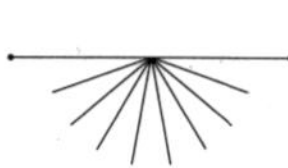

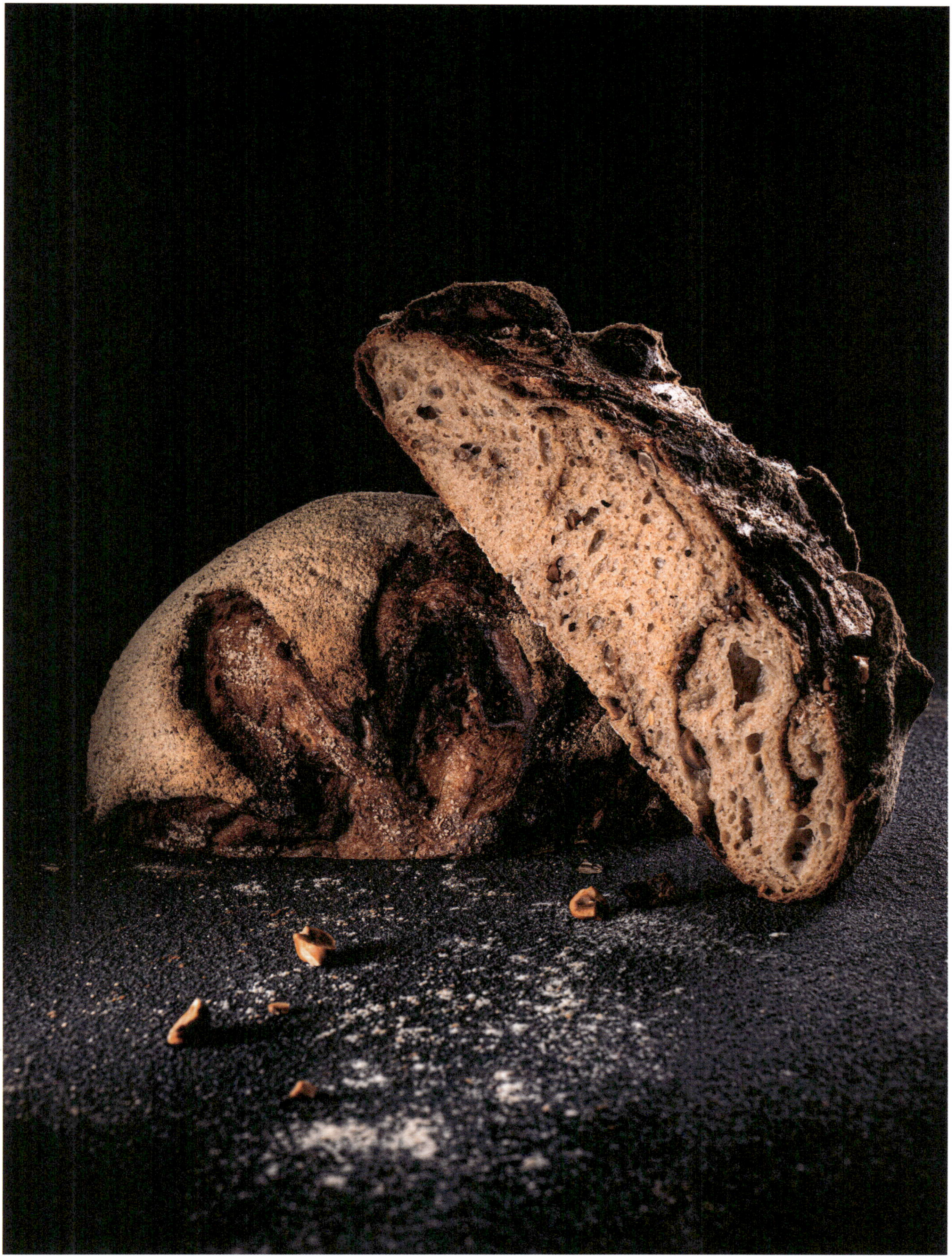

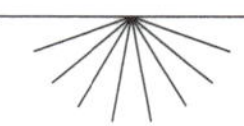

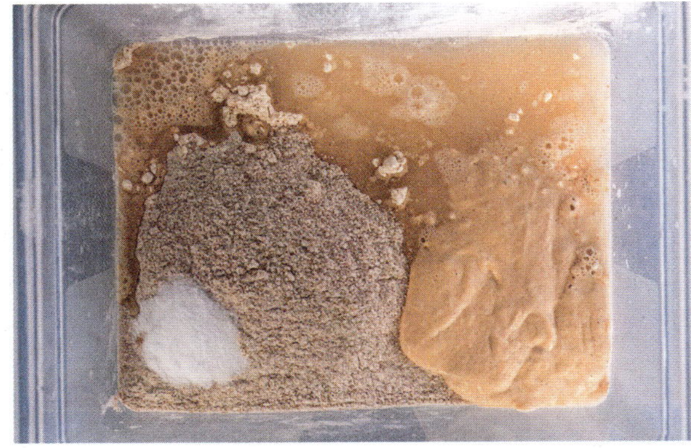

1.

Mix the flours, water, salt and levain.

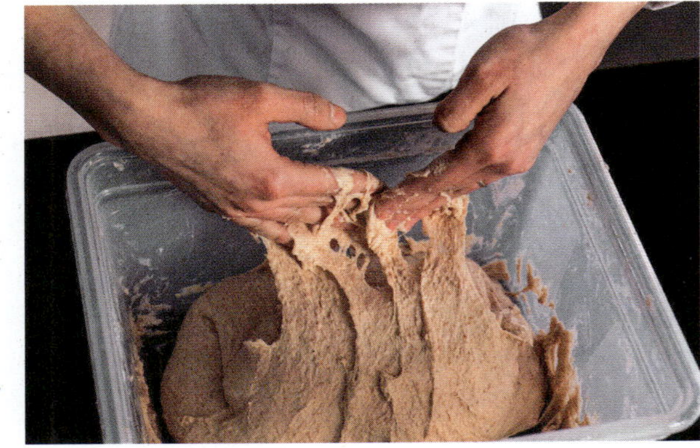

2.

Rest the dough for 2 hours, then stretch and fold.

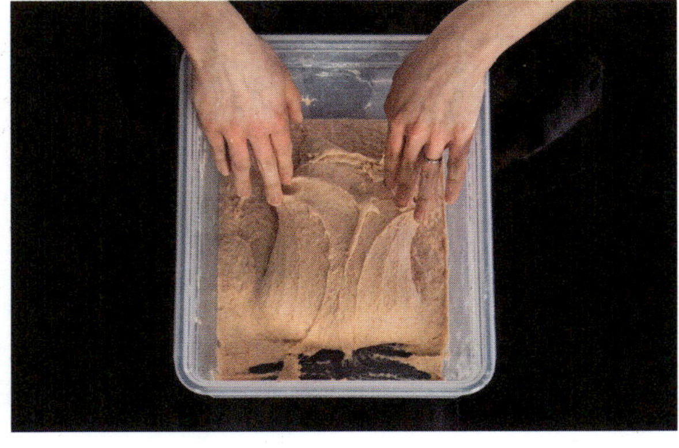

3.

Allow to rest for a further 2 hours and stretch and fold again, then repeat the operation a third time.

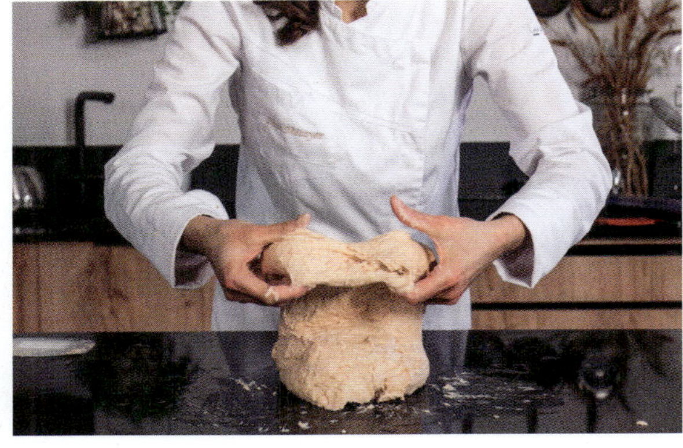

4.

Add the chopped hazelnuts and the homemade cocoa nib praline. Mix well. Shape 500-g portions of the dough into balls.

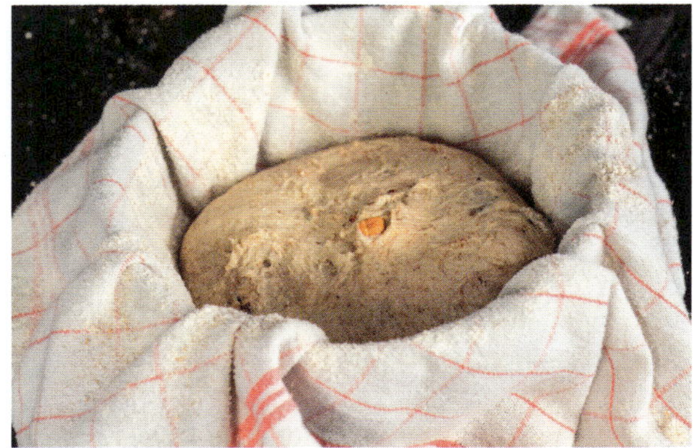

5.

Prove the loaves for 3 hours at room temperature in large containers, wrapped in a cloth.

'I love this bread; I think it's my favourite. Beautiful and deliciously indulgent, it's perfect at any time of the day. Simply spread it with a little butter and rhubarb jam for breakfast, add a small piece of chocolate for afternoon tea, or enjoy it with cheese at the end of a meal.'

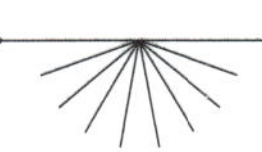

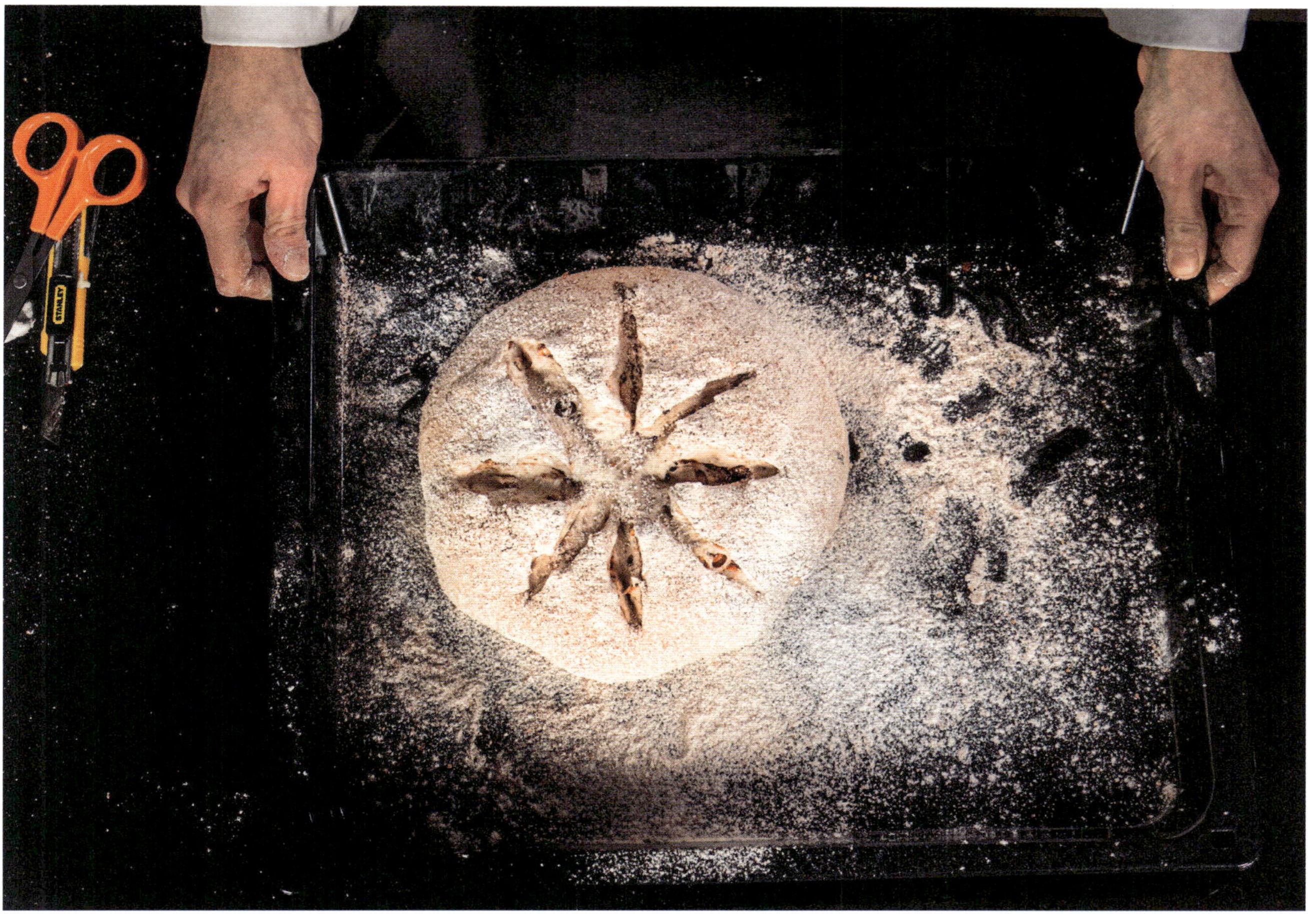

6.

Score the top of each loaf with a box cutter.

Makes 5 baguettes

Preparation	Resting	Proving	Baking
30 minutes	18 hours	2–3 hours	12 minutes

Baguette

200 g levain
(see recipe on p. 194)
400 g T80 (stoneground white)
   flour
600 g T55 (plain) flour
2 g fresh yeast
23 g salt
650 g water

To make the levain, feed the sourdough mother 6 hours before use. To do this, add 75 g of T55 flour and 75 g of water to 50 g of sourdough mother (1) - see the recipe for sourdough mother on p. 194. In a stand mixer fitted with a dough hook, mix all the ingredients and knead the dough for about 12 minutes on low speed until it develops good elasticity. This can also be done by hand: mix the ingredients (2) and knead the dough by slapping it on the work surface (3) and folding it over. Then rotate the dough 90 degrees and repeat the operation for several minutes until it develops good elasticity (4). Transfer the dough to a large container and rest it in the fridge for 12 hours.

Weigh out 350-g portions of dough and shape them into baguettes (5). Lay the baguettes on a cloth and prove them for 2–3 hours at room temperature (ideally 24°C) covered with a lid (6).

Preheat the oven to 250°C. Splash the bottom of the oven with the equivalent of a bowl of water, then score the baguettes, arrange them on baking trays and place in the oven. Lower the oven temperature to 230°C(7). Bake for about 12 minutes, adjusting the time if necessary (8).

Transfer the baguettes to a rack and allow to cool before serving.

'Always make two or three baguettes more than needed. The smell of the freshly baked, warm and crusty baguette will always make them disappear faster than you expect. If you have any left over, heat the oven to 140°C, then cut the baguette in half lengthways, rub over with a clove of garlic and cut everything into small croutons. Sprinkle the croutons with olive oil and bake for 40 minutes. Then allow them to cool before storing them in an airtight jar in a dry place. You can use them to enliven soups and salads.'

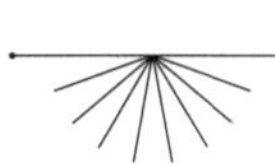

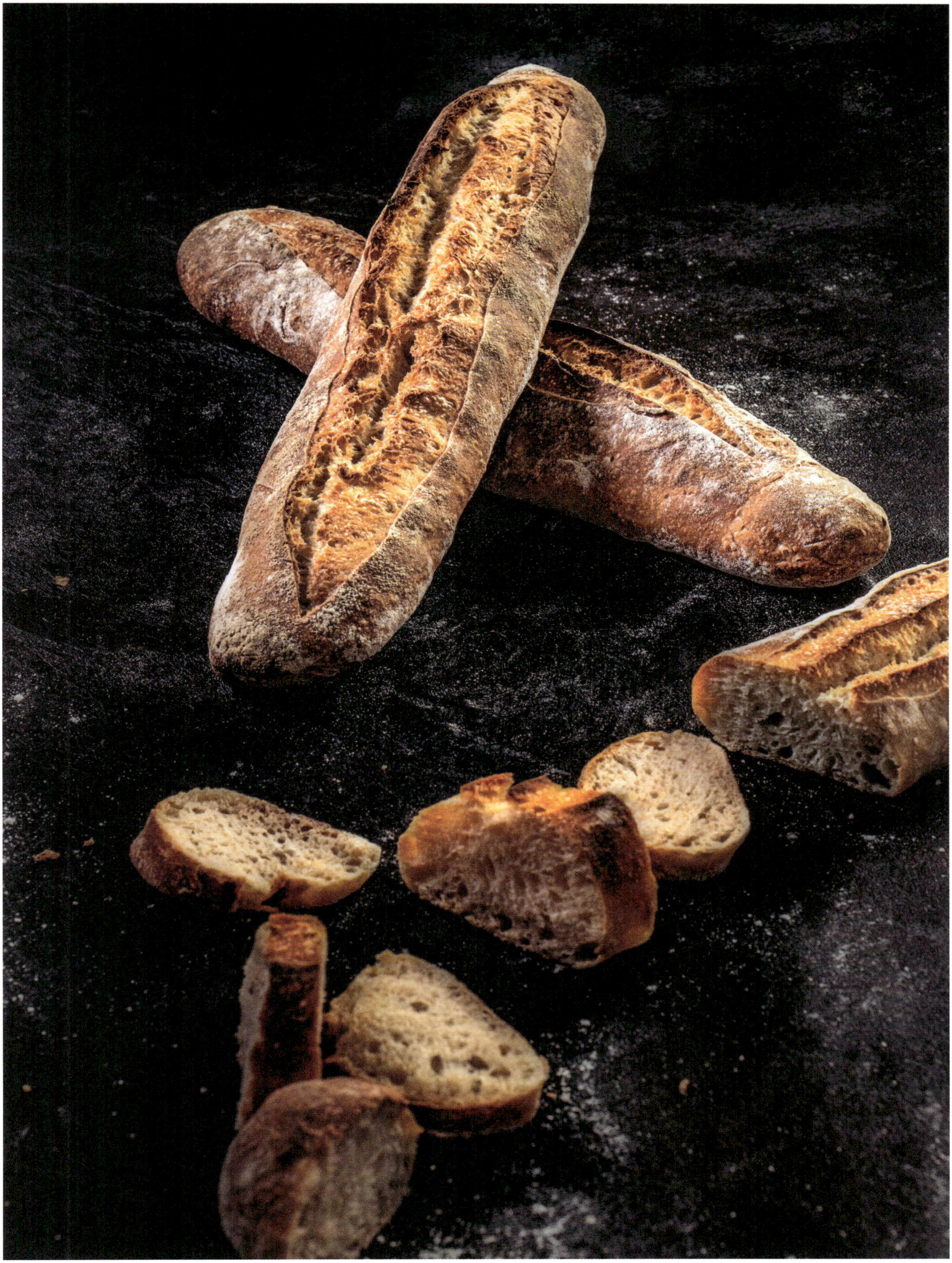

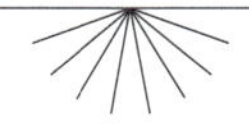

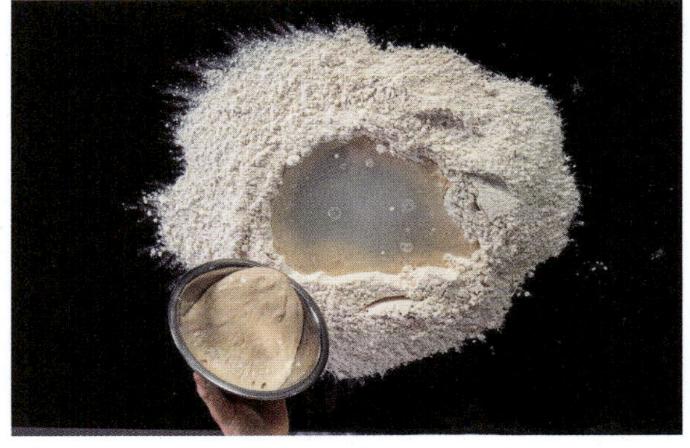

To make the levain, feed 50 g of sourdough mother with 75 g of T55 flour and 75 g of water 6 hours before kneading.

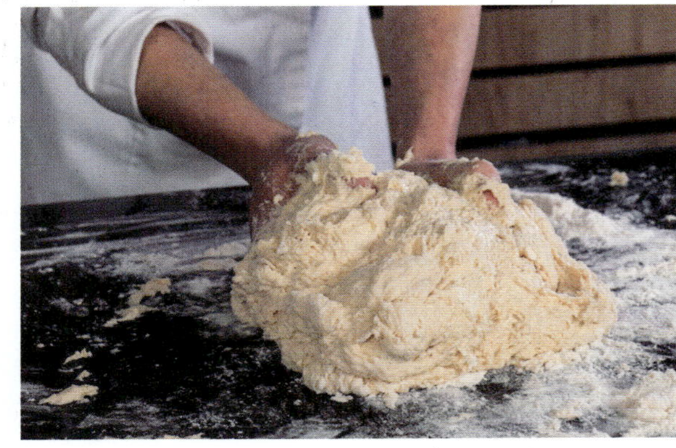

Mix the ingredients together.

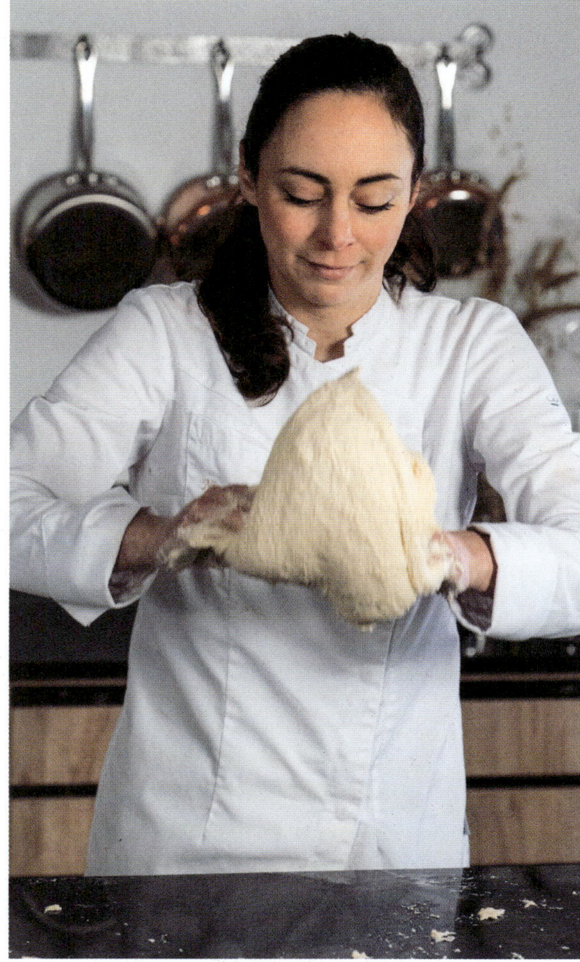

Knead the dough by slapping it on the work surface.

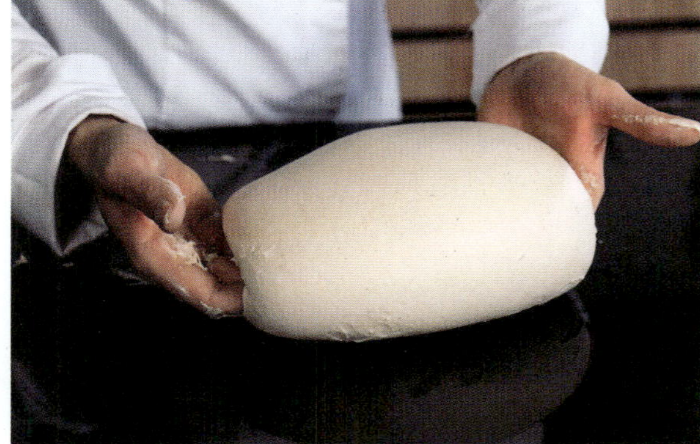

Fold the dough over and turn it 90 degrees. Repeat the operation for several minutes until it develops good elasticity. Transfer the dough to a large container and rest it in the fridge for 12 hours.

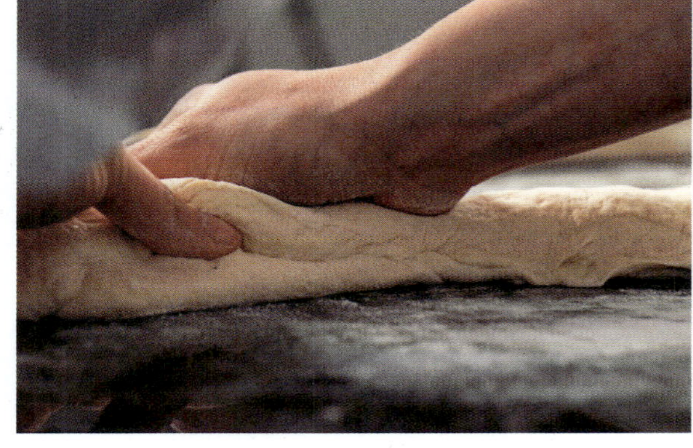

Weigh out 350-g portions of dough and shape them into baguettes.

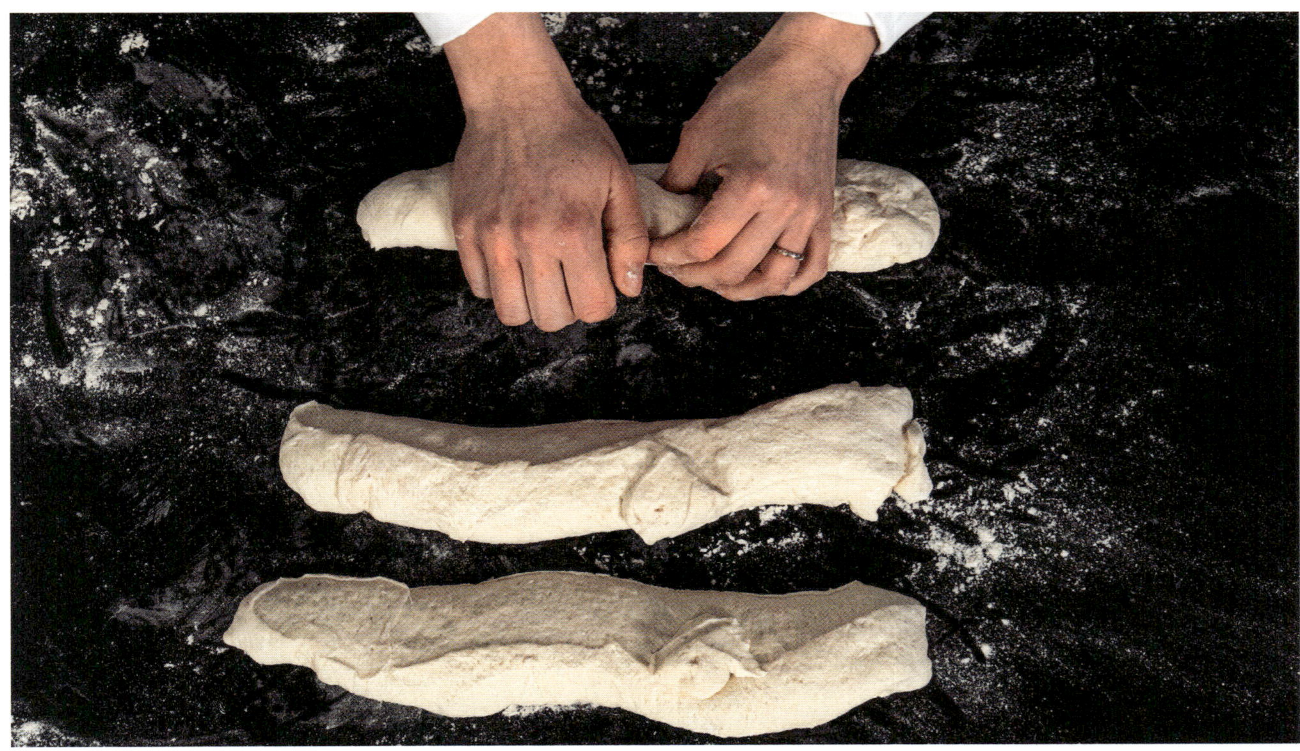

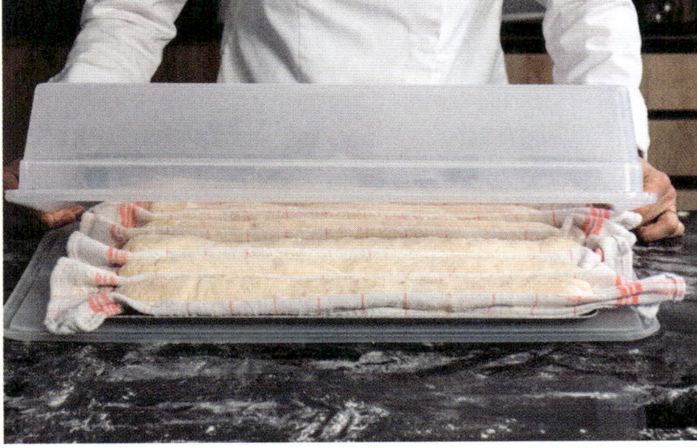

6.

Lay the baguettes on a cloth and prove them for 2—3 hours at room temperature (ideally 24°C) covered with a lid.

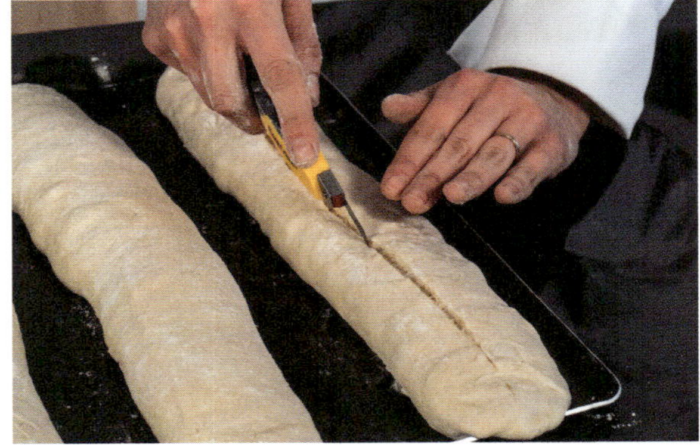

7.

Preheat the oven to 250°C. Splash the bottom of the oven with the equivalent of a bowl of water, then score the baguettes, arrange them on baking trays and place in the oven. Lower the oven temperature to 230°C.

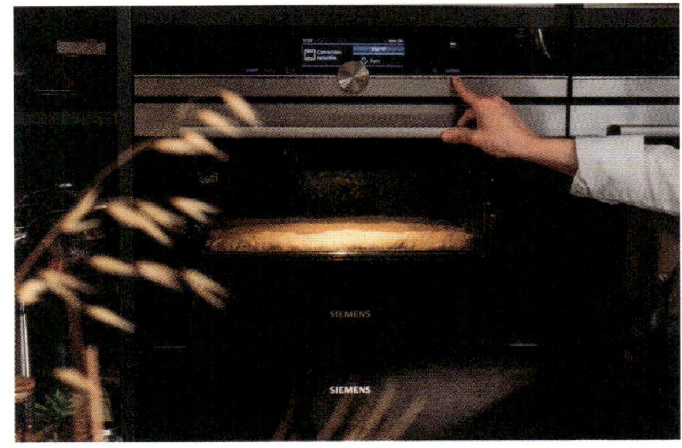

8.

Bake for about 12 minutes, adjusting the time if necessary.

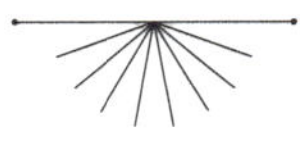

Makes 2 large brioches	**Preparation**	**Resting**	**Proving**	**Baking**
to serve 5 people	30 minutes	12 hours	2 hours	30 minutes

Brioche

30 g fresh yeast

70 g milk

650 g T45 (soft white) flour

450 g T55 (plain) flour

20 g salt

50 g honey

6 eggs

350 g unsalted butter, cold

20 g muscovado sugar

130 g light brown soft sugar

300 g milk levain

(see recipe on p. 195)

Egg wash

1 egg

2 g salt

Dissolve the yeast in the milk.

In a stand mixer fitted with a dough hook (or by hand), mix the flour, salt, honey, eggs and milk and yeast mixture for 5 minutes to form a dough (1).

Knead the dough until it pulls away from the bowl or becomes smooth (2). Add the cold butter in small pieces and both types of sugar (3). Knead again on speed 1 for about 30 minutes, until the dough is very elastic and its gluten structure is well developed (4).

Rest the dough in the fridge for 12 hours.

Shape the dough into two large brioches (5) and prove them at 28°C for about 2 hours (6). Place them in 18-cm diameter moulds. Brush the brioches with egg wash and bake them at 160 °C for 30 minutes (7). Take them out of the oven and wait 5 minutes before turning them out of the moulds.

'I recommend making large batches of brioches. Then cut them into thick slices and keep them in the freezer. You will love the feeling of toasting brioche slices in the oven or a toaster on a Sunday morning a few weeks later. Spread them with lots of butter, homemade praline or jam. You can even make delicious French toast on a rainy day when friends drop by unexpectedly for afternoon tea.'

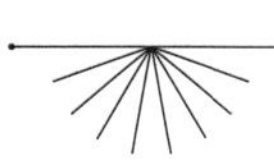

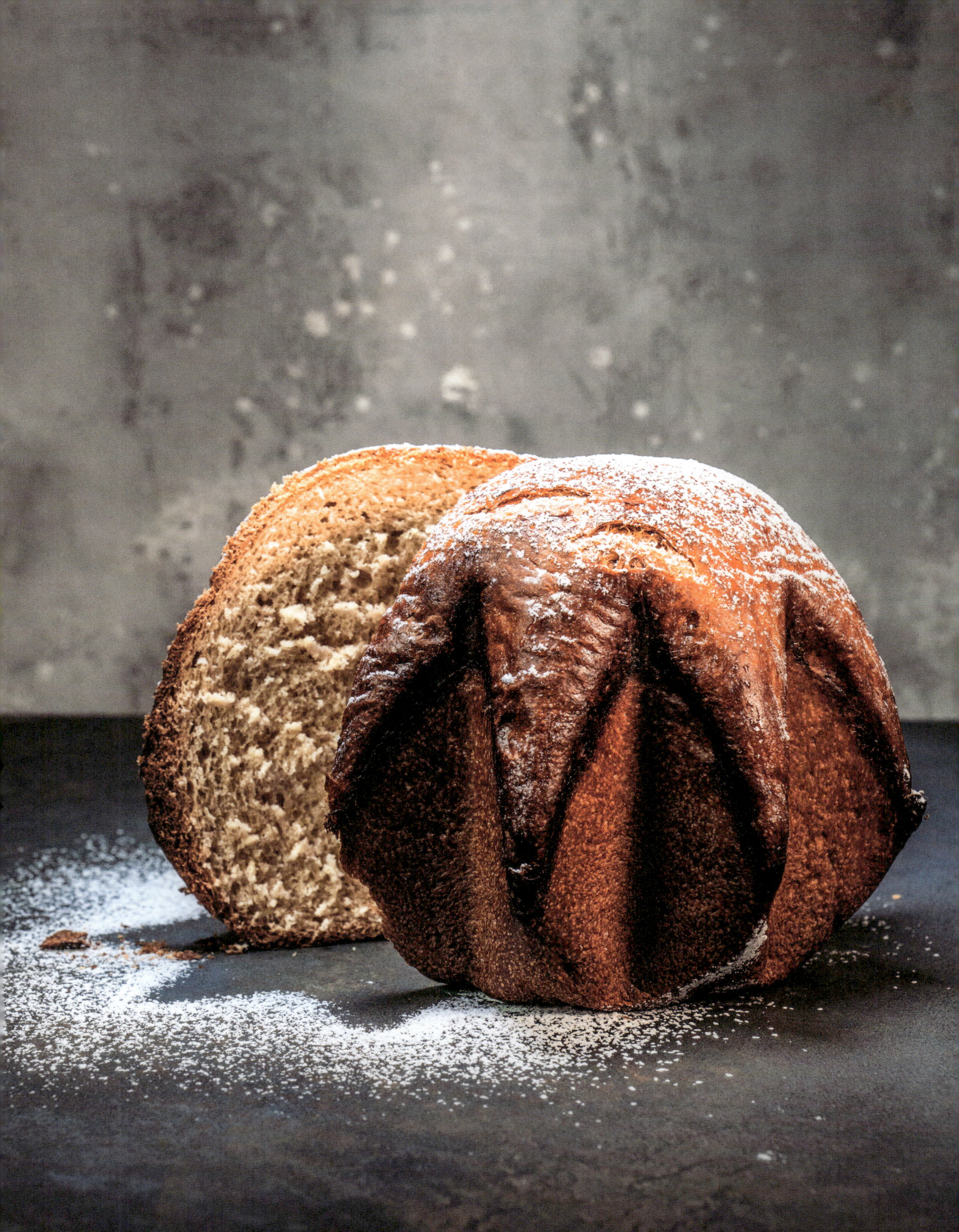

1. 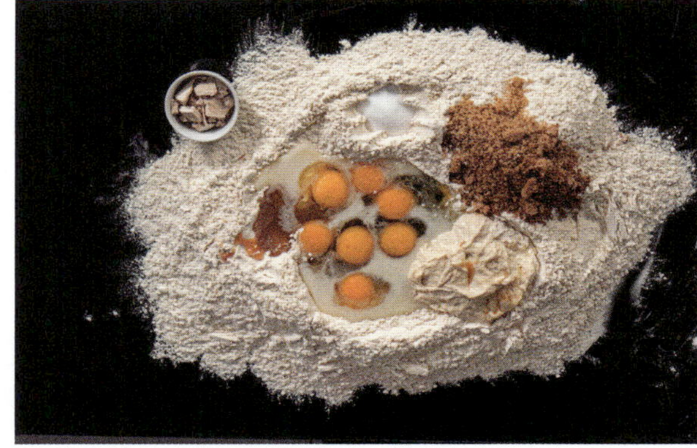

Mix the flour, salt, honey, eggs and milk and yeast mixture for 5 minutes to form a dough.

2. 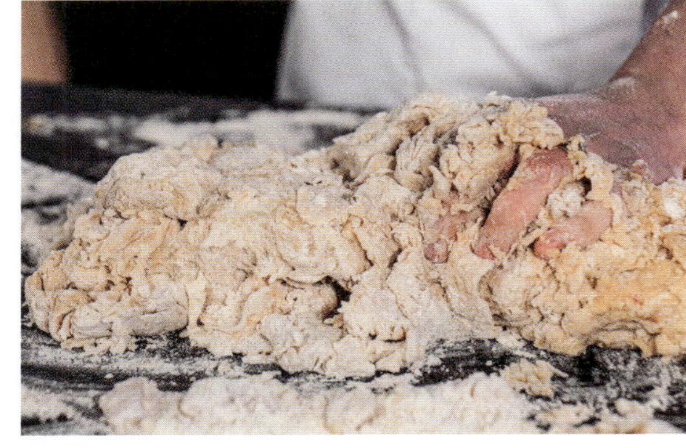

Knead the dough until it pulls away from the bowl or becomes smooth.

3. 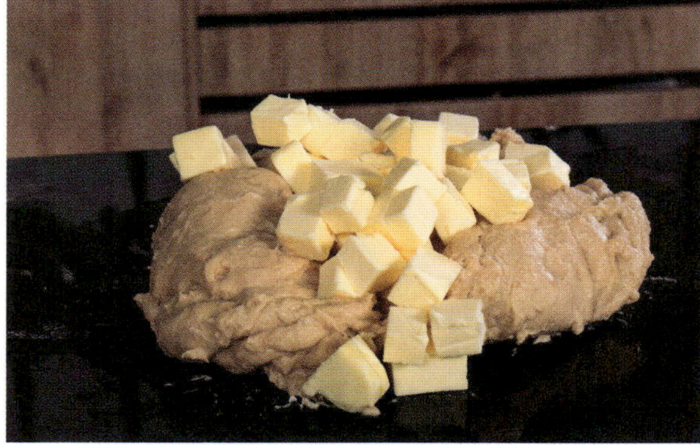

Add the cold butter in small pieces and both types of sugar.

4. 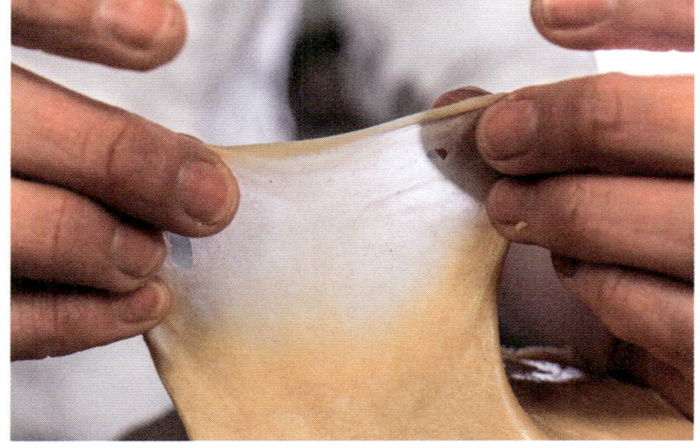

Knead again for about 30 minutes, until the dough is very elastic and its gluten structure is well developed.

5. 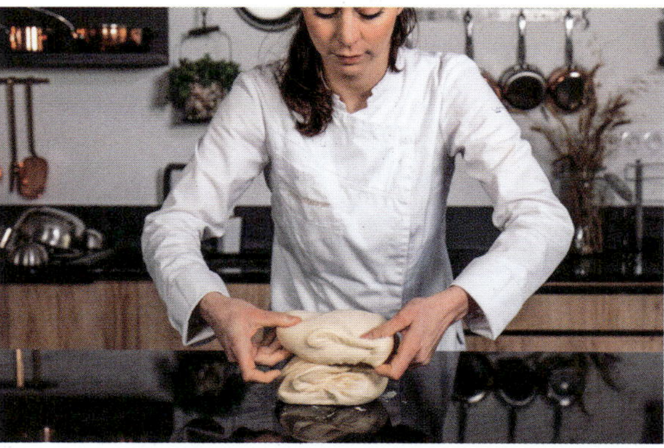

Rest the dough in the fridge for 12 hours. Shape into two large brioches.

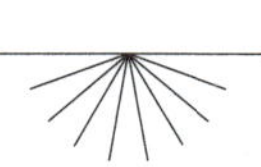

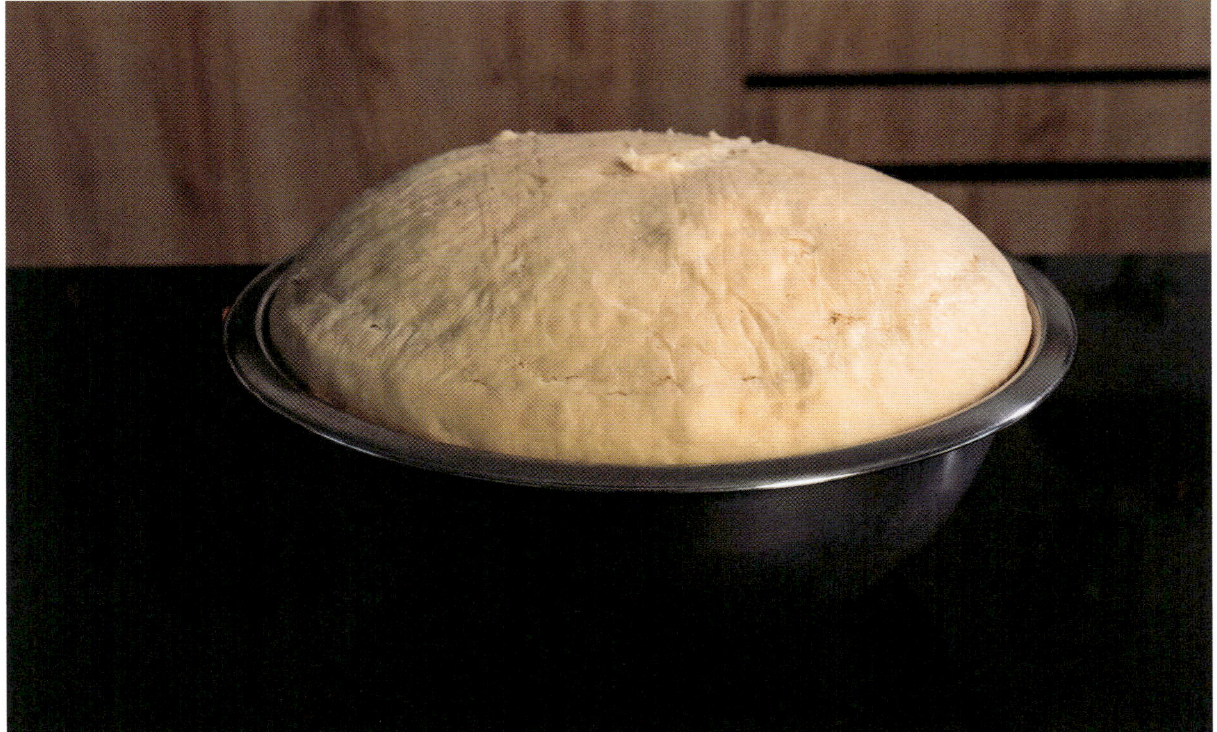

6.

Prove at 28°C for about 2 hours.

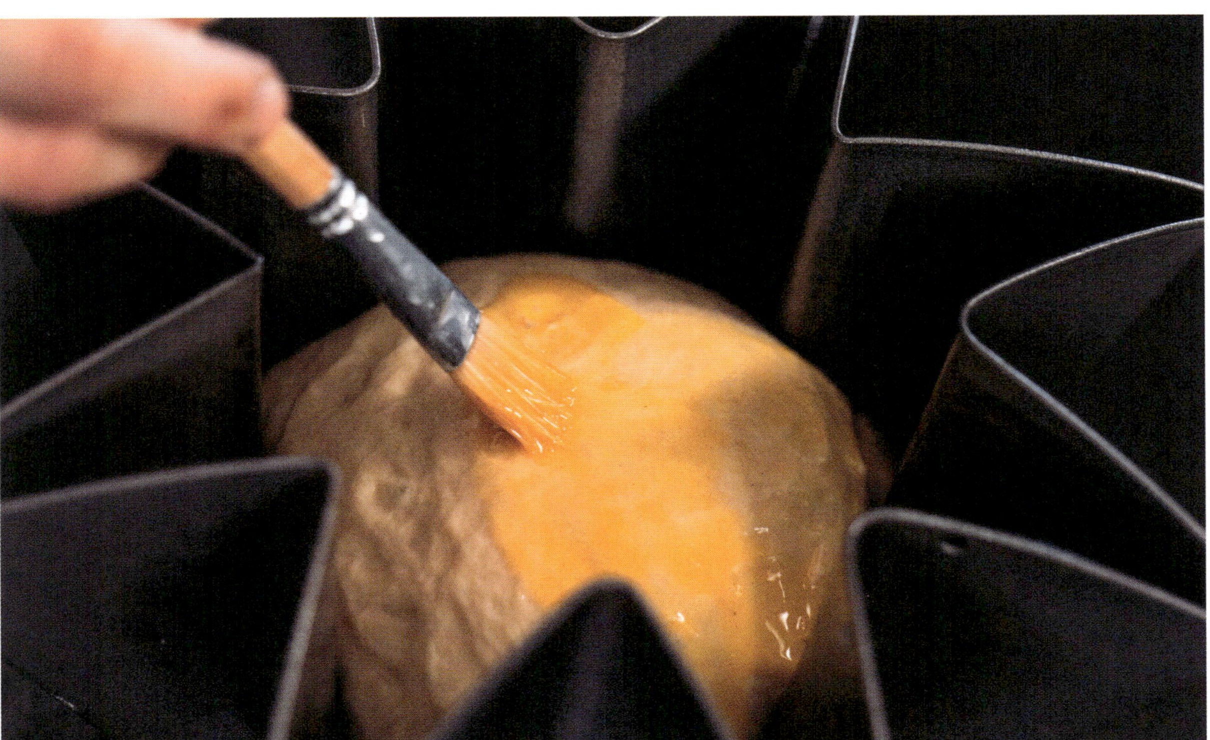

7.

Place the brioches in 18-cm diameter moulds. Brush them with egg wash and bake at 160 °C for 30 minutes.

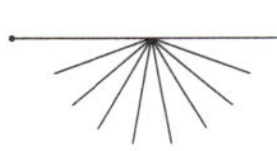

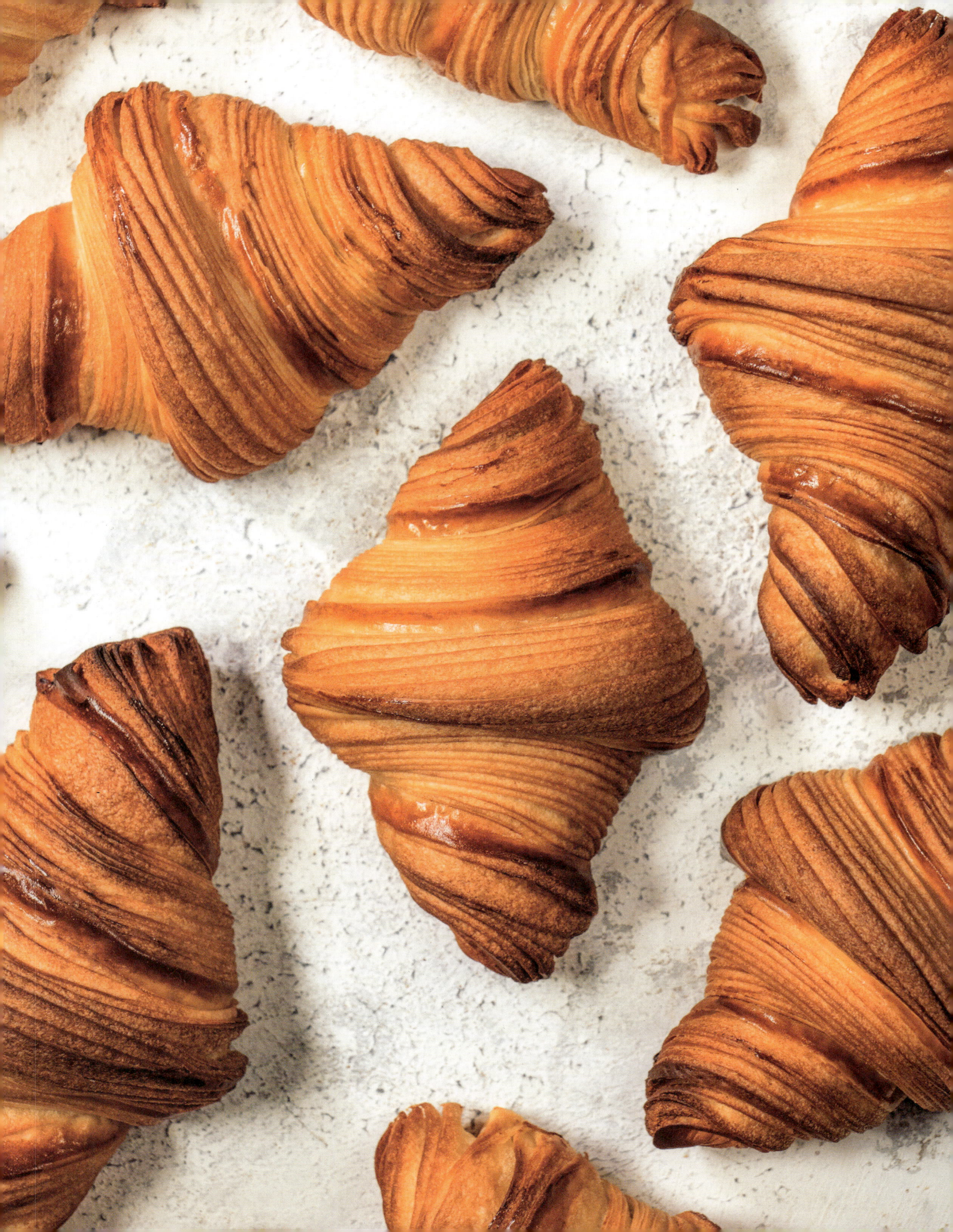

Makes 20 croissants		Preparation	Resting	Proving	Baking
		1 hour	18 hours 30 minutes	3 hours	12 minutes

Croissants

100 g milk levain
  (see recipe on p. 195)
254 g T45 (soft white) flour
500 g T55 (plain) flour
100 g light brown soft sugar
24 g salt
200 g water
160 g milk
112 g unsalted butter, melted
20 g fresh yeast
450 g dry butter

egg wash

1 egg
1 pinch of salt

The day before, prepare the milk levain by feeding the sourdough mother with the flour and milk. Allow the levain to rest for 4 hours at about 20°C. In a stand mixer fitted with a dough hook, mix both types of flour with the sugar, salt, water, milk and melted butter. Then incorporate the levain and yeast into the dough. Knead for 5 minutes on speed 1, then for 2 minutes on speed 2. Rest the dough at 4°C for about 15 hours 30 minutes.

On the day, roll out the dry butter into a sheet 5-mm thick (1). Roll out the dough into a sheet twice the size of the butter (2). Encase the butter in the dough (3) and roll out to a 5-mm thickness (4), then perform a single turn by folding the dough into thirds, like a letter, (5) to make 3 stacked layers. Rest the dough at 4°C for 1 hour 30 minutes, then turn it 90 degrees and roll out to a 5-mm thickness.

Fold in half (6), then fold in half again to obtain four successive layers of dough (7). Leave to rest for 1 hour at 4°C. Roll out to a thickness of 3-mm and cut triangles 8-cm wide and 20-cm long (8). Make a small cut in the centre of the base of each croissant, gently stretch the base and roll up the croissant (9). Leave to prove at 25°C for approximately 3 hours (10).

Make the egg wash by beating the egg with the salt and carefully brush it over the croissants (11). Bake at 180 °C for about 12 minutes (12).

'There's nothing more rewarding than making your own croissants. However, you'll need to be well organised. Here are 2 alternatives.
— Either make your croissants the day before (as far as step 10) and refrigerate them overnight, then get up early the next morning, 4 hours before everyone else, and leave them next to a radiator to prove (NB: as the croissants are cold, this step will take longer).
— Or let them prove directly and bake them in the evening, before reheating them in the oven the next morning. Preheat the oven to 180°C, put the croissants in for 10 minutes and then take them out. Wait 10 minutes before eating them.'

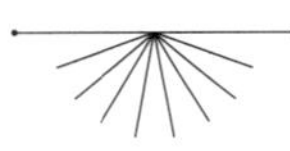

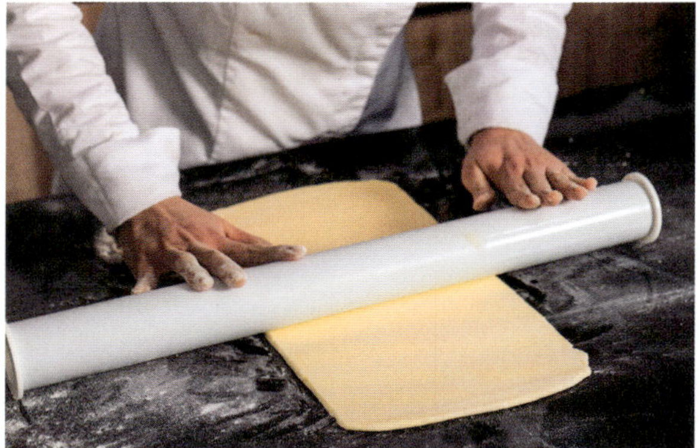

Roll out the dry butter into a sheet 5-mm thick.

1.

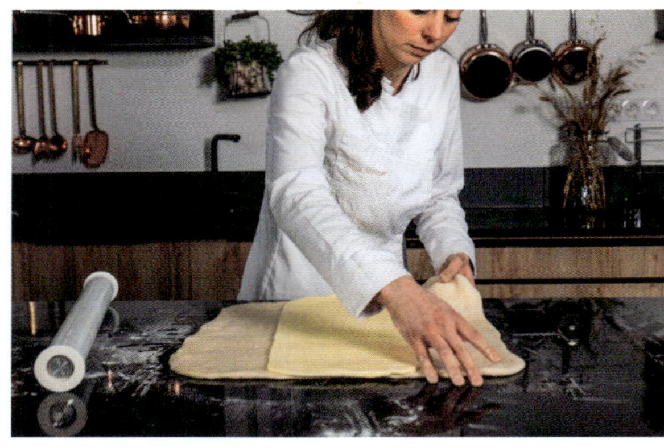

Roll out the dough into a sheet twice the size of the butter.

2.

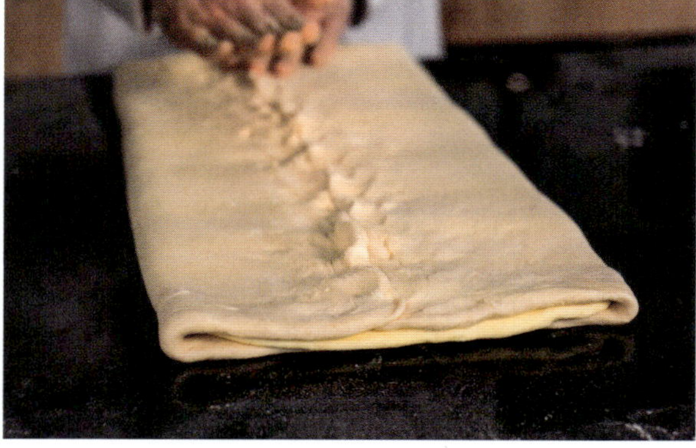

Encase the butter in the dough.

3.

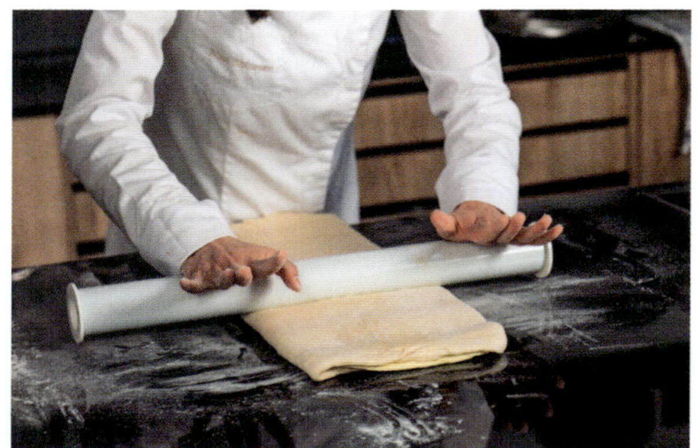

Roll out to a 5-mm thickness.

4.

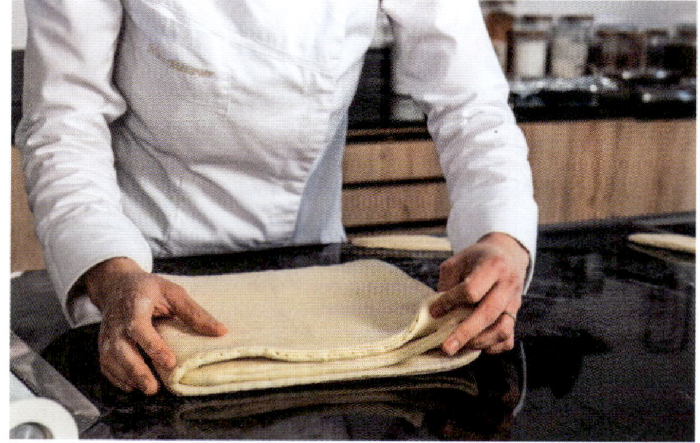

Fold in thirds (single turn) to make 3 stacked layers. Rest the dough at 4°C for 1 hour 30 minutes.

5.

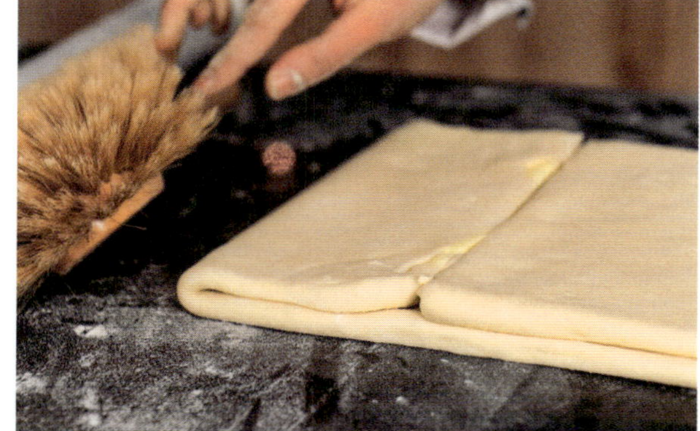

Turn the dough 90 degrees and roll out to a 5-mm thickness. Fold the dough over.

6.

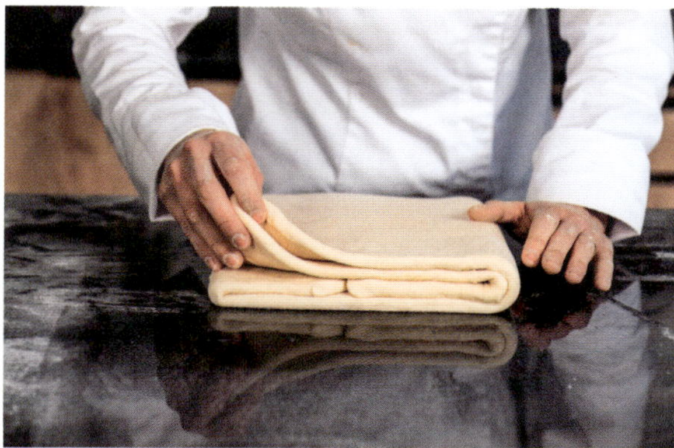

Fold the dough over again (double turn) to make 4 stacked dough layers. Rest in the fridge at 4°C for 1 hour.

7.

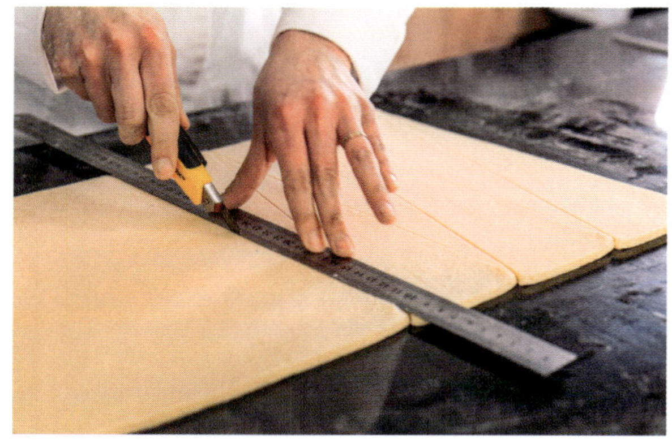

Roll out the dough to a 3-mm thickness and cut it into triangles 8 cm wide by 20 cm long.

8.

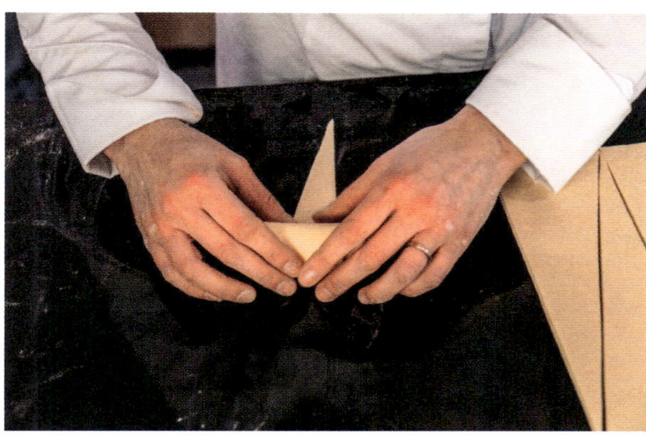

9.

Cut a small notch in the centre of the bottom edge, stretch the edge slightly and roll up the croissants.

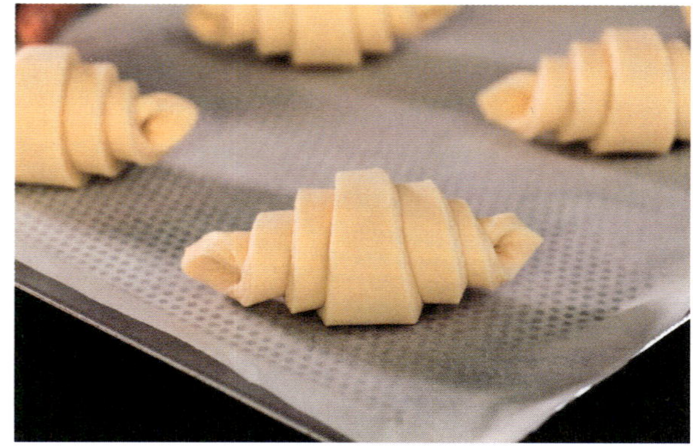

10.

Prove at 25°C for about 3 hours.

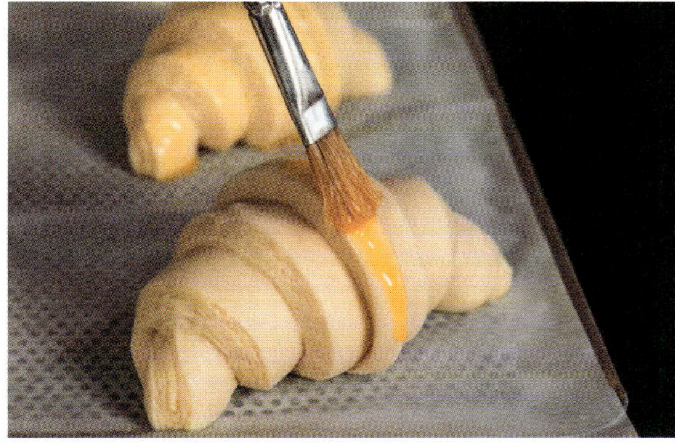

11.

Carefully brush the croissants with egg wash.

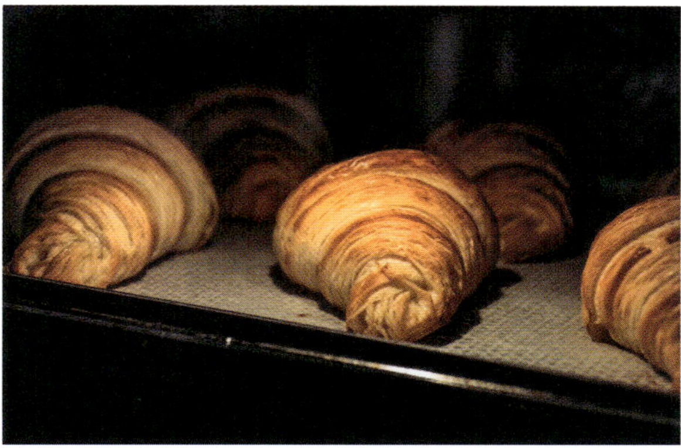

12.

Bake at 180°C for about 12 minutes.

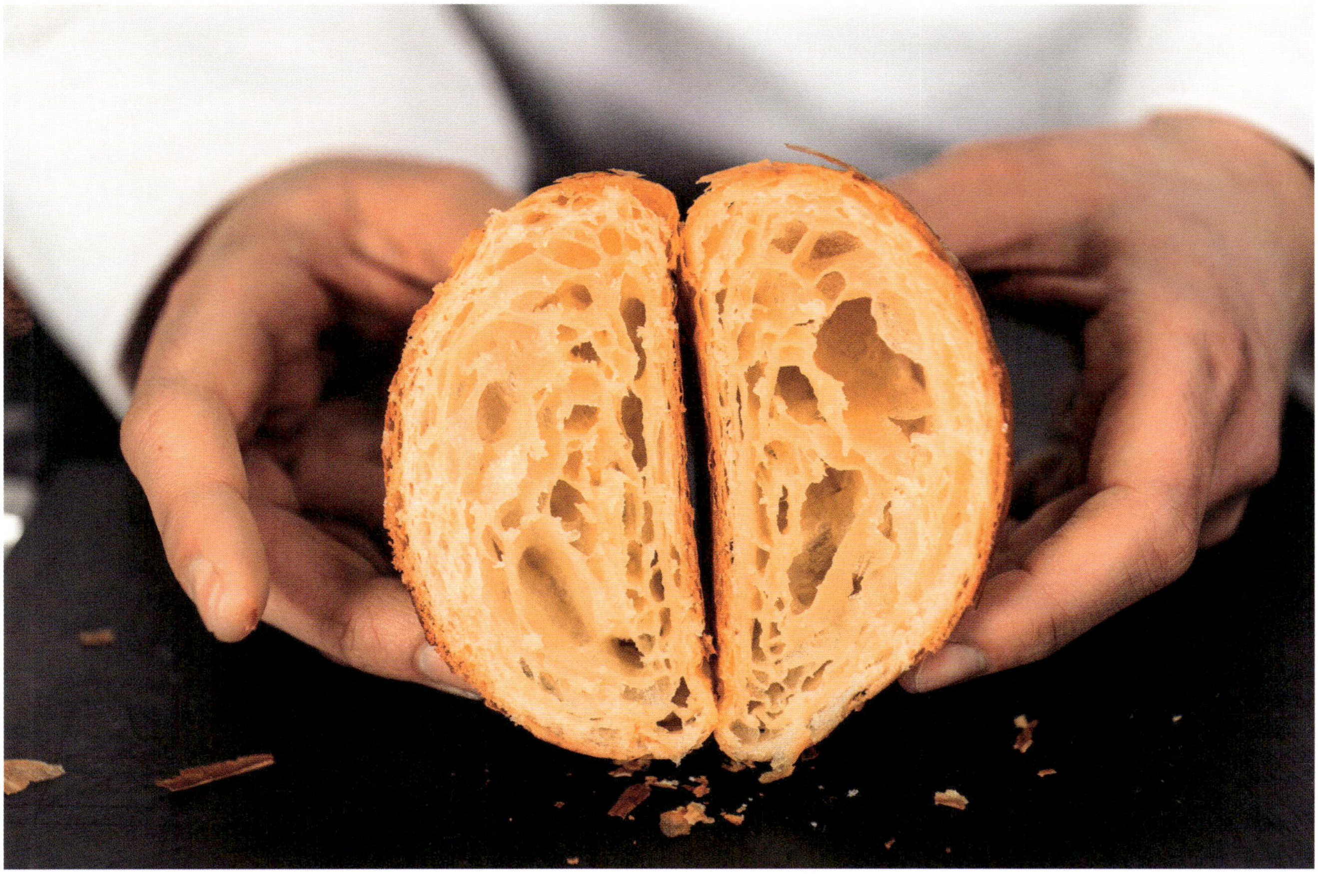

Makes 10 turnovers

Preparation
2 hours

Resting
12 hours

Baking
30 minutes

Peach and verbena turnovers

Puff pastry

For the beurre manié

225 g Charentes-Poitou PDO
    unsalted butter
100 g T55 (plain) flour

For the dough

187 g T55 flour
85 g water
85 g Charentes-Poitou PDO
    unsalted butter
8 g salt
2.5 g white vinegar

Make the beurre manié. In a stand mixer fitted with a paddle attachment, mix the butter with the flour, then roll out the beurre manié to an even thickness.

Make the dough by mixing all the ingredients, then roll it out to an even thickness and place it over the beurre manié. Rest the assembled pastry in the fridge for at least 6 hours.

Perform a double turn by rolling out the pastry to a 5-mm thickness and folding it over twice to make 4 stacked layers (double turn). Rest the pastry at 4°C for at least 6 hours.

Repeat the operation to perform a total of 3 double turns.

'I always keep any puff pastry trimmings in the freezer. Whenever I have fruit that's starting to overripen, I take out the puff pastry trimmings and make turnovers with the leftover fruit. Children and grown-ups alike love them. I like to leave the fruit inside as a surprise and let them guess the filling. Warm turnovers are always a hit.'

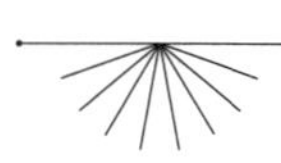

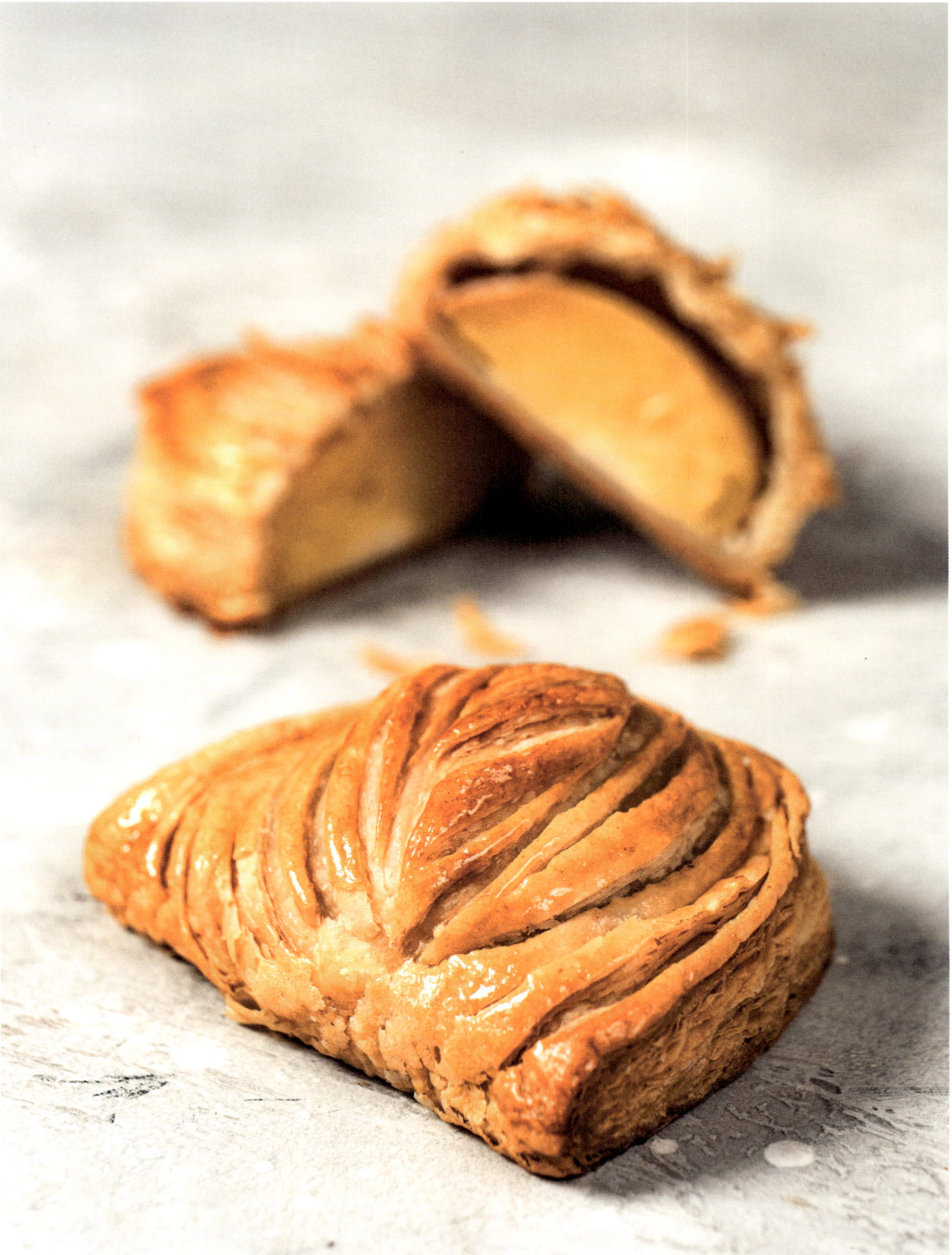

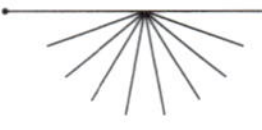

Filling

5 peaches

10 verbena leaves

1 egg

Assembly

Roll out the puff pastry to 3.5-mm thickness and chill until well relaxed. Cut out 10-cm-diameter discs and lightly roll over the centre with a rolling pin to stretch them into an oval shape (1).

To peel the peaches, blanch them in boiling water for 30 seconds (2), refresh them in iced water and carefully remove the skin (3). Halve the peaches and remove the stone.

Arrange a peach half and 2 verbena leaves on one side of each pastry oval. Lightly brush the edges of the pastry with water (4), fold it over the filling and seal the turnover.

Rest the turnovers in the fridge for at least 30 minutes and then brush with beaten egg (5).

Using a box cutter or a knife, score the surface with an attractive pattern (6).

Bake at 170°C for about 30 minutes.

'You can also make a larger version in the form of a pie, similar to a galette des rois, to share for afternoon tea in summer. Cut out 2 puff pastry discs, each with a 20-cm diameter. Spread a thin layer of almond cream over one disc to absorb the moisture from the peach (or apricot) halves, then top with verbena leaves. Moisten around the edges and cover the filling with the second puff pastry disc. Brush with beaten egg and bake at 160°C for about 50 minutes.'

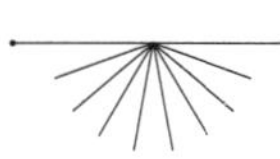

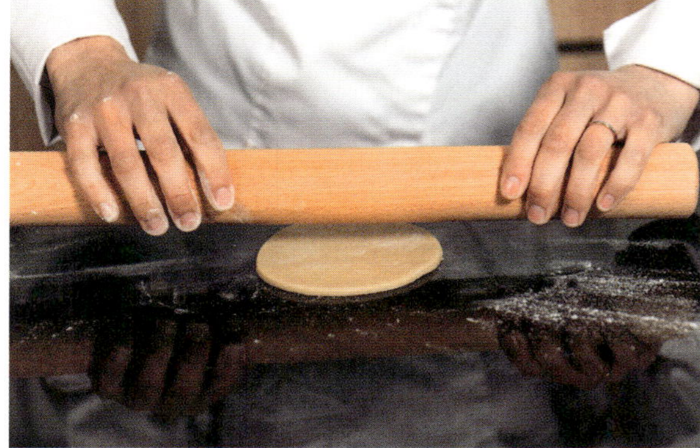

1.

Cut out 10-cm-diameter puff pastry discs and lightly roll over the centre with a rolling pin to stretch them into an oval shape.

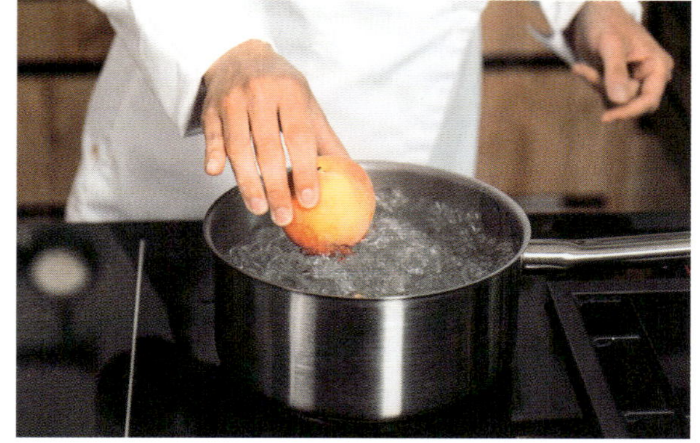

2.

Blanch the peaches in boiling water for 30 seconds.

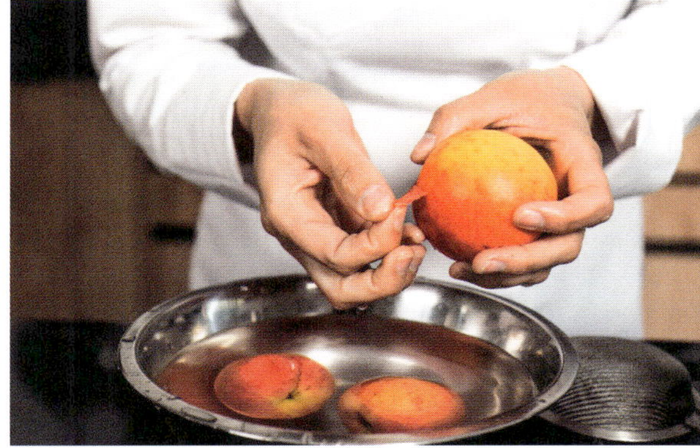

3.

Refresh the peaches in iced water and carefully peel off the skin.

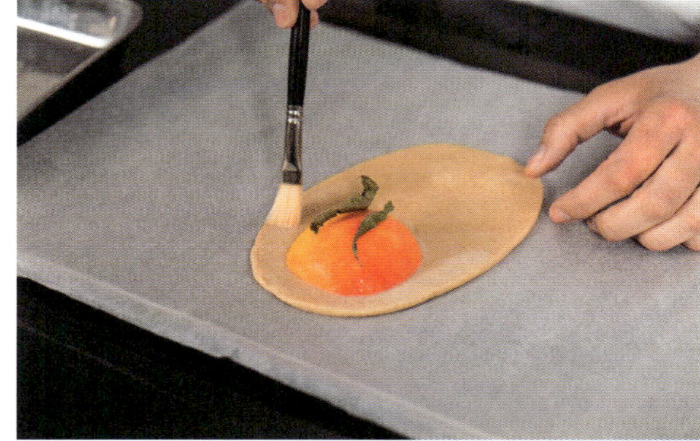

4.

Halve the peaches and remove the stone, then arrange one peach half and 2 verbena leaves on one side of each oval. Lightly brush the edges of the pastry with water.

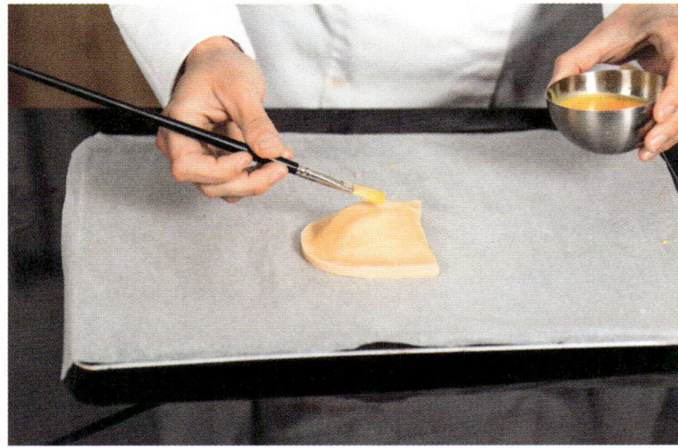

5.

Seal the turnovers, rest them in the fridge for 30 minutes and then brush with beaten egg.

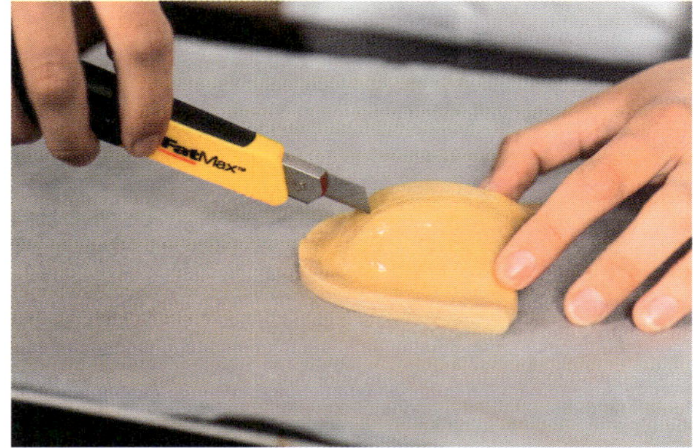

6.

Using a box cutter or a knife, score the surface with an attractive pattern.

Makes 12 rolls

Preparation	Resting	Baking
3 hours	14 hours	15 minutes

Cherry rolls

Croissant dough

50 g milk levain
(see recipe on p. 195)
127 g T45 (soft white) flour
250 g T55 (plain) flour
100 g water
80 g milk
12 g salt
50 g light brown soft sugar
56 g unsalted butter, melted
10 g fresh yeast
200 g dry butter

Cherry confit

376 g fresh cherries
60 g light brown soft sugar
5 g fresh rosemary
10 g unsalted butter
8 g caster sugar
8 g pectin
10 g lemon juice

Egg wash

1 egg
1 pinch of salt

Croissant dough The day before, prepare the milk levain by feeding the 17 g of sourdough mother with 17 g of T55 flour and 17 g of milk. Allow the levain to rest for 4 hours at about 20°C. In a stand mixer fitted with a dough hook, mix both types of flour with the levain, water, salt, sugar, melted butter and yeast. Knead for 5 minutes on speed 1, then for 2 minutes on speed 2. Rest the dough at 4°C overnight. On the day, roll out the dry butter into a sheet 5-mm thick. Roll out the dough into a sheet twice the size of the butter. Encase the butter in the dough and roll it out to a 5-mm thickness, then fold the dough into thirds, like a letter (single turn) to make 3 stacked layers. Rest the dough for 1 hour 30 minutes at 4°C, then turn it 90 degrees and roll it out to a 5-mm thickness. Fold the dough over, then over again (double turn) to make 4 stacked layers. Rest the dough for 1 hour at 4°C.

Cherry confit Quarter the cherries. Melt the brown sugar in a frying pan and add the cherries, fresh rosemary and butter. Cook for 4 minutes, then remove from the heat and blend. Heat to 40°C, then add the caster sugar and pectin mixed together. Bring to the boil and allow to cook for 1½ minutes. Stir in the lemon juice. Transfer the jam to a tray and cool quickly. Then loosen the jam and transfer it to a piping bag.

Assembly

Make the egg wash by beating the egg with the salt. Roll out the dough to a 2.5-mm thickness and cut into 30-cm-long and 4-cm-wide strips. Spread jam over the strips, roll them up to form spirals and carefully brush with egg wash. Place each roll inside a 10-cm-diameter pastry ring and bake at 170°C for 10 minutes, until nicely coloured. Garnish with fresh cherries and rosemary flowers.

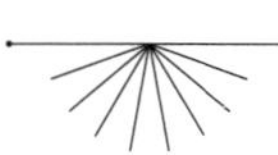

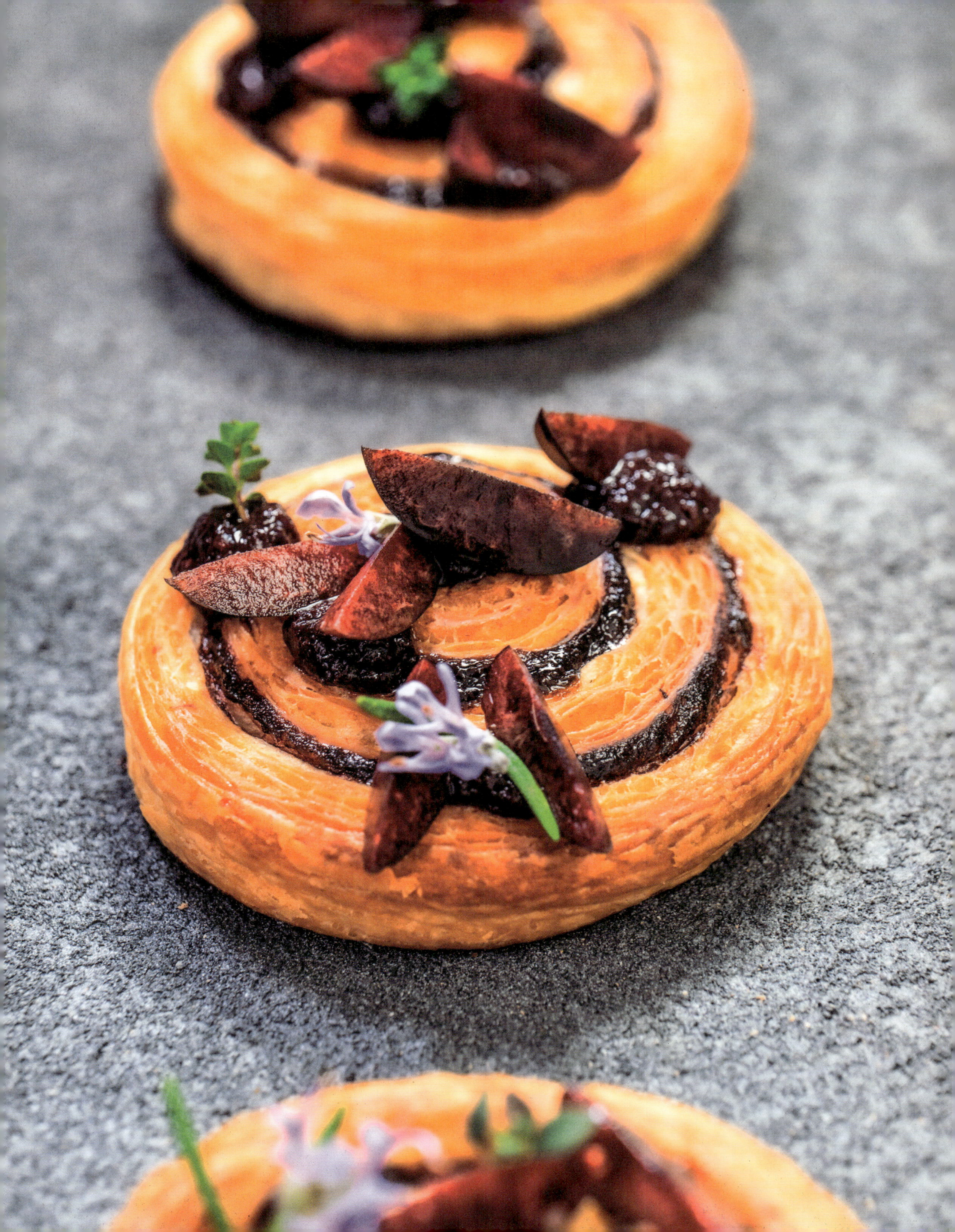

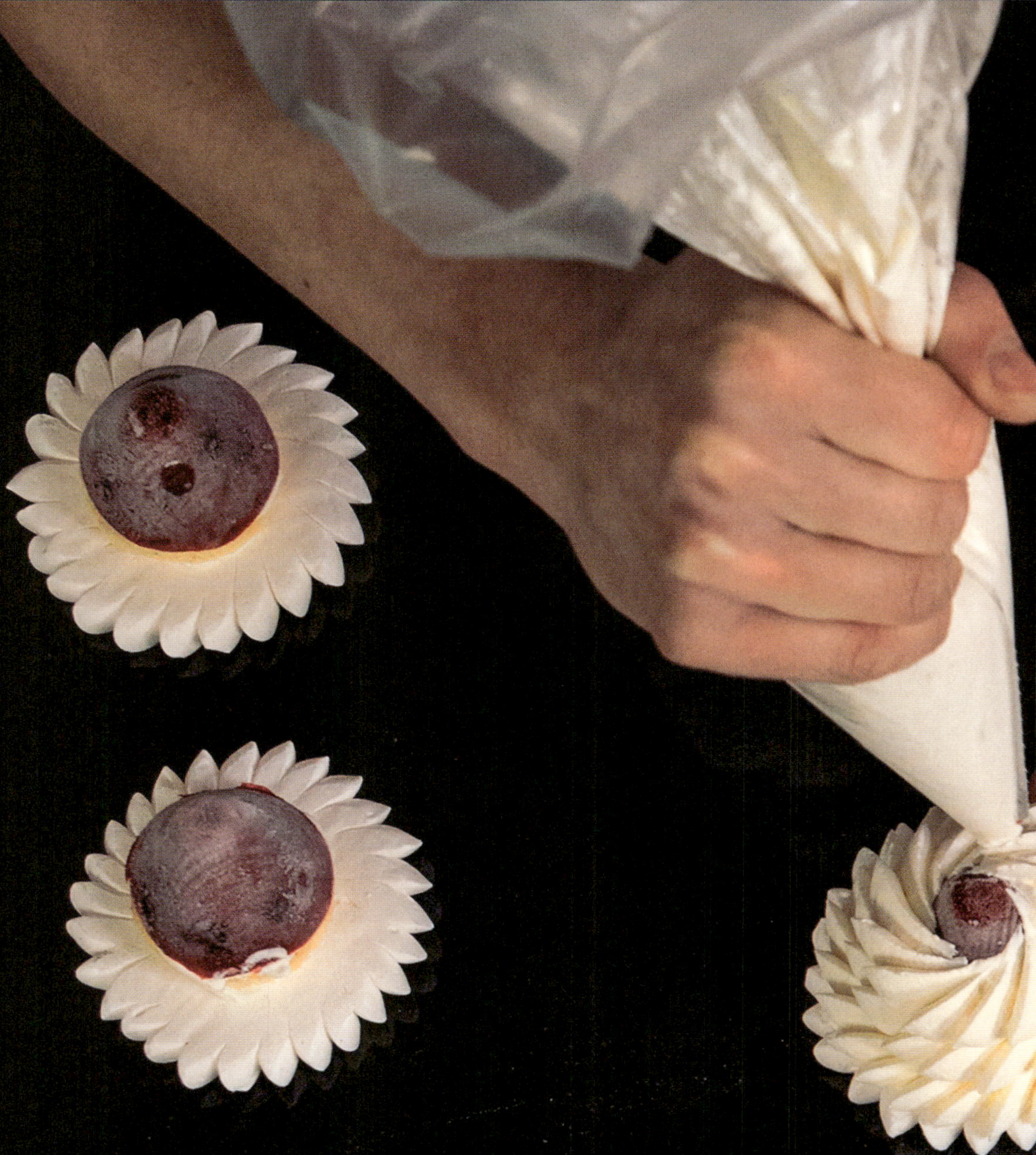

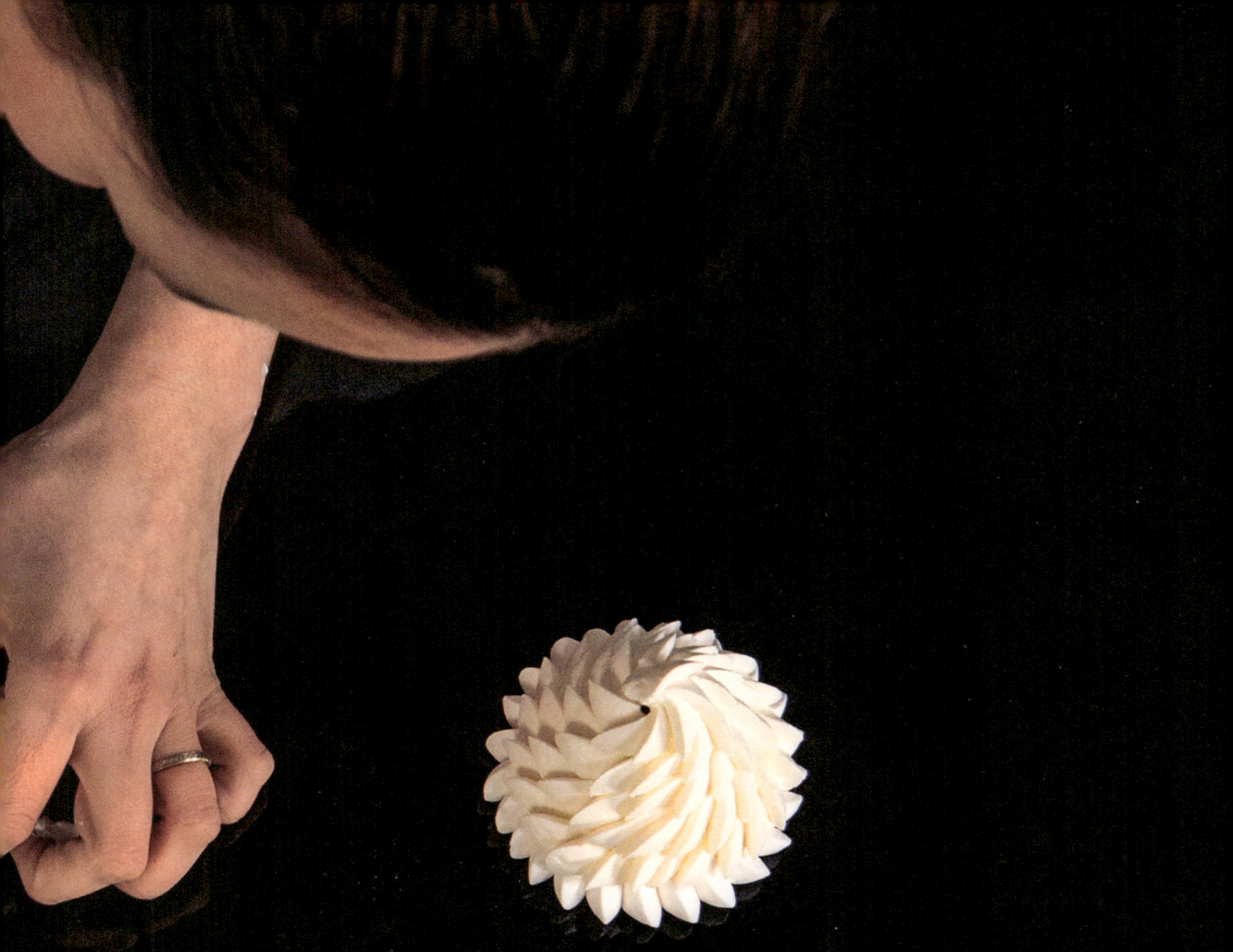

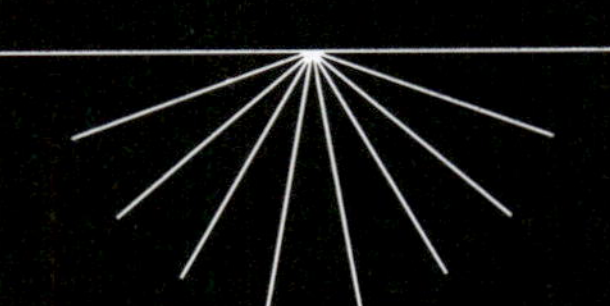

Plated desserts

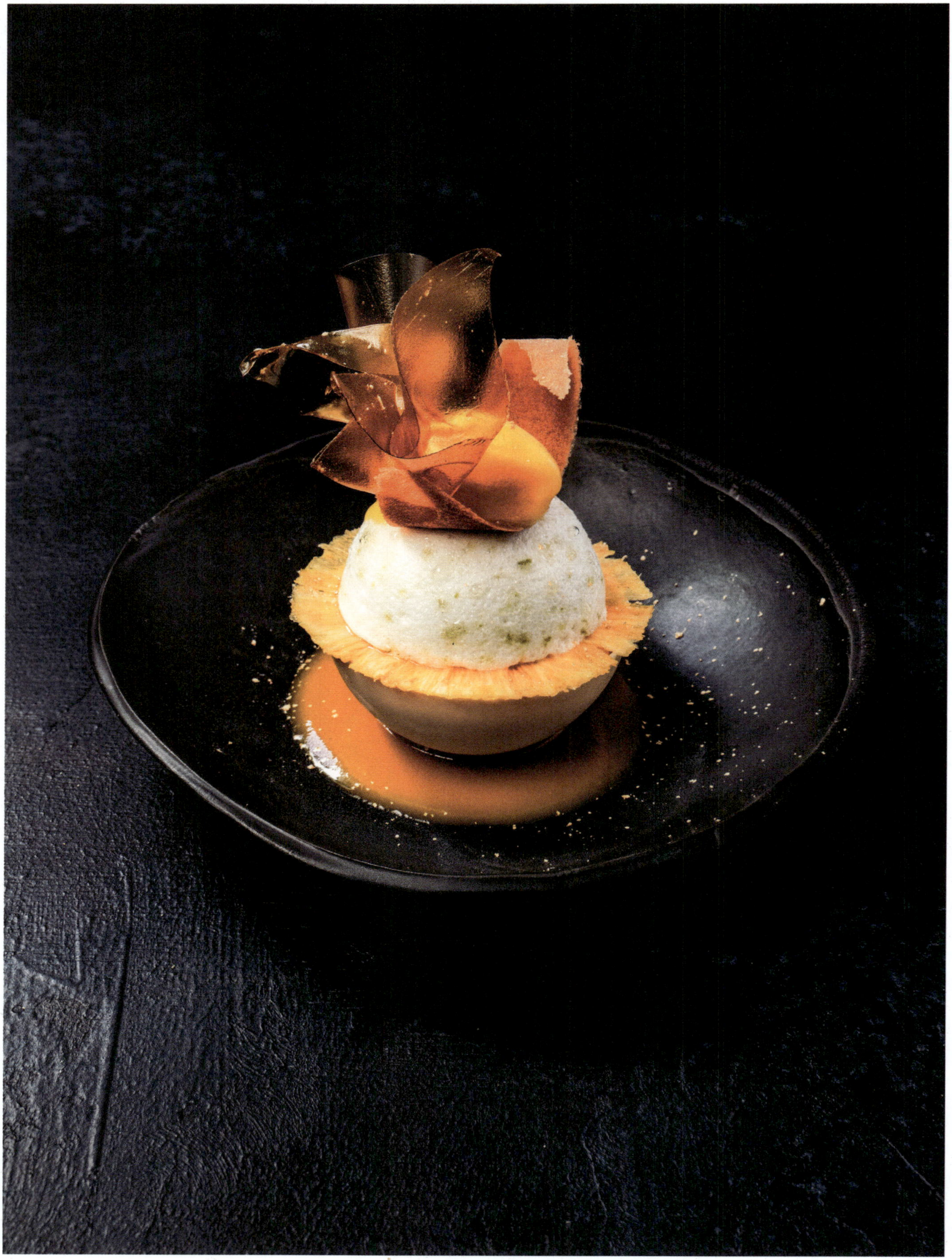

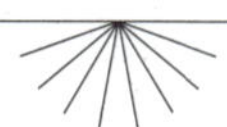

Serves 6

Preparation	Resting	Cooking
3 hours	8 hours 10 minutes	7 hours 20 minutes

Exotic île flottante

Passion fruit paper

1½ gelatine leaves
125 g water
63 g mango purée
125 g passion fruit purée
25 g caster sugar
1.5 g pectin NH325

White chocolate shells

250 g white chocolate

Passion fruit and mango insert

1 g fresh ginger
125 g mango purée
50 g passion fruit purée
0.5 g agar-agar

Passion fruit and mango coulis

250 g mango purée
35 g orgeat syrup
50 g passion fruit purée

Hazelnut dacquoise

113 g egg whites
37 g caster sugar
100 g ground hazelnuts
113 g icing sugar

Passion fruit paper The day before, soak the gelatine in iced water for 10 minutes, then squeeze to drain. Put the water, mango purée and passion fruit purée into a saucepan and place over the heat. Mix the caster sugar with the pectin, add this mixture to the fruit purées and bring to the boil for 1 minute. Dissolve the gelatine in the mixture. Refrigerate for 6 hours. On the day, preheat the oven to 250°C with non-stick trays inside, then transfer the mixture to the very hot trays. Bake for 3 hours at 85°C with the oven in fan mode, then cut out 5–6-cm-diameter discs, detach them from the tray and crumple them up. Store them in an airtight container with a moisture absorber.

White chocolate shells Temper the chocolate using the temperature curve method: melt the chocolate at 45°C, cool over an ice bath to 26°C and reheat to 28°C in a bain-marie.

Prepare 8-cm-diameter chocolate hemisphere moulds, ensuring they are very clean. Using a brush, apply a coat of chocolate to the cavities and allow it to harden for a few minutes, then apply a second coat to achieve an even thickness. Allow the chocolate shells to harden in the fridge for 1 hour, then remove them from the moulds. Heat a 2-cm-diameter biscuit cutter with a blowtorch and use it to cut off the bottom of the shells.

Passion fruit and mango insert Grate the ginger and mix it with the purées. Add the agar-agar, bring to the boil for 1 minute and pour the mixture into-3 cm-diameter hemisphere moulds. Freeze.

Passion fruit and mango coulis Mix all the ingredients together and refrigerate.

Hazelnut dacquoise Beat the egg whites to soft peaks, then gradually add the sugar while beating to stiff peaks. Sift the icing sugar with the ground hazelnuts, then carefully fold the dry ingredients into the beaten egg whites. Spread the mixture over a sheet of baking paper and bake at 180°C for 5 minutes. Allow to cool on a rack. Cut out dacquoise discs using a 3-cm-diameter biscuit cutter.

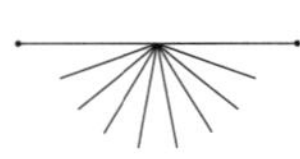

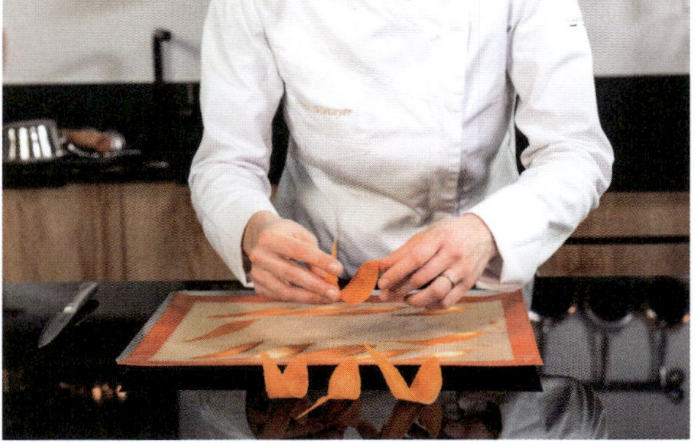

1\.

To make the mango tuile, use an angled palette knife to spread neat teardrops about 8 cm long on a baking mat.

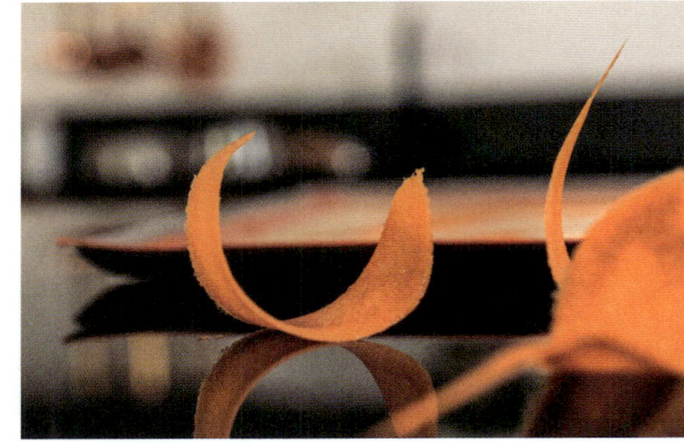

2\.

Bake at 170°C for 8 minutes, until evenly coloured. Once out of the oven, shape the tuiles into a curve.

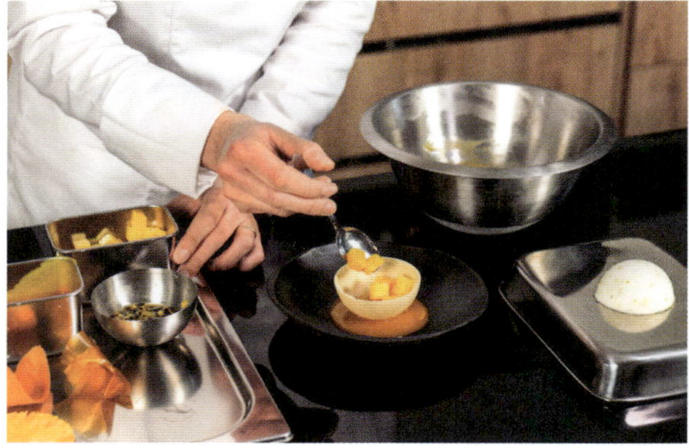

3\.

To assemble, spread a little mango coulis inside a bowl, arrange a white chocolate shell held in place with a little almond paste and fill with a dacquoise disc and the diced fruit mixture.

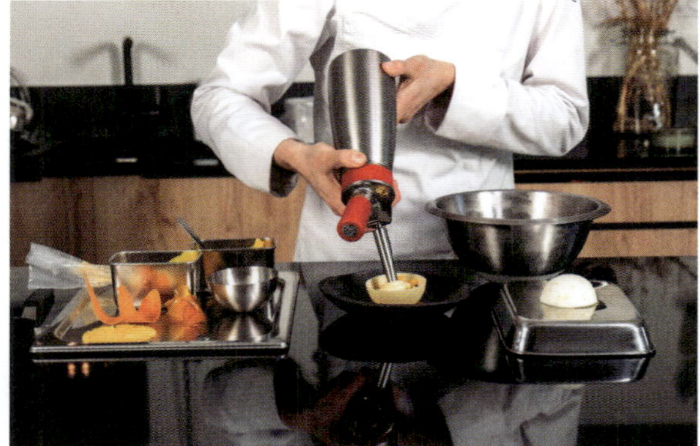

4\.

Cover with passion fruit foam.

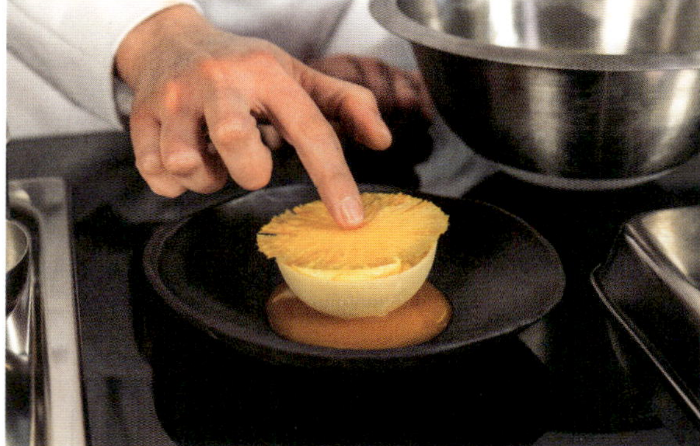

5\.

Top with a pineapple crisp.

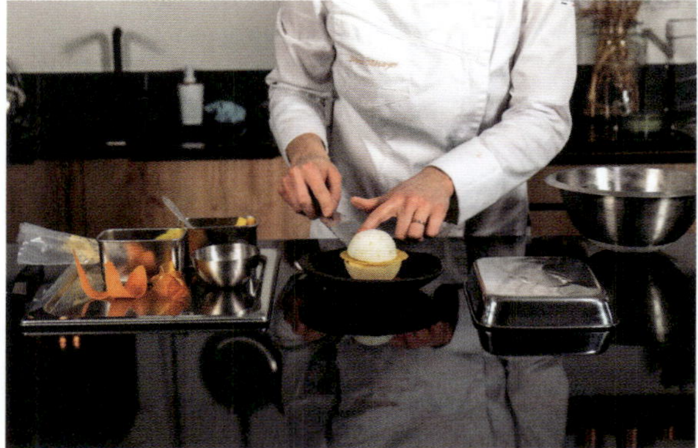

6\.

Place a lime meringue dome on top of the crisp.

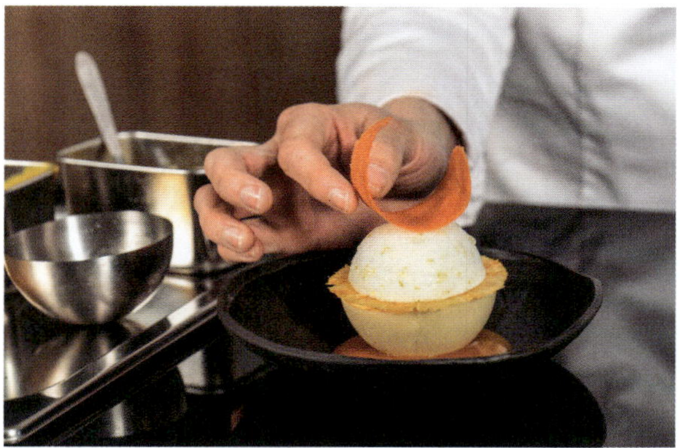

7\.

Add a mango tuile, then a quenelle of banana and passion fruit sorbet, and finish with a light dusting of gold powder.

Pineapple crisps
½ fresh pineapple
40 g water
54 g caster sugar

Lime meringue domes
6 egg whites
100 g caster sugar
Grated zest of 2 limes

Mango tuiles
90 g caster sugar
32 g T55 (plain) flour
68 g unsalted butter, melted
22 g mango nectar
45 g water

Passion fruit and banana sorbet
200 g bananas
125 g passion fruit pulp
8 g orange juice
75 g caster sugar
112 g water
15 g honey
1 g guar gum

Passion fruit foam
200 g passion fruit purée
125 g whipping cream (35% fat)
25 g icing sugar

Filling
1 mango
½ pineapple
1 passion fruit

Decoration
Edible gold powder (as needed)

Pineapple crisps Make a syrup by combining the water and sugar in a saucepan and bringing to the boil. Using a meat slicer, cut the pineapple into thin slices and lay them on a baking mat. Brush the slices with a very thin coat of syrup. Bake at 80°C with the oven in fan mode for 4 hours, then set aside in a drying oven or in a dry place.

Lime meringue domes Beat the egg whites to soft peaks, then gradually add the sugar while beating to stiff peaks. Fold in the zest. Pipe the mixture into greased hemisphere moulds and press a frozen insert into the centre of each mould, cover over and smooth the surface with a palette knife. Grease the surface of the moulds and cover in cling film. Cook the meringue in a steam oven at 75°C for 14 minutes.

Mango tuiles Mix all the ingredients together and refrigerate for 1 hour.

Using an angled palette knife, carefully spread the batter to form neat teardrops about 8 cm long on a baking mat. Bake at 170°C for 8 minutes, until evenly coloured. Once out of the oven, shape the tuiles into a curve (1–2).

Passion fruit and banana sorbet Purée the bananas with the passion fruit pulp and orange juice, then strain through a conical sieve. Make a syrup with the water, sugar, honey and guar gum and add it to the purée. Blend until smooth, then churn the sorbet.

Passion fruit foam Mix all the ingredients, transfer to a siphon and insert one gas charger.

Assembly Cut the mango and pineapple into 8-mm dice and mix with the passion fruit pulp.

Spread 2 tablespoons of mango coulis in the bottom of each bowl. Arrange a white chocolate shell in the coulis and use a little almond paste to hold it in place. Place a dacquoise disc in the centre. Fill the shell with the diced pineapple, mango and passion fruit mixture (3). Cover with passion fruit foam (4) and cover with a pineapple crisp (5). Arrange a lime meringue dome over the crisp (6). Top with a mango tuile (7). Add a quenelle of banana and passion fruit sorbet. Arrange a piece of passion fruit paper on top of the tuile. To finish, sprinkle with gold powder.

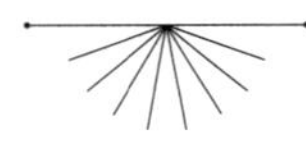

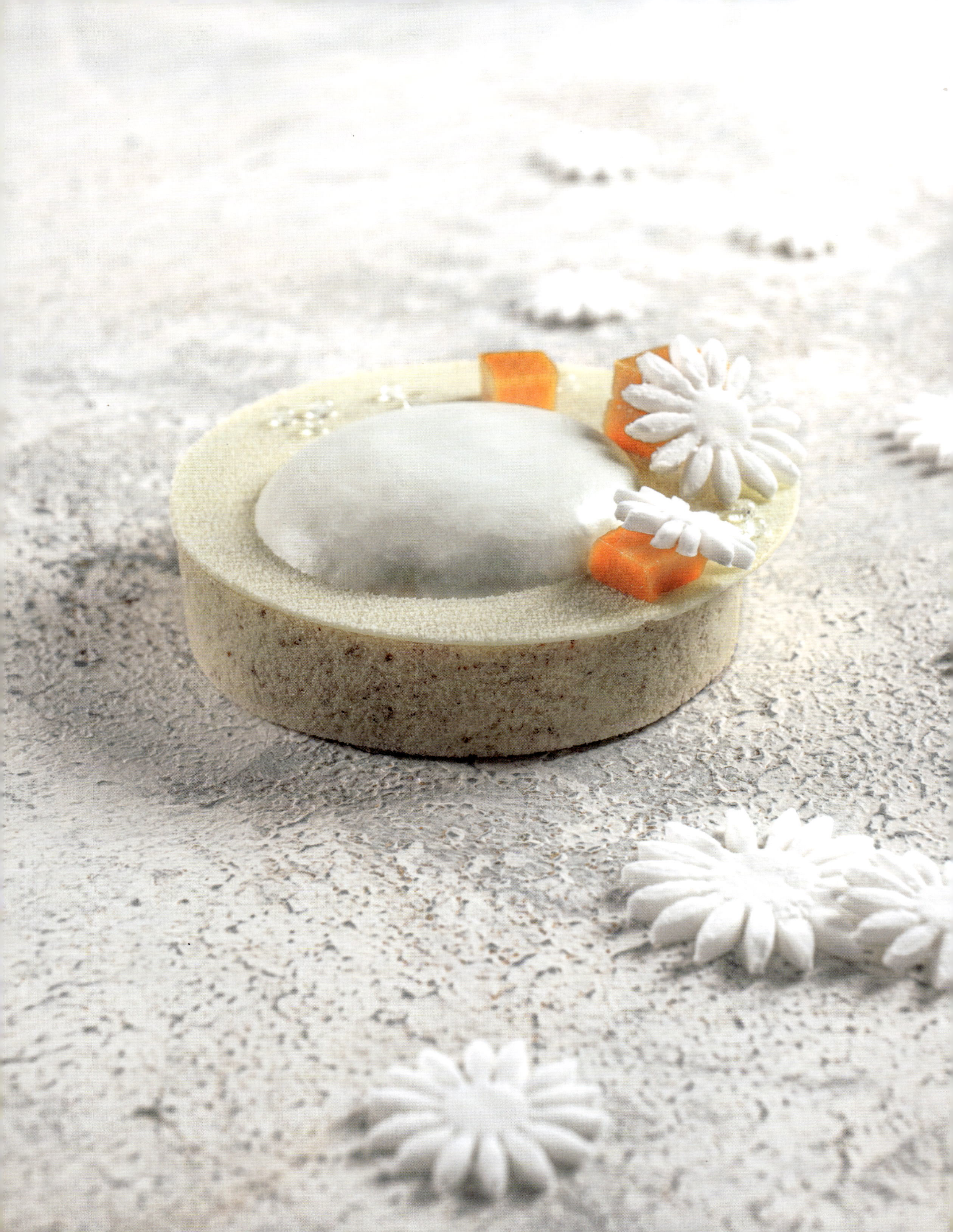

Serves 6

Preparation
3 hours

Cooking
50 minutes

Rice pudding

Joconde sponge

100 g eggs

75 g icing sugar

75 g ground almonds

20 g T55 (plain) flour

15 g unsalted butter

65 g egg whites

10 g caster sugar

Viennese shortbread

62 g unsalted butter, softened

25 g icing sugar

10 g egg white

75 g T55 flour

1 g salt

1 g vanilla powder

Reconstituted Viennese shortbread

85 g white chocolate couverture

150 g Viennese shortbread

60 g feuillantine

1 g fleur de sel

Rice pudding

60 g pudding rice

350 g milk

1 vanilla pod

7 g jasmine tea

15 g light brown soft sugar

2 egg yolks

70 g whipping cream (35% fat)

Joconde sponge In a stand mixer fitted with a whisk attachment, beat the eggs with the icing sugar and ground almonds. In the meantime, sift the flour and melt the butter. Beat the egg whites to soft peaks, then gradually add the sugar while beating to stiff peaks. Gently combine the different mixtures and then spread the batter to a 3-mm thickness in a baking tray lined with baking paper. Bake for 5 minutes at 190°C.

Viennese shortbread In a stand mixer fitted with a paddle attachment, mix the butter with the sifted icing sugar, then add the egg white, sifted flour, salt and vanilla powder. Break the pastry up into crumbs. Bake at 150°C for 23 minutes. Check the colour and adjust the cooking time if necessary. After baking, crumble the pastry again and set aside in a dry place.

Reconsistuted Viennese shortbread Melt the chocolate in a bain-marie, then gently mix with the baked Viennese shortbread, feuillantine and fleur de sel.

Rice pudding Blanch the rice for 3 minutes in boiling water and rinse until the water runs clear. Bring the milk to the boil, add the seeds scraped from the vanilla pod and the tea. Allow to steep for 15 minutes. Strain the milk through a conical sieve, then weigh and top up if needed to make up its original weight. In a saucepan, cook the rice with a third of the infused milk over a medium heat. When the liquid in the pan is almost completely absorbed, gradually add the remaining milk and repeat the process. Add more milk if necessary. When the rice is cooked, remove the pan from the heat and add the egg yolks and sugar. Mix well. Transfer to a container and allow to cool. Whip the cream and gently fold it into the cold rice pudding.

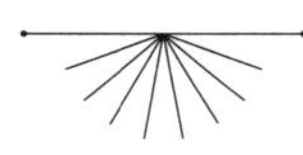

Caramel cubes

110 g whipping cream
75 g caster sugar
9 g glucose syrup
½ vanilla pod
27 g egg yolks
25 g gelatine mass
(3 g gelatine power
    and 22 g cold water)
0.5 g salt

Sugar paste flowers

180 g icing sugar
10 g potato starch
10 g white vinegar
10 g gelatine mass
(1.5 g gelatine powder
    and 8.5 g cold water)

Decoration

150 g whipping cream
10 g caster sugar
100 g white chocolate
10 g neutral glaze

Caramel cubes In a saucepan, heat the cream over a low heat. Make a dry caramel with the sugar until slightly smoking, then add the hot cream to stop the cooking process. Add the glucose. Bring the mixture to the boil, pour it over the egg yolks and mix, then add the seeds scraped from the vanilla pod. Transfer the mixture to the saucepan and cook to a sauce consistency and the temperature reaches 83°C. Add the gelatine mass and salt and blend until smooth. Pour the caramel into a greased container to a 1-cm thickness. Allow the caramel to set in the fridge, then cut it into 1-cm cubes.

Sugar paste flowers Sift the icing sugar with the potato starch. In a saucepan, heat the vinegar and gelatine mass over a low heat and mix with the icing sugar and potato starch. Allow the sugar paste to rest and thicken to the desired consistency. Then use a biscuit cutter to cut out small flowers.

Decoration Make a Chantilly cream by whipping the cream with the sugar. Transfer to a piping bag fitted with a 10-mm plain nozzle and set aside. Temper the white chocolate. Spread the chocolate thinly over an acetate sheet, allow to harden for a few minutes and cut out rings with an 8.5-cm outer diameter and a 5-cm inner diameter. If desired, chill the rings in the freezer and then spray them with a flocking made by mixing cocoa butter and white chocolate to give them a fine velvety texture.

Assembly

Cut the joconde sponge into 2.5-cm-wide and 24-cm-long strips. Line 8-cm-diameter pastry rings with the sponge strips. If necessary, join the two ends of the strip with a small dot of white chocolate.

Cover the bottom of the ring with 6 g of reconstituted shortbread and refrigerate.

Soft-whip the cream and incorporate it into the rice pudding.

Fill the lined pastry rings with rice pudding (1).

Pipe a mound of Chantilly cream over the rice pudding (2).

Arrange the white chocolate ring on top (3), then decorate with dots of glaze, caramel cubes (4) and sugar paste flowers (5).

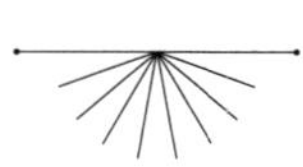

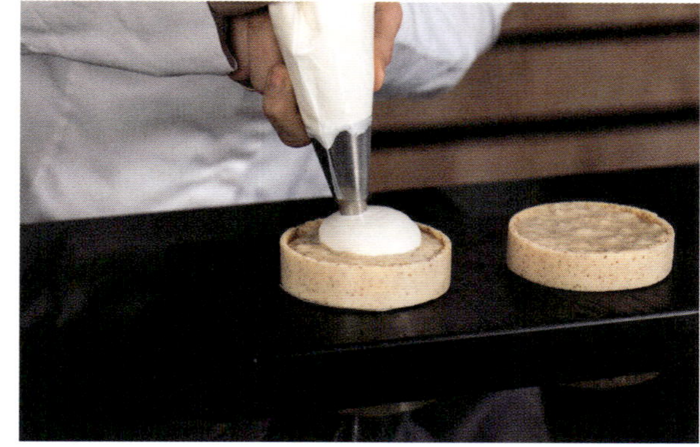

2.

Pipe a mound of Chantilly cream on top.

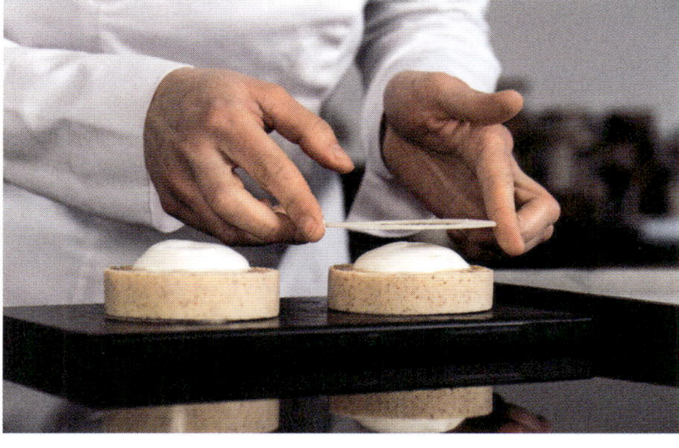

1.

Cover the bottom of the sponge-lined pastry rings with 6 g of reconstituted shortbread and refrigerate, then fill with rice pudding.

3.

Arrange the white chocolate ring on top.

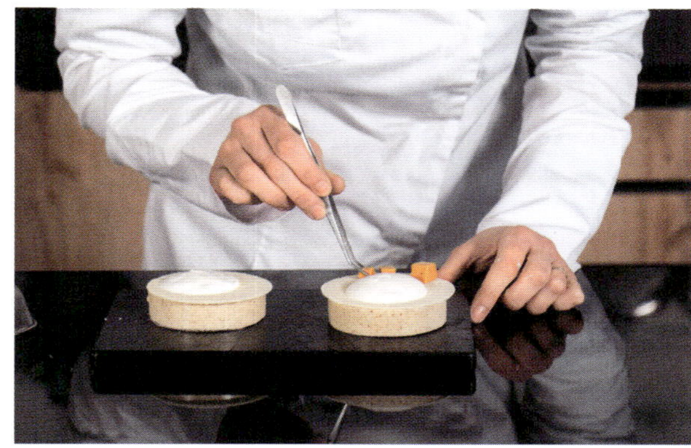

4.

Decorate with dots of neutral glaze, caramel cubes...

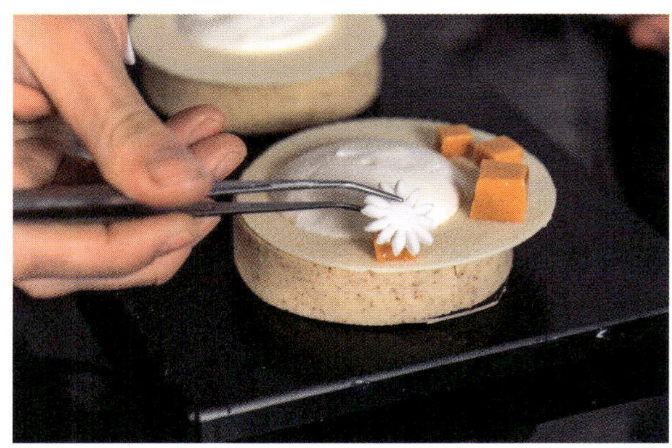

5.

...and sugar paste flowers.

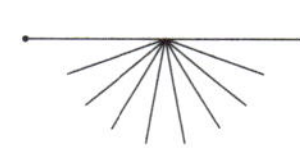

Serves 8

Preparation	**Resting**	**Cooking**
2 hours 30 minutes	2–3 hours	5 hours 10 minutes

Strawberry and raspberry pavlova

Swiss meringue
100 g egg whites
100 g caster sugar
100 g icing sugar

Strawberry confit
350 g fresh strawberries
3 g pectin
10 g light brown soft sugar
1 gelatine leaf
75 g fresh raspberries
120 g fresh blueberries

Pain de Gênes sponge
50 g unsalted butter
160 g almond paste
2 eggs
30 g T55 (plain) flour
2 g baking powder

Swiss meringue In the bowl of a stand mixer, whisk the egg whites and caster sugar by hand in a bain-marie while heating to 70°C, then return the bowl to the mixer, fit with a wire whisk attachment and beat briskly until cool (1). Fold the sifted icing sugar into the beaten egg whites. Transfer the meringue to a piping bag and pipe 7-cm-diameter flowers. To do this, draw 7-cm circles on a sheet of baking paper, then turn the sheet over. Snip off the end of the piping bag on a diagonal and pipe petals of Swiss meringue to fill the circles (2). Bake for 5 hours at 80°C.

Strawberry confit Soak the gelatine leaf in cold water. Purée the fresh strawberries and gently heat the purée to 40°C. Mix the pectin with the sugar and add to the purée. Bring to the boil for 1 minute, then dissolve the gelatine in the mixture. Pour the confit into cone-shaped moulds and add one raspberry and three blueberries to each one, pressing lightly to press the fruit inside. Freeze at -20°C.

Pain de Gênes sponge Melt the butter. In a stand mixer, mix the almond paste with the eggs and beat to a ribbon consistency. Incorporate the sifted flour and baking powder into the mixture, followed by the melted butter. Pour the batter into a silicone cake mould to a depth of 1 cm and bake at 170°C for 8 minutes. Cut the sponge into 4.5-cm-diameter discs.

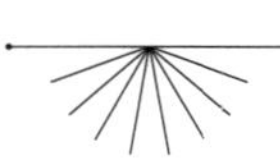

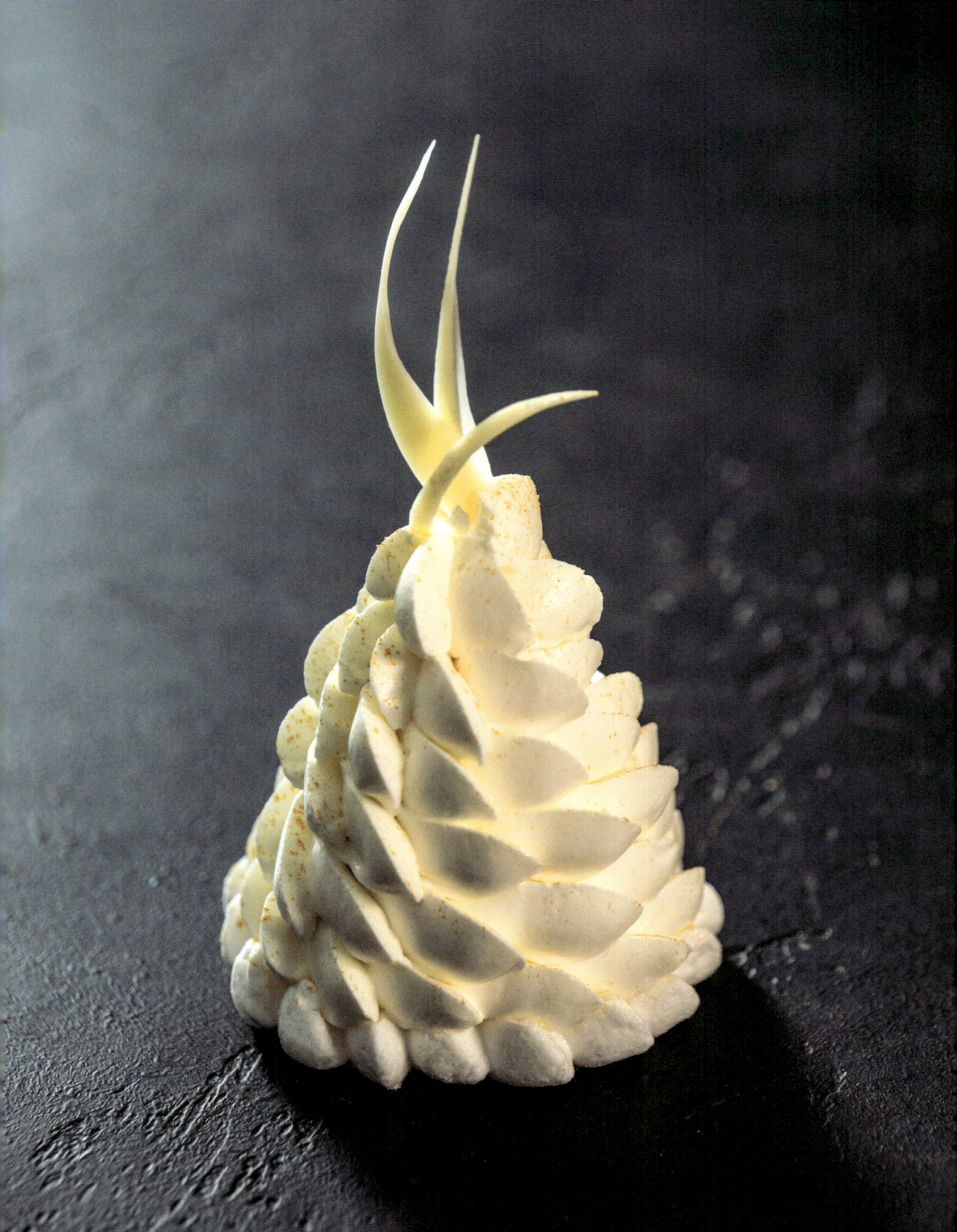

Orange blossom Chantilly cream
375 g whipping cream (35% fat)
100 g mascarpone cheese
15 g icing sugar
2.5 g orange blossom water

Decoration
100 g white chocolate
10 g edible silver or gold glitter

Orange blossom Chantilly cream Make a Chantilly cream by whipping the cream with the mascarpone and icing sugar. Then gently fold in the orange blossom water. Transfer the cream to a piping bag and snip off the end on a diagonal.

Assembly

Prepare the Swiss meringue flowers and strawberry jam inserts. Temper the white chocolate. Using the back of a knife, make white chocolate teardrops on a 5-cm-wide acetate strip (3), insert the strip lengthways into a tube and allow them to harden in the fridge (4). Then sprinkle the teardrops with 5 g of glitter.

Whip the Chantilly cream. Attach a sponge disc to each meringue with a small dot of the cream, then attach a frozen strawberry jam cone to the sponge with a little more cream (5).

Pipe petals of Chantilly cream all around the cone (6). Decorate the top of each pavlova with three white chocolate teardrops. Use a brush to gently apply 5 g of glitter to the pavlovas.

Chill the pavlovas at 4°C for 2–3 hours before serving.

'Pavlova is one of my favourite desserts. It's a fresh and light dessert that is easy to make and can adapt to each season. For instance, you can use pears and an almond syrup-flavoured Chantilly cream in winter, chestnuts and a rum Chantilly cream in autumn, and white peaches, redcurrants and a verbena-infused Chantilly cream in summer.'

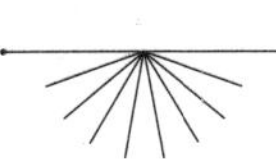

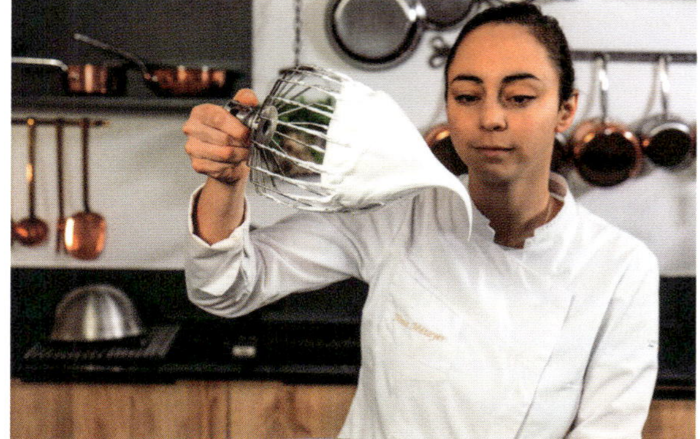

I.

Make the Swiss meringue: it is ready when it forms stiff peaks.

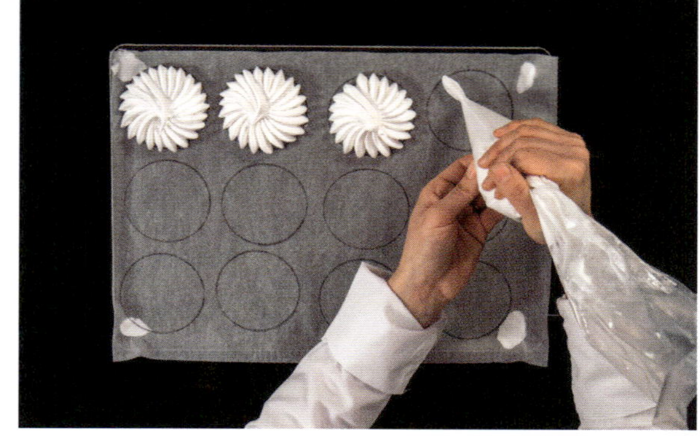

2.

Draw 7-cm circles on a sheet of baking paper, then turn the sheet over and pipe petals of Swiss meringue to fill the circles using a piping bag with its end snipped off on a diagonal.

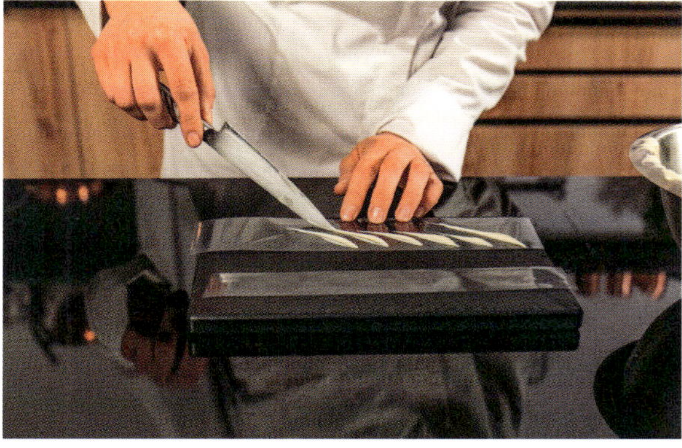

3.

To decorate, temper the white chocolate and make teardrops along a 5-cm-wide acetate strip using the back of a knife. Insert the strip into a tube and refrigerate.

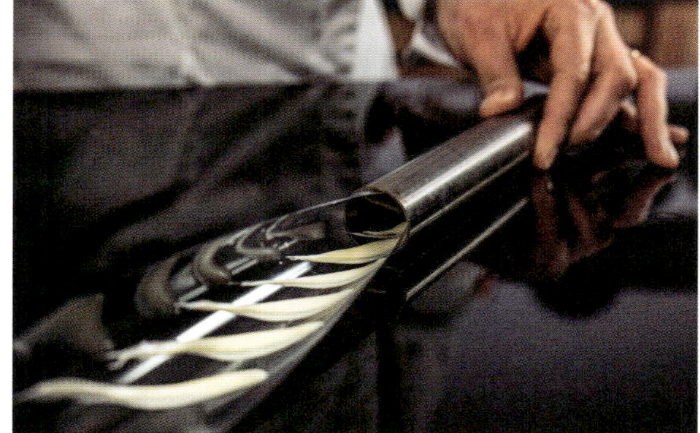

4.

Then brush the chocolate teardrops with glitter.

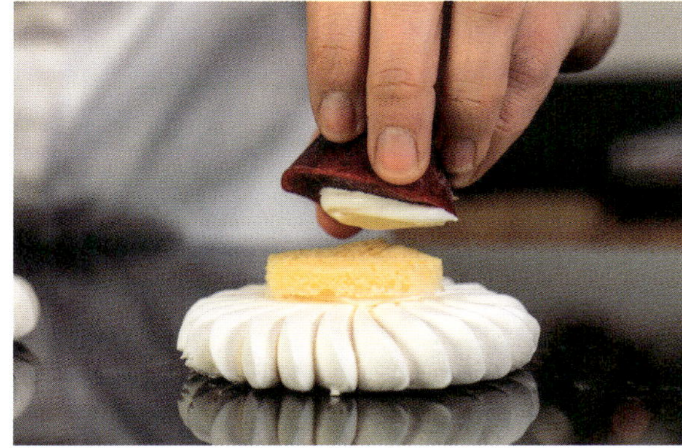

5.

To assemble, attach a sponge disc to each meringue with a small dot of Chantilly cream, then attach the strawberry jam cone to the sponge.

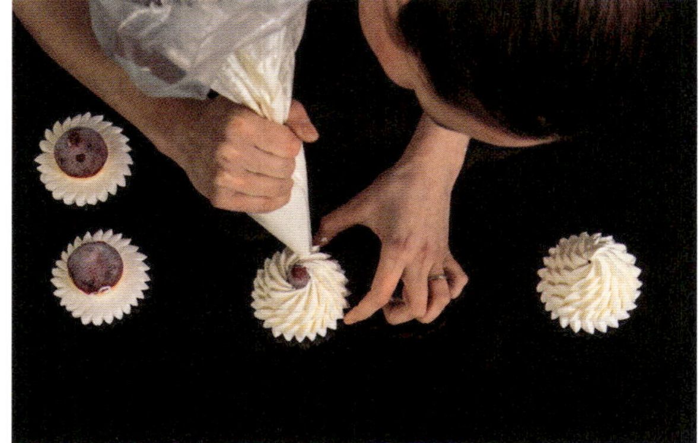

6.

Using a piping bag with the end snipped off on a diagonal, pipe petals of Chantilly cream all around the cone, then decorate.

Serves 6

Preparation	Resting	Cooking
1 hour 30 minutes	2 hours 30 minutes	36 minutes

Cherry clafoutis

Sweet pastry

70 g unsalted butter, at room
   temperature
45 g icing sugar
120 g T55 (plain) flour
10 g ground almonds
25 g egg
0.7 g salt

Clafoutis

200 g whipping cream (35% fat)
150 g double cream (40% fat)
1 egg
3 egg yolks
60 g light brown soft sugar
10 g T55 flour
70 g ground almonds
2 g salt
100 g pitted cherries

Sweet pastry flower tuiles

50 g T55 flour
25 g egg
12 g coconut sugar
0.2 g salt

Sweet pastry Mix the butter with the icing sugar either by hand or in a stand mixer fitted with a paddle attachment. Add the flour, ground almonds, egg and salt. Mix to a smooth dough. Wrap the pastry in cling film and allow it to rest in the fridge for 2 hours. Roll out the pastry to a 2-mm thickness. Using a 9-cm-diameter biscuit cutter, cut out 6 pastry discs. Bake for 10 minutes at 160°C, until golden.

Clafoutis Whisk both creams with the whole egg and yolks (1). Incorporate the sugar, flour, ground almonds and salt. Fill 8-cm-diameter silicone moulds with the clafoutis batter (2). Arrange cherries in each clafoutis (3) and bake for 10 minutes at 180°C.

Sweet pastry flower tuiles Make the pastry by mixing all the ingredients together. Roll out the pastry as thinly as possible and allow to dry for 30 minutes (4). Cut very thin strips of pastry (5) and arrange them into flowers with stems (6–7). Bake at 110°C for 15 minutes.

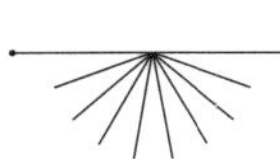

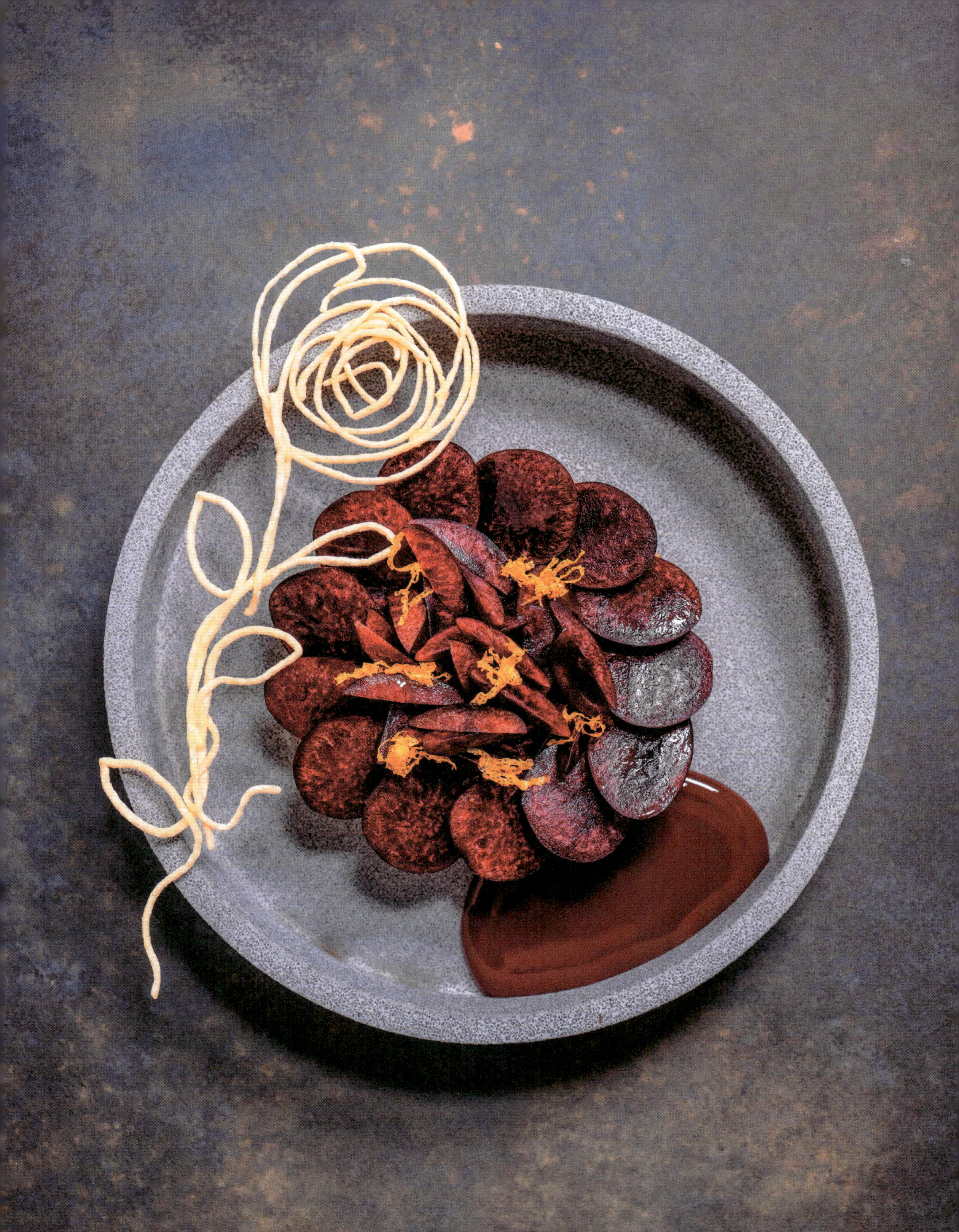

Cherry confit

300 g black cherries
30 g light brown soft sugar (1)
50 g unsalted butter
1 g salt
Juice of 1 lemon
10 g verbena leaves
40 g light brown soft sugar (2)
4 g pectin

1 lemon
300 g pitted cherries

Cherry confit Halve and pit the cherries. Make a caramel in a hot frying pan by melting the sugar (1), then add the butter and salt. Cook the cherries in the caramel. When the cherries are cooked, add the lemon juice. Drain the fruit and collect the sauce.

Using an immersion blender, purée the cooked cherries, then heat to 40°C and add the sugar (2) mixed with the pectin. Bring to the boil and allow to cook for 1½ minutes. Transfer the confit to a tray and cool quickly in the freezer. When cold, blend the confit. Set aside in the fridge.

Assembly Grate the lemon zest. Allow the grated zest to dry out at room temperature for about 1 hour. Cut some of the cherries into pretty slices and other into small segments. Arrange a clafoutis in the centre of each plate. Cover it with a sweet pastry disc. Place a tablespoon of cherry confit on top and spread it carefully with the spoon. Arrange cherry slices overlapped in a ring over the jam and fill the centre with small segments. Decorate with dried lemon zest. Carefully arrange the flower tuile on the plate and serve with the warmed cherry sauce.

'The sweet pastry flower tuiles takes a long time to make. You can replace them by making flowers in pâte à cigarette and using your own silicone mould. This will allow you to make them more quickly and in larger numbers and serve your dessert at others' dinner parties. Detailed instructions with step-by-step illustrations can be found on pages 214 and 215.'

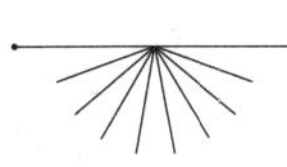

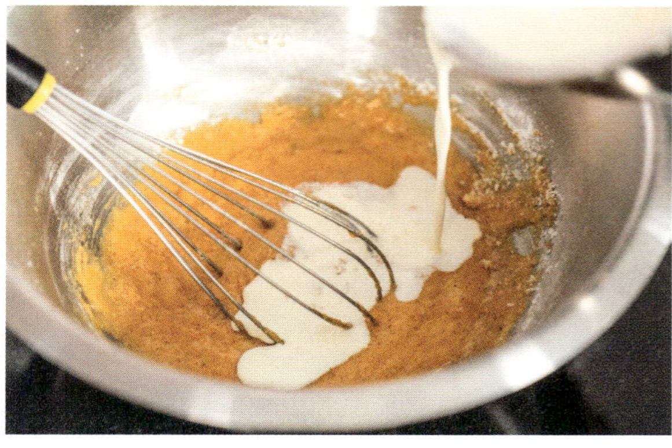

To make the clafoutis, whisk both creams with the whole egg and yolks. Incorporate the sugar, flour, ground almonds and salt.

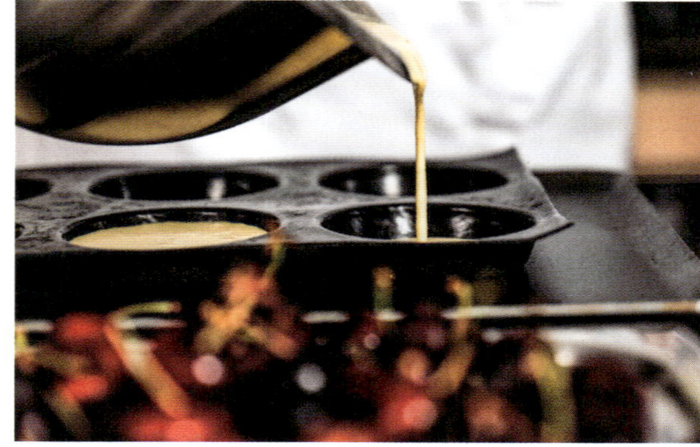

Fill 8-cm-diameter silicone moulds with the clafoutis batter.

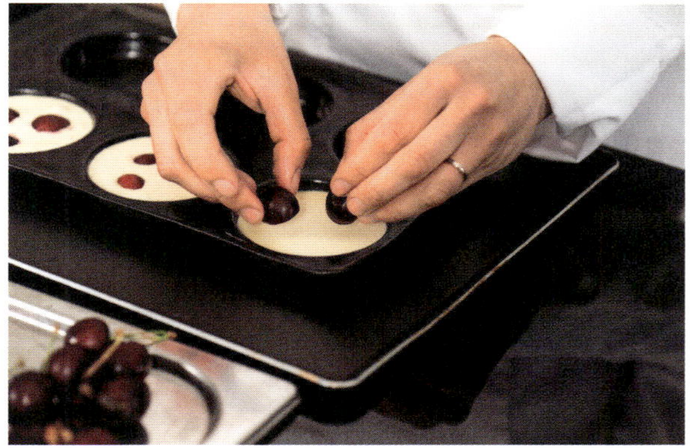

Arrange cherries in each clafoutis and bake for 10 minutes at 180°C.

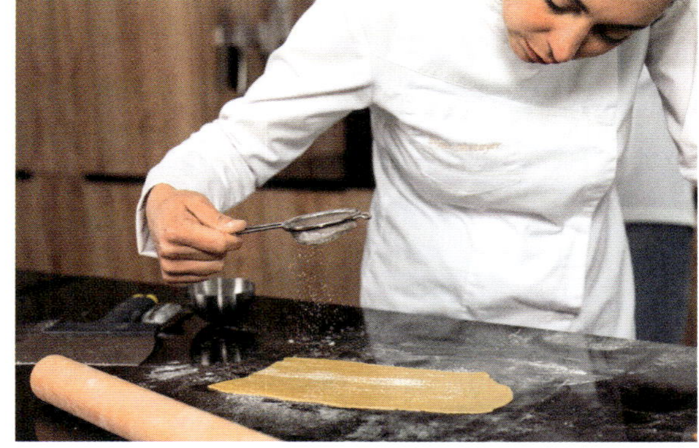

To make the tuiles, roll out the pastry as thinly as possible and allow to dry for 30 minutes.

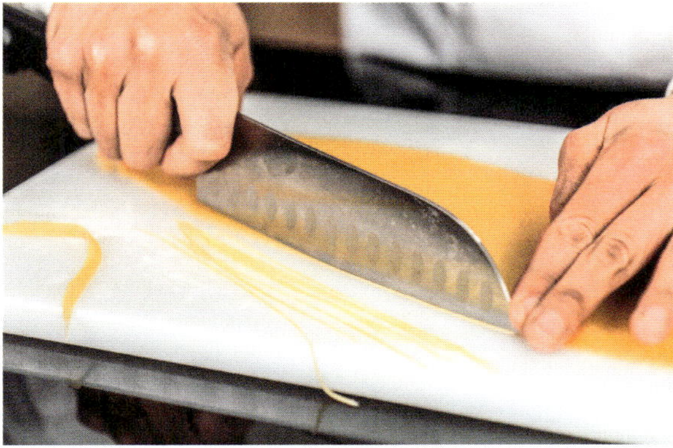

Cut very thin strips of pastry.

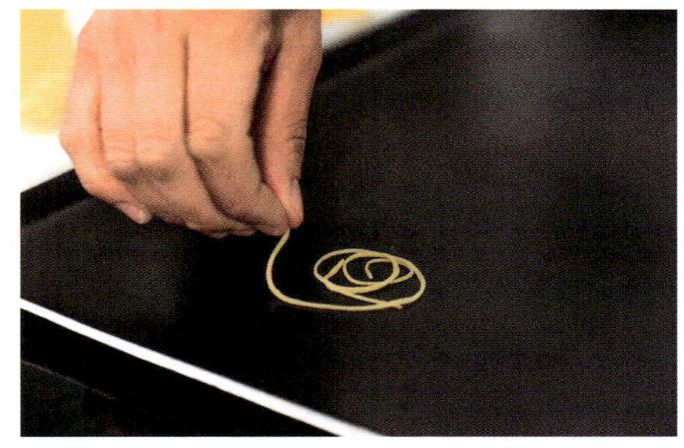

Arrange the strips into...

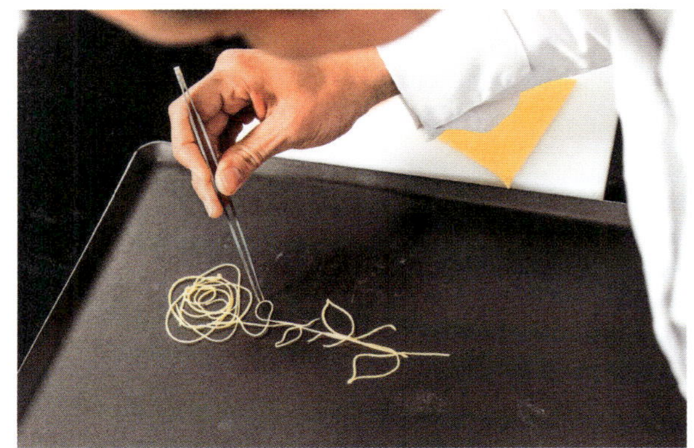

...flowers with stems. Bake at 110°C for 15 minutes.

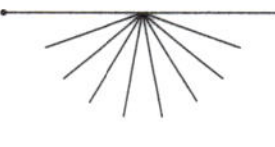

Serves 6

Preparation
30 minutes

Cooking
25 minutes

My Mum's crumble

4 apples

4 pears

1 lemon

1 g salt

30 g caster sugar

30 g unsalted butter

Crumble topping

200 g unsalted butter, at room
   temperature

200 g light brown soft sugar

100 g ground hazelnuts

100 g ground almonds

2 g fleur de sel

1 g ground cinnamon

Peel and chop the apples and pears. Grate lemon zest over the fruit pieces. Squeeze the lemon and drizzle the fruit with the juice to keep from turning brown.

In a saucepan, make a caramel with the sugar and butter, then add the fruit, zest and salt. Allow the fruit to caramelise for a few minutes over a medium heat, stirring regularly.

Crumble topping Cut the butter into pieces and put it into a large mixing bowl together with the sugar, ground nuts, fleur de sel and cinnamon. Using the tips of your fingers, rub the butter into the other ingredients to form a crumbly dough.

Preheat the oven to 180°C. Spread the caramelised fruit in an ovenproof dish and sprinkle the crumble over the top. Bake in the oven for about 20 minutes, until nice and golden.

Serve warm with vanilla ice cream.

'This is my favourite dessert, which my mum used to make. I can still smell her crumble baking in the oven and whetting my appetite — I couldn't wait for dessert! My mum would change the fruit to match the season. I love this dessert, which combines sweetness and indulgence, with its warm and juicy fruit topped with the buttery and crispy crumble. And it's so easy that the whole family can make it together.'

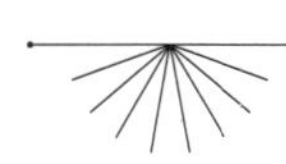

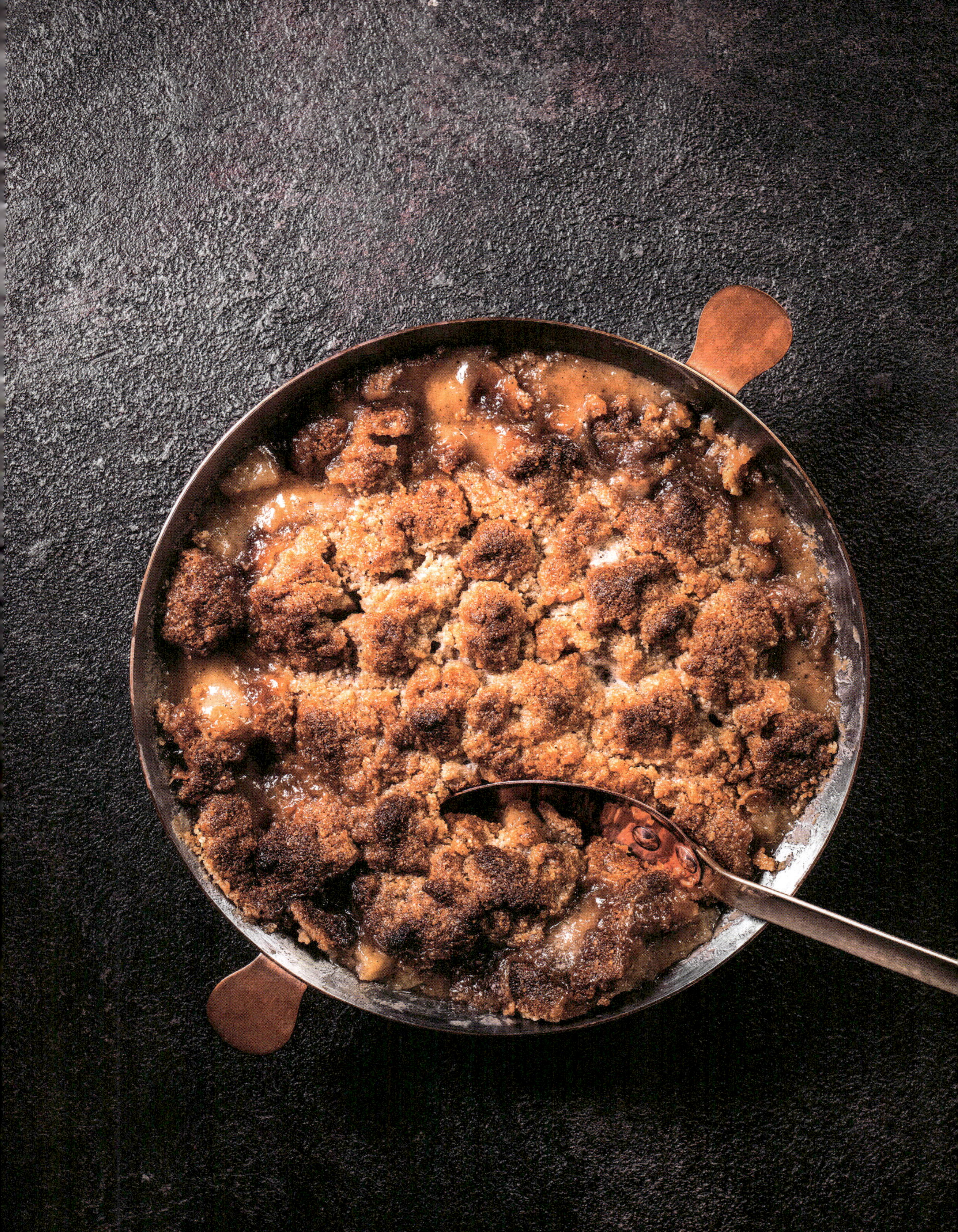

Serves 6

Preparation	Resting	Cooking
2 hours 30 minutes	20 hours	30 minutes

Chocolate and rosemary flower

Chocolate mousse foam

35 g caster sugar

50 g water

2 g cocoa powder

75 g dark chocolate (70% cocoa)

225 g whipping cream (35% fat)

Caraïbe chocolate crémeux

125 g full-fat milk

125 g whipping cream

2 egg yolks

12 g light brown soft sugar

117 g Valrhona® Caraïbe dark
 chocolate (66% cocoa)

0.5 g salt

Chocolate shortbread

62 g unsalted butter, at room
 temperature

55 g icing sugar

10 g egg yolk

1 g salt

75 g T55 (plain) flour

10 g cocoa powder

40 g ground almonds

Chocolate mousse foam The day before, bring the sugar and water to the boil in a saucepan, then add the cocoa and blend with an immersion blender. In a saucepan, bring the cream to the boil over a low heat and pour it over the chocolate. Mix well until smooth and thick. Then combine both mixtures. Strain through a conical sieve and blend until smooth. Refrigerate overnight at 4°C, then transfer to a siphon and insert two gas chargers.

Caraïbe chocolate crémeux In a saucepan, bring the milk and cream to the boil. Whisk the egg yolks with the sugar until thick and pale. Carefully add part of the cream and milk mixture to the blanched egg yolks. Stir well. Transfer the mixture back to the saucepan and cook it until the temperature reaches 85°C and it is thick enough to coat a spoon. Then add the custard into the dark chocolate a third or quarter at a time. Add the salt and mix with a silicone spatula to combine, then blend with an immersion blender until very smooth and thick. Allow to set in the fridge for 5 hours before use.

Chocolate shortbread In a stand mixer fitted with a paddle attachment, mix the butter with the icing sugar. Add the egg yolk and salt, then incorporate the sifted dry ingredients to form a dough. Roll the pastry out to a 2-mm thickness and freeze (1). Then cut out rings with a 4-cm outer diameter and a 3-cm inner diameter (2). Bake at 155°C for 25 minutes. Make 3 rings for each individual dessert (3).

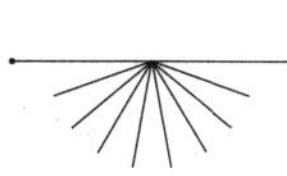

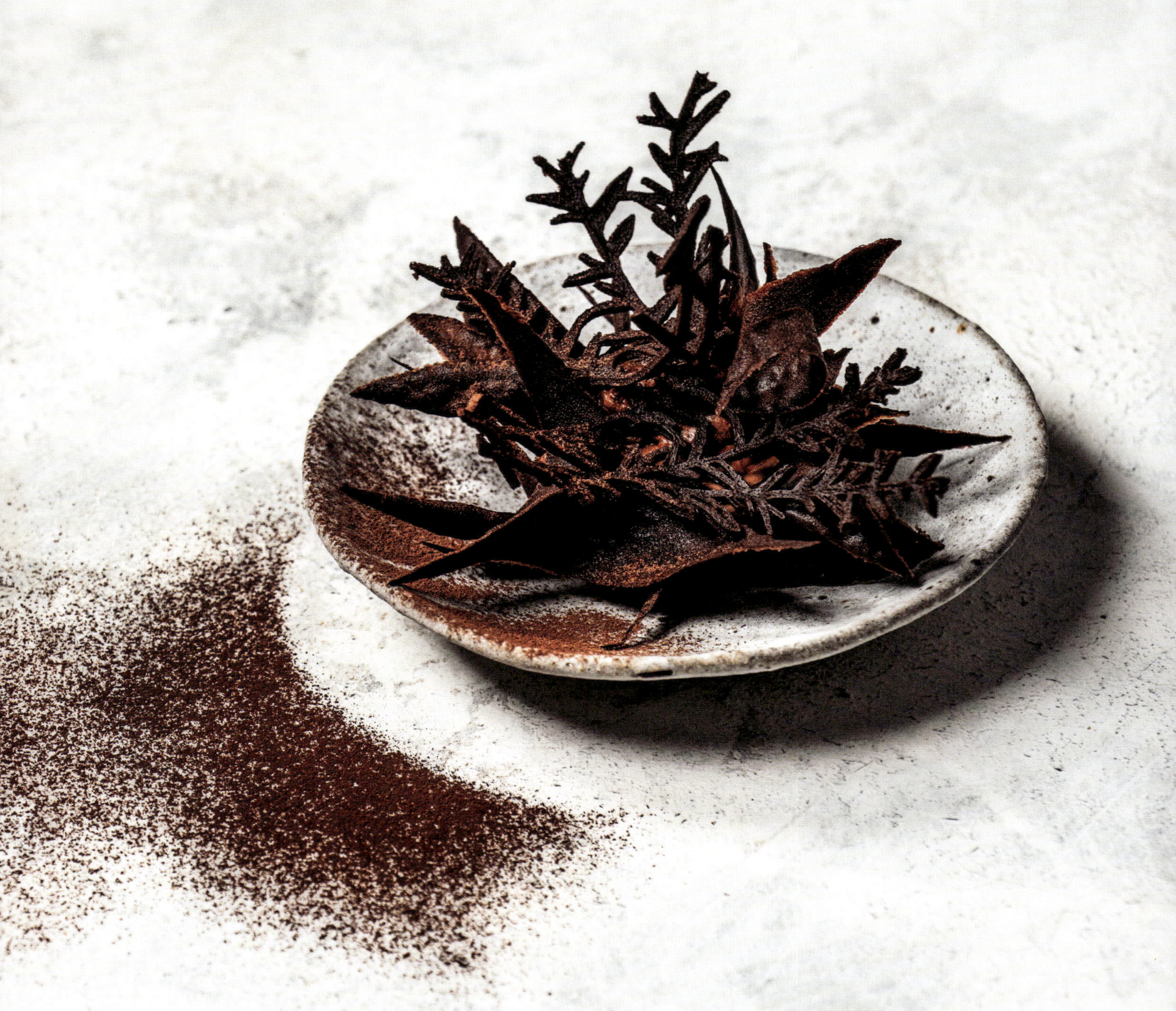

Rosemary fromage blanc sorbet

112 g water

100 g light brown soft sugar

40 g lemon juice

250 g fromage blanc

5 g rosemary

Marinated lemon zest segments

2 lemons

40 g lemon juice

110 g water

70 g light brown soft sugar

1 sprig rosemary

Cocoa tuiles

60 g unsalted butter

60 g caster sugar

40 g T55 flour

20 g cocoa powder

2 egg whites

Rosemary fromage blanc sorbet Make a syrup with the water, sugar and lemon juice. Add the rosemary, cover and allow to steep for 30 minutes. Strain the infused syrup through a conical strainer and mix with the fromage blanc. Churn the sorbet base in an ice-cream maker.

Marinated lemon zest segments Remove the zest from the lemons in segments, then squeeze the zested lemons. In a saucepan, make a syrup with the water, lemon juice and sugar then add the rosemary and allow to steep for 30 minutes. Strain the syrup through a conical sieve. Marinate the lemon zest segments in the syrup for at least 2 hours.

Cocoa tuiles Melt the butter, then add the sugar, followed by the flour, cocoa and egg whites. Mix to a paste. Allow it to rest, then make teardrop-shaped tuiles on a baking mat (4). Bake for 4 minutes at 180°C. As soon as they come out of the oven, shape the tuiles into a curve in a yule log tin, or by hand if you don't mind the heat too much (5–6).

Assembly

To make this dessert, start by making the mousse foam mixture. Next, make the chocolate crémeux. Then make the shortbread rings. Make the fromage blanc sorbet base and churn in an ice-cream maker. Prepare the marinated lemon segments and make the tuiles.

Then proceed to assemble all the components. Place a shortbread ring in the centre of a plate and pipe a ring of crémeux over it. Cover the crémeux with a second shortbread ring, cover with more crémeux and top with a last shortbread ring (7).

Fit the piping bag with a 4-mm nozzle and pipe a spiral of crémeux around the shortbread assembly (8).

Pipe fromage blanc sorbet into the centre (9), add marinated lemon zest segments and pipe chocolate mousse foam over the top (10). Decorate the dessert with cocoa tuiles (11–12) and dust with cocoa. Serve immediately.

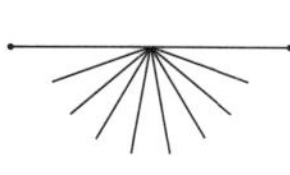

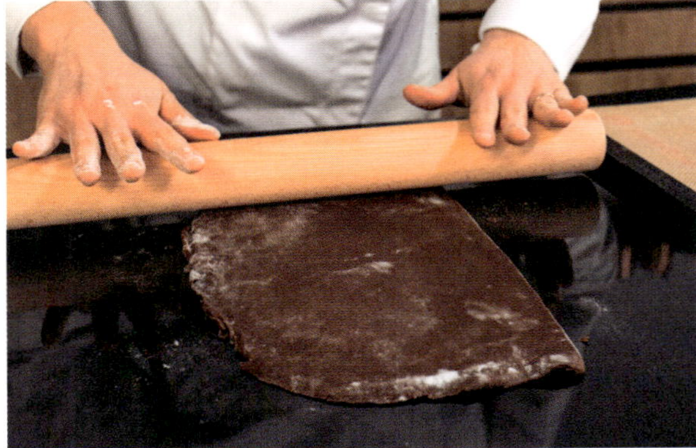

I. To make the chocolate shortbread rings, roll out the pastry to 2 mm and freeze.

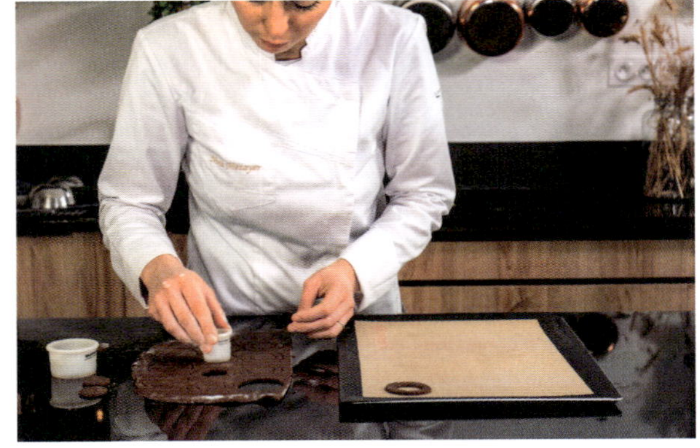

2. Cut out rings with a 4-cm outer diameter and a 3-cm inner diameter.

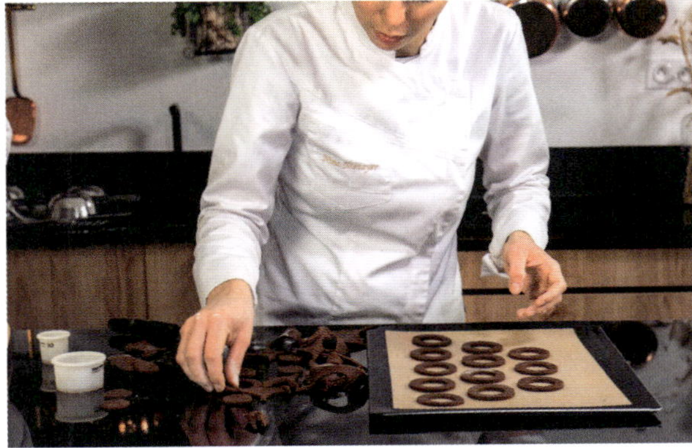

3. Make 3 rings per dessert. Bake at 155°C for 25 minutes.

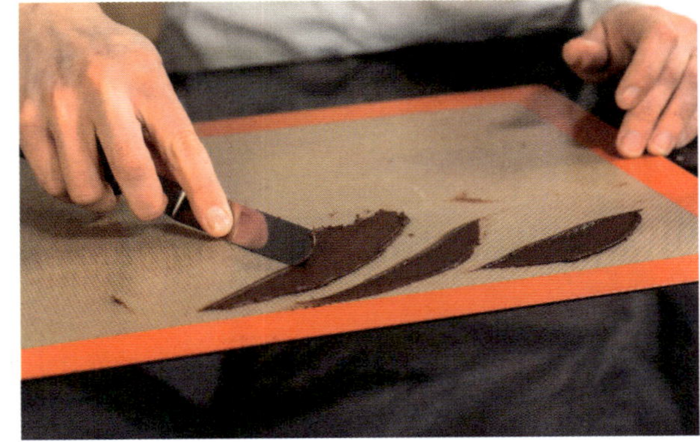

4. To make the cocoa tuiles, spread the paste to make teardrop shapes on a baking mat.

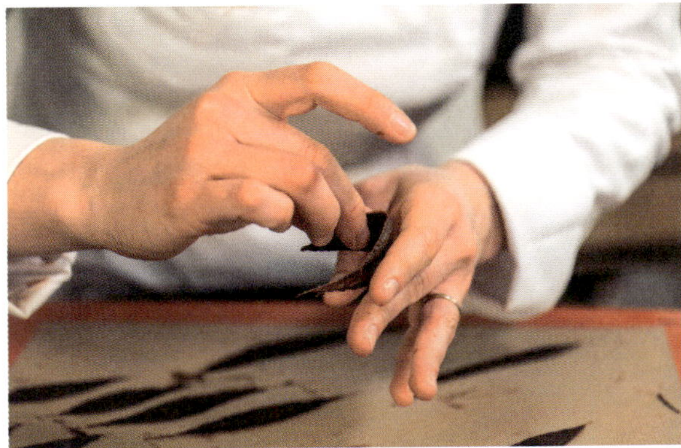

5. Bake for 4 minutes 180°C and shape the tuiles into a curve in a yule log tin as soon as they come out of the oven.

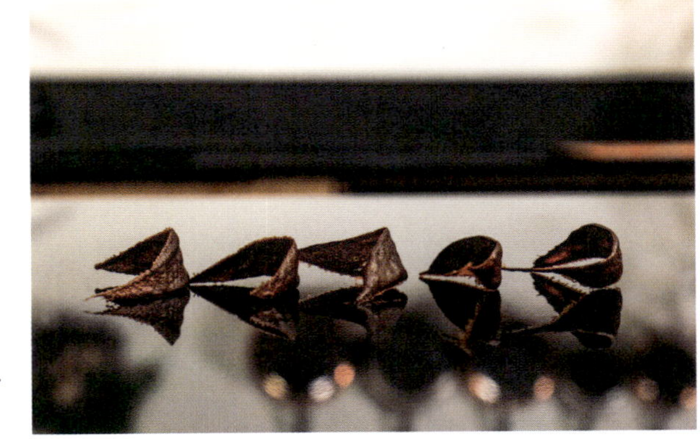

6. The finished tuiles.

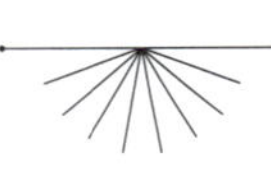

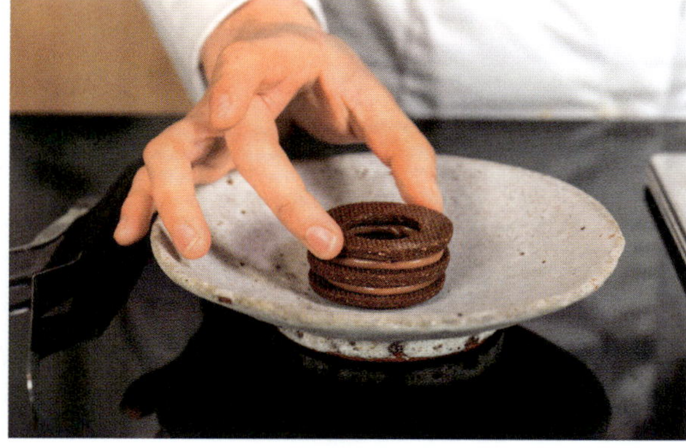

7.

To assemble the dessert, place a shortbread ring in the centre of a plate and pipe a ring of crémeux over it. Cover the crémeux with a second shortbread ring, cover with more crémeux and top with a last shortbread ring.

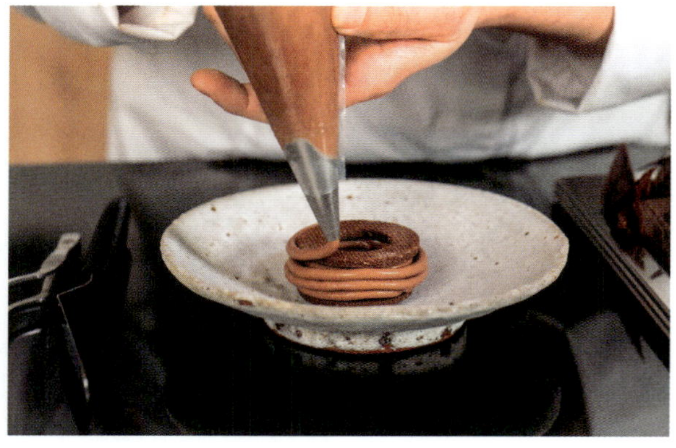

8.

Using a piping bag fitted with a 4-mm nozzle, pipe a crémeux spiral around the shortbread assembly.

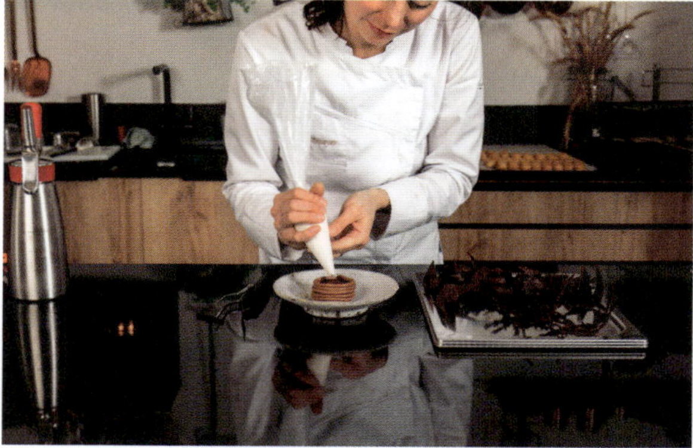

9.

Pipe fromage blanc sorbet into the centre.

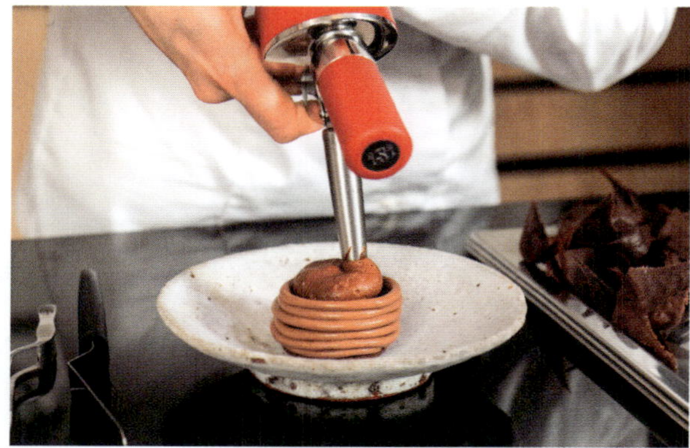

10.

Arrange marinated lemon segments and pipe chocolate mousse foam over the top.

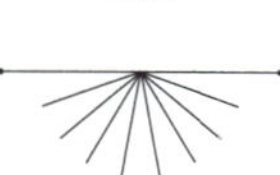

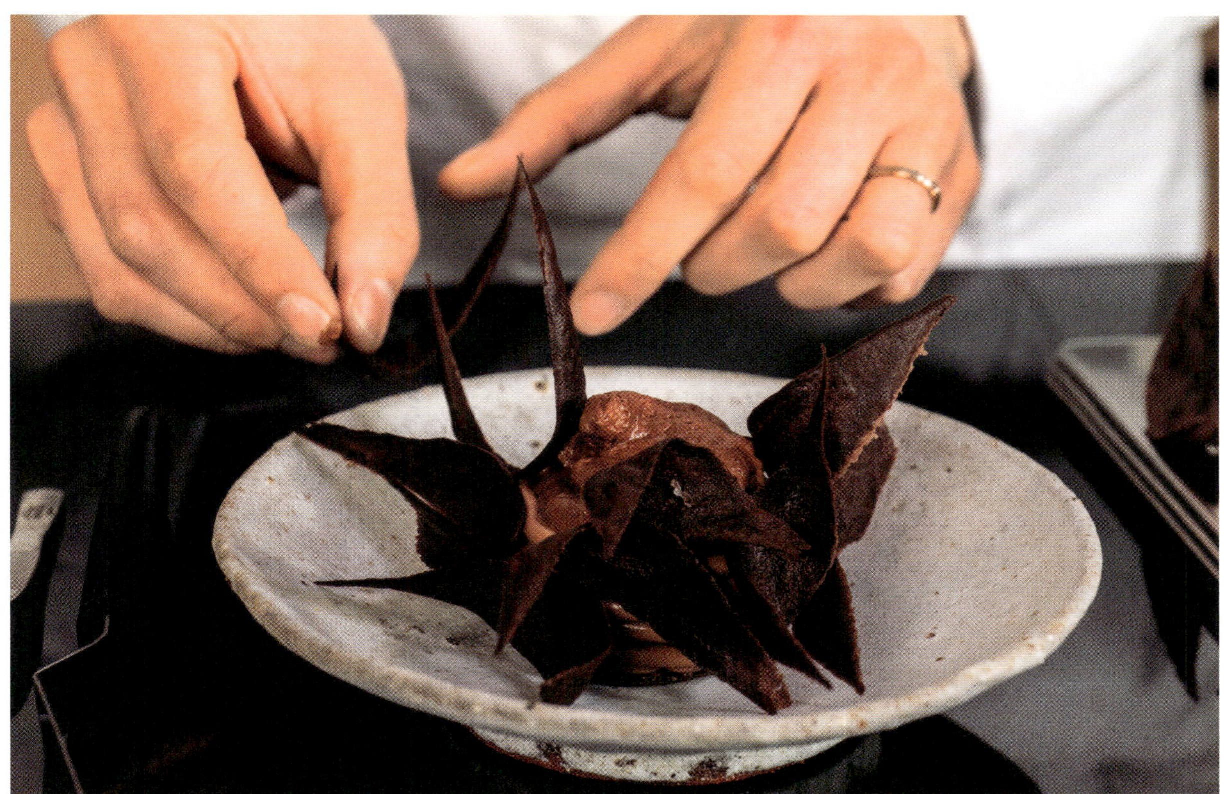

II.

Decorate the dessert with cocoa tuiles...

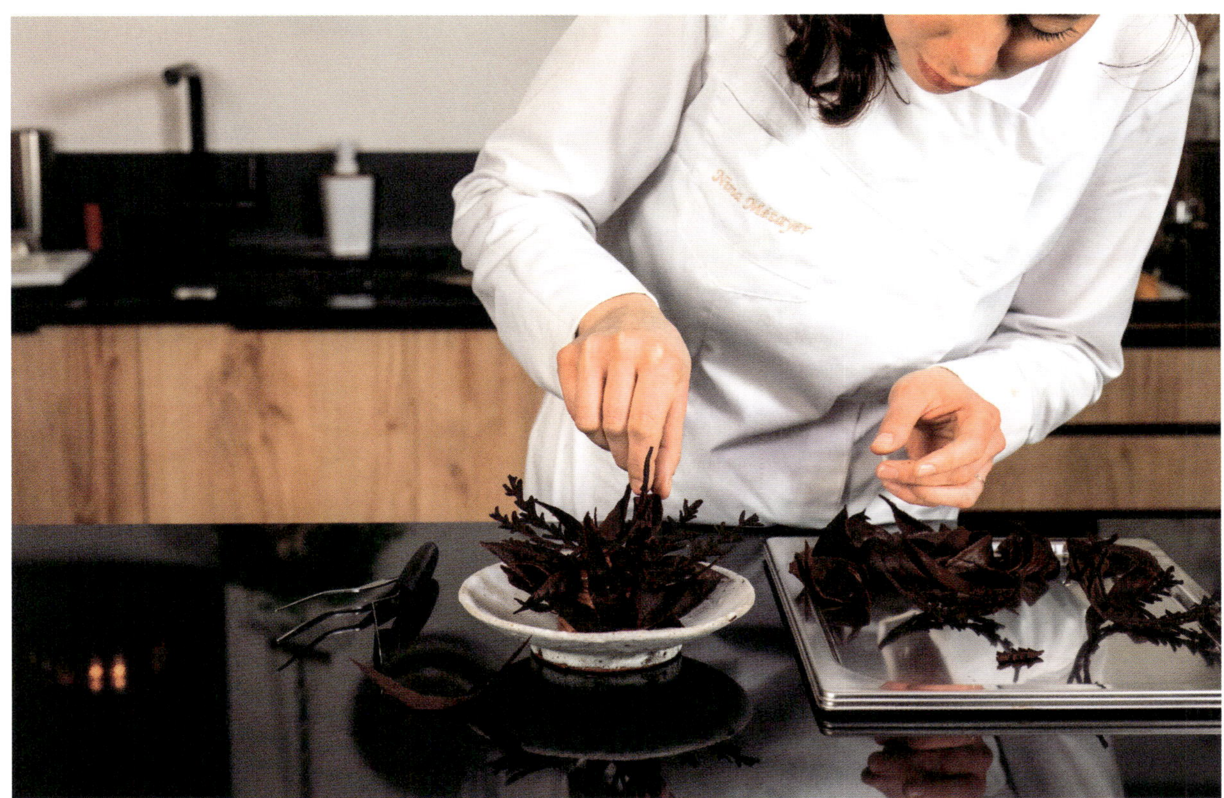

I2.

...before dusting with cocoa. Serve immediately.

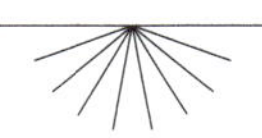

Makes 6 soufflés

Preparation
1 hour 30 minutes

Cooking
13 minutes

Chocolate and pear soufflé

Caramelised pears

3 Comice pears
100 g caster sugar
Juice of 1 lemon

Chocolate soufflé

160 g dark chocolate (64% cocoa)
150 g full-fat milk
10 g cornflour
40 g caster sugar
1 egg yolk
3 egg whites

Decoration

100 g dark chocolate (72% cocoa)
2.5 g edible gold glitter

Assembly

100 g unsalted butter, softened
100 g caster sugar

Caramelised pears Peel the pears and cut out 1.5-cm-thick discs with a slightly smaller diameter than that of the soufflé dishes. In a saucepan, make a dry caramel with the sugar and stop the cooking process with half the lemon juice. Add the pears and caramelise for 5 minutes, then drain.

Chocolate soufflé Melt the chocolate in a bain-marie. Blend the milk and cornflour, then add the sugar and egg yolk and cook to the consistency of a pastry cream. Pour the mixture into the melted chocolate, half at a time, and whisk until smooth. Beat the egg whites to soft peaks and gently fold into the soufflé mixture. Transfer the mixture to a piping bag.

Decoration Temper the chocolate by heat to 55°C, cooling to 28°C and reheating slightly to 31°C. Thinly spread the chocolate over an acetate sheet and cut it into 5-mm-wide strips. Allow the chocolate to harden. Peel off the chocolate strips and brush them with gold glitter.

Assembly Work the butter with a spatula until smooth. Grease 8-cm-diameter and 6-cm-deep soufflé dishes by brushing with the butter and then coating with sugar.

Place a slice of caramelised pear in the bottom of each dish and pipe over with soufflé mixture. Bake the soufflés for 8 minutes at 180°C. Once out of the oven arrange tempered chocolate strips on top of the soufflé and serve.

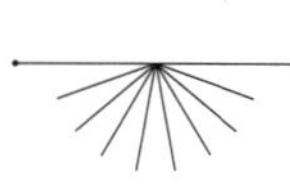

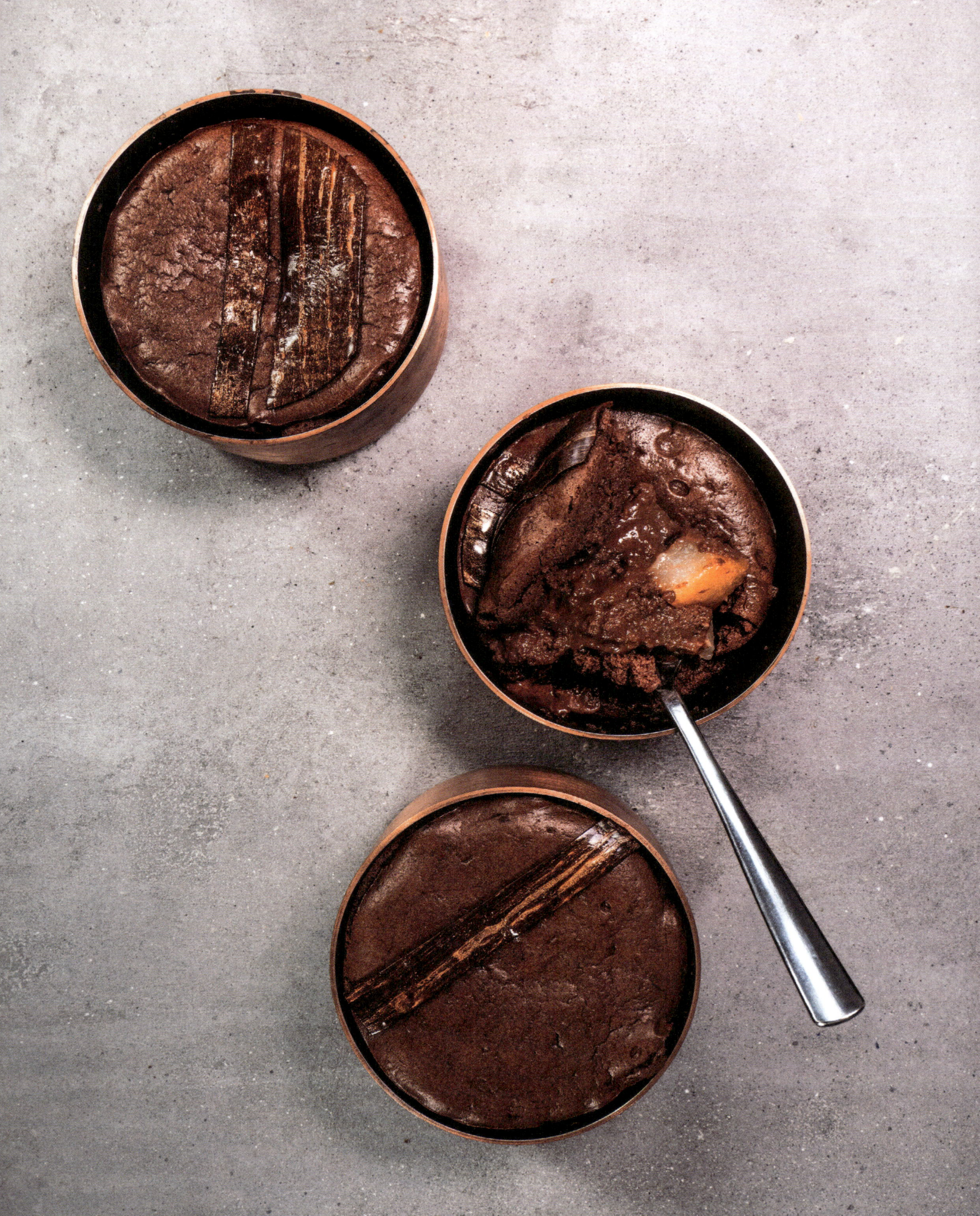

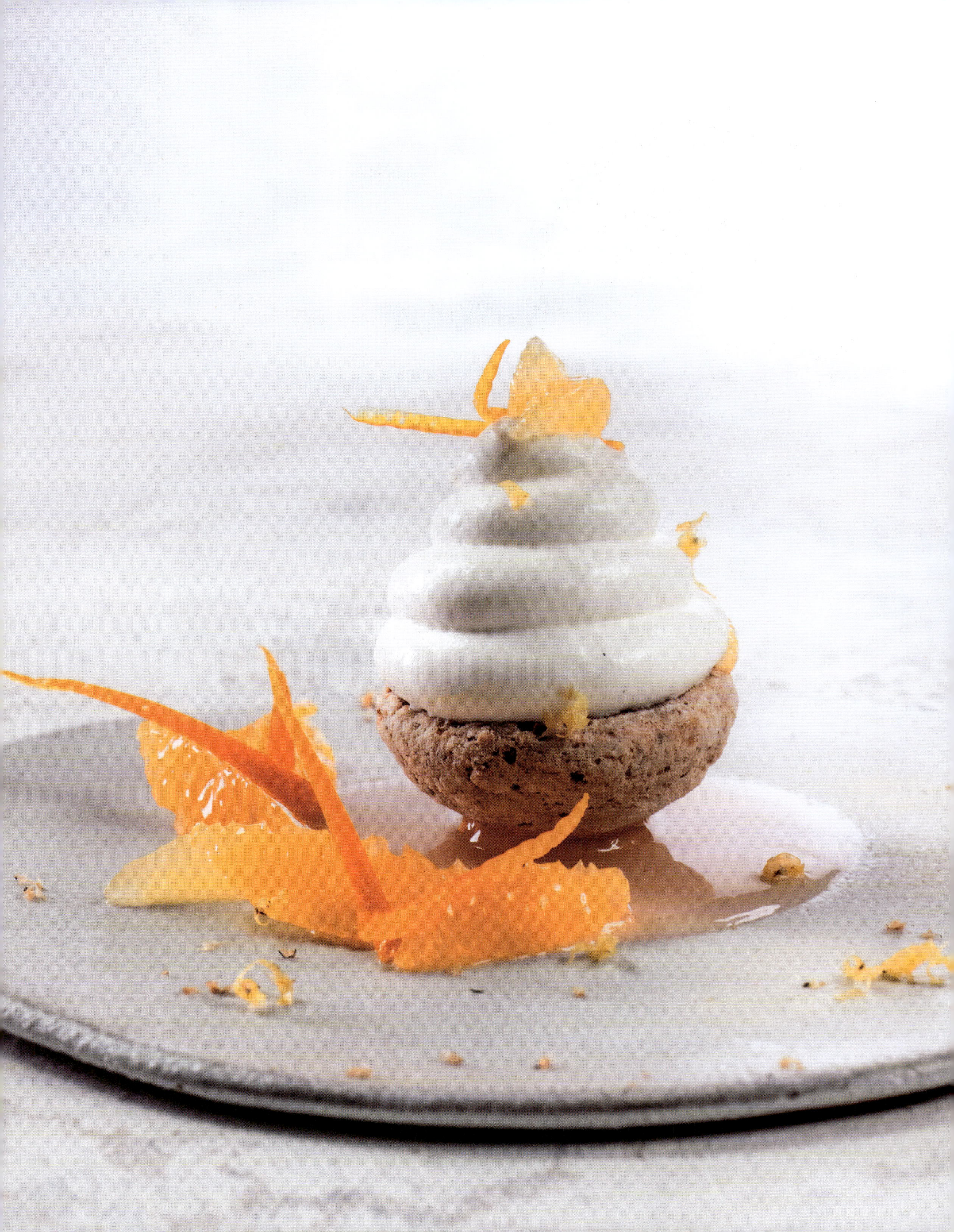

Serves 6	Preparation	Resting	Cooking
	2 hours	15 hours	2 hours 45 minutes

Meringue with grapefruit and Chantilly cream

Grapefruit and vanilla sorbet

158 g water

77 g caster sugar

3 g guar gum

1 vanilla pod

368 g grapefruit juice

Almond meringue shells

100 g egg whites

100 g caster sugar

50 g icing sugar

50 g ground almonds

Grapefruit jelly

210 g grapefruit juice

20 g gelatine mass

(3 g gelatine powder

   and 17 g cold water)

Tonka bean Chantilly cream

½ tonka bean

250 g whipping cream (35% fat)

11 g icing sugar

50 g mascarpone cheese

Candied grapefruit zest

½ grapefruit

100 g grapefruit juice

100 g caster sugar

Grapefruit and vanilla sorbet The day before, heat the water in a saucepan to 50°C. Dissolve the sugar and guar gum mixture. Add the split vanilla pod and scraped-out seeds to the syrup and bring to the boil. Allow to cool, then mix in the grapefruit juice. Refrigerate the sorbet base for 12 hours at 4°C, then churn in an ice-cream maker.

Almond meringue shells In a stand mixer, beat the egg whites to soft peaks, then gradually add the caster sugar while beating to stiff peaks. Sift the icing sugar and ground almonds and fold into the beaten egg whites (1–2). Pipe neat and uniform domes of meringue on a baking tray (3), dust with icing sugar (4) and bake for 30 minutes at 160°C. Then dry out the meringues at 100°C for 2 hours. Allow to cool.

Grapefruit jelly In a saucepan, heat the grapefruit juice and dissolve the gelatine mass. Allow to set in the fridge at 4°C.

Tonka bean Chantilly cream Grate the tonka bean and mix it with the cream. Allow to steep for 3 hours, then strain through a conical sieve. Mix in the sugar and mascarpone and then whip to a Chantilly cream using a whisk.

Candied grapefruit zest Peel the zest from the grapefruit, making sure to remove any remaining pith. Cut the zest into very thin julienne strips and blanch them 3 times, starting from cold water each time. In a saucepan, make a syrup with the grapefruit juice and sugar over a low heat. Then candy the zest by simmering in the syrup for about 15 minutes and drain.

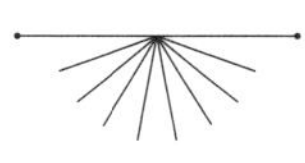

20 g almond paste

3 grapefruits

2 g dried grapefruit
zest

2 g vanilla powder

Assembly

Chill the plates well in the freezer. Once the meringues are completely dry (5), hollow them into shells using a Dremel® Multi-Tool (available from DIY stores) (6–7).

Gently melt the grapefruit jelly. Place a 10-cm-diameter pastry ring in the centre of a chilled plate and fill it with jelly. When the jelly sets slightly, remove the ring. Place a dot of almond paste in the centre of the jelly and attach a meringue shell.

Fill the meringue with grapefruit sorbet and add a few fresh grapefruit segments. Transfer the tonka bean Chantilly cream to a piping bag fitted with a 12-mm plain nozzle and pipe a swirl of cream over the filling.

Decorate the plate with candied grapefruit zest, fresh grapefruit segments and vanilla powder.

Serve immediately.

'This very light and delicate dessert is a great way to end a good meal. It's a simple and elegant dessert of meringue, fruit and Chantilly cream. I learnt this technique and meringue recipe from Camille Lesecq, the former head pastry chef at Le Meurice hotel. He's a chef who I greatly appreciate and has given me a great deal.'

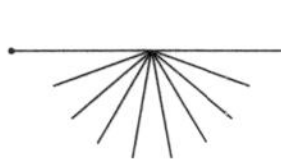

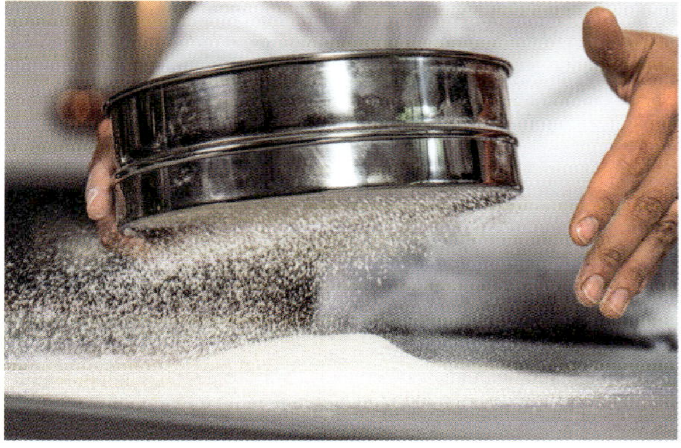

1.

To make the almond meringue shells, sift the dry ingredients.

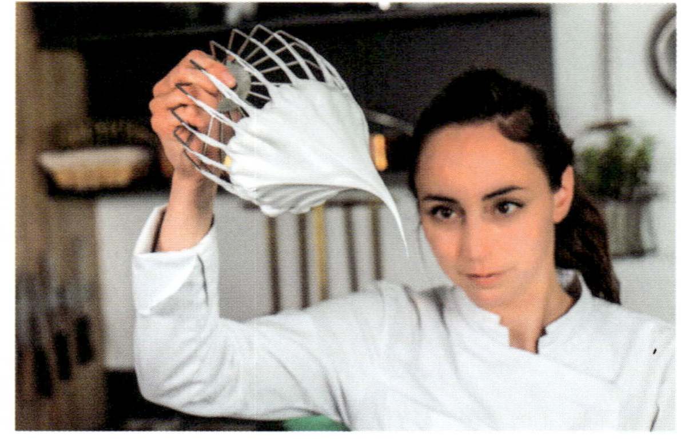

2.

In a stand mixer, beat the egg whites to soft peaks, then gradually add the caster sugar while beating to stiff peaks. Then fold in the icing sugar and ground almonds.

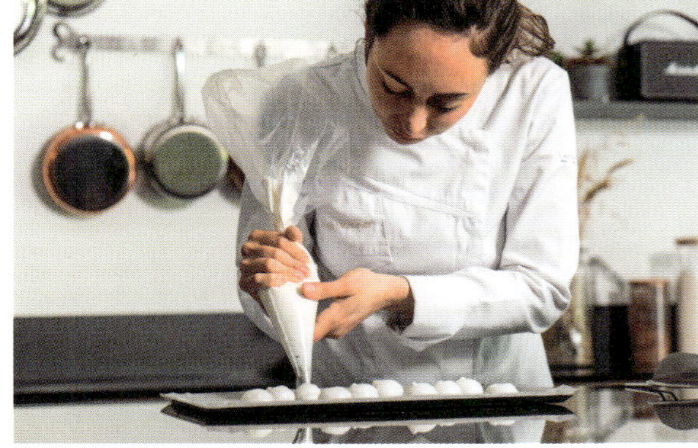

3.

Pipe neat and uniform domes of meringue on a baking tray.

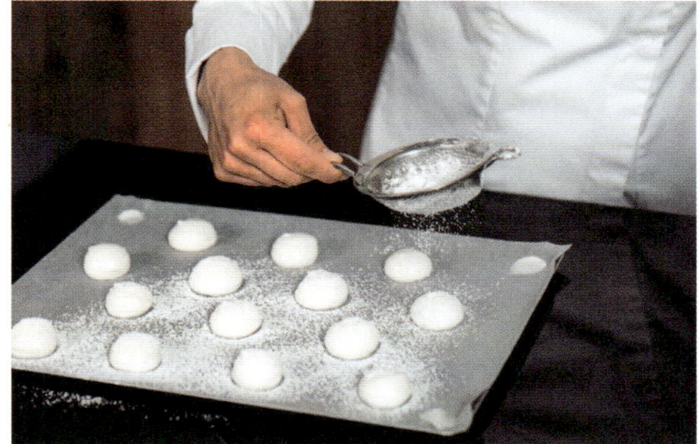

4.

Dust the meringues with icing sugar and bake for 30 minutes at 160°C, then dry them out at 100°C for 2 hours.

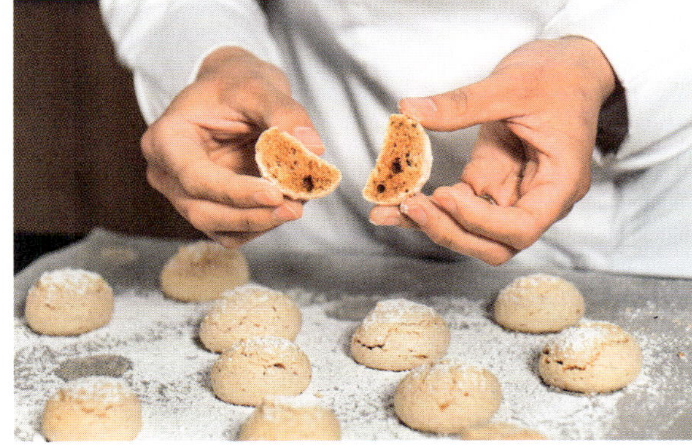

5.

Once completely dry...

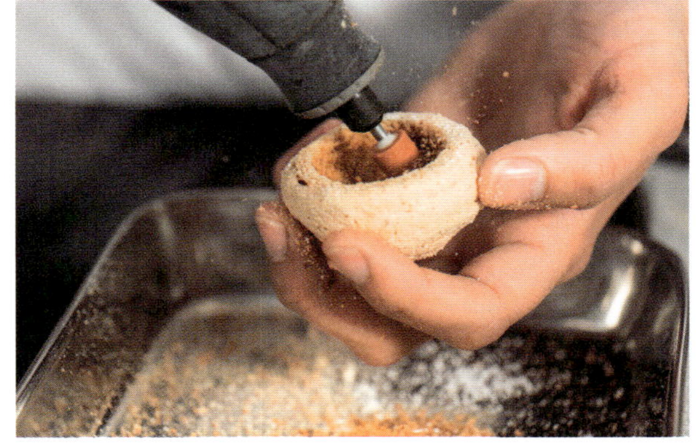

6.

...hollow the meringue into shells with a Dremel® Multi-Tool.

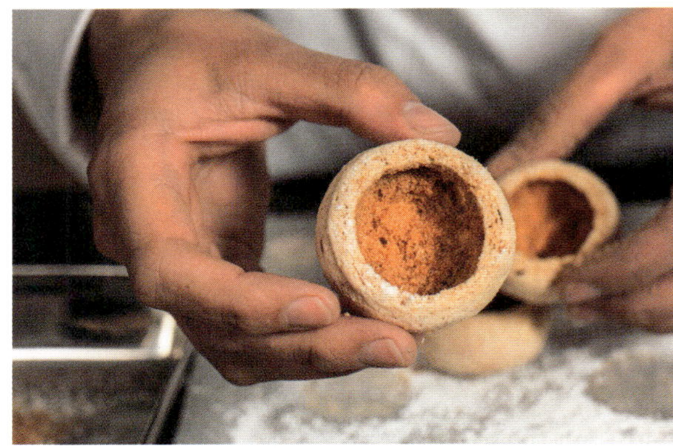

7.

The finished meringue shells. There you go.

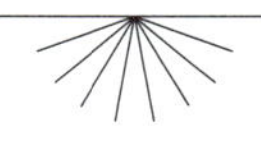

Serves 8

Preparation	Resting	Cooking
3 hours	1 hour	1 hour

Tarte Tatin

Rough puff pastry

200 g T55 (plain) flour
240 g unsalted butter, cold
8 g caster sugar
3 g salt
90 g water

Hazelnut sponge

16 g unsalted butter
40 g icing sugar
40 g ground almonds
40 g ground hazelnuts
3 egg whites
30 g caster sugar

Rough puff pastry Cut the butter into pieces and mix with the flour, sugar and salt. Add the water and work to a smooth dough but with small pieces of butter still visible. Wrap the dough in cling film and rest it in the fridge for 1 hour, then perform 5 single turns. Rest the pastry in the fridge between turns if necessary.

Roll out the pastry to a 3.5-mm-thick sheet. Place the pastry sheet on a baking tray and prick it all over with a fork. Cover with another baking tray and bake at 160°C. After 10 minutes, remove the trays from the oven and cut out 8-cm-diameter discs in the pastry (1). Cover the pastry with a tray again, return it to the oven and bake again for about 25 minutes, until evenly coloured (2). Dust the discs with icing sugar and bake for 8 minutes at 180°C (3), then raise the oven temperature to 240°C for a few seconds until the puff pastry turns glossy all over (4).

Hazelnut sponge Melt the butter in a saucepan. Sift the icing sugar and ground nuts into a bowl. In a stand mixer, beat the egg whites to soft peaks, then gradually add the caster sugar while beating to stiff peaks. Gently fold in the ground nuts and icing sugar mixture and then incorporate the melted butter. Using an angled palette knife, spread the batter very thinly over a baking mat, lightly deflating, and bake for 8 minutes at 180°C. Using a biscuit cutter, cut out 7-cm-diameter discs.

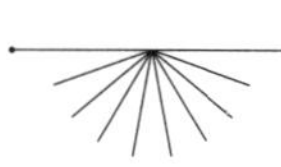

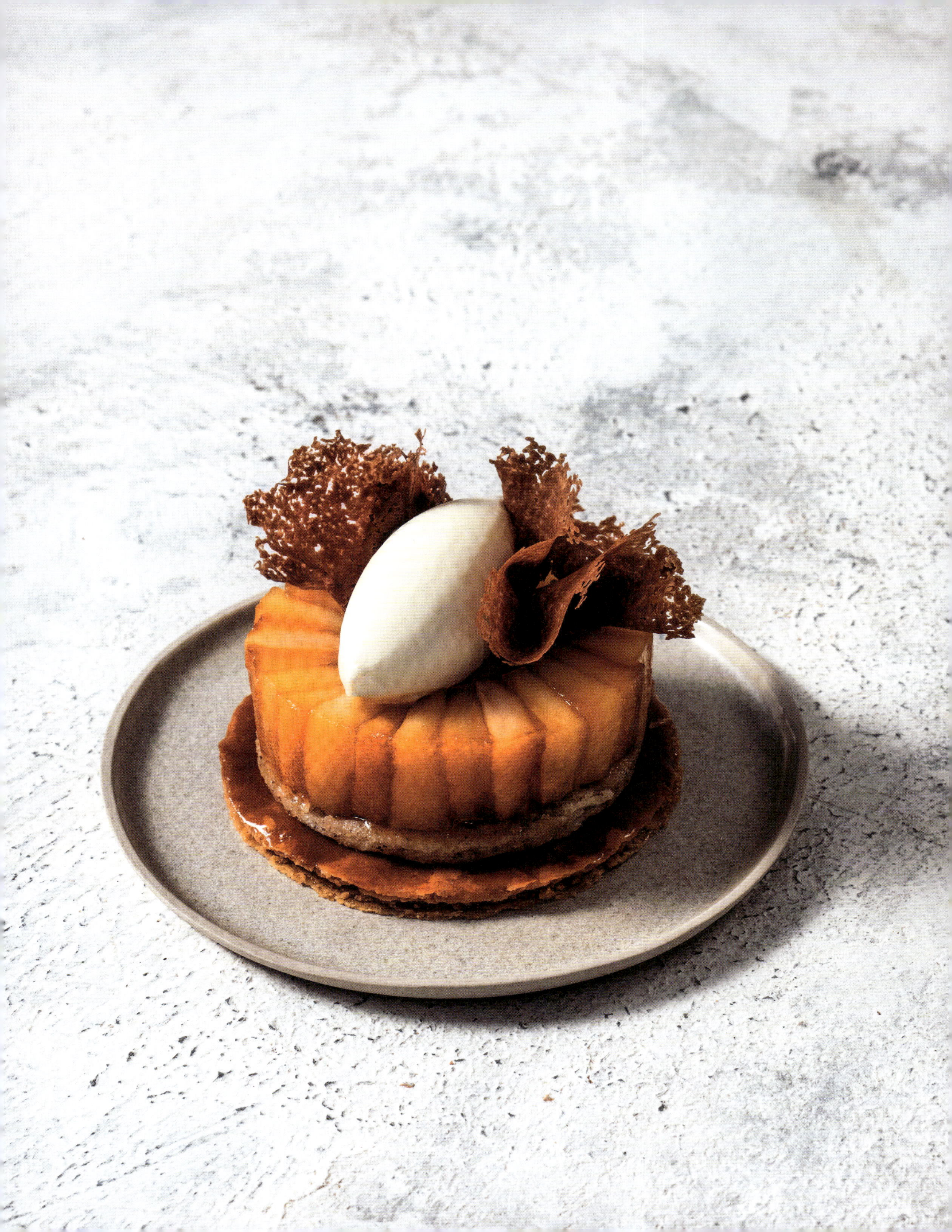

Caramelised apples

8 apples

60 g caster sugar

40 g unsalted butter

20 g lemon juice

40 g water

Decoration

Chocolate opaline tuiles

200 g glucose syrup

300 g fondant icing

200 g milk chocolate

Quenelle

250 g crème fraîche

Caramelised apples Peel, core and cut the apples into 10 wedges. In a frying pan, make a caramel with the sugar, then add the butter, lemon juice and water. Cook the fruit in the caramel for 3 minutes on each side, then drain (5–6). Arrange the apple wedges in a hemisphere mould and allow to cool and firm up in the freezer.

Chocolate opaline tuiles In a saucepan, cook the glucose and fondant icing until the temperature reaches 155°C, then add the chocolate. Transfer the mixture to a clean silicone baking mat and allow to cool. Then grind to a powder. Sift the powder to form uniform discs on a baking mat using a 7-cm-diameter stencil (7). Bake at 180°C until the powder melts, which should take about 2 minutes. Lift off the tuiles immediately, then pinch the centre and lift the edges to form a flower quickly while still warm (8–9). Return the opaline tuiles to the oven and reheat when too cold (10).

Assembly

(11) Arrange a caramelised puff pastry disc on a plate and place a hazelnut sponge disc (12) on top. Turn out the caramelised apples from the moulds. Cut into 2-cm-thick slices (13) and arrange them in a circle on the hazelnut sponge disc (14-15). Serve with a quenelle of crème fraîche. Decorate the desserts with the opaline tuiles (16).

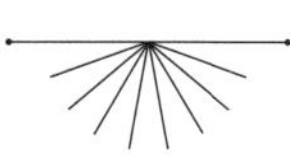

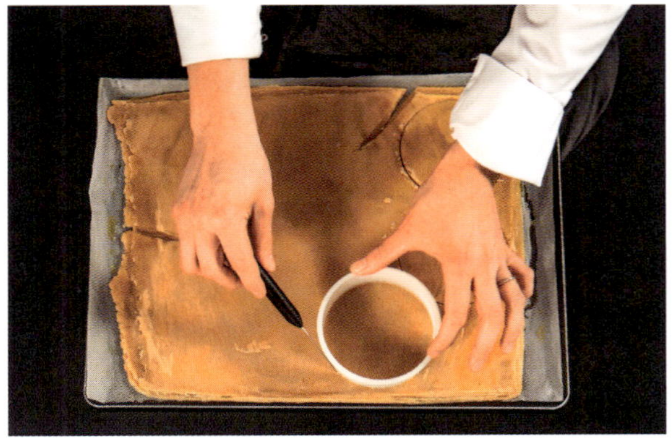

I.

Make the puff pastry. After 10 minutes of baking at 160°C between 2 baking trays, remove the trays from the oven and cut out 8-cm-diameter circles in the pastry.

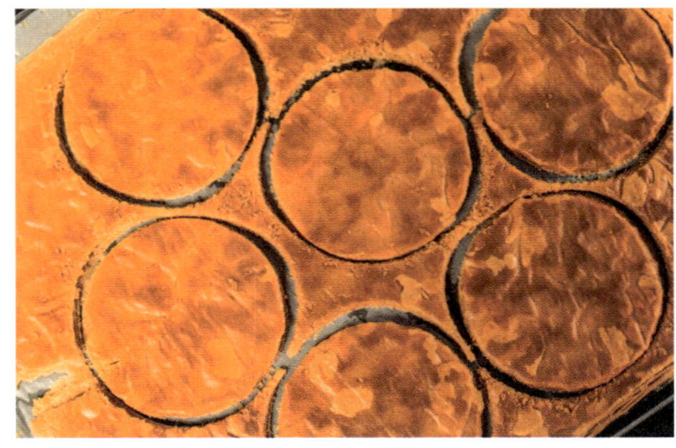

2.

Cover the pastry with a tray again, return it to the oven and bake again for about 25 minutes, until evenly coloured.

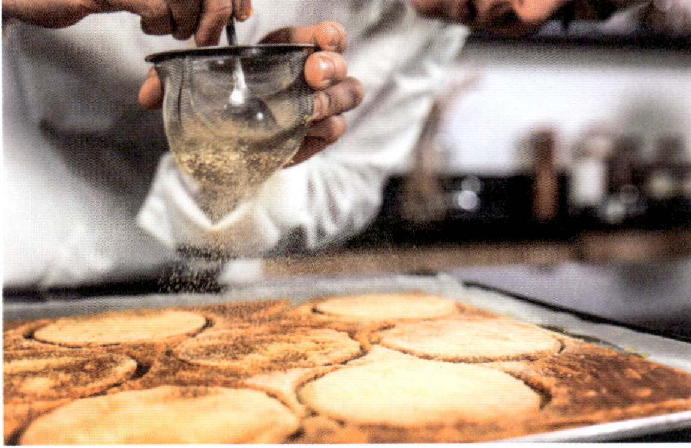

3.

Dust with icing sugar and bake for 8 minutes at 180°C.

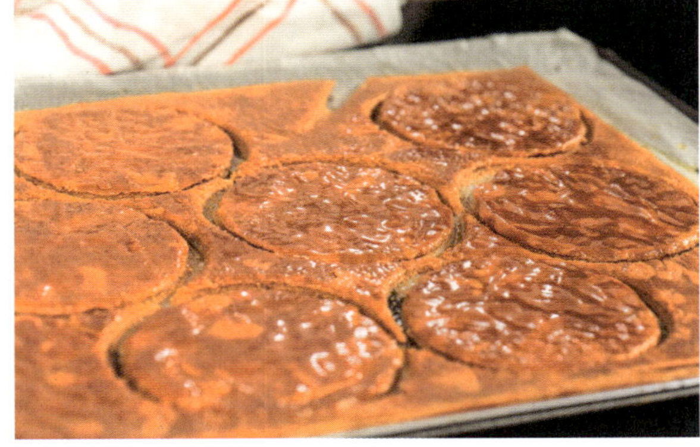

4.

Raise the oven temperature to 240°C for a few seconds, until the puff pastry is glossy all over.

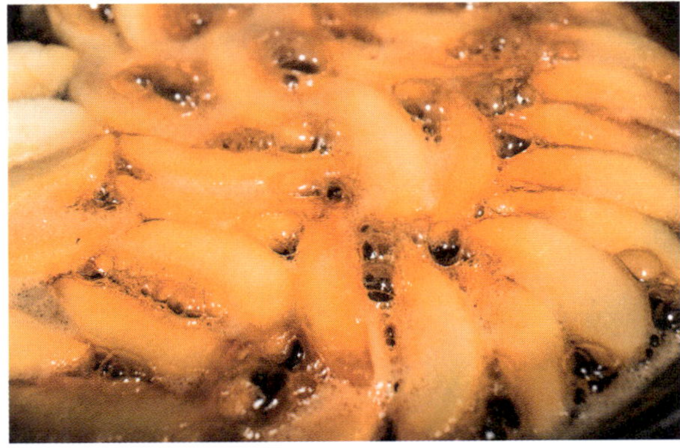

5.

Cook the apple wedges in the caramel for 3 minutes on each side.

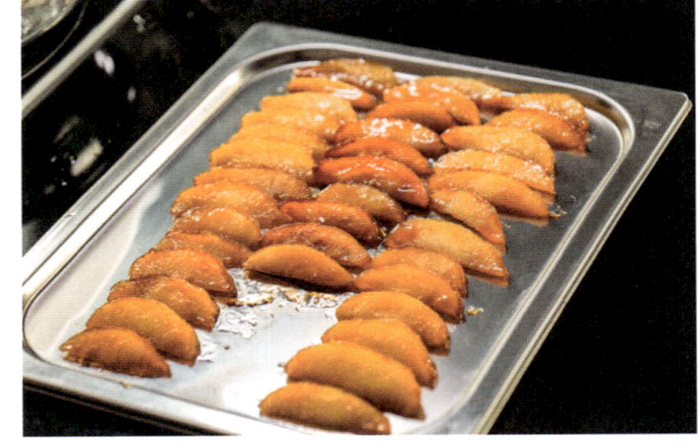

6.

Drain the apples, arrange them in a semi-spherical mould and allow to cool and firm up in the freezer.

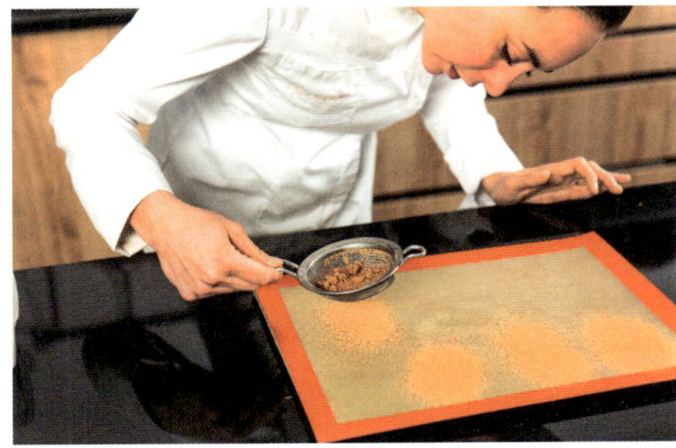

7.

To make the opaline tuiles, sift the powder to form uniform discs on a baking mat using a 7-cm-diameter stencil.

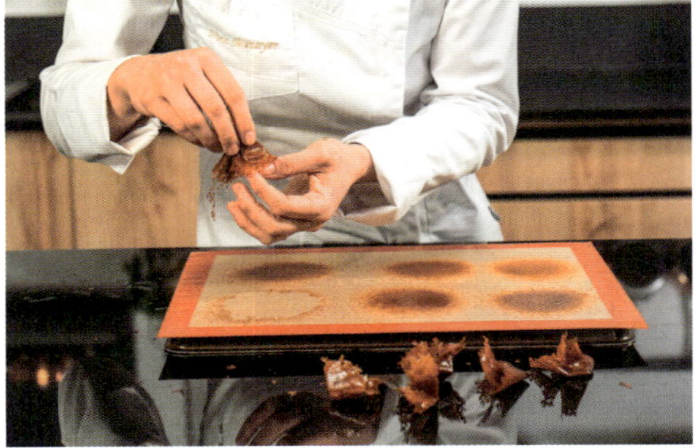

8.

Bake in the oven at 180°C until the powder melts, which should take about 2 minutes. Lift off the tuiles immediately…

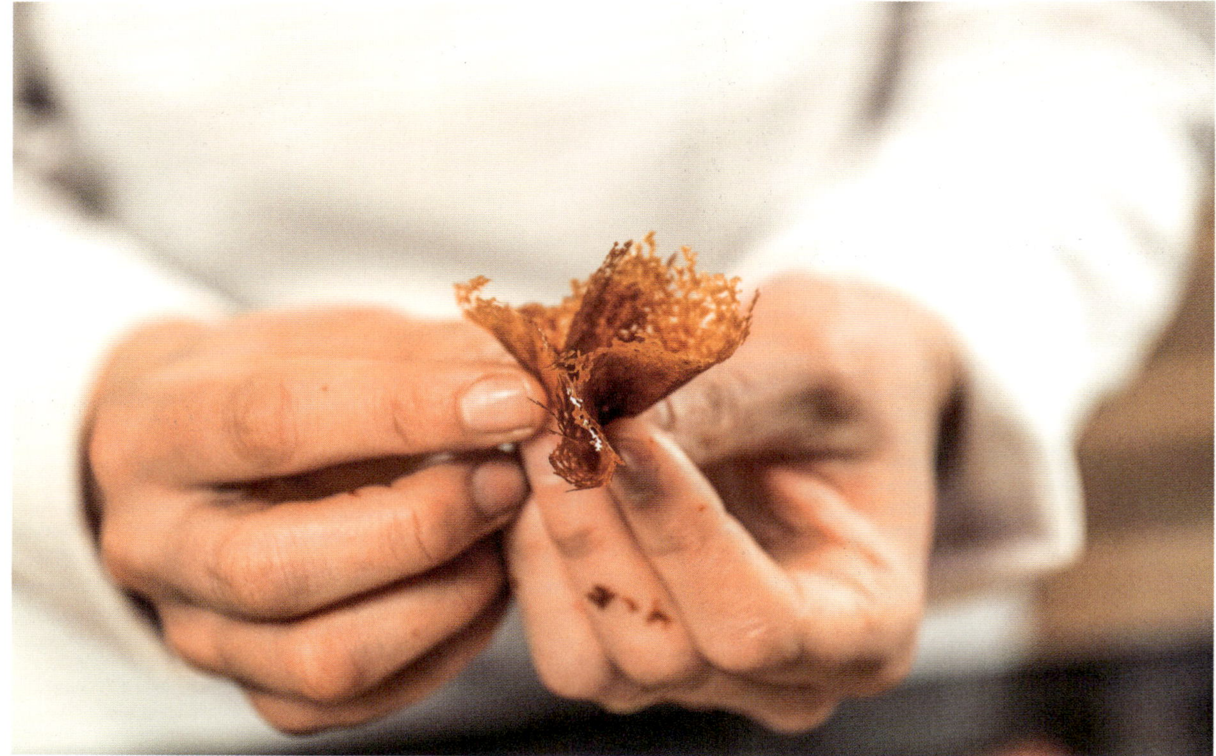

9.

...pinch the centre and lift the edges to form a flower quickly while still warm.

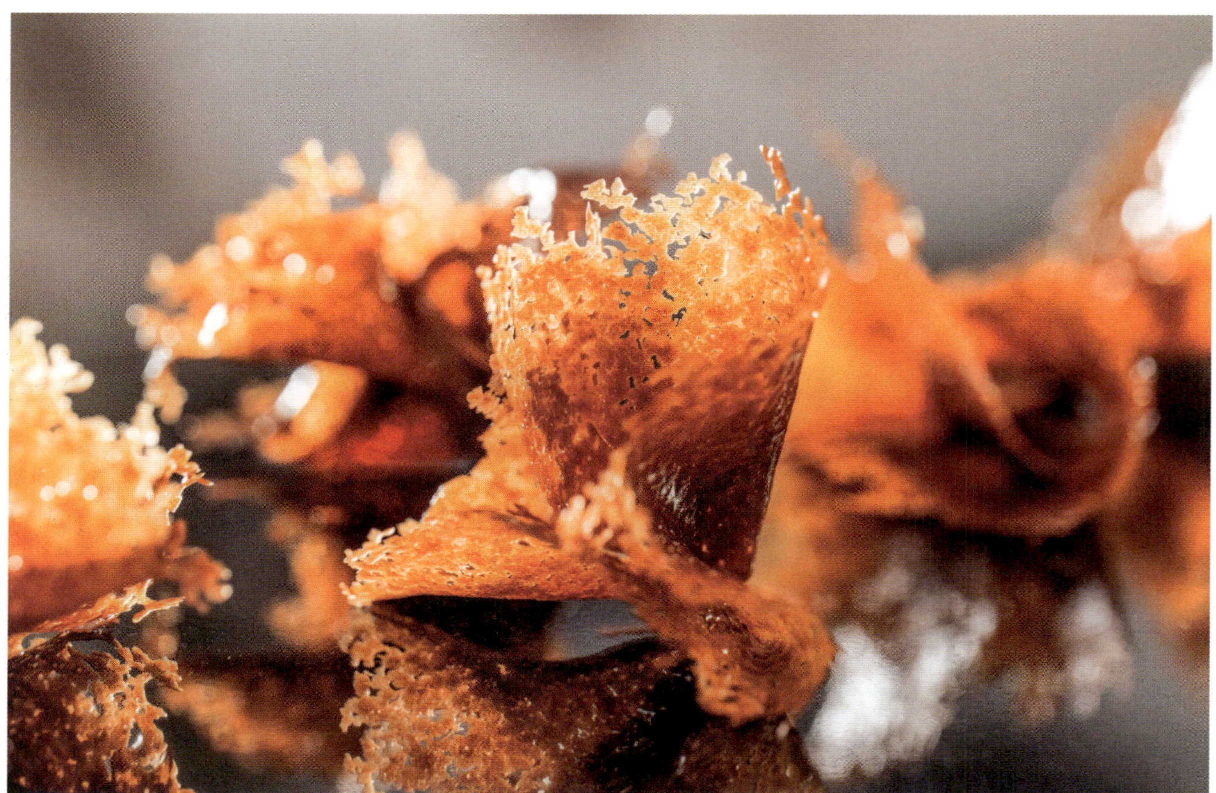

10.

Return the opaline tuiles to the oven and reheat when too cold.

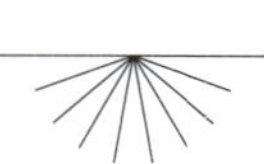

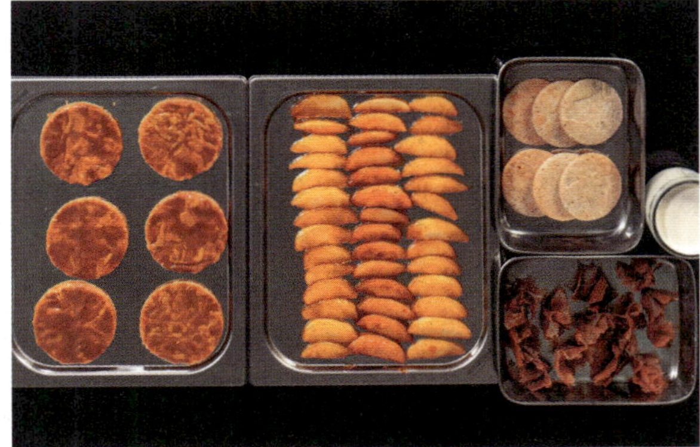

11.

Prepare to assemble the dessert.

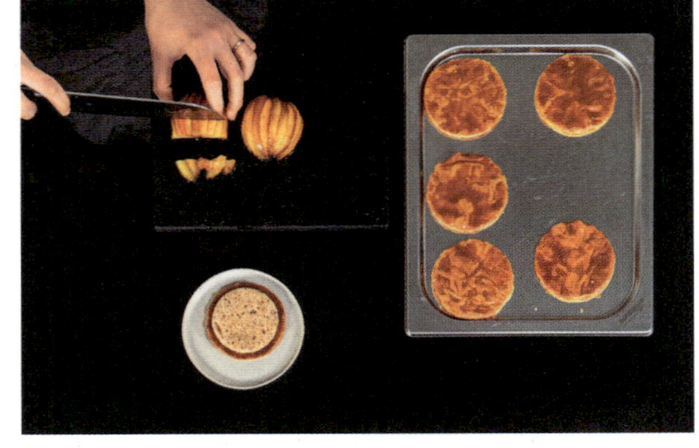

12.

Arrange a caramelised puff pastry disc on a plate and place a hazelnut sponge disc on top.

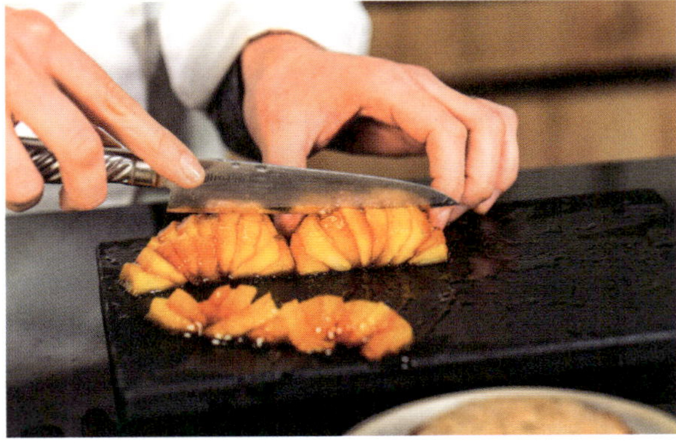

13.

Turn out the caramelised apples from the moulds. Cut them into 2-cm-thick slices.

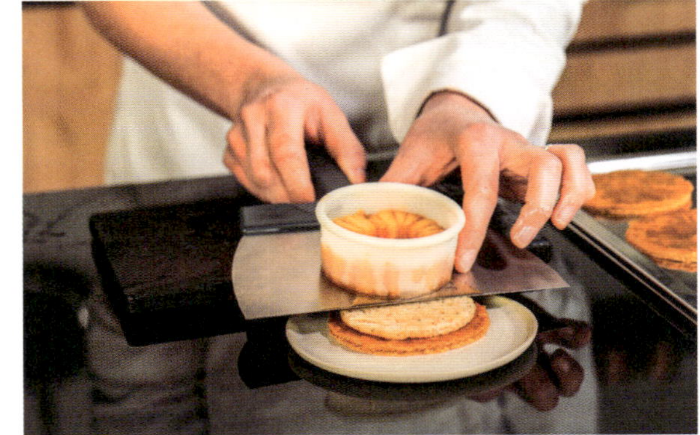

14.

Arrange the apple pieces in a circle...

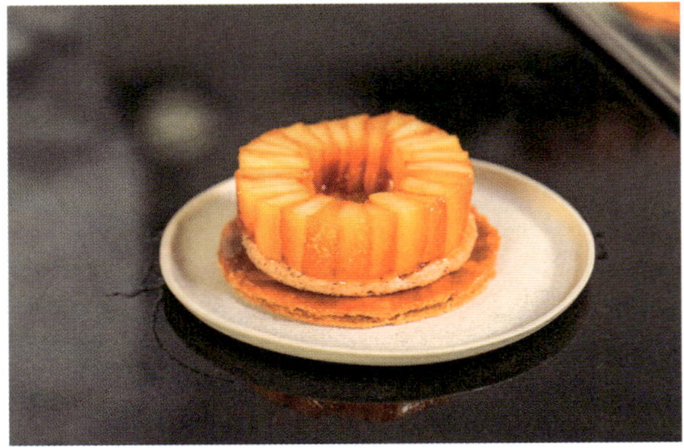

15.

...on the hazelnut sponge disc.

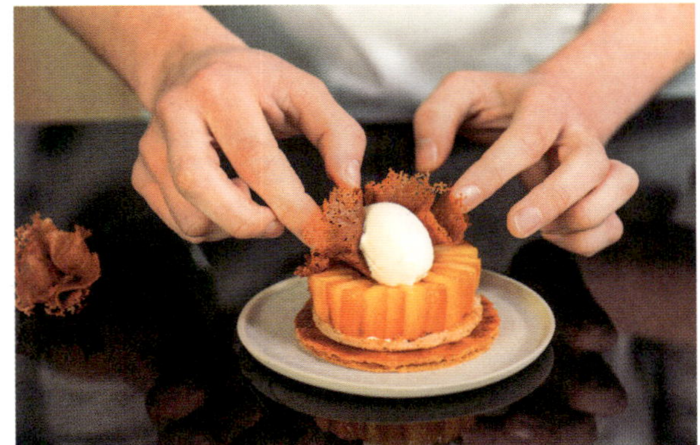

16.

Serve with a quenelle of crème fraîche. Decorate with the opaline tuiles.

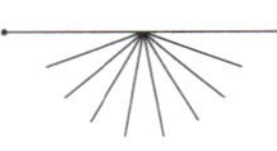

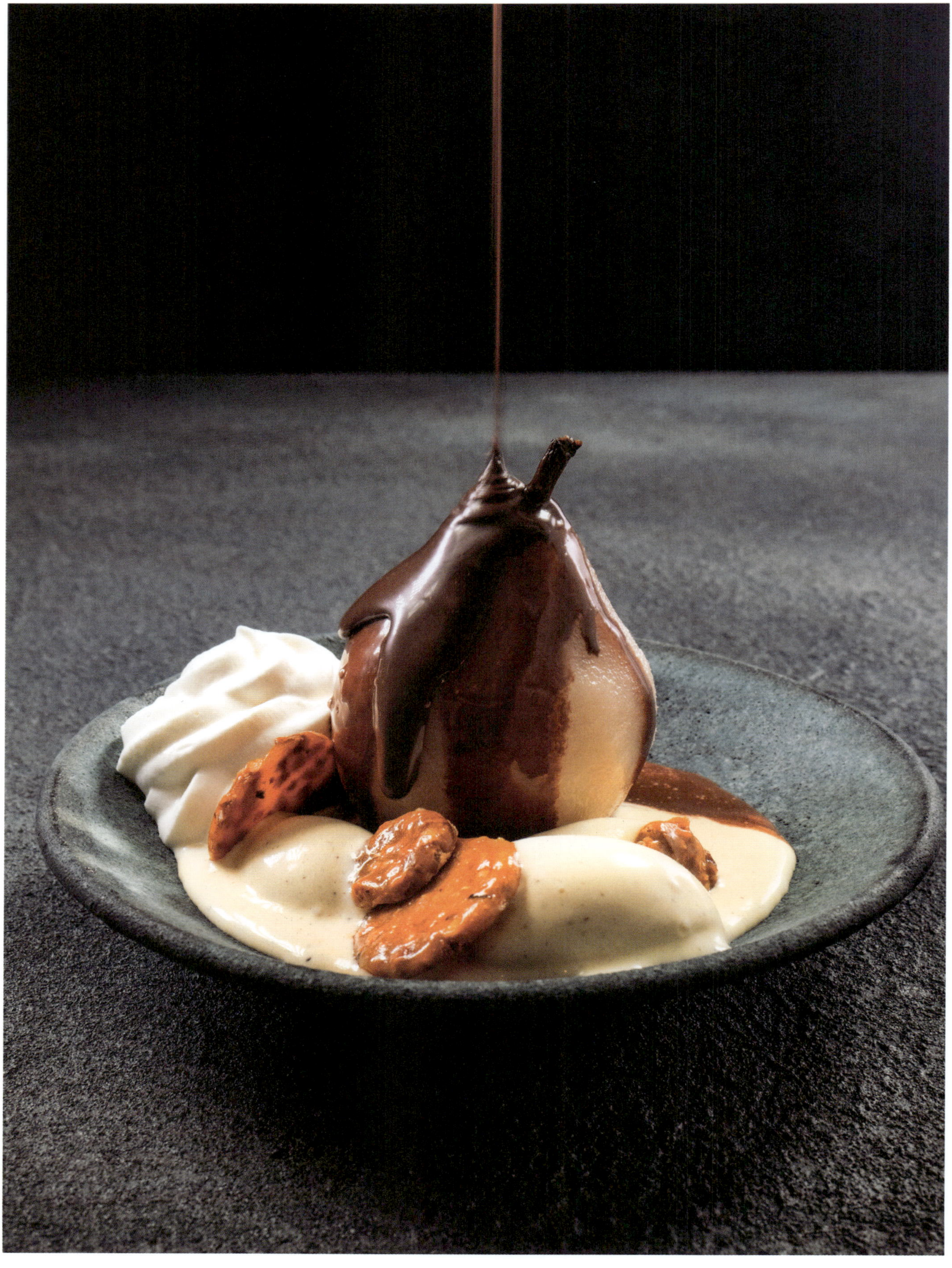

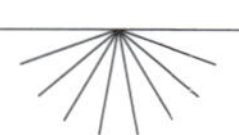

Serves 6

Preparation	Cooking	Resting
1 hour 30 minutes	50 minutes	1 hour 25 minutes

My Dad's Belle-Hélène pear

Pears in syrup

6 Comice pears
Juice of 1 lemon
1 litre water
250 g light brown soft sugar
1 vanilla pod
1 cinnamon stick
2 star anise
30 g lemon juice
3 g lemon zest

Almond nougatine

36 g milk
88 g unsalted butter
36 g glucose syrup
100 g caster sugar
1.5 g pectin NH
125 g chopped almonds

Vanilla ice cream

250 g milk
37 g whipping cream (35% fat)
1 vanilla pod
2 egg yolks
50 g light brown soft sugar
17 g milk powder
20 g honey

Chocolate sauce

125 g milk
62 g whipping cream
35 g light brown soft sugar
150 g dark chocolate (66% cocoa)
12 g unsalted butter

Chantilly cream

1 vanilla pod
250 g whipping cream
8 g icing sugar

Pears in syrup Peel the pears and rub them with lemon juice to keep from browning. In a saucepan, make a syrup by combining the water, sugar, split vanilla pod and scraped-out seeds, spices, lemon juice and zest and bring to the boil over a high heat. Then poach the pears in the syrup over a low heat for 30 minutes, depending on their degree of ripeness. Remove the pears from the syrup and allow to cool in the fridge.

Almond nougatine Put the milk, butter and glucose into a saucepan and bring to the boil over a high heat. Mix the sugar with the pectin, add to the mixture and bring to the boil for 1½ minutes. Add the almonds. Using a rolling pin, roll out the mixture between two baking mats to a 3-mm thickness. Freeze for 1 hour. Then remove the top baking mat and bake the nougatine at 160°C for 20 minutes. Using round biscuit cutters in different sizes, cut out discs while the nougatine is still hot.

Vanilla ice cream In a saucepan, bring the milk and cream to the boil over a high heat. Add the split vanilla pod and scraped-out seeds, strain and leave to infuse for 25 minutes. Strain through a conical sieve and reheat over a low heat. Mix the egg yolks, sugar and milk powder and add the cream and milk mixture. Return the mixture to the saucepan and cook until the temperature reaches 82°C and the mixture is thick enough to coat a spoon. Add the honey and allow to cool. Churn the ice-cream base in an ice-cream maker.

Chocolate sauce In a saucepan, bring the milk, cream and sugar to the boil and add the mixture to the chocolate. Mix with a silicone spatula to combine, then blend in the butter using an immersion blender. Set aside.

Chantilly cream Split the vanilla pod, then scrape out the seeds and mix them with the cream and icing sugar. Whip the Chantilly cream using a mixer.

Assembly Poach the pears in the syrup. In the meantime, make the almond nougatine, vanilla ice cream and chocolate sauce. Immediately before serving, whip the Chantilly cream and reheat the chocolate sauce. Arrange a poached pear in the middle of each plate. Transfer the Chantilly cream to a piping bag fitted with a fluted tip and pipe a swirl of whipped cream. Add a few quenelles of vanilla ice cream. Pour chocolate sauce over the pear and arrange nougatine discs on the plate. Serve immediately.

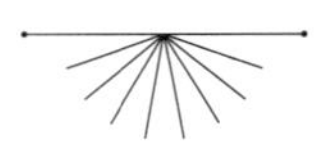

Serves 6

Preparation
2 hours 30 minutes

Resting
8 hours 20 minutes

Cooking
40 minutes

Fresh citrus and fromage blanc

Marinated pomelo

100 g water
100 g light brown soft sugar
100 g grapefruit juice
3 g hibiscus flowers
20 g fresh ginger
Juice and zest of 1 yuzu
30 g rice vinegar
½ pomelo

Fromage blanc mousse foam

75 g whipping cream (35% fat)
50 g acacia honey
25 g gelatine mass
(4 g gelatine powder and 21 g
   cold water)
200 g fromage blanc

Lemon sponge

120 g light brown soft sugar
75 g eggs
60 g double cream
15 g lemon juice
1.5 g lemon zest
90 g T55 (plain) flour
1.5 g baking powder
30 g olive oil
0.5 g salt

Marinated Pomelo Combine the water, sugar, grapefruit juice, yuzu juice, hibiscus flowers, grated ginger and yuzu zest in a saucepan and bring to the boil. Cover and allow to steep for 15 minutes. Strain through a conical sieve, mix in the vinegar and add the half pomelo. Refrigerate and allow to marinate for at least 6 hours.

Fromage blanc mousse foam In a saucepan, heat the cream with the honey over a low heat, then add the gelatine mass and stir until completely dissolved. Add the fromage blanc and whisk to incorporate, then transfer the mixture to a siphon, insert two gas chargers and shake vigorously. Refrigerate for at least 2 hours before use.

Lemon sponge In a stand mixer, beat the sugar with the eggs, then add the cream, lemon juice and zest, followed by the sifted flour and baking powder. Finally, incorporate the olive oil and salt. Place a baking frame on a baking tray lined with baking paper and pour in the batter to a depth of 5 mm. Bake for 20 minutes at 170°C. Using suitable biscuit cutters, cut out rings with an 8-cm outer diameter and a 5-cm inner diameter.

Citrus Confit Mix the caster sugar with the pectin. Zest the fruits and squeeze and measure out their juice. In a saucepan, heat all the juice with the brown sugar and zest over a low heat. When the temperature of the mixture reaches about 40°C, add the sugar and pectin mixture. Then bring to the boil for 2 minutes. To test the confit, place a drop on a very cold plate and wait 3 minutes, then check its consistency: if it is too runny, cook further before adding the gelatine mass. Mix until dissolved. Transfer to a container and allow to set in the fridge.

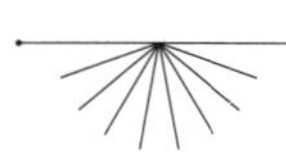

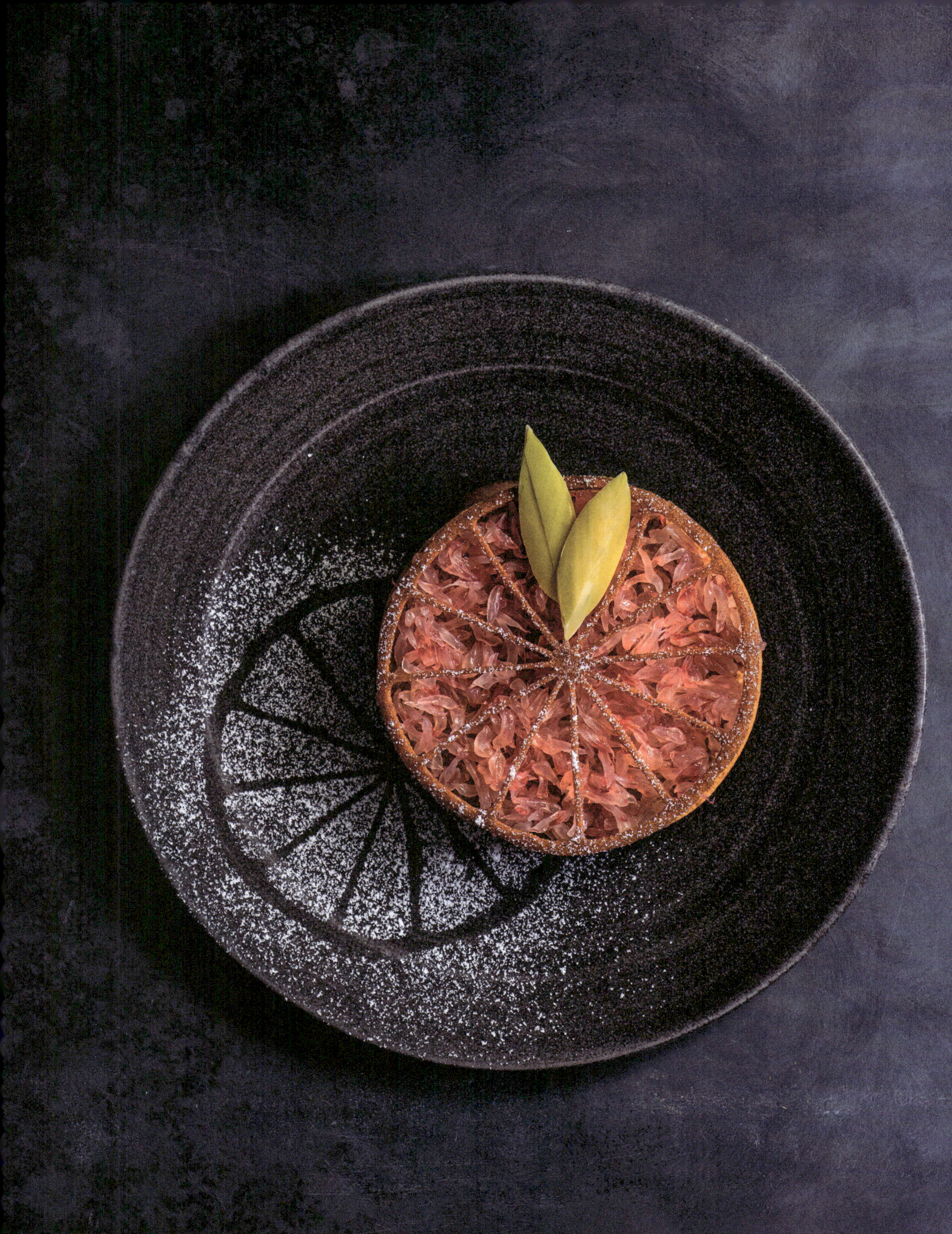

Citrus confit

50 g caster sugar

4.5 g pectin

200 g orange juice

80 g grapefruit juice

12 g lemon juice

70 g light brown soft sugar

80 g gelatine mass

(11 g gelatine powder
   and 69 g cold water)

Sweet pastry

90 g unsalted butter

55 g icing sugar

17 g ground almonds

0.5 g salt

1 g vanilla powder

145 g T80 (stoneground white)
   flour

1 egg

Pâte à cigarette tuiles

50 g egg whites

50 g caster sugar

50 g T55 flour

50 g unsalted butter, melted

Plating
Citrus segments

1 mandarin

1 orange

1 grapefruit

1 lime

20 g neutral glaze

50 g icing sugar

Chocolate leaves

200 g white chocolate

100 g cocoa butter

1 g blue fat-soluble food
   colouring

2 g yellow fat-soluble food
   colouring

Sweet pastry Rub the butter into the sugar, ground almonds, salt, vanilla powder and flour until the mixture resembles fine breadcrumbs. Incorporate the egg. Once smooth, allow the pastry to rest in the fridge. Then roll it out to a 1.5-mm thickness. Using a 9-cm-diameter biscuit cutter, cut out 6 discs. Bake at 160°C for 10 minutes.

Pâte à cigarette tuiles Preheat the oven to 150°C. Mix the egg whites with the sugar, then add the sifted flour and finish by incorporating the butter. Lightly grease the lace mould before adding the batter. Bake in the oven at 150°C for around 8 minutes.

Assembly

Marinate the pomelo. Make the fromage blanc mousse and allow to set in the fridge. Using an 8-cm-diameter biscuit cutter, cut out a sponge disc, then cut a hole in the middle with a 5-cm-diameter biscuit cutter. Blend the citrus confit and transfer to a piping bag. Segment the different citrus fruitss. Bake the tuiles, then bake the sweet pastry discs. Temper the white chocolate and make the leaves.

Chocolate leaves

Melt the cocoa butter in a bain-marie, mix in both food colourings and allow the mixture to cool to 35°C. Cut out two large acetate strips and lay them side by side. Brush the coloured cocoa butter diagonally over the acetate, alternating the brush strokes in opposite directions to create the veins of a grapefruit leaf. Melt and temper the white chocolate, then spread a thin layer over the coloured cocoa butter with a spatula. Using a cocktail stick, trace leaf shapes in the chocolate, then allow the leaves to harden before peeling them off the acetate.

Plating

Lay the tuile on one side of each plate and dust with icing sugar. Carefully lift off the tuile, taking care not to disturb the pattern left on the plate. Arrange a lemon sponge ring on the plate slightly offset from the pattern left by the tuile. Pipe a little confit in the hole and fill with the fromage blanc mousse foam (1). Make an attractive arrangement with the citrus segments around the sponge (2). Place the shortbread disc on top of the sponge and cover with marinated pomelo segments. Then arrange the tuile on top (3) and decorate with white chocolate leaves and a few drops of neutral glaze.

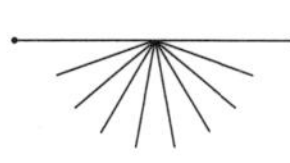

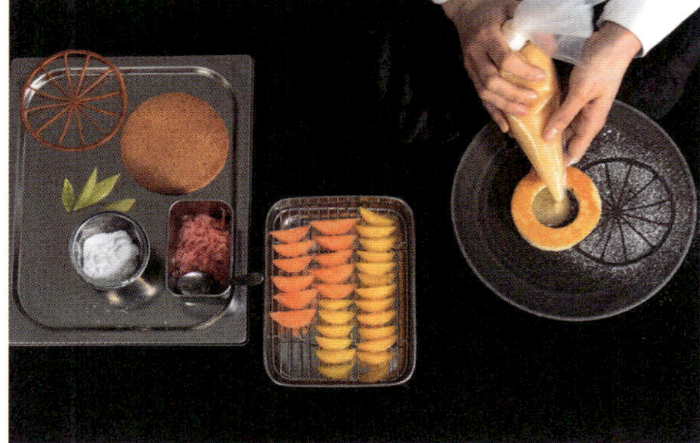

I.

Using the tuile as a stencil, dust with icing sugar to leave an outline of its design. Place the lemon sponge ring on the plate and pipe a little confit inside the hole.

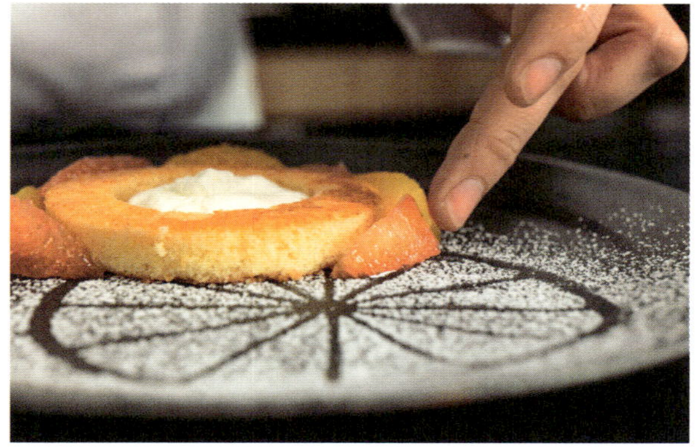

2.

Add the fromage blanc mousse foam to the confit. Make an attractive arrangement with the citrus segments around the sponge ring.

3.

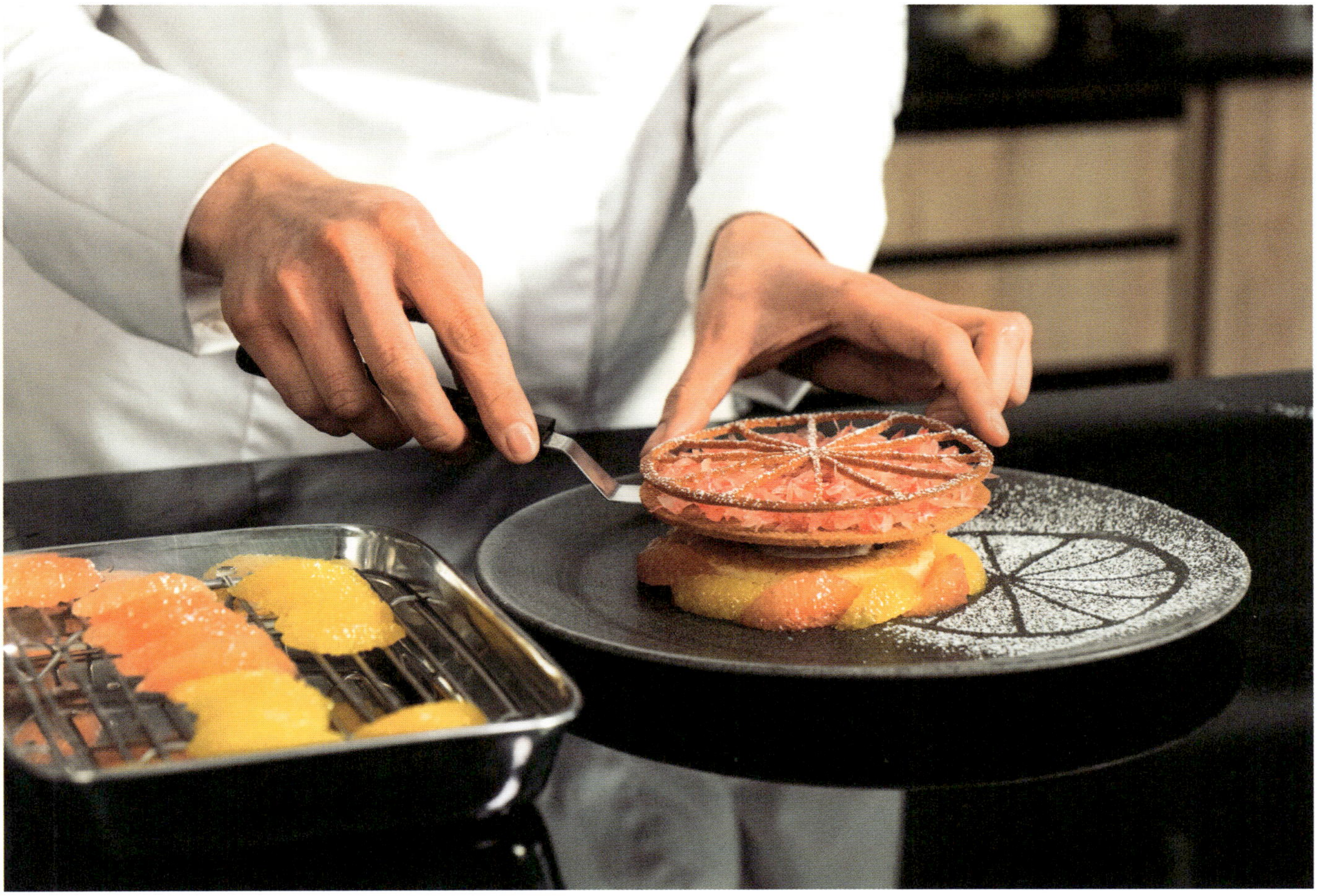

Place the sweet pastry disc covered with pomelo kernels over the filled sponge ring and arrange the tuile on top. Decorate with white chocolate leaves and a few drops of neutral glaze.

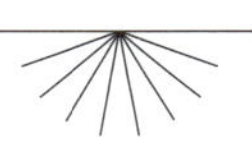

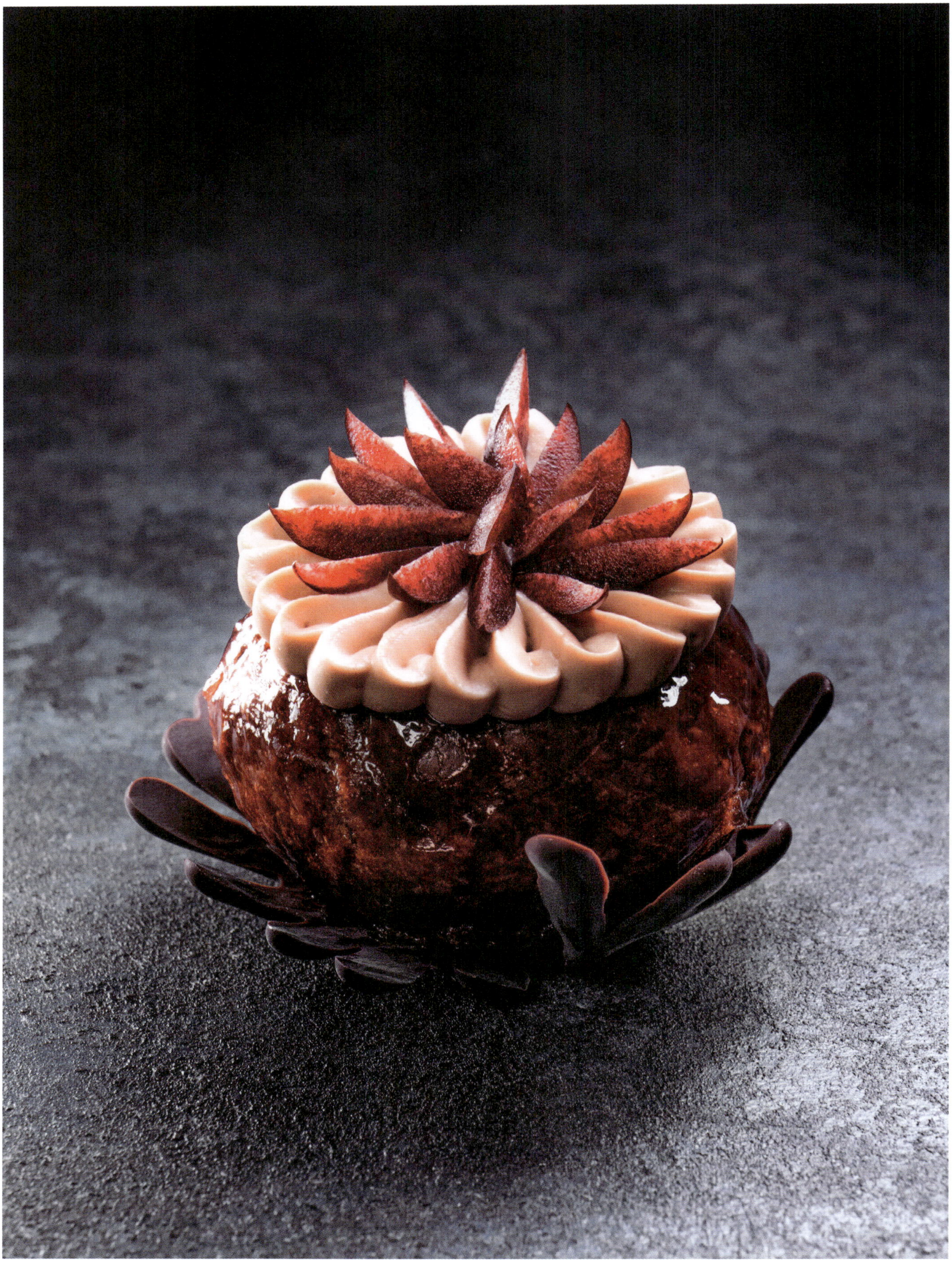

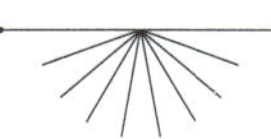

Serves 10	Preparation 3 hours	Resting 43 hours	Proving 1 hour 30 minutes	Cooking 35 minutes

Wolfberger® cherry and chocolate brioche

Chocolate Chantilly cream

150 g whipping cream (35% fat)

100 g milk chocolate

10 g syrup from Wolfberger®
Griottissimo® morello cherries in
kirsch syrup

Brioche

270 g T55 (plain) flour

30 g cocoa powder

8 g salt

35 g light brown soft sugar

10 g fresh yeast

4 eggs

120 g unsalted butter, cold

Jellied syrup

5.5 g lemon zest

250 g water

100 g caster sugar

30 g lemon juice

3 gelatine leaves

100 g Wolfberger® Chocolat
liqueur

Chocolate Chantilly cream The day before, put the cream into a saucepan and bring to the boil over a medium heat, then pour it over the chocolate a third at a time, blending until thick and smooth. Refrigerate at 4°C for 24 hours. On the day, whip the cream in a stand mixer fitted with a whisk attachment, then add the Griottissimo® syrup, gently whisk to combine and transfer to a piping bag fitted with a small Saint-Honoré nozzle.

Brioche The day before, mix the flour, cocoa, salt, sugar, baking powder and eggs to a dough in a stand mixer on a slow speed for about 20 minutes. When the dough pulls away from the sides of the bowl, add the cold butter cut into small pieces and continue to knead until the cough pulls away again. Wrap the dough in cling film and rest it in the fridge for 10 hours, then cut it into 35-g portions each and roll them into balls. Place the dough balls in 6-cm-diameter Flexipan® silicone hemisphere moulds, cover with a cloth and prove for 1 hour 30 minutes at about 22°C(near a radiator). Bake the brioches at 165°C for 35 minutes. Check for doneness and adjust the cooking time if necessary. Allow the brioches to cool a little before using a melon baller to hollow them out.

Jellied syrup Using a vegetable peeler, remove the zest from the lemon. In a saucepan, bring the water and sugar to the boil, then add the lemon juice and lemon zest. Cover and allow to steep for 3 hours, then remove the zest. Set aside the syrup. Soak the gelatine in iced water for 10 minutes. Heat the syrup to about 50°C, then add the squeezed gelatine and chocolate liqueur. Soak the still-warm brioches with the warm jellied syrup. Allow to set in the fridge at 4°C for 2 hours.

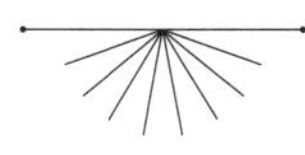

Black cherry confit

½ gelatine leaf
188 g black cherry purée (or
    cooked and puréed black
    cherries)
30 g light brown soft sugar
4 g pectin NH
20 g lemon juice
40 g Wolfberger® Griottissimo®
    morello cherries in syrup

Chocolate decorations

300 g dark chocolate
    couverture
3 g edible gold glitter

150 g neutral glaze
30 fresh black cherries

Black cherry confit Soak the gelatine in iced water for 10 minutes.

In a saucepan, heat the cherry purée over a low heat to 40°C, then stir in the sugar mixed with the pectin. Bring to the boil for 1 minute, then add the squeezed gelatine and lemon juice. Blend and allow to cool in the fridge at 4°C. Then blend again. Coarsely chop the Griotissimo® morello cherries and mix them with the cherry confit. Transfer to a piping bag and set aside at 4°C.

Chocolate decorations Temper the chocolate by heating it to 50°C, cooling it to 28°C and then lightly reheating it for use at 31°C. Turn the 6-cm-diameter Flexipan® hemisphere moulds upside down, cover each mould with a circle of crumpled baking paper and pipe the tempered chocolate over the top, allowing it to run down the sides. Allow the chocolate to harden before removing it from the mould and then dust with gold glitter powder.

Assembly Start by making the chocolate Chantilly cream. Next, make the cherry confit, followed by the chocolate decorations. Make the brioche dough, then bake and allow to cool a little. Meanwhile, make the jellied syrup and allow to cool a little. Once the brioche and syrup are just warm, cut off the top of the brioches and use a small knife or melon baller to hollow them out. Return the brioches to the moulds, pour over 20 g of jellied syrup and allow to set in the fridge for 4 hours. Melt the glaze and brush it over the brioches. Arrange the brioches inside the chocolate decorations and pipe them full of cherry confit.

Whip the chocolate Chantilly cream and pipe an attractive petal design over the brioches. Then quarter the cherries and arrange them harmoniously on the dessert.

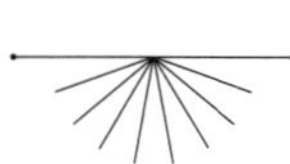

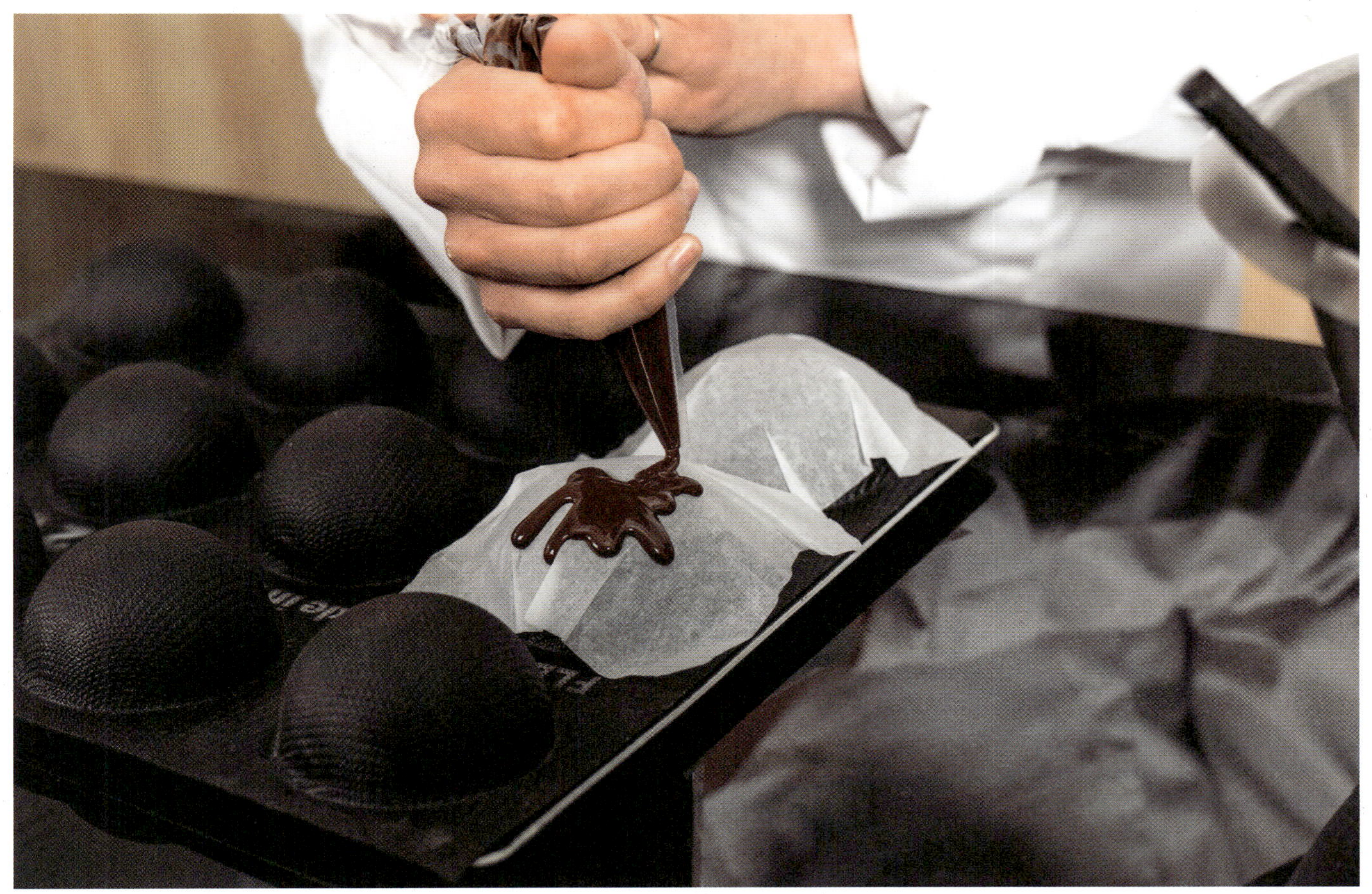

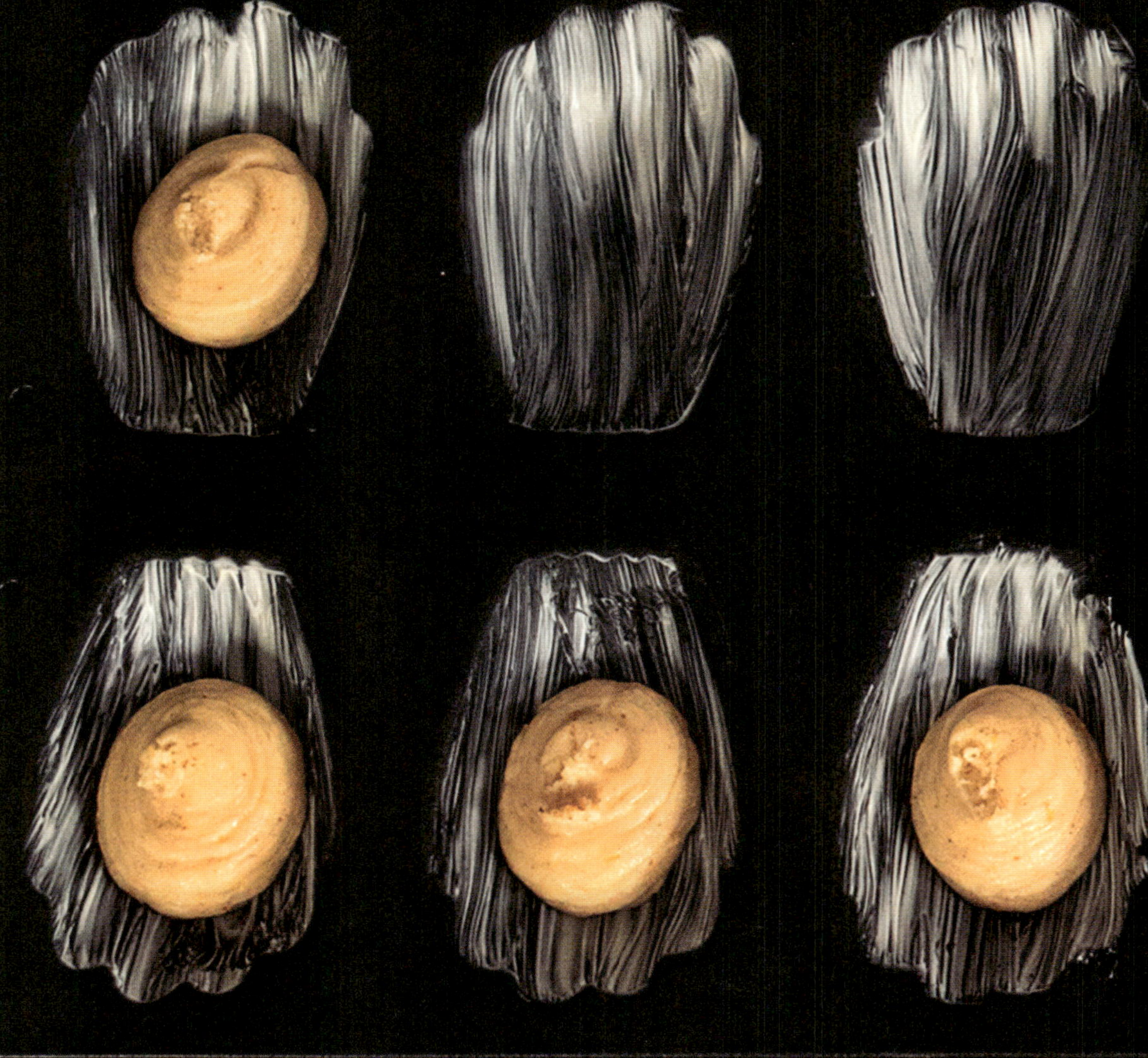

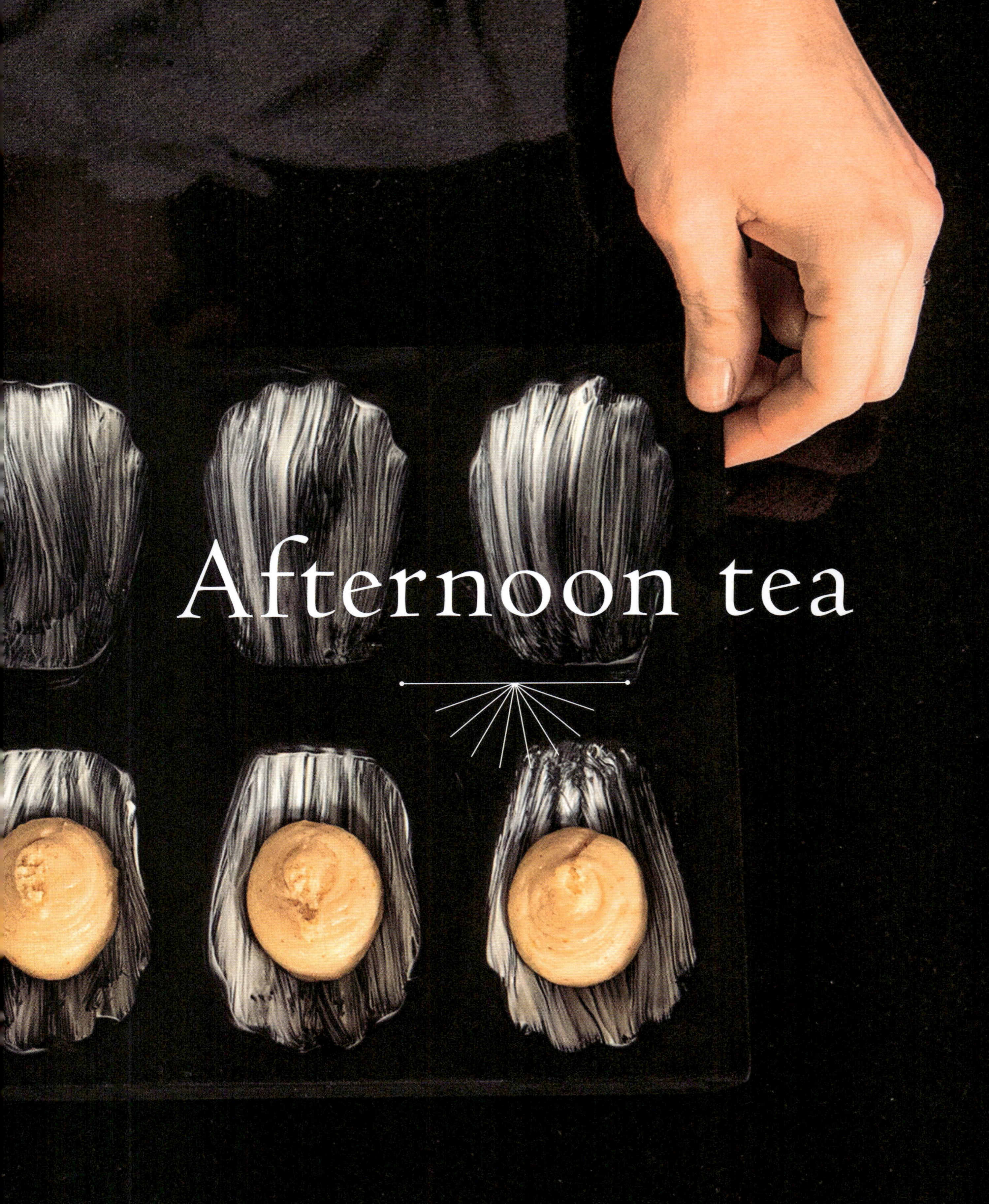

Afternoon tea

Makes 10 cookies

Preparation
10 minutes

Baking
5 minutes

Anastasia's cookies

80 g unsalted butter, softened
50 g light brown soft sugar
130 g T55 (plain) flour
2 g baking powder
2 g salt
1 small egg
120 g chocolat, chopped
50 g hazelnuts

Rub the butter into the sugar, then add the flour, baking powder, salt and egg. Mix to combine, before adding the chocolate. Roll the dough into small balls, arrange them on a baking mat and press gently to flatten. Decorate the cookies with roasted hazelnut halves.

Bake for 5 minutes at 180°C.

'This is what Anastasia loves most for afternoon tea. She loves eating them as much as she does making them. If you'd like to see the recipe made step by step, Anastasia has put together a video tutorial. It was her first video, which she was very proud to make with her dad. So even though the kitchen ends up messy, baking with the kids is something I love so much that it's worth the effort of tidying up afterwards.'

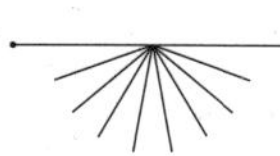

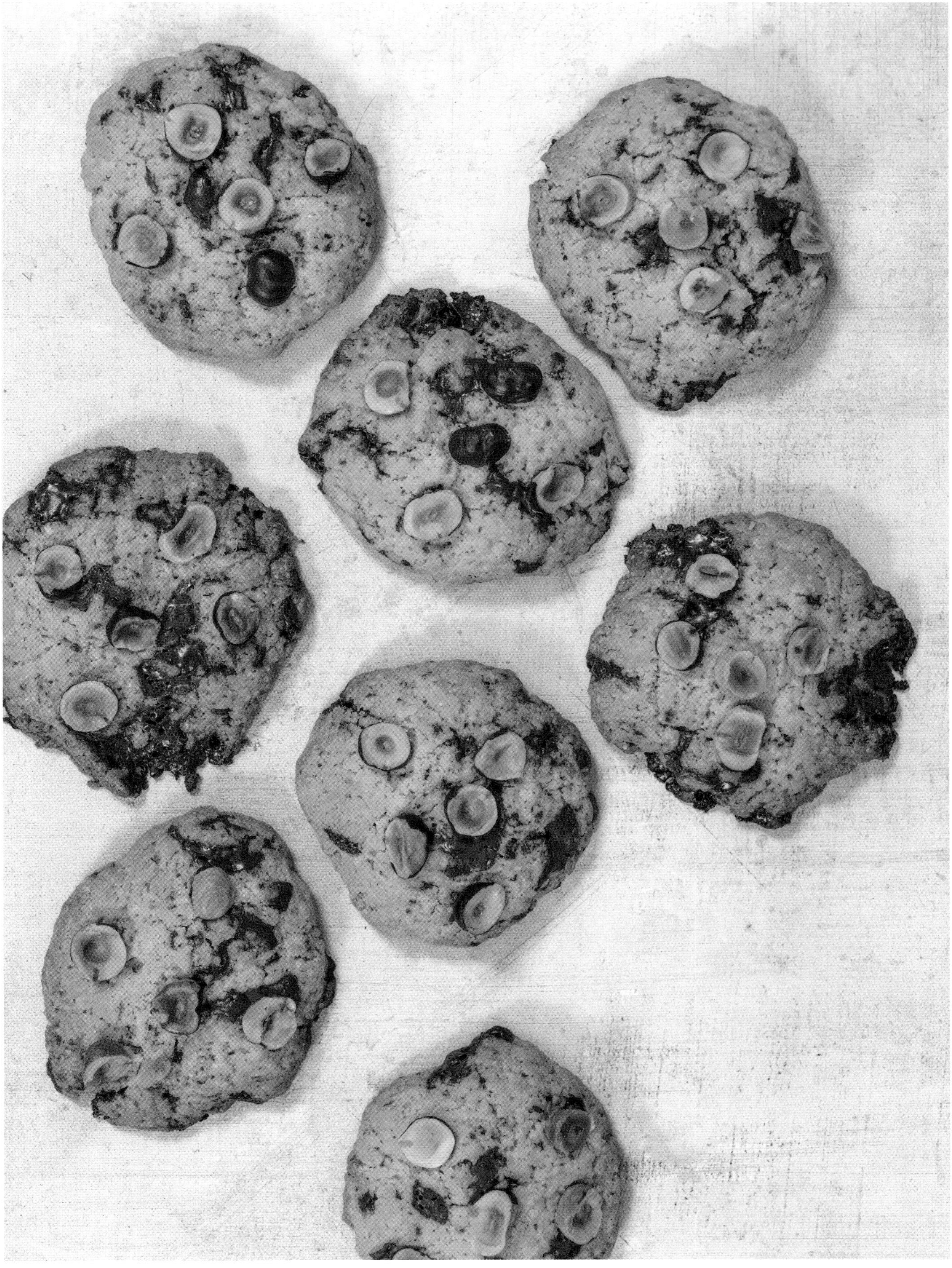

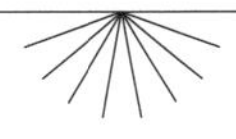

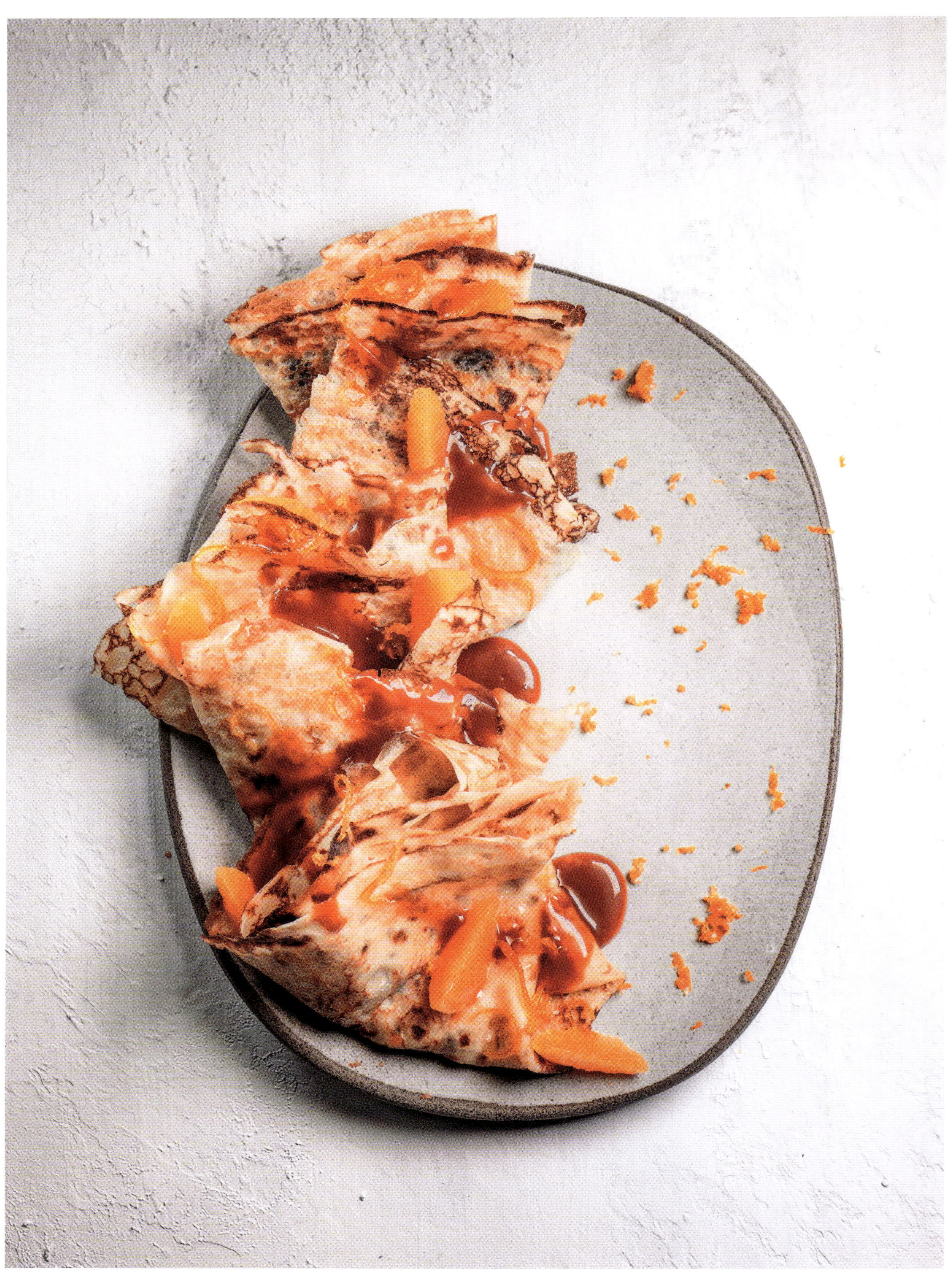

Makes 10 crêpes

Preparation
30 minutes

Resting
6 hours

Cooking
15 minutes
+ 3 minutes per
crêpe

Crêpes

Crêpe batter

25 g unsalted butter
238 g full-fat milk
40 g whipping cream (35% fat)
Grated zest of 1 mandarin
20 g mandarin juice
¼ tonka bean
50 g light brown soft sugar
125 g T55 (plain) flour
1 g salt
2 eggs
12 g rum

Oranges and mandarins

2 oranges
4 mandarins
100 g caster sugar

Crêpe batter Make beurre noisette by putting the butter into a saucepan over a low heat while stirring with a whisk until it turns dark and nutty.

In a saucepan, lightly heat the milk, cream, mandarin zest, mandarin juice and grated tonka bean. Mix the sugar with the flour and salt and pour over the warm cream mixture. Whisk until smooth, then add the eggs, rum and beurre noisette. Blend the batter until smooth, then allow to rest in the fridge for 6 hours. Cook the crêpes in a hot frying pan greased with butter.

Oranges and mandarins Peel the zest from the oranges and mandarins, making sure to remove any remaining pith. Separate a few segments from each fruit as a garnish and accompaniment for the crêpes. Carefully remove them from their membranes. Squeeze the remainder of the oranges and mandarins and make a syrup by mixing the resulting juice with the sugar in a saucepan and bringing to a simmer.

Cut the zest into very thin julienne strips and blanch them 3 times, starting from cold water each time. Candy the zest by simmering in the syrup for about 15 minutes. Collect the zest from the syrup using a small sieve. Reduce the syrup until lightly caramelised as a sauce to pour over the crêpes before serving.

Assembly

Arrange the crêpes on a plate and decorate with the fresh orange and mandarin segments and candied zest. Pour over the warm sauce immediately before serving.

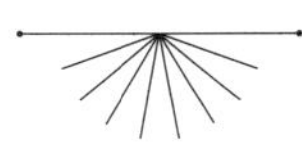

Makes 10 waffles

Preparation	Resting	Cooking
20 minutes	10 hours	10 minutes per waffle

Sourdough waffles

70 g sourdough mother
(see recipe on p. 194)
300 g T55 (plain) flour
450 g full-fat milk
30 g light brown soft sugar
100 g unsalted butter, melted
2 eggs
1 g salt

Make a levain starter by feeding 24 g of T55 flour and 24 g of milk to 24 g of sourdough mother and allowing it to rest at 20°C for 4 hours.

Mix the flour, milk, sugar, melted butter and levain. Allow to rest in the fridge at 4°C for 6 hours.

Whisk the eggs with the salt and gently fold into the previous mixture.

Heat a waffle iron. Fill the waffle iron with a small ladle of batter and cook for 5 minutes on each side. Serve the waffles with a little whipped cream, melted chocolate or chocolate chips, or simply sugar.

'This is what our afternoon tea is like in winter. As soon as the weather starts to get cold, I look forward to these afternoon waffles. Mathieu, my husband, comes from the north of France, and his cousins gave us their grandparents' waffle iron. Now we can't get enough of these waffles, which we cook in the fireplace. The taste of the wood fire is absolutely delicious. It takes all afternoon because you have to keep the embers burning, but they're so worth the effort! The waffles must be eaten immediately, piping hot. They're so scrumptious that I love them plain.'

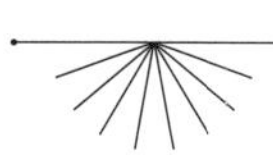

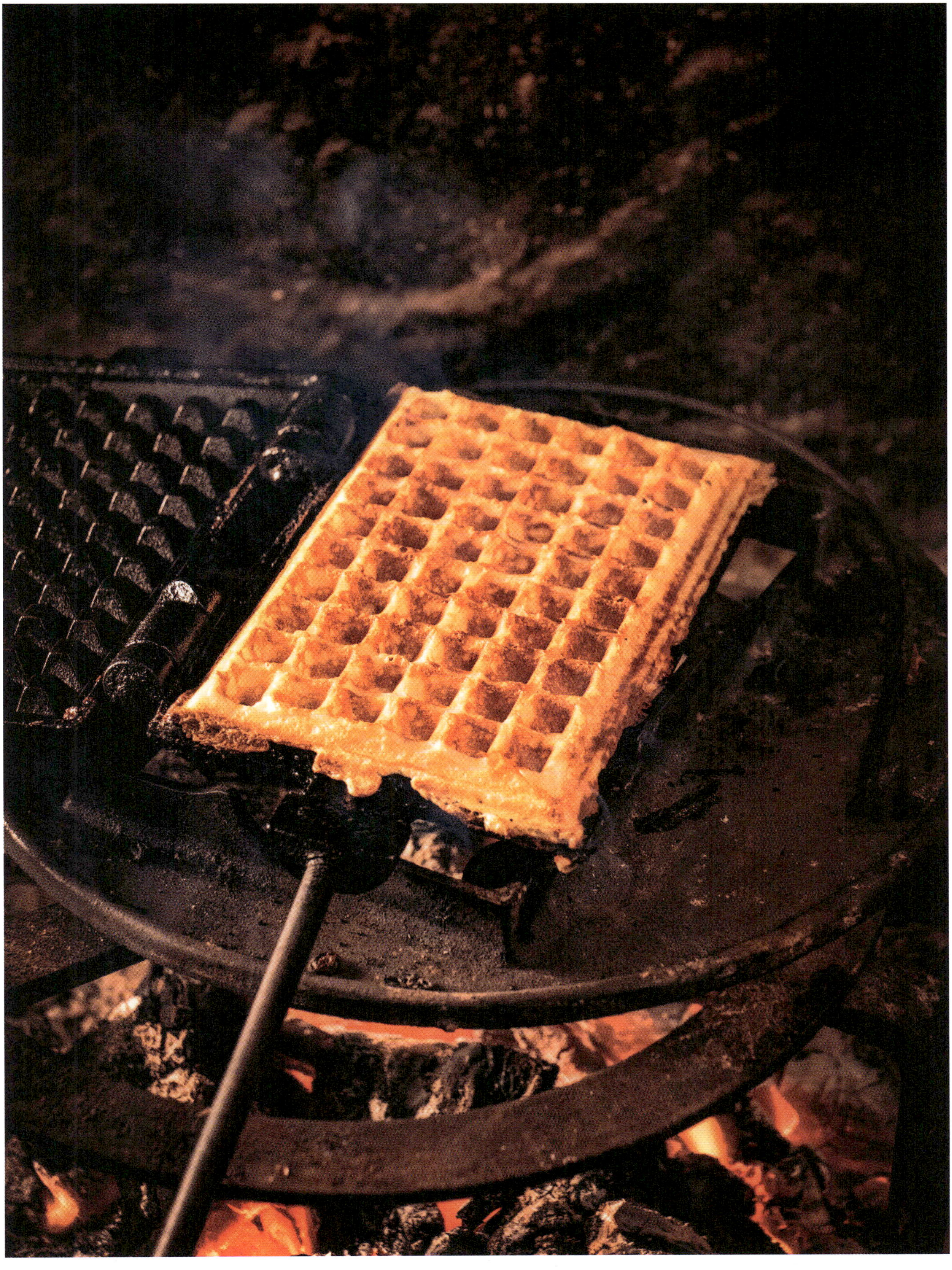

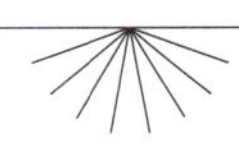

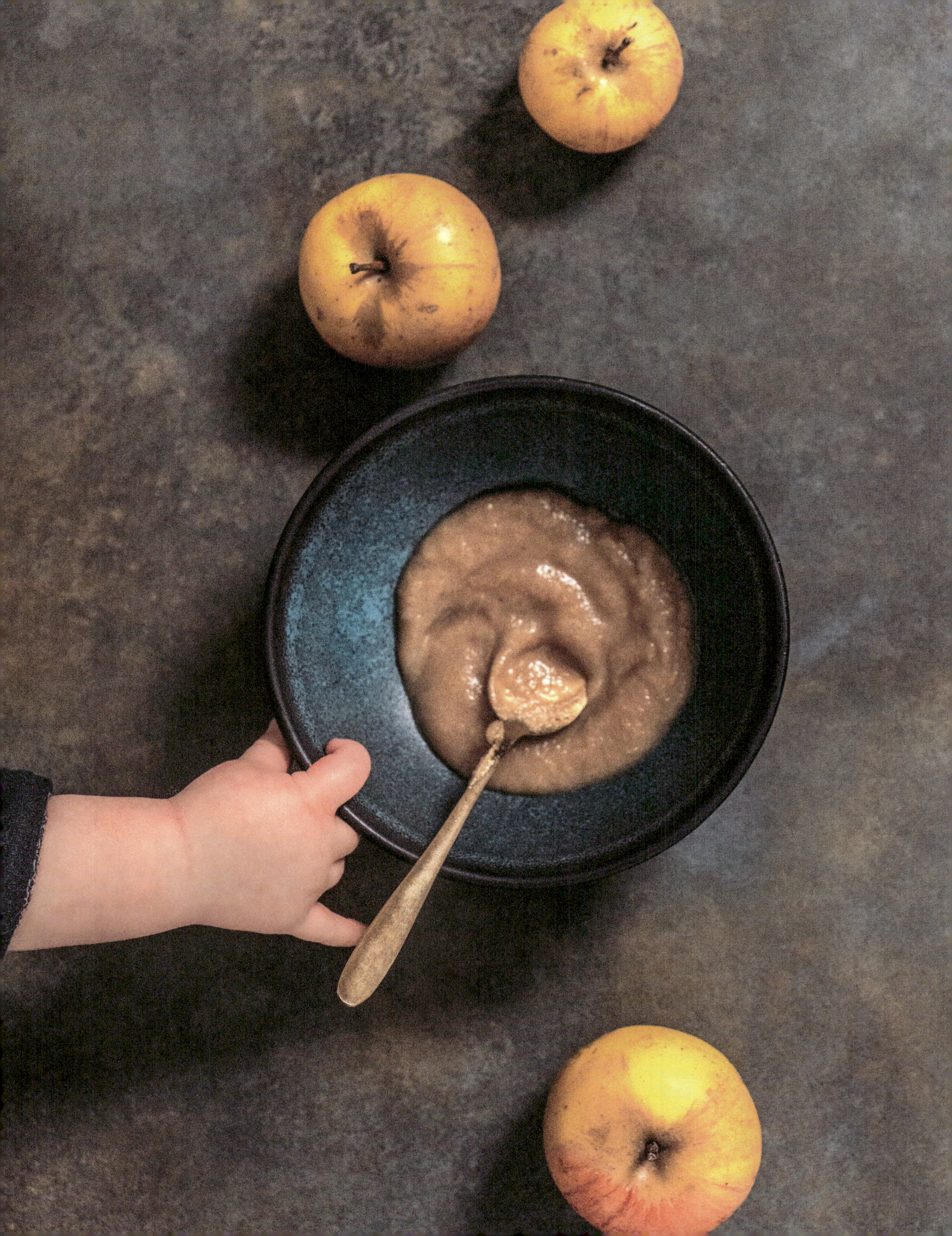

Ingredients

10 organic apples
1 lemon
100 g light brown soft sugar
1 cinnamon stick

Serves 5 babies

Preparation
10 minutes

Cooking
50 minutes

Adèle's compote

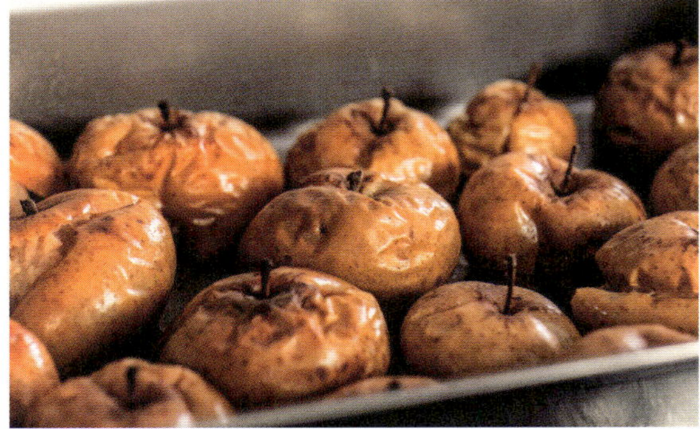

1.

Bake the whole apples in the oven at 180°C for 45 minutes.

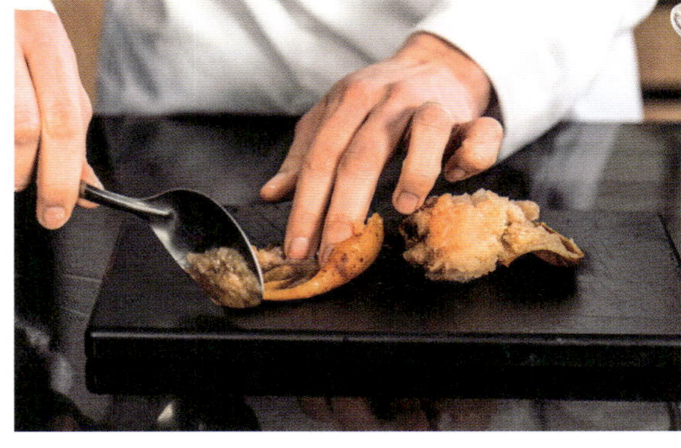

2.

Remove the cooked flesh and discard the core and skin.

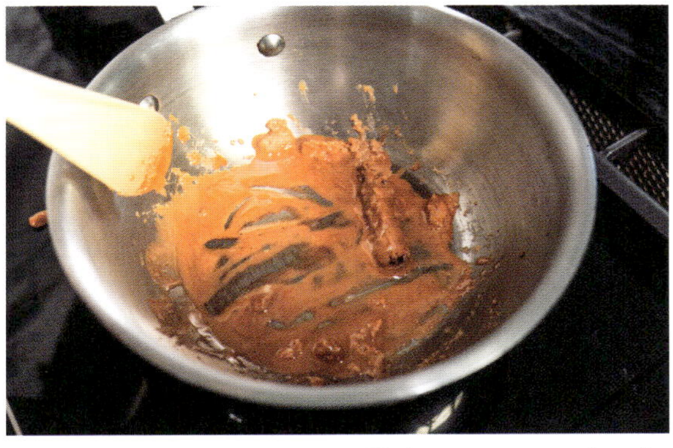

3.

In a saucepan, melt the sugar, add the cinnamon stick and caramelise for 20 seconds.

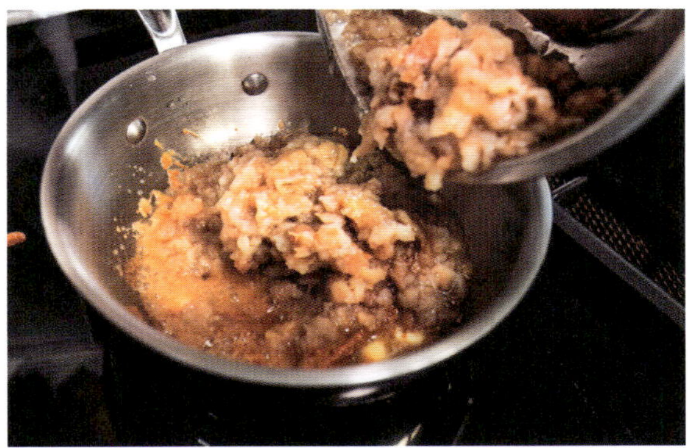

4.

Add the apple flesh and cook until soft.

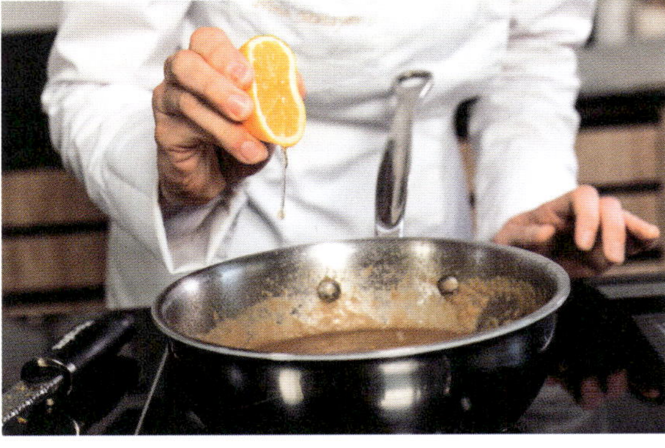

5.

Squeeze the lemon juice into the compote. Remove the cinnamon stick.

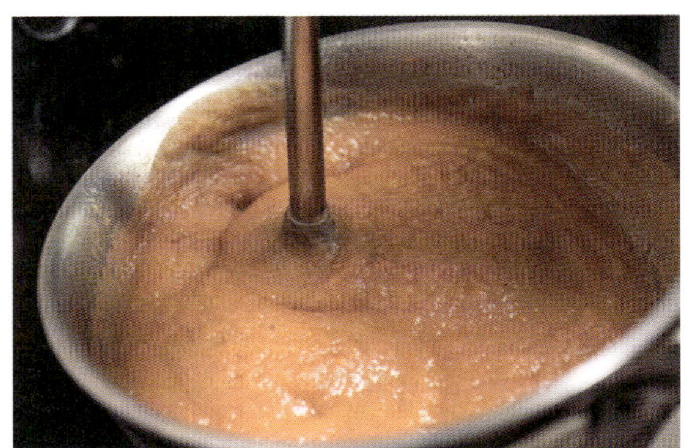

6.

Blend until smooth with an immersion blender. Allow to cool down before serving.

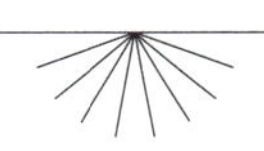

Makes 8

Preparation
30 minutes

Baking
9 minutes

Brownies

60 g shelled walnuts
40 g pecan nuts
150 g unsalted butter
80 g dark chocolate
2 egg yolks
90 g light brown soft sugar
40 g T55 (plain) flour
10 g cocoa powder
2 g salt
3 egg whites

Chop the walnuts and pecans.

Melt the butter and chocolate together in a bain-marie over a low heat. Whisk together the egg yolks and sugar.

Sift the flour, cocoa and salt. Mix the melted butter and chocolate with the sifted ingredients and incorporate the mixture into the egg yolk and sugar mixture. Whisk the egg whites to soft peaks and gently fold into the previous mixture, then add the walnuts and pecans.

Transfer the batter to a piping bag, fill 6-cm-diameter silicone moulds and bake at 180°C for 9 minutes.

'Brownies are a welcome treat at any time of day. You can have them for breakfast, to accompany your coffee after lunch, for afternoon tea, or to finish a good evening meal on a sweet note... I always make more than I need, which I freeze so that I can slip one into Anastasia's school bag from time to time as an afternoon snack; she loves it!'

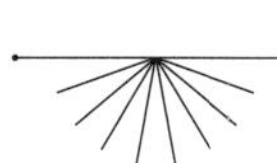

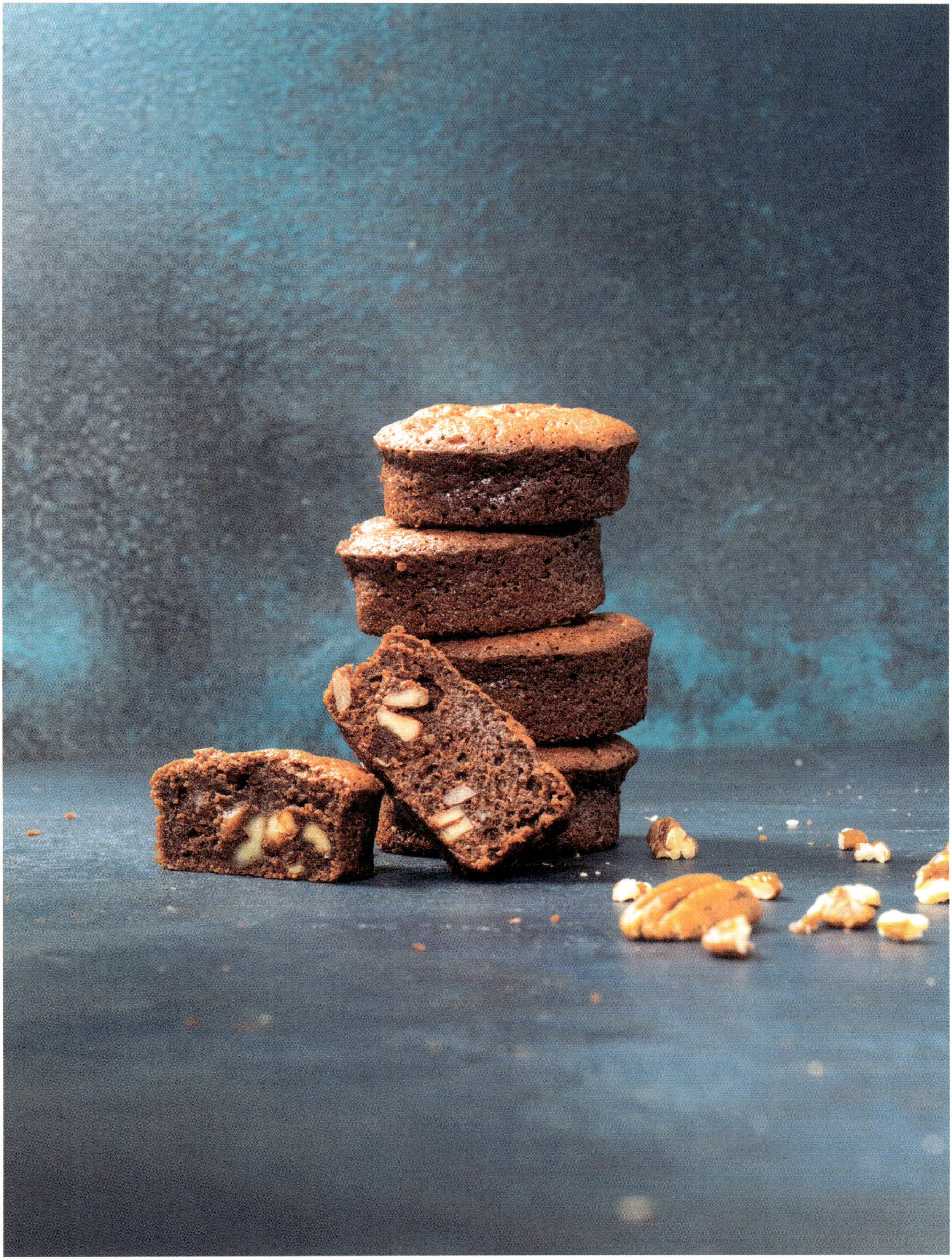

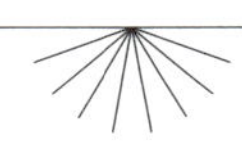

Makes 20 madeleines

Preparation
20 minutes

Baking
5 minutes

Madeleines

190 g unsalted butter
190 g T55 (plain) flour
12 g baking powder
3 eggs
125 g light brown soft sugar
½ vanilla pod
4 g orange zest
57 g full-fat milk
30 g forest honey (1)
50 g forest honey (2)

Preheat the oven to 210°C.

Make beurre noisette by cooking the butter in a saucepan while stirring constantly until it turns dark and nutty.

Sift the flour with the baking powder. Whisk the eggs with the sugar, then add the flour and baking powder. Scrape the seeds out of the vanilla pod half and incorporate the seeds, orange zest, milk, honey (1) and beurre noisette into the batter. Transfer to a piping bag.

Grease the madeleine moulds with butter. Pipe a small amount of batter into each mould. Lower the oven temperature to 200°C and bake the madeleines for 5 minutes.

Using a piping bag, fill the freshly baked madeleines with honey (2) through the bottom.

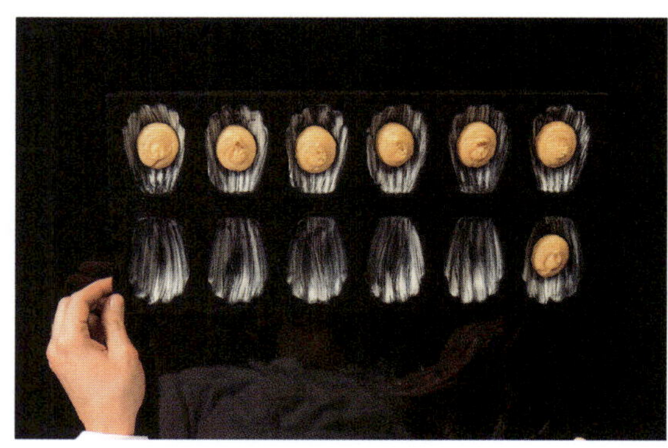

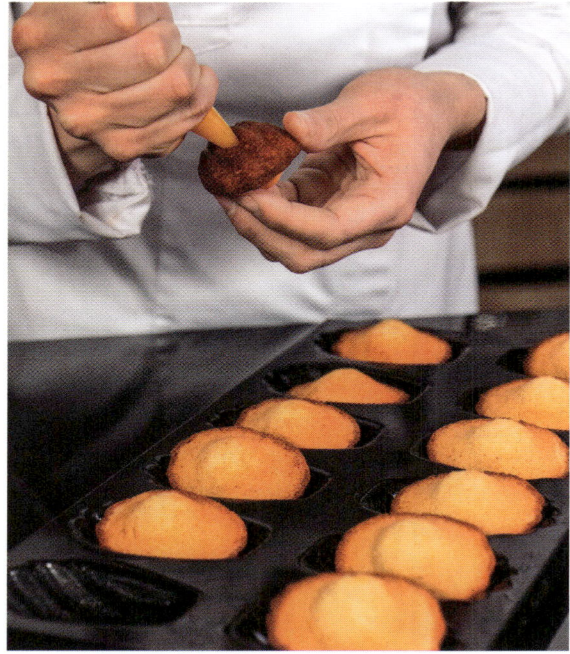

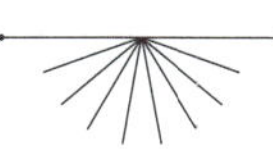

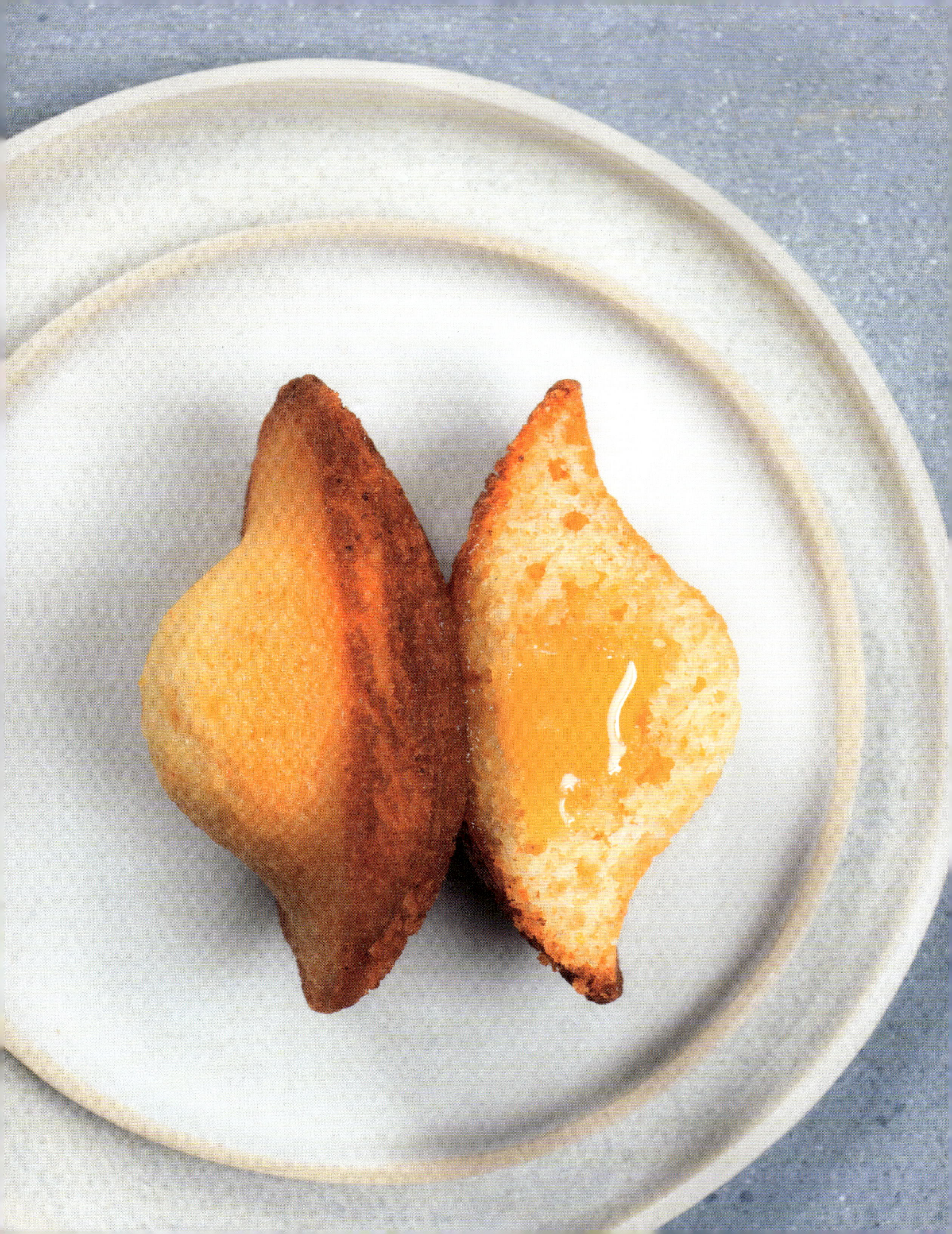

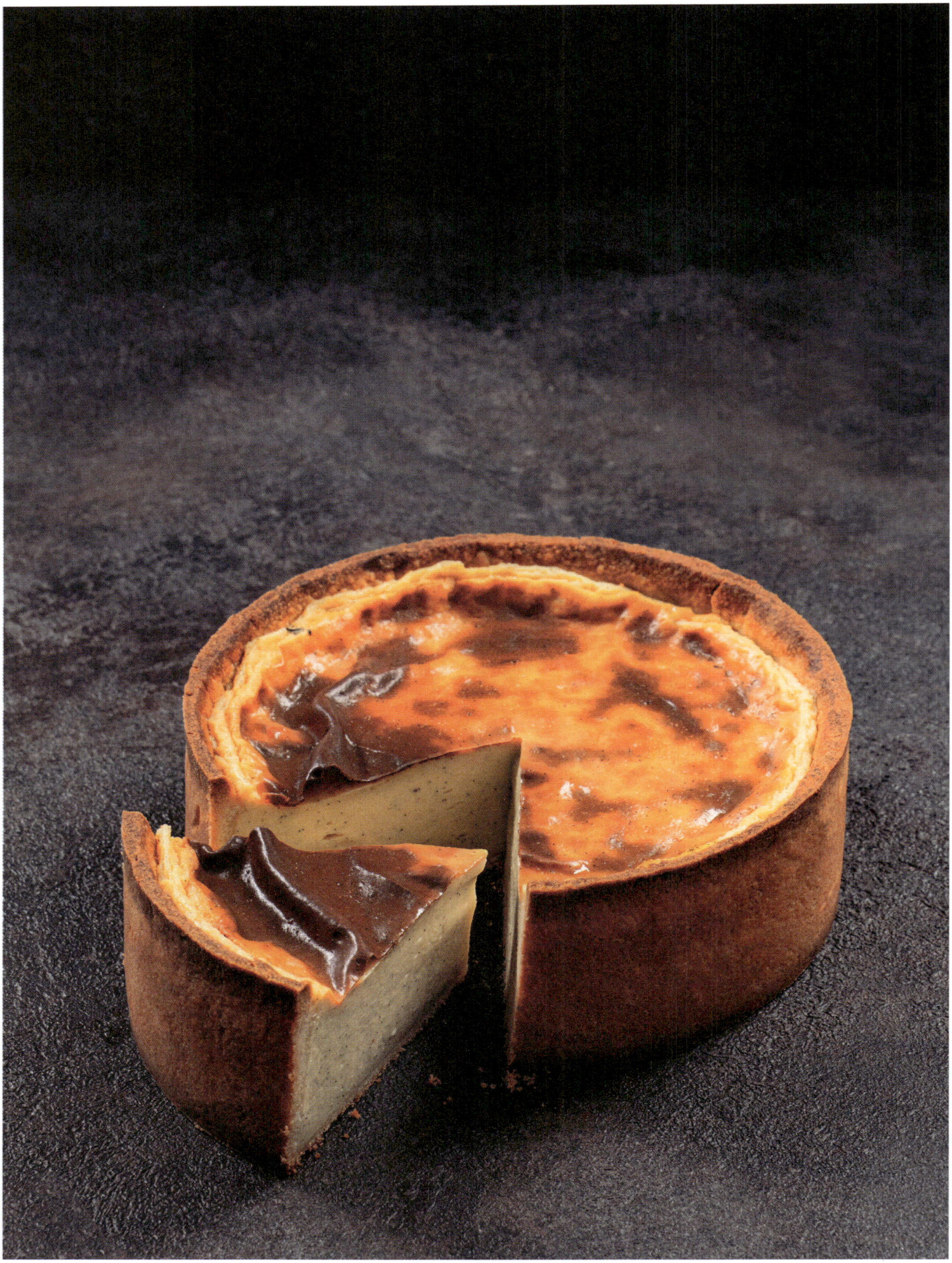

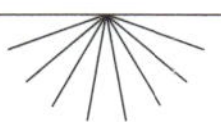

Serves 6	Preparation	Resting	Baking
	1 hour	5 hours 30 minutes	45 minutes

Tonka bean flan

Sweet pastry

150 g unsalted butter, at room
 temperature
90 g icing sugar
30 g ground almonds
2.5 g salt
1 g vanilla powder
270 g T55 (plain) flour
1 egg

Custard

450 g full-fat milk
130 g whipping cream (35% fat)
½ tonka bean
79 g caster sugar
65 g egg yolks
39 g cornflour
65 g unsalted butter

Sweet pastry By hand or in a stand mixer fitted with a paddle attachment, rub the butter into the sugar, ground almonds, salt, vanilla powder and flour until the mixture resembles fine breadcrumbs. Incorporate the egg. When the pastry is smooth, wrap it in cling film and refrigerate for 2 hours. Grease a tart ring 18 cm in diameter and 6 cm deep. Roll out the pastry to a 3-mm thickness. Cut out an 18-cm-diameter disc for the base and a 6-cm-wide strip of pastry for the sides. Line the tart ring with the pastry. Freeze for 30 minutes.

Put the milk, cream and grated tonka bean into a saucepan and bring to the boil.

Custard Whisk the egg yolks with the sugar until thick and pale and incorporate the cornflour. Add the hot milk and cream to the egg yolk mixture, whisk to combine and then return it to the saucepan. Cook over a low heat, stirring constantly with a whisk. Bring the custard to a simmer and continue to cool for 1 minute. Remove from the heat and incorporate the butter in small pieces.

Take the tart shell out of the freezer and fill it directly with the pastry cream. Chill the flan in the freezer for 1 hour, then bake at 180°C for 45 minutes.

As soon as the flan comes out of the oven, allow it to cool to room temperature in the ring, then take it out and refrigerate for 2 hours.

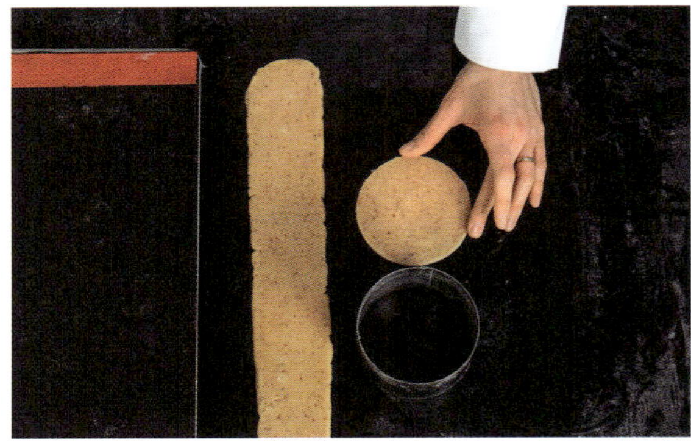
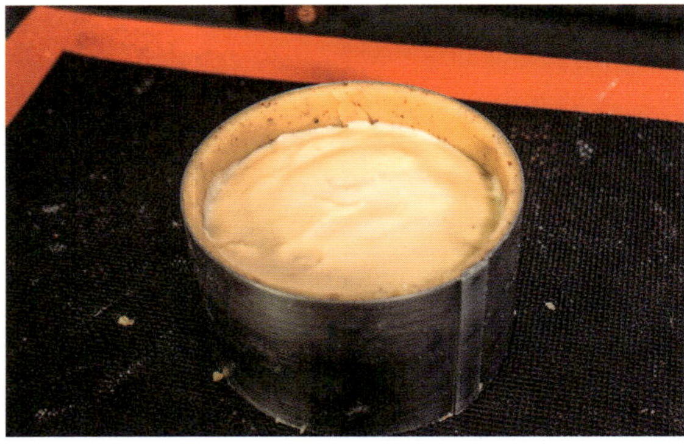

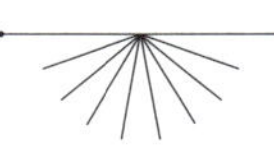

Makes 30 macarons

Preparation
1 hour

Resting
1 hour 25 minutes

Baking
20 minutes

Chocolate macarons

Macaron shells

330 g icing sugar
210 g ground almonds
30 g cocoa powder
6 (180 g) egg whites
68 g caster sugar

Chocolate ganache

160 g whipping cream (35% fat)
100 g dark chocolate
50 g milk chocolate
50 g praline
1.5 g fleur de sel

Macaron shells Sift the icing sugar, ground almonds and cocoa (1). Beat the egg whites to soft peaks and add the sugar just before the end. Beat the egg whites with the sugar for a further 30 seconds. Gently fold the dry ingredients into the beaten egg whites (2). Lightly deflate the batter with the spatula (3). Using a piping bag fitted with an 8-mm-diameter plain nozzle, pipe small and uniform macaron shells in staggered lines on a sheet of baking paper (4). Allow the shells to dry for 40 minutes, then bake at 160°C for 20 minutes (5).

Chocolate ganache Chop the different chocolates and place in a bowl. Bring the cream to the boil in a saucepan, then pour it over the chopped chocolates, stir and blend. Add the praline and fleur de sel and mix until smooth. Allow to set in the fridge for 45 minutes.

Assembly
Loosen the ganache with a spatula, then transfer it to a piping bag fitted with an 8-mm plain nozzle. Pipe ganache onto half the shells, then complete the macarons by covering the filling with another shell of similar size (6).

'Your macarons will be even better after 6 hours in the fridge, as the ganache will moisten the shells slightly, making them even softer. You can also freeze them; they keep very well when frozen and will be soft when thawed.'

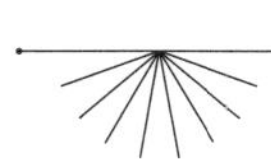

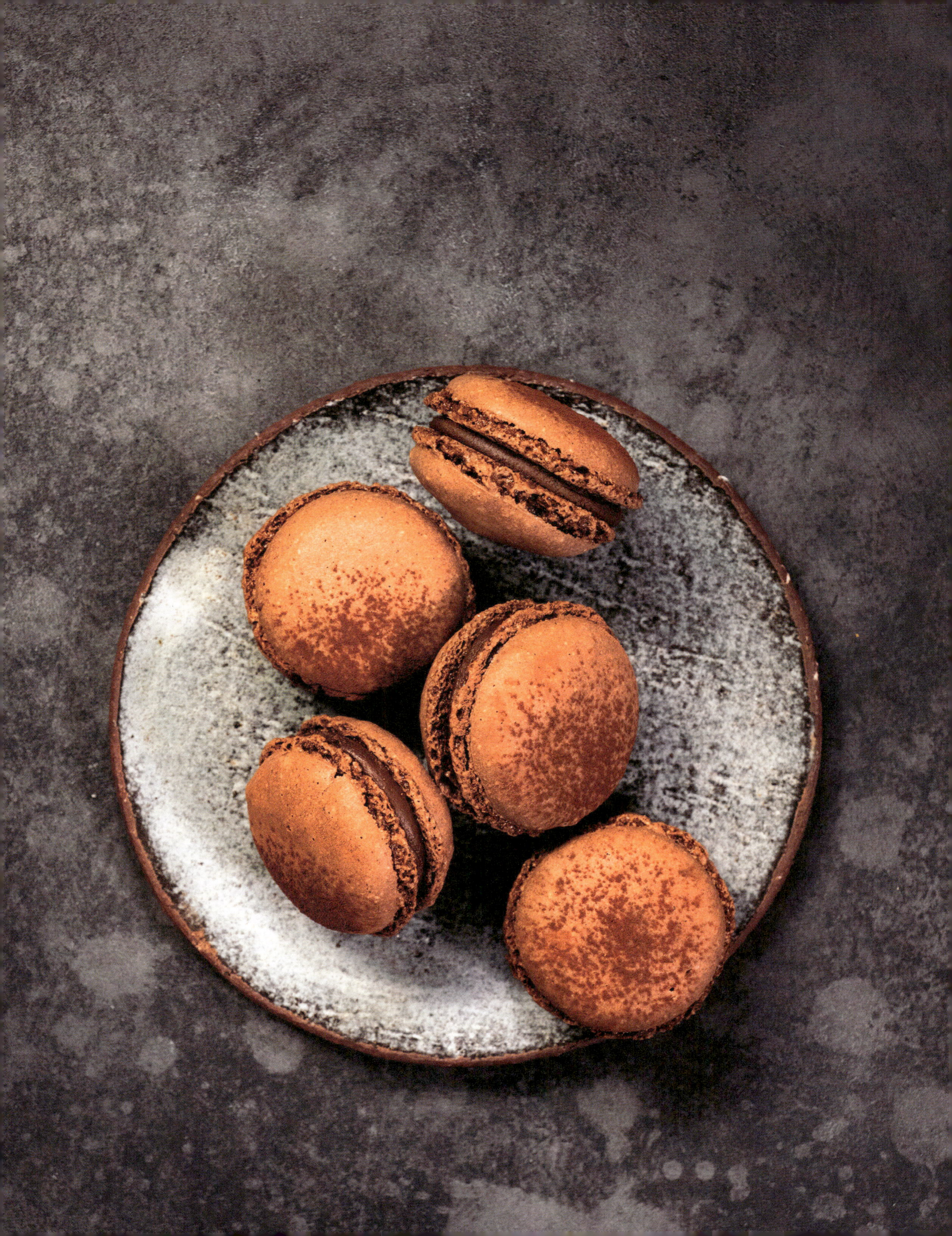

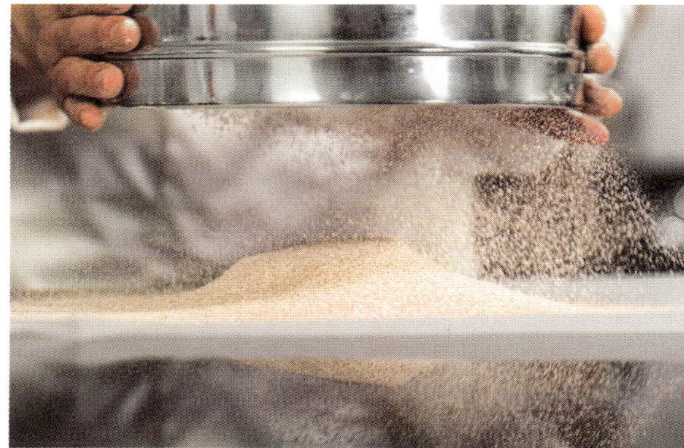

I. Sift the icing sugar, ground almonds and cocoa.

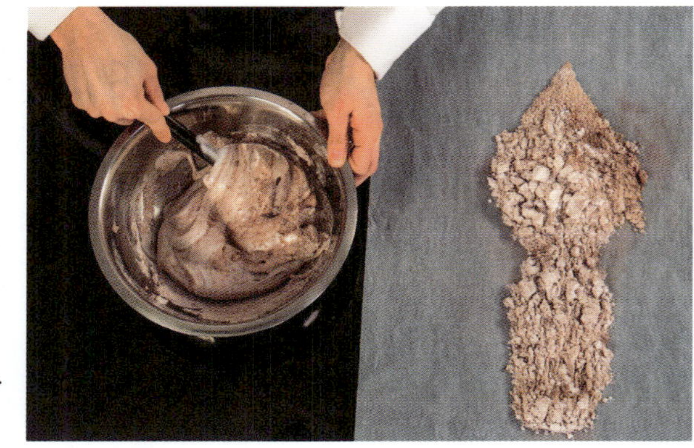

2. Beat the egg whites to stiff peaks and add the caster sugar just before the end, then gently fold in the dry ingredients.

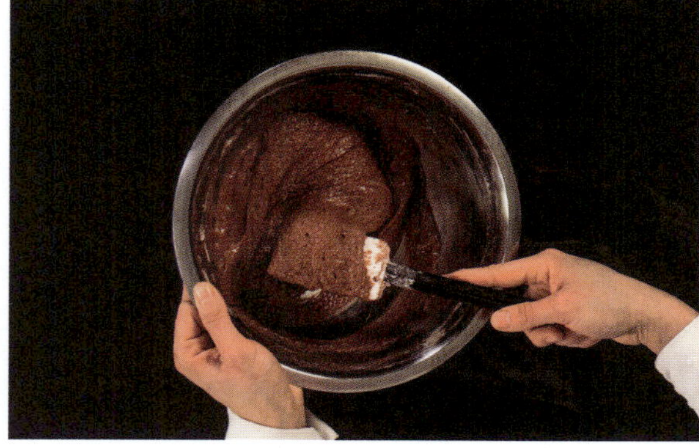

3. Lightly deflate the batter with the spatula.

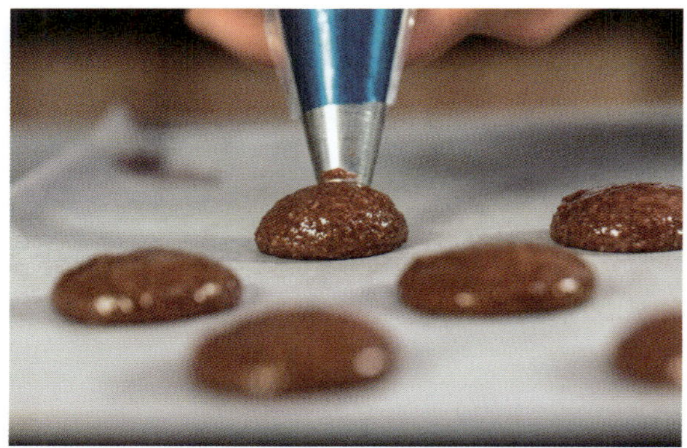

4. Using a piping bag fitted with an 8-mm-diameter plain nozzle, pipe small and uniform macaron shells in staggered lines on a sheet of baking paper.

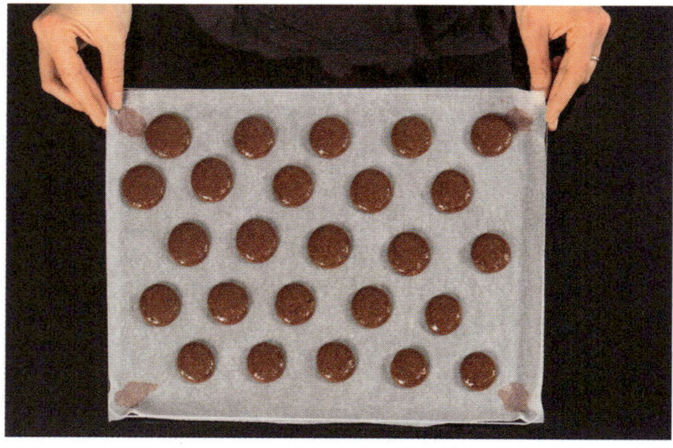

5. Leave to dry for 40 minutes, then bake at 160°C for 20 minutes.

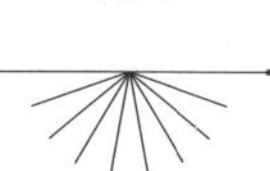

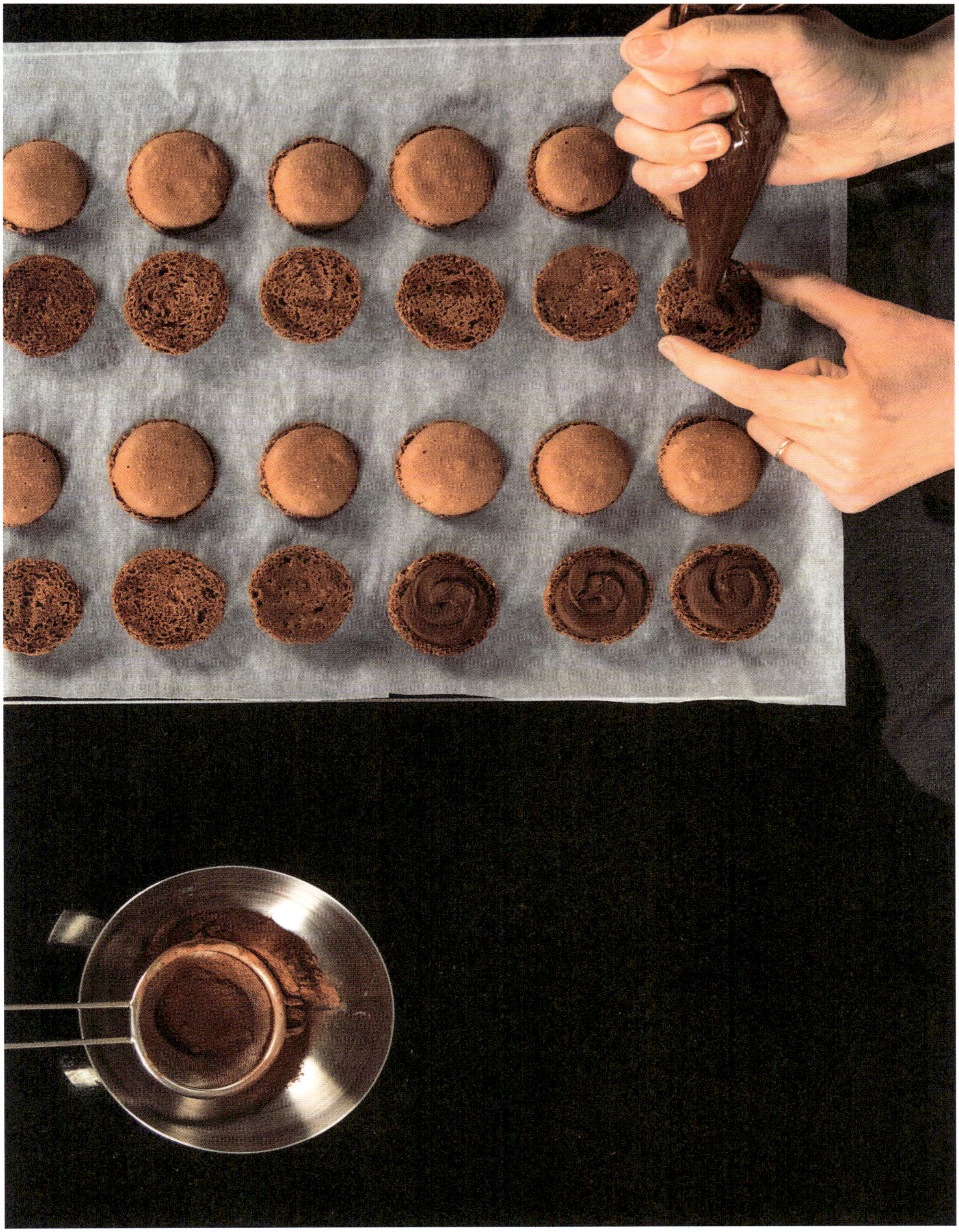

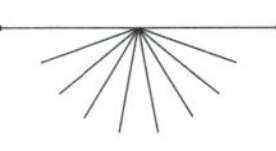

6.

Using a piping bag fitted with an 8-mm plain nozzle, pipe ganache onto half the shells, then complete the macarons by covering the filling with another shell of similar size.

Makes 10 shortbread biscuits

Preparation
1 hour

Resting
12 hours

Baking
10 minutes

Christmas shortbread biscuits

Shortbread

125 g unsalted butter, at room
   temperature
28 g light brown soft sugar
18 g muscovado sugar
75 g T150 (wholemeal) flour
75 g T55 (plain) flour
1 g fleur de sel
½ tonka bean
1 g ground cinnamon
Zest of ½ lemon
30 g egg white

Royal icing

150 g icing sugar
10 g egg white
1 g white vinegar

Shortbread Mix together the brown sugars, flours, fleur de sel, tonka bean, cinnamon and lemon zest, then rub in the butter and incorporate the egg white. Mix by hand or in a stand mixer until the dough is smooth. Roll up the dough, wrap it in cling film and allow to rest in the fridge for 12 hours. Roll out the dough to a 3-mm thickness. Use Christmas-themed biscuit cutters to shape the shortbread. Arrange the shortbread biscuits on a baking tray lined with baking paper or a baking mat and bake for 10 minutes at 175°C.

Royal icing Sift the icing sugar, then mix in the egg white and vinegar with a palette knife until the icing has the desired consistency. Add a little icing sugar if the icing is too runny, and add a little egg white if the icing is too thick. Make a piping bag out of baking paper. Fill the piping bag with icing and pipe decorations on the shortbread biscuits.

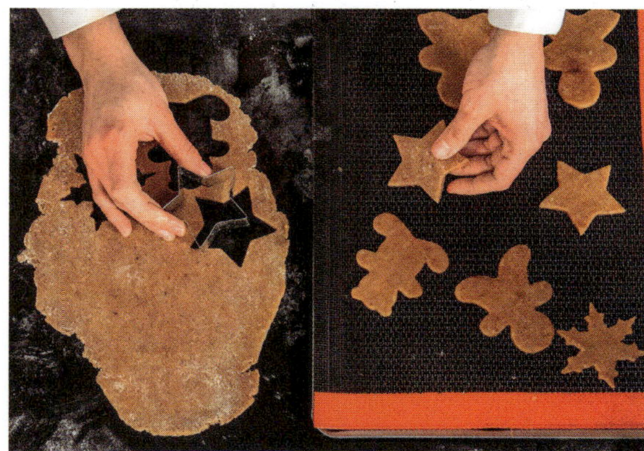
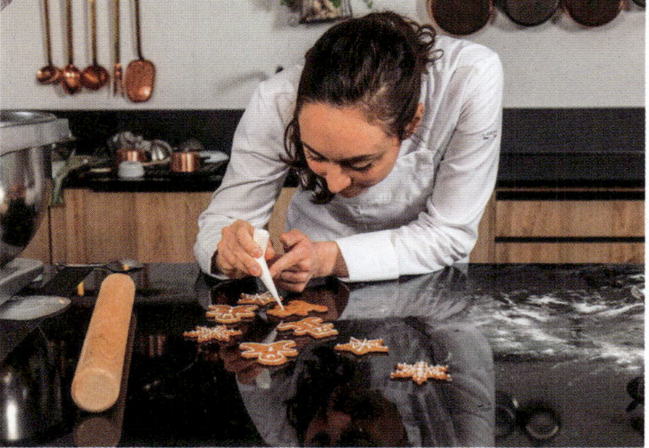

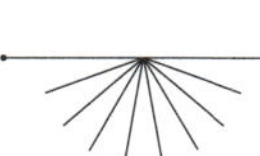

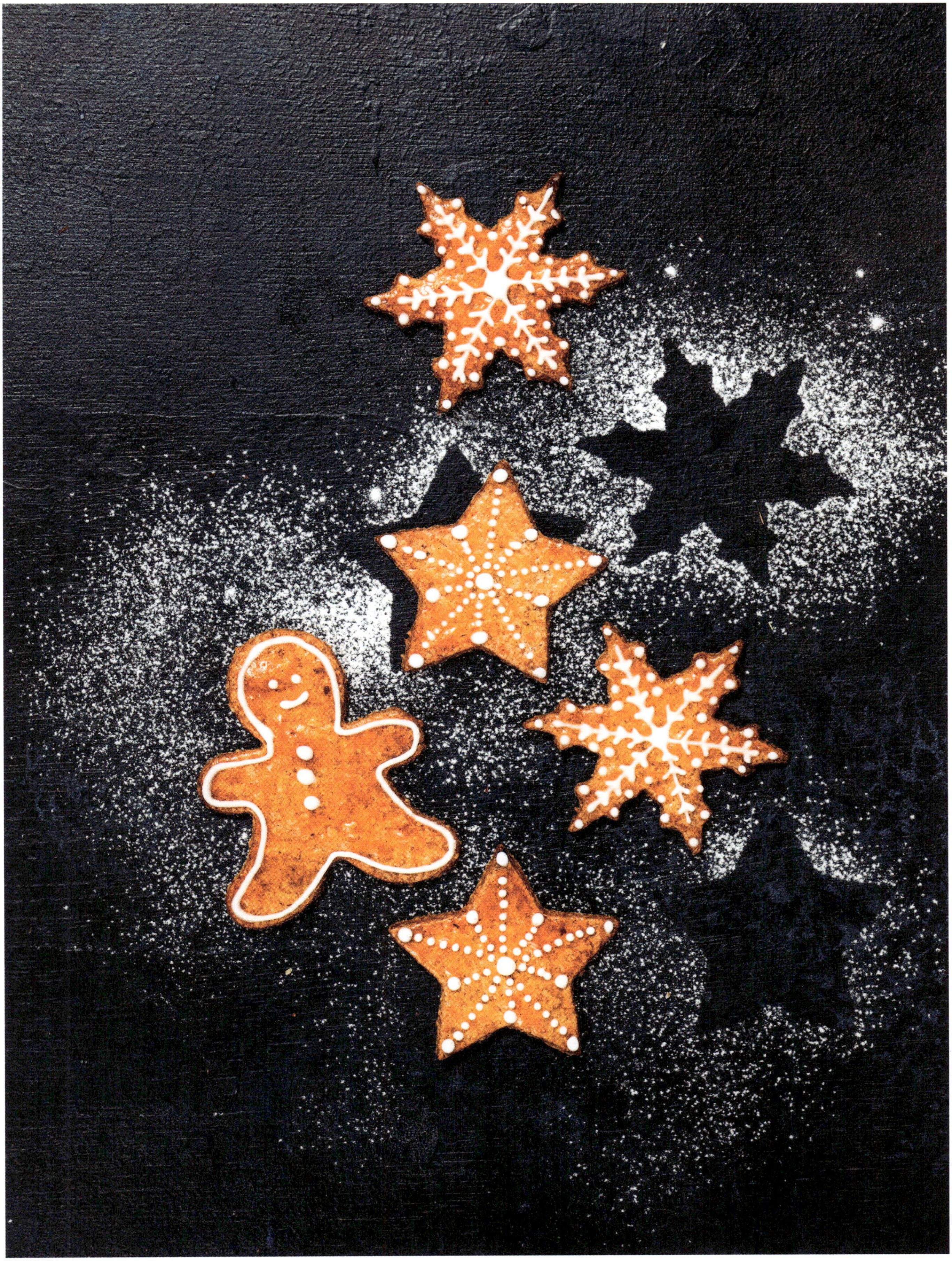

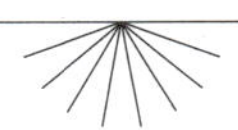

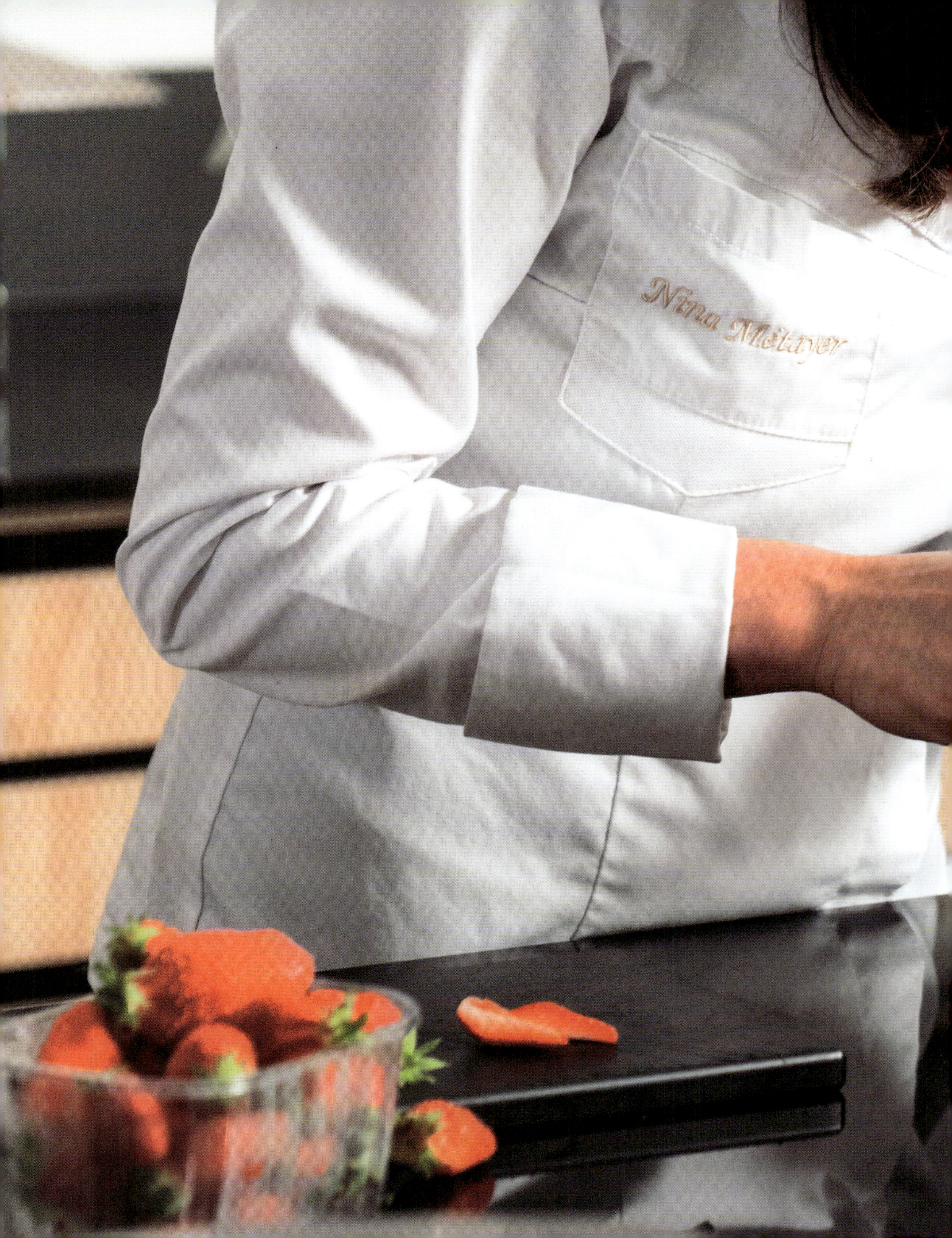
Nina Métayer

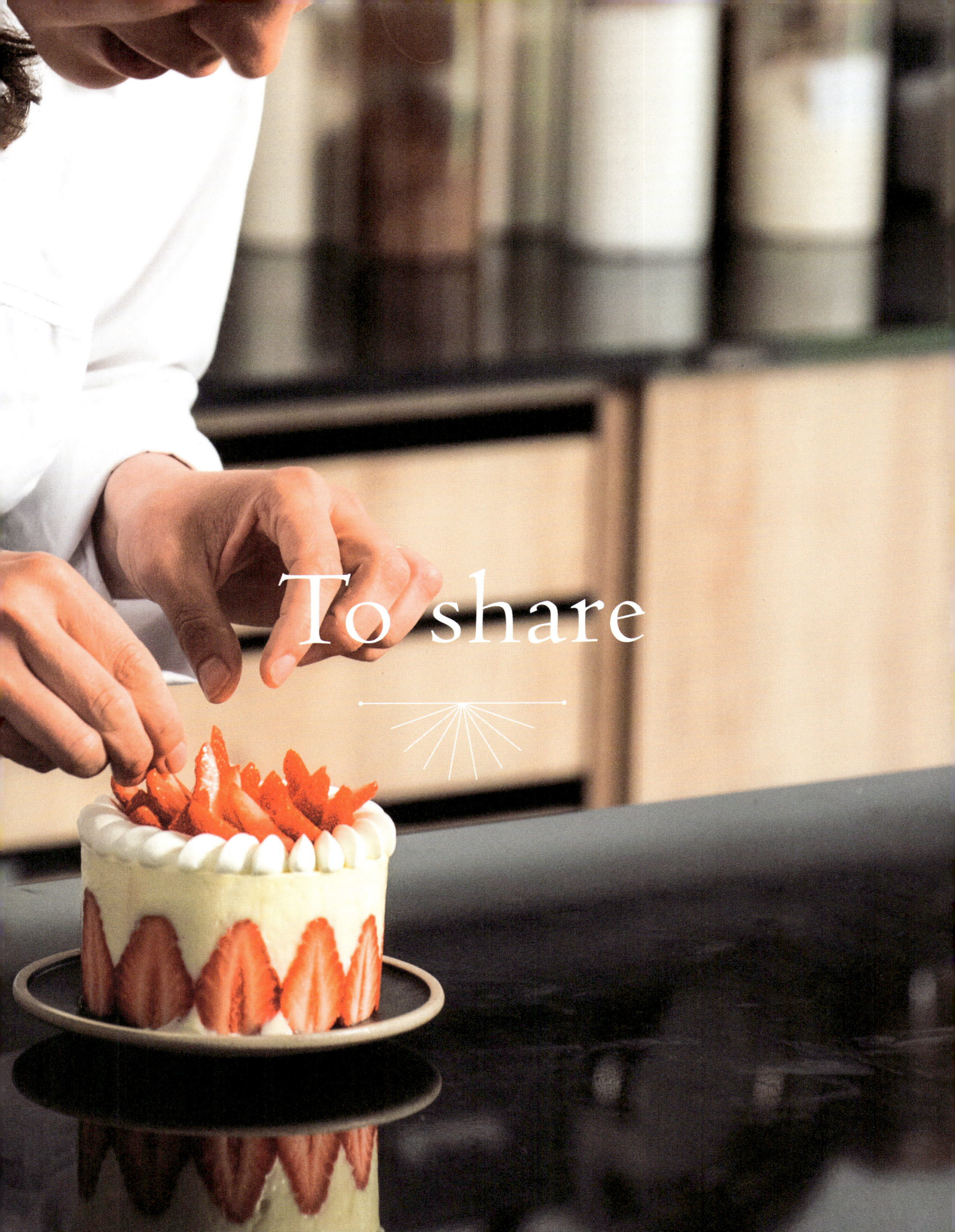
To share

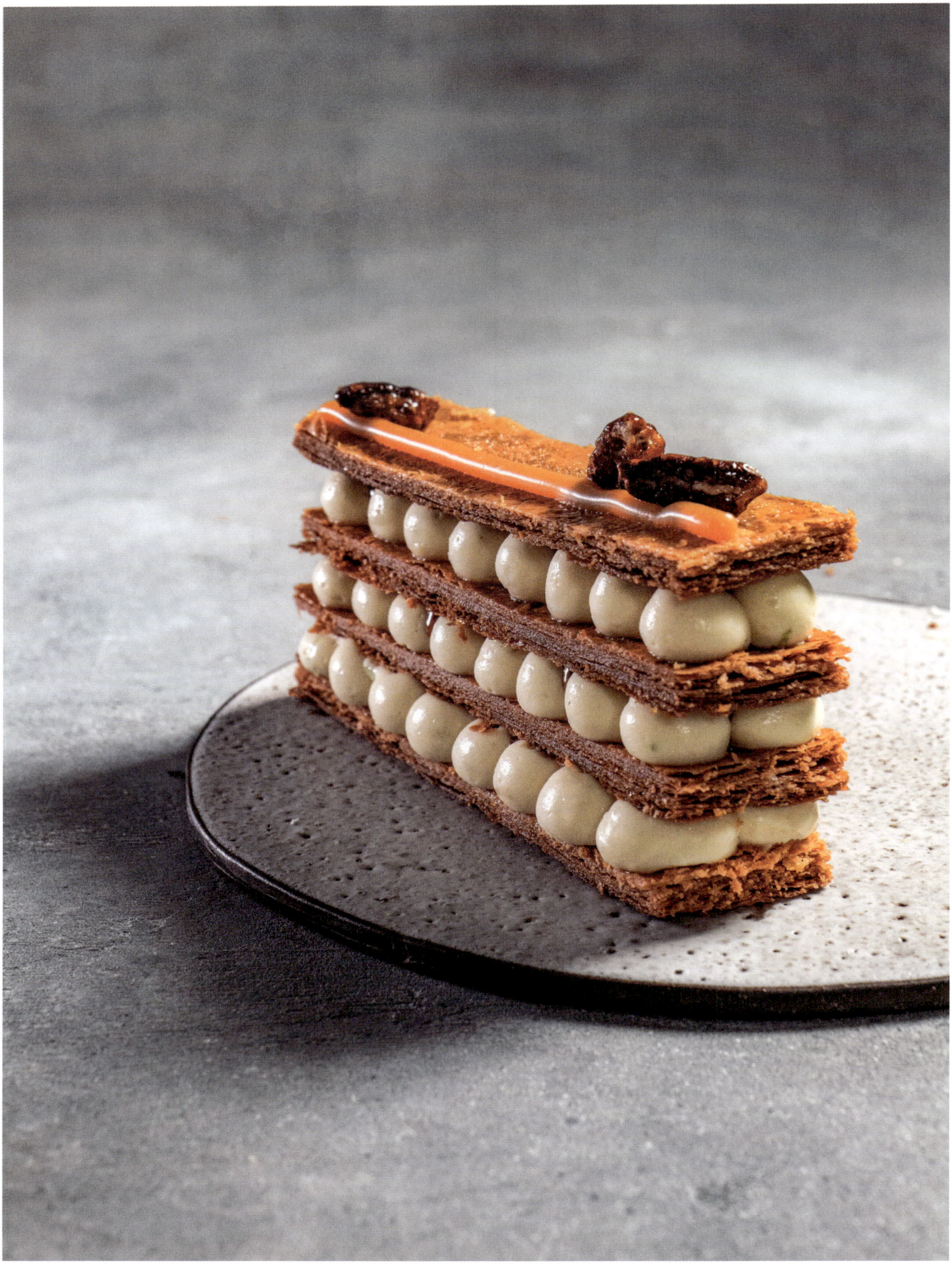

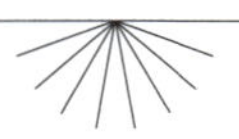

Serves 8

Preparation	Resting	Cooking
2 hours 30 minutes	20 hours	1 hour 15 minutes

Millefeuille

Inverse puff pastry
Beurre manié
338 g unsalted butter
150 g small spelt flour

Dough
282 g T80 (stoneground white)
    flour
127 g water
90 g unsalted butter
12 g salt
4 g white vinegar

Pastry cream
280 g full-fat milk
140 g whipping cream
1 vanilla pod
2 eggs
70 g light brown soft sugar
35 g potato starch
12 g T55 (plain) flour
15 g unsalted butter

Crème légère
425 g pastry cream
170 g whipping cream
23 g gelatine mass
(3 g gelatine powder
    and 20 g cold water)
Grated zest of 1 lime

Caramel powder
25 g water
60 g caster sugar
6 g glucose syrup

Beurre Manié The day before, mix the butter with the spelt flour and roll out the mixture to an even thickness.

Dough Make the dough by mixing all the ingredients, then roll it out to an even thickness and place it over the beurre manié. Rest the assembled pastry in the fridge for at least 6 hours. Perform a double turn by rolling out the pastry to a 5-mm thickness and folding it over twice to make 4 stacked layers (double turn). Rest the pastry in the fridge at 4°C for at least 6 hours. Repeat the operation to perform a total of 3 double turns. Roll out the puff pastry to a 2-mm thickness and chill until well relaxed.

Pastry cream In a saucepan, bring the milk and cream to the boil, add the split vanilla pod and scraped-out seeds. Cover with cling film and allow to steep for 10 minutes. Beat the eggs with the sugar until thick and pale, then add the potato starch and flour. Bring the vanilla-infused mixture back to the boil and immediately mix it into the beaten egg mixture. Then return everything to the saucepan and bring to the boil for 3 minutes. Remove from the heat and add the butter. Transfer the pastry cream to a deep baking tray lined with cling film and cool quickly.

Crème légère Loosen the cold pastry cream with a whisk. Whip the cream in a stand a mixer. Heat a small amount of pastry cream and dissolve the gelatine mass in it. Incorporate the cold pastry cream a little at a time into the hot mixture, making sure not to allow the gelatine to set. Gently fold in the whipped cream and lime zest. Refrigerate for 4 hours.

Caramel powder Put the water and sugar into a saucepan and bring to the boil, then add the glucose and cook until the temperature reaches 170°C. Pour the caramel onto a baking mat and allow to cool. Then grind to a powder in a blender.

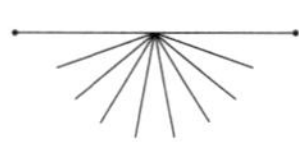

Caramel sauce
50 g whipping cream
120 g caster sugar
80 g unsalted butter, cold
1 vanilla pod
2 g fleur de sel

Hazelnut and cocoa nib praline
125 g hazelnuts
63 g caster sugar
20 g water
30 g grape seed oil
2.5 g fleur de sel
50 g cocoa nibs

Caramelised pecans
40 g water
120 g caster sugar
130 g pecan nuts

Caramel sauce Split the vanilla pod and scrape out the seeds. Heat the cream with the vanilla pod and seeds. Make a dry caramel with the sugar and add the hot cream to stop the cooking process. Cook until the temperature reaches 106°C, then blend in the cold butter. Add the fleur de sel. Transfer the caramel to a container and allow to set in the fridge.

Hazelnut and cocoa nib praline Roast the hazelnuts in the oven at 140°C for 40 minutes. In a saucepan, cook the sugar and water to a caramel over a low heat and transfer to a baking mat. Put the hazelnuts, cooled caramel and oil into a blender and blend to a smooth liquid, then add the fleur de sel and cocoa nibs.

Caramelised pecans In a saucepan, cook the sugar with the water until the temperature reaches 110°C, then stir in the pecans then heat until caramelised. Spread out the caramelised pecans on an oiled work surface, spacing well apart, and allow to cool.

Assembly
Make the puff pastry.

Make the pastry cream and then the crème légère. Allow the crème légère to rest in the fridge at 4°C. In the meantime, roll out the puff pastry to a 2-mm thickness, prick it all over with a fork and bake between 2 baking trays at 170°C for 30 minutes (1). Check every 10 minutes: if the pastry has risen, press down on the top tray. Cut out 13-cm-long and 2.5-cm-wide puff pastry rectangles (2–3), dust with caramel powder through a sieve and caramelise in the oven for 3 minutes at 175°C (4). Allow to cool.

Make the caramel sauce, praline and caramelised pecans.

Pipe 2 rows of 8 small balls of crème légère onto 3 puff pastry rectangles and add a dot of praline between each ball. Using a 2-mm diameter plain nozzle, pipe a line of caramel sauce on a fourth pastry rectangle (5).

Stack three pastry and crème légère rectangles (6). Close the millefeuille with the rectangle containing the line of caramel sauce on top.

Decorate the top with caramelised pecans.

You can also place caramelised pecans between the balls of crème légère. Chill in the fridge at 4°C, then serve.

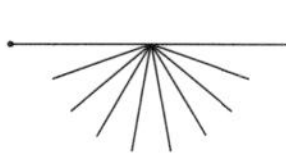

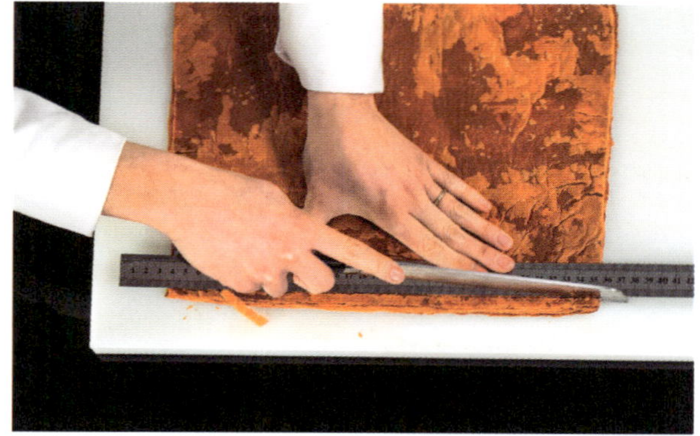

I.

Roll out the puff pastry to a 2-mm thickness, prick it all over and bake between 2 baking trays at 170 °C for 30 minutes. Check every 10 minutes: if the pastry has risen, press down on the top tray.

2.

Cut out puff pastry rectangles...

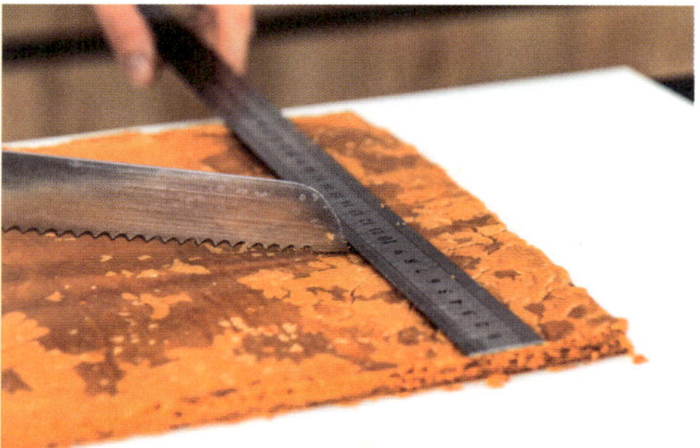

3.

...13 cm long and 2.5 cm wide.

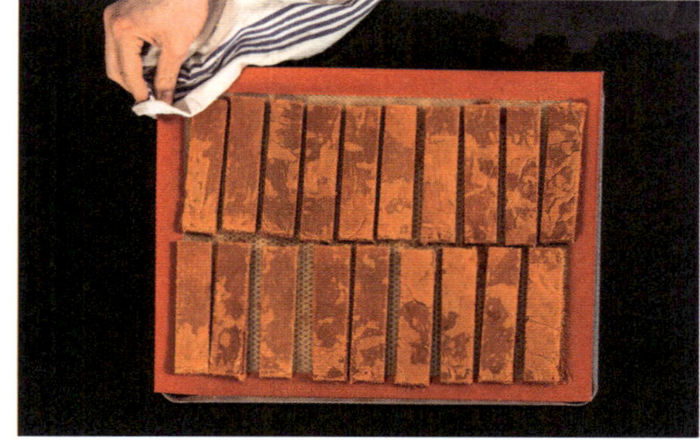

4.

Dust with caramel powder through a sieve and caramelise in the oven for 3 minutes at 175 °C.

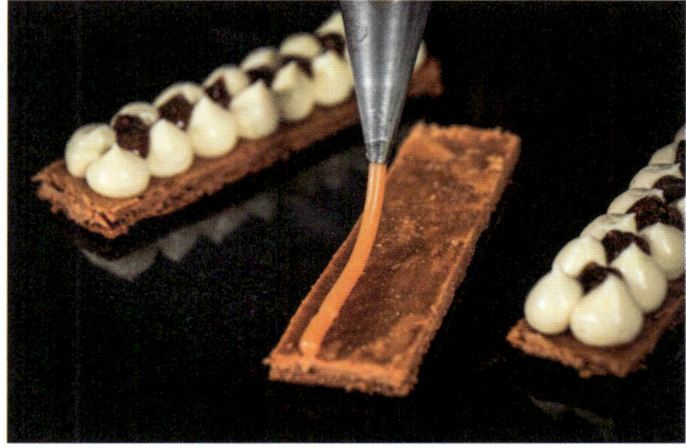

5.

Pipe 16 small balls of crème légère on 3 puff pastry rectangles and add a dot of praline between each ball. Pipe a line of caramel sauce on a fourth puff pastry rectangle.

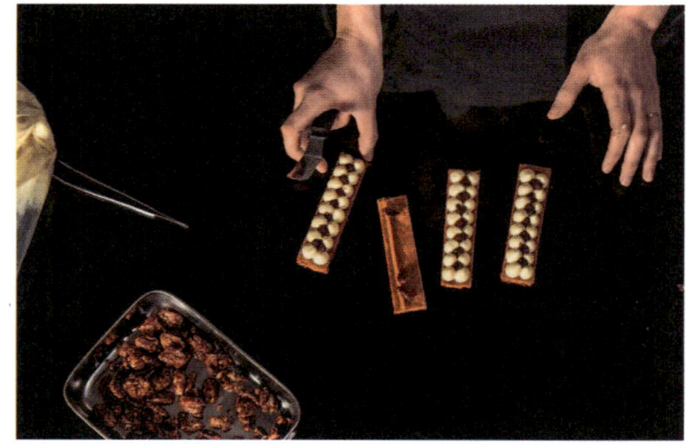

6.

Stack three pastry and crème légère rectangles, then close the millefeuille with the rectangle containing the line of caramel sauce on top. Decorate the top with caramelised pecans.

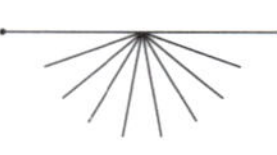

Serves 8

Preparation	Resting	Cooking
5 hours	2 days	1 hour 25 minutes

L'éveil

Cocoa ganache

1 gelatine leaf
100 g whipping cream (1)
14 g deZaan Crimson Red
   cocoa powder
0.3 g salt
100 g whipping cream (2)
40 g white chocolate

Cocoa glaze

2 gelatine leaves
45 g water
40 g glucose syrup
106 g caster sugar
30 g deZaan True Dark
   cocoa powder
78 g whipping cream
12 g honey

Kumquat and
kalamansis confit

20 g bergamot zest
100 g kumquats
100 g kalamansis
100 g satsumas
50 g light brown soft sugar

Hazelnut and cocoa nib praline

125 g hazelnuts
63 g caster sugar
20 g water
17 g grape seed oil
2.5 g fleur de sel
50 g cocoa nibs

Cocoa ganache Soak the gelatine in iced water for 10 minutes. Put the cream (1) and cocoa in a saucepan, bring to the boil and blend with an immersion blender. Squeeze the gelatine to drain, add with the salt and pour the mixture over the white chocolate. Mix with a silicone spatula. Then add the second measure of cream (2) and blend again. Refrigerate overnight.

Cocoa glaze Soak the gelatine in iced water for 10 minutes and squeeze to drain. In a saucepan, make a syrup by bringing the water, glucose and sugar to the boil, then stir in the sifted cocoa. In another saucepan, bring the cream and honey to the boil and add to the syrup. Bring back to the boil again, remove from the heat and add the gelatine. Blend until smooth without forming any bubbles. Refrigerate overnight.

Kumquat and kalamansis confit Using a vegetable peeler, remove the zest from the bergamot. Blanch the kumquats, kalamansi, bergamot zest and satsumas together 3 times, changing the water each time. Save the last batch of blanching water. Mix the fruit with the sugar, then blend everything, making sure to keep chunks of fruit. Dilute with a little blanching water if necessary.

Hazelnut and cocoa nib praline Roast the hazelnuts at 140 °C for 40 minutes. In a saucepan over a low heat, cook the sugar and water to a caramel and transfer to a baking sheet. Put the hazelnuts, cooled caramel and oil into a blender and blend to a smooth liquid, then add the fleur de sel and cocoa nibs, blend for a further 30 seconds and transfer to a container.

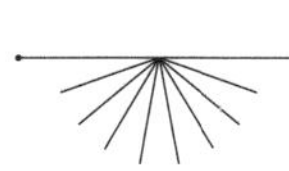

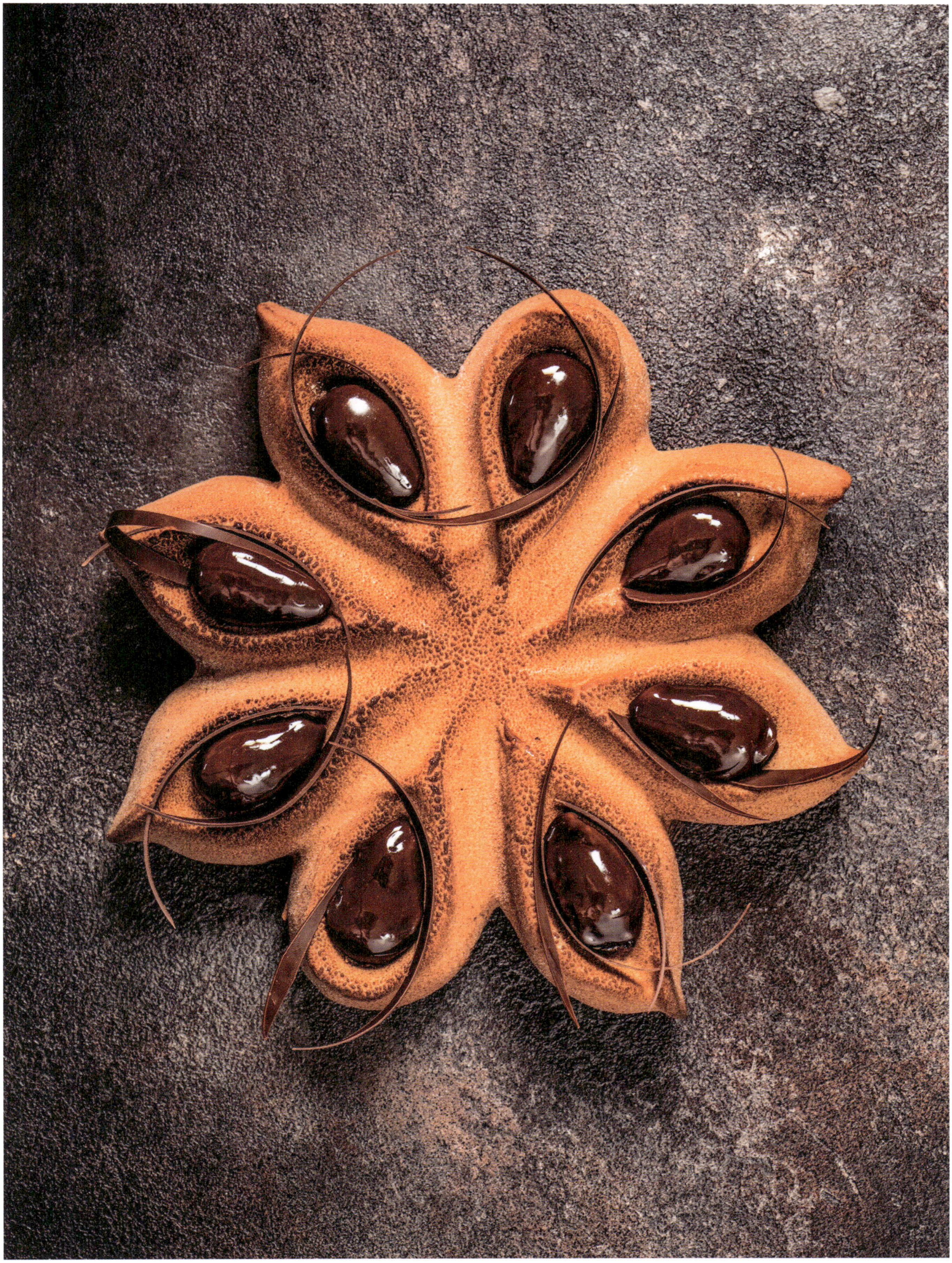

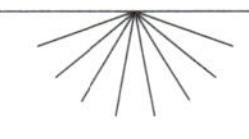

Cocoa pain de Gênes sponge

130 g almond paste (50%)

134 g eggs

48 g unsalted butter

13 g deZaan Rich Terracotta
cocoa powder

0.5 g salt

9 g T55 (plain) flour

15 g potato starch

Sweet pastry

69 g unsalted butter

44 g icing sugar

14 g ground almonds

0.5 g salt

17 g deZaan True Gold
cocoa powder

0.5 g vanilla powder

100 g T80 (stoneground white)
flour

25 g egg

Rich chocolate mousse

120 g whipping cream (1)

130 g milk

40 g deZaan True Gold
cocoa powder

3 egg yolks

40 g light brown soft sugar

150 g dark chocolate (66%
cocoa)

674 g whipping cream (2)

Black flocking

200 g cocoa butter

200 g dark chocolate (72%
cocoa)

Chocolate decorations

100 g dark chocolate (72%
cocoa)

Cocoa pain de Gênes sponge In a blender, blend the almond paste with a third of the eggs, then transfer to a stand mixer and beat. Melt the butter and gently fold it into the almond mixture. Sift the cocoa, salt, flour and potato starch and fold them into the mixture. Spread the batter in a baking tray lined with baking paper to a 1-cm thickness. Bake the sponge for 8 minutes at 180 °C, then check that it is cooked using the tip of a knife. Adjust the cooking time if necessary.

Sweet pastry Rub the butter into the sugar, ground almonds, salt, cocoa, vanilla powder and flour until the mixture resembles fine breadcrumbs. Incorporate the egg. Once smooth, allow the pastry to rest in the fridge. Roll out the pastry to a 4-mm thickness and chill in the freezer. Using a knife and a template previously drawn on cardboard, cut out a pastry flower and bake at 150 °C for 35 minutes.

Rich chocolate mousse Heat the cream (1) and milk in a saucepan, add the cocoa and blend until very smooth with an immersion blender. Add the cream and milk mixture to the egg yolks and sugar, then return everything to the saucepan and cook, until the temperature reaches 82 °C, stirring constantly. Pour the mixture over the melted chocolate. Stir well. Whip the second measure of cream (2) and incorporate into the mousse mixture.

Black flocking Melt the cocoa butter and chocolate. Blend and set aside.

Chocolate decorations Temper the chocolate using the temperature curve method: melt the chocolate at 55 °C, cool over an ice bath to 28 °C and reheat to 30–31°C in a bain-marie. Spread the chocolate thinly over an acetate strip (1) and score the surface with rhomboid shapes (2). Shape the chocolate strip into a curve in a yule log tin (3). Allow the chocolate to harden (4) before separating the rhomboids.

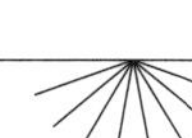

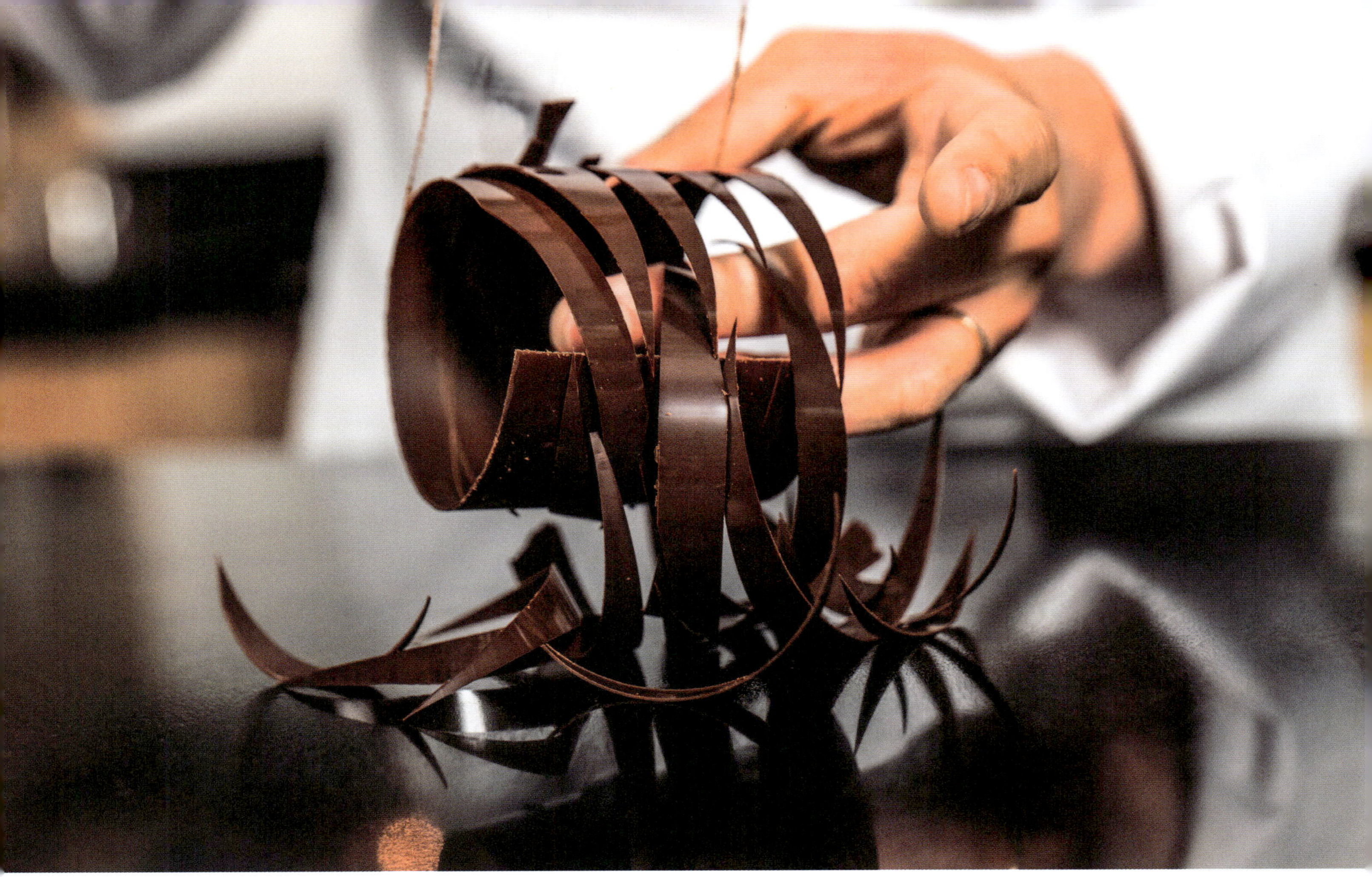

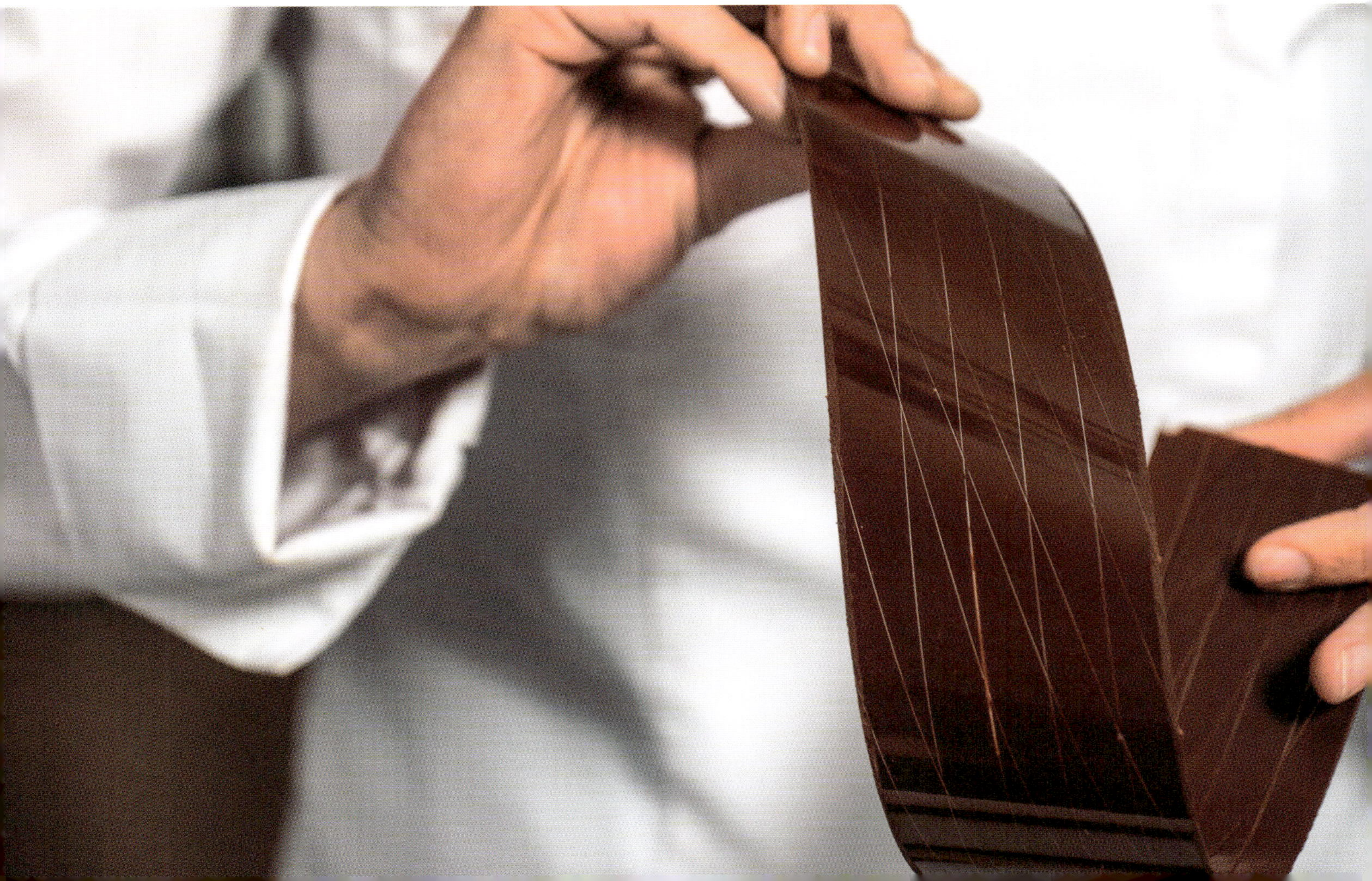

Assembly

The day before, make the ganache and refrigerate overnight.

Make the chocolate icing and refrigerate overnight.

Make the confit, praline and pain de Gênes for the inserts. Pour 200 g of confit into custom-made silicone moulds and allow to harden in the freezer. Cover the confit in the moulds with 200 g of praline and return the mould to the freezer. Cut petals out of the pain de Gênes sponge using biscuit cutters. Lay the Genoa bread petals on top of the praline in the moulds and return them to the freezer. Make the sweet pastry, cut into a flower shape and bake. Set aside.

Remove the inserts from the moulds. Make the rich chocolate mousse, pour it into the moulds and spread mousse up the sides of the mould to prevent air bubbles from forming. Place the inserts in the mousse in the moulds, pressing lightly so that the mousse rises a little. Then smooth the mousse to cover the insert and freeze the entremets overnight.

On the day, whip the chocolate ganache with a mixer until soft, then pipe teardrop shapes over a baking tray and freeze for 2 hours.

Melt part of the glaze in a bain-marie, then blend the melted glaze with the cold glaze to a smooth and creamy consistency (5). Cover the frozen ganache drops with glaze (6).

Make the chocolate decorations.

When the individual entremets are frozen, remove them from the moulds, spray with the black flocking and arrange them on the pastry flower. Cover them with the glazed ganache teardrops and arrange the chocolate decorations over the dessert.

Chill the dessert in the fridge at 4°C for 6 hours before serving.

'This is a dessert that I created for Easter. I wanted a shape that symbolised spring, so I sculpted a flower out of chocolate. I developed my flower idea over a period of several weeks to find the balance between aesthetics and flavour. To go with it, I worked with citrus and cocoa. I used several different cocoas and chose particular citrus fruits so that I could bring out and enhance their shared notes of acidity, bitterness, spice and freshness.'

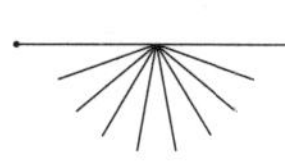

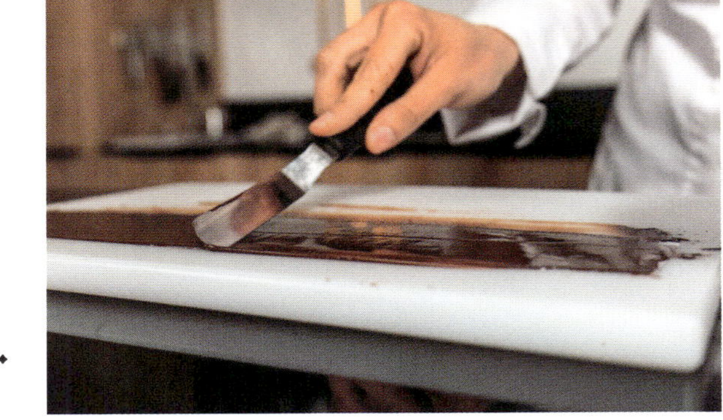

I.

For the chocolate decorations, temper the chocolate and spread thinly over an acetate sheet.

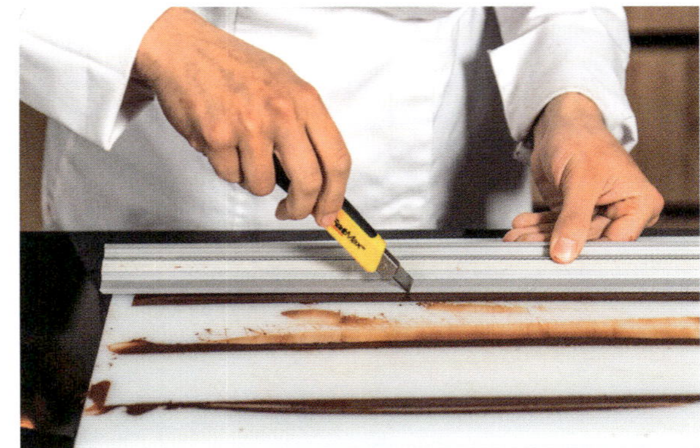

2.

Score the chocolate with rhomboid shapes.

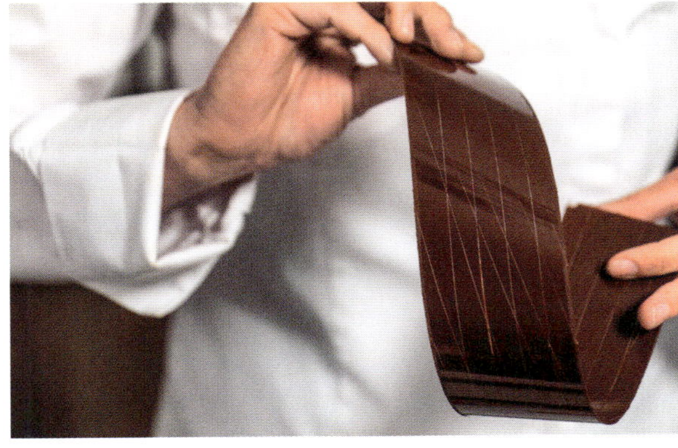

3.

Curve the chocolate using a yule log tin to give shape to the chocolate decorations.

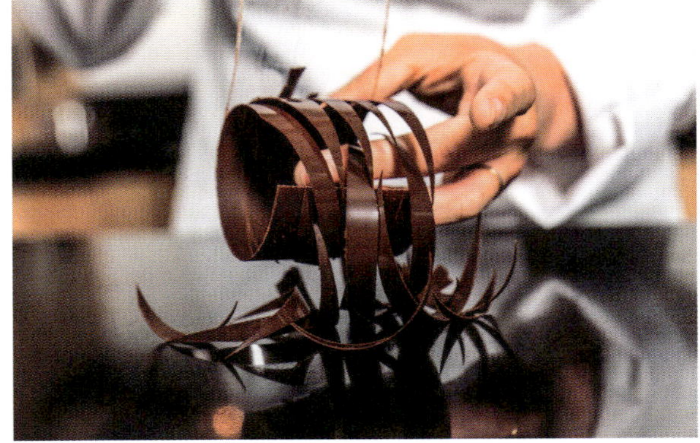

4.

Allow the chocolate to harden before peeling the chocolate off the acetate and separating the decorations.

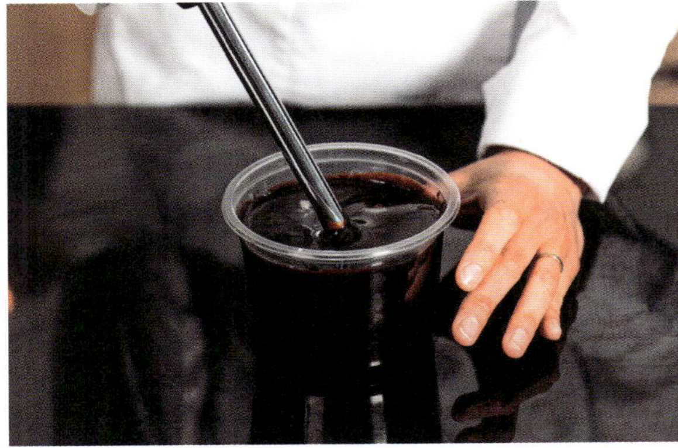

5.

Melt part of the glaze in a bain-marie, then blend the melted glaze with the cold glaze to a smooth and creamy consistency.

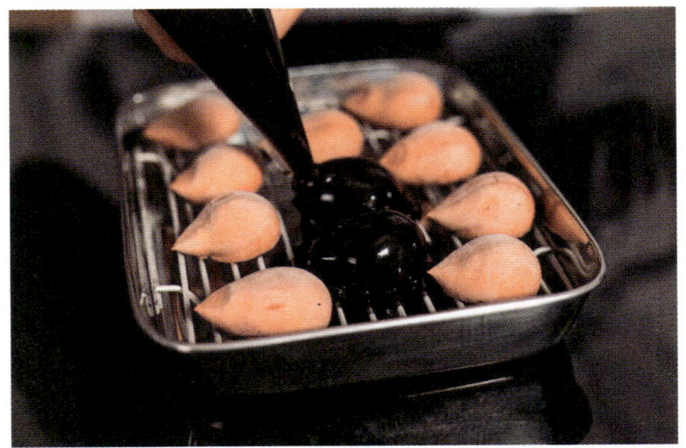

6.

Glaze the frozen ganache drops.

Serves 6

Preparation	Resting	Cooking
1 hour	2 hours 15 minutes	1 hour 15 minutes

Paris-Brest

Choux pastry

125 g milk

125 g water

112 g unsalted butter

2.5 g caster sugar

5 g salt

1 vanilla pod

137 g T55 (plain) flour

4½ eggs

Hazelnut and cocoa nib praline

125 g hazelnuts

62 g caster sugar

20 g water

35 g grape seed oil

2.5 g fleur de sel

50 g cocoa nibs

Pastry cream

390 g milk

52 g egg yolks

30 g light brown soft sugar

40 g custard powder

40 g unsalted butter

Praline cream

2½ gelatine leaves

200 g whipping cream

500 g pastry cream

80 g cocoa nib praline

Put the milk, water, butter, sugar and salt into a saucepan, add the scraped-out vanilla seeds and bring to the boil. Sift the flour and incorporate into the mixture. Allow the pastry to dry well for a few minutes. Transfer the pastry to a stand mixer fitted with a paddle attachment and beat on low speed for a few minutes to dry out before gradually adding the eggs. Check the consistency and add more egg if necessary.

Hazelnut and cocoa nib praline Roast the hazelnuts at 140 °C for 40 minutes. In a saucepan over a low heat, cook the sugar and water to a caramel and transfer to a baking sheet. Put the hazelnuts, cooled caramel and oil into a blender and blend to a smooth liquid, then add the fleur de sel and cocoa nibs, blend for further 30 seconds and transfer to a container.

Pastry cream Bring the milk to the boil in a saucepan. Whisk the egg yolks with the sugar and custard powder. Add a little boiling milk to the mixture, then add it to the remainder of the milk in the saucepan and stir briskly until the mixture comes to the boil. Allow the mixture to boil for 1 minute while stirring constantly. Whisk in the butter and quickly cool the pastry cream.

Praline cream Soak the gelatine in cold water for 15 minutes and squeeze to drain. Whip the cream and set aside in the refrigerator. Incorporate the praline into the pastry cream, then heat a little of the mixture over a low heat to dissolve the gelatine. Add the mixture to the remainder of the pastry cream and whisk to combine. When smooth, gently fold in the whipped cream (1). Refrigerate for 2 hours before use.

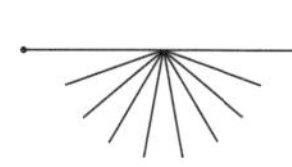

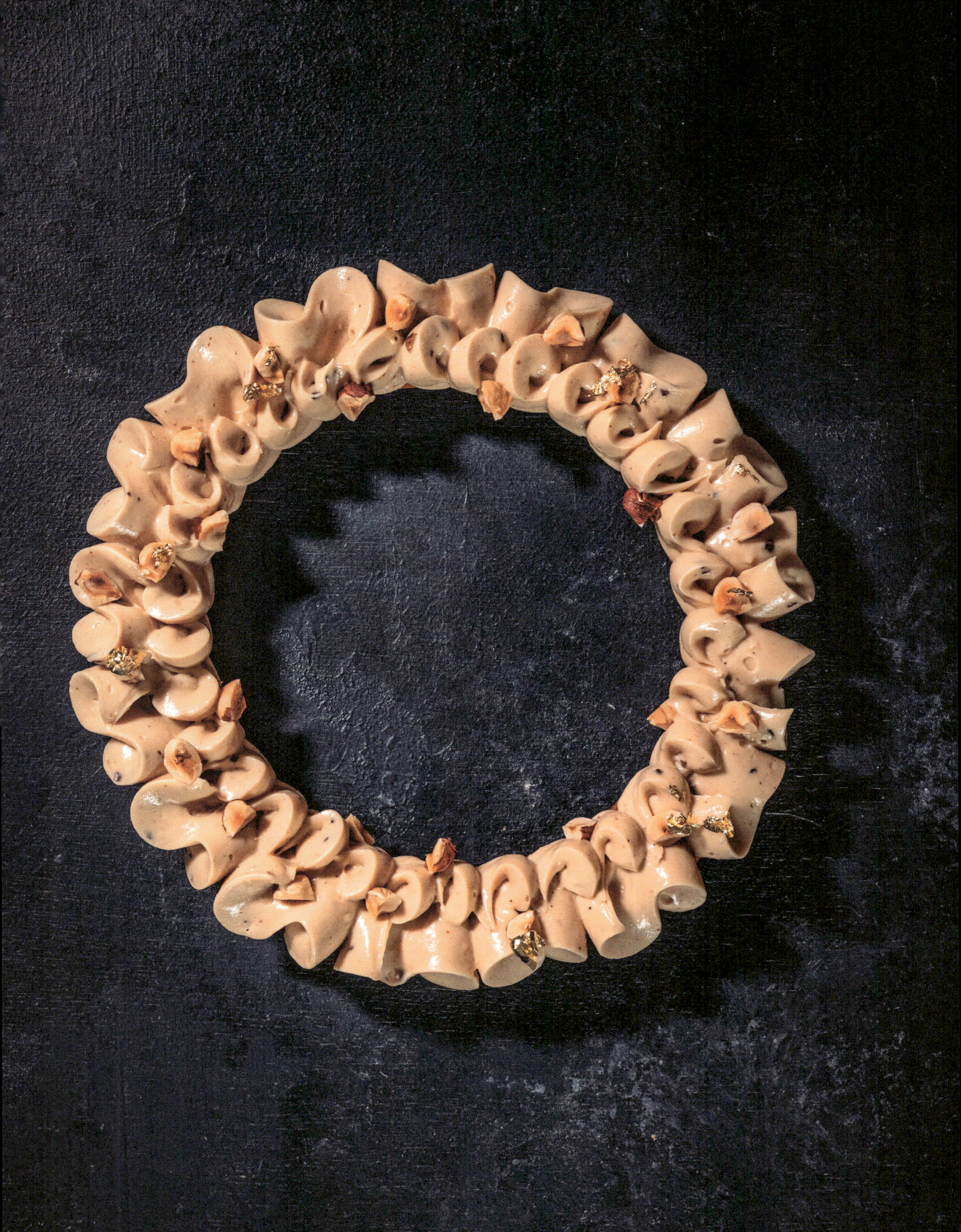

For decoration

100 g roasted hazelnuts
1 sheet edible gold leaf

Assembly

Make the choux pastry. Arrange 22-cm-diameter and a 16-cm-diameter greased pastry rings on a non-stick baking tray. Using a piping bag, pipe the choux pastry between the two rings (2). Bake at 170 °C for about 35 minutes (3). Adjust the cooking time if necessary. Remove the pastry rings while still hot (4). Make the praline. Make the praline cream.

Using a serrated knife, cut off the top of the choux pastry ring (5).

Pipe a little praline cream over the bottom part of the choux pastry and cover it with praline. Then using a Saint-Honoré nozzle, pipe a decorative layer of praline cream over the top (6).

Decorate with a few roasted hazelnuts and gold leaf.

Chill in the fridge.

'I love Paris-Brest! I love its melt-in-the-mouth choux pastry, crunchy, praline filling, and light and delicious cream with roasted hazelnut pieces. Because it's such a simple dessert, all the steps have to be performed carefully, right through to the presentation. Take your time when piping the cream and decorate it beautifully. This will show just how much effort you've put into making it.'

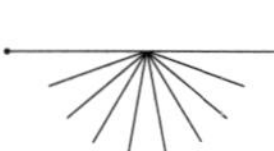

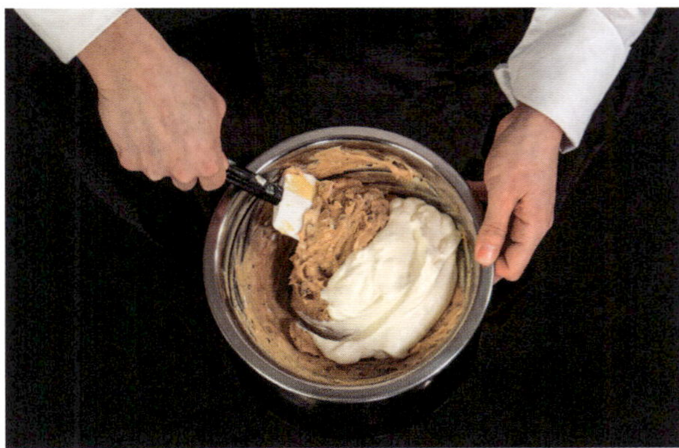

1. Make the praline cream.

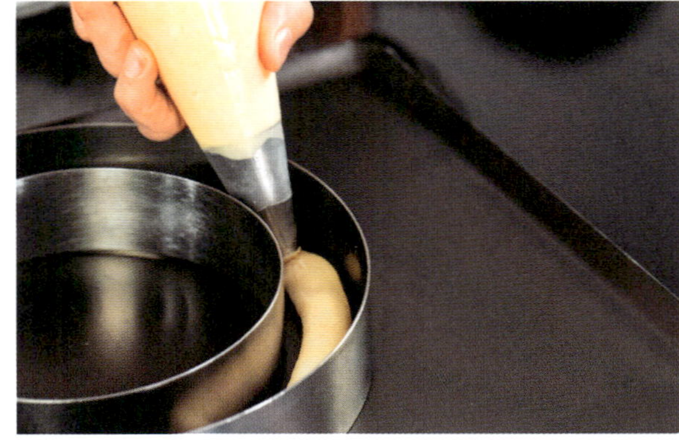

2. Make the choux pastry. Arrange 22-cm-diameter and 16-cm-diameter greased pastry rings on a non-stick baking tray. Pipe choux pastry between the two rings.

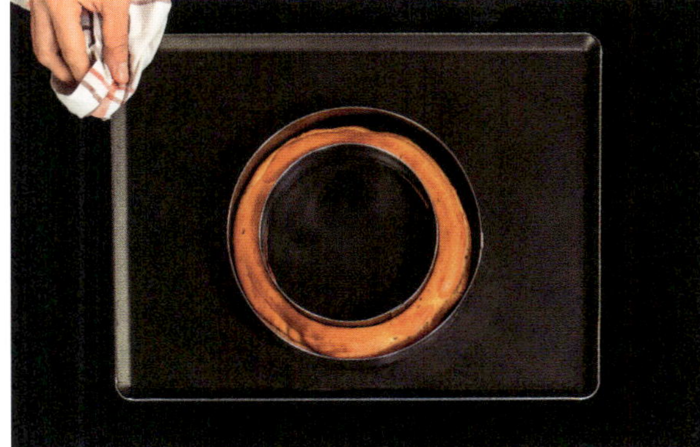

3. Bake at 170 °C for about 35 minutes.

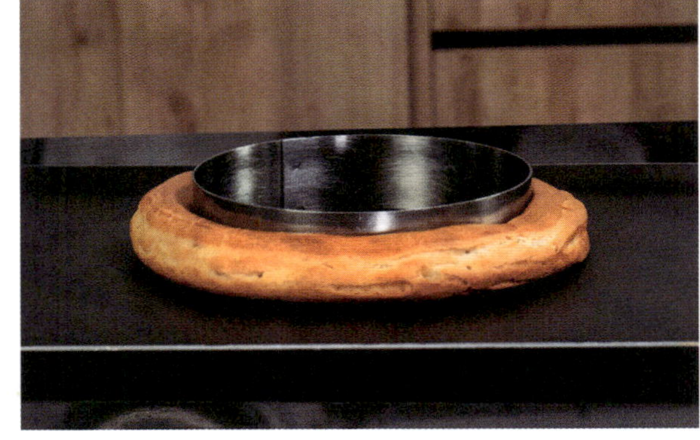

4. Remove the pastry rings while still hot.

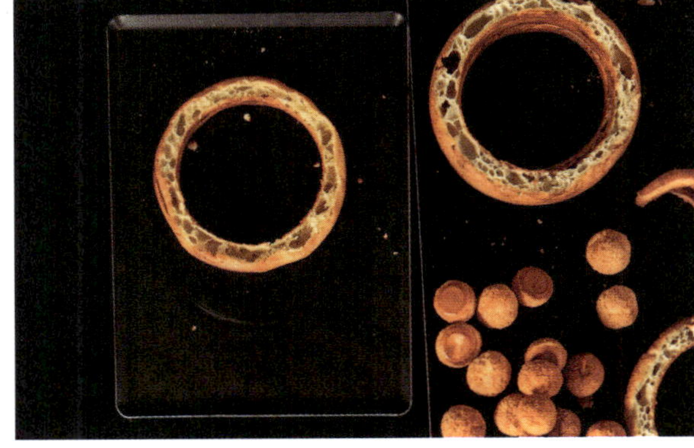

5. Using a serrated knife, cut off the top of the choux pastry ring.

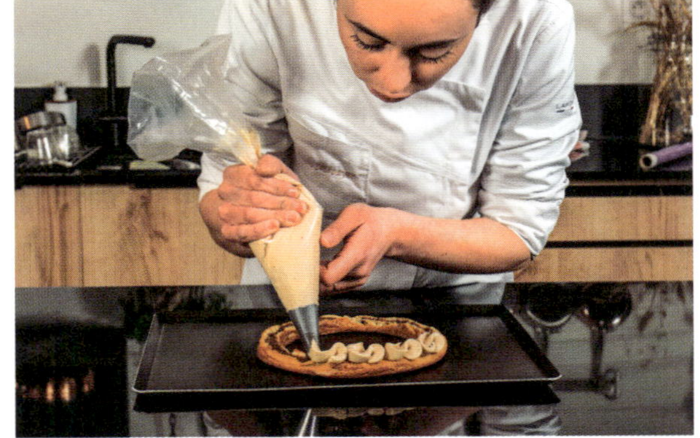

6. Pipe a little praline cream over the bottom part of the choux pastry and cover it with praline. Then using a Saint-Honoré nozzle, pipe a decorative layer of praline cream over the top.

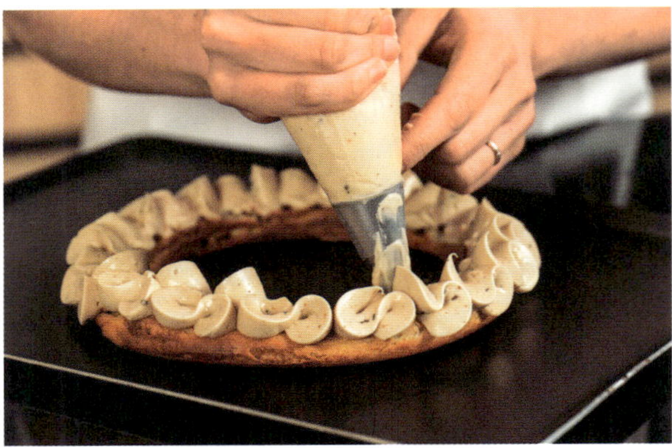

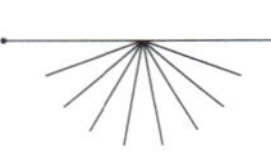

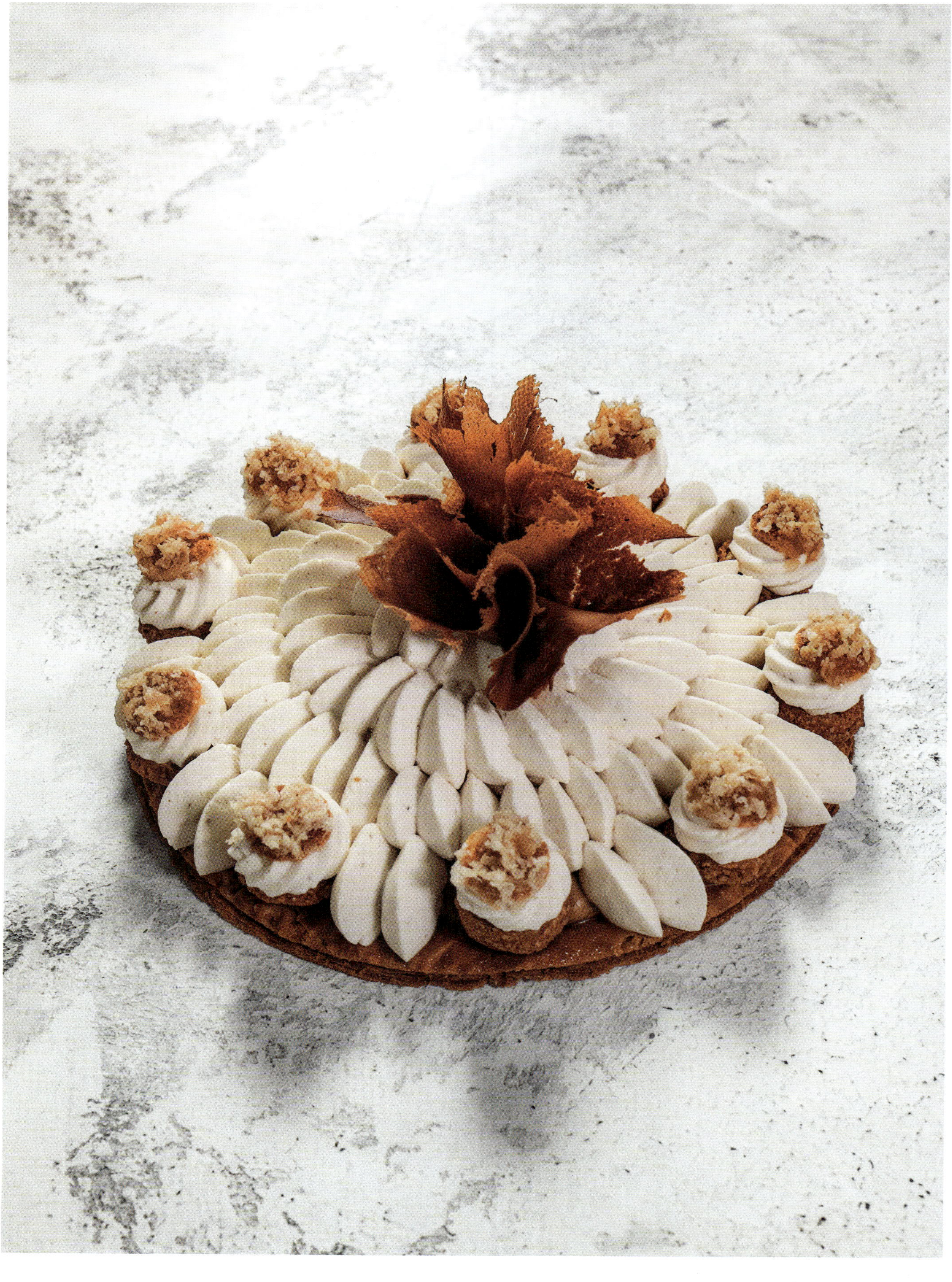

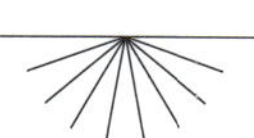

Makes 1 Saint-Honoré to serve 6

Preparation
3 hours

Resting
7 hours 10 minutes

Cooking
1 hour 20 minutes

Chestnut gâteau Saint-Honoré

Rough puff pastry

200 g T55 (plain) flour
240 g unsalted butter, cold
8 g caster sugar
3 g salt
90 g water
Icing sugar

Chestnut tuile

200 g crème de marrons
(chestnut cream)
200 g pâte de marrons (chestnut
paste)

Chestnut ganache

253 g whipping cream
47 g pâte de marrons
70 g chestnut tuile powder
35 g white chocolate

Rough puff pastry Mix the flour, butter cut into pieces, sugar and salt either by hand or in a stand mixer fitted with a paddle attachment. Add the water and work to a smooth dough but with small pieces of butter still visible. Wrap the pastry in cling film and rest it in the fridge for 1 hour, then perform 5 single turns. Rest the pastry in the fridge between turns if necessary. Roll out the pastry to a 3-5-mm thickness. Place the pastry sheet on a baking tray and prick it all over with a fork. Cover with another baking tray and bake at 160 °C. After 10 minutes, remove the trays from the oven and cut out an 18-cm-diameter disc. Return the disc to the oven between the two trays and bake for about 25 minutes, until evenly coloured. Dust the disc with icing sugar and bake for 8 minutes at 180 °C, then raise the oven temperature to 240 °C for a few seconds until the pastry turns glossy all over.

Chestnut tuile Preheat the oven to 180 °C. Using a spatula, mix the crème de marrons and pâte de marrons until smooth. Make each tuile by spreading 2 teaspoons of the chestnut mixture into the desired shape on a baking mat (1). Spread the rest of the mixture in a thin layer over another baking mat. Bake at 180 °C for about 15 minutes, until evenly coloured (2). As soon as they come out of the oven, peel the tuiles off the mat and crumple them up (3). Allow the tuile sheet to cool, then grind it to a fine powder in a blender to make the chestnut ganache.

Chestnut ganache In a saucepan, blend the cream with the pâte de marrons, then bring to the boil. Incorporate the tuile powder into part of the cream and pour the rest over the white chocolate (4). Then blend everything together. Refrigerate at 4°C for 6 hours. Then lightly whip the chilled ganache.

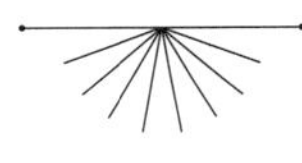

Plain craquelin

50 g unsalted butter, softened
65 g light brown soft sugar
50 g T55 flour

Choux buns

125 g milk
125 g water
5 g salt
2.5 g light brown soft sugar
110 g unsalted butter
140 g T55 flour
225 g eggs

Candied chestnuts

100 g candied chestnuts in syrup

Chestnut Chantilly cream

240 g whipping cream
60 g crème de marrons

Plain craquelin Mix all the ingredients with a spatula. Roll out the mixture thinly and evenly between two baking mats. Freeze the craquelin for 10 minutes, then cut out discs slightly larger than the diameter of the choux buns.

Choux buns Preheat the oven to 180 °C. Put the milk, water, salt, sugar and butter into a saucepan and bring to the boil. Then remove from the heat and add all the flour in one go. Stir briskly to incorporate, then dry the pastry for 2 minutes over a low heat. Gradually incorporate the eggs either in a stand mixer fitted with a paddle attachment or by hand with a spatula. Using a piping bag fitted with an 8-mm-diameter nozzle, pipe small choux buns onto a baking tray (5). Top each choux bun with a craquelin disc. Bake at 180 °C for about 20 minutes (6). Take care not to open the oven during this time as the choux buns could collapse and not rise again.

Drain the candied chestnuts.

Chestnut Chantilly cream Mix the cold ingredients, then blend with an immersion blender. Transfer the mixture to the well-chilled bowl of a stand mixer and whip the cream.

Assembly

Make the puff pastry, then roll out, bake, cut into discs, finish baking and glaze the tops. Make the whipped ganache and refrigerate at 4°C for 6 hours. Make the craquelin, then the choux pastry. Bake the craquelin-topped choux buns at 180 °C for about 20 minutes, adjusting the cooking time if necessary depending on your oven. Cut the choux buns in half.

Once the ganache has cooled, whisk it lightly. Transfer the ganache to a piping bag and fill the choux bun bases. Pipe a 1-cm-thick spiral of ganache over the pastry disc, starting at the centre and leaving 1.5 cm uncovered around the edge (7). Arrange the choux bun bases evenly along the edge of the pastry. Place a small piece of candied chestnut in the centre of each ganache-filled choux bun base. Arrange a few candied chestnut pieces over the chestnut ganache on the puff pastry, keeping a few pretty pieces for decoration. Use a whisk to whip the chestnut Chantilly cream and pipe a swirl on each filled choux bun base. Using a Saint-Honoré nozzle, pipe petals of Chantilly cream over the gâteau (8). Gently grate candied chestnuts over the Chantilly cream swirl on the choux bun bases before covering them with the top halves.

Decorate the centre of the gâteau with chestnut tuiles and pieces of candied chestnut.

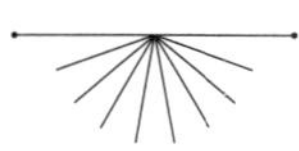

I.

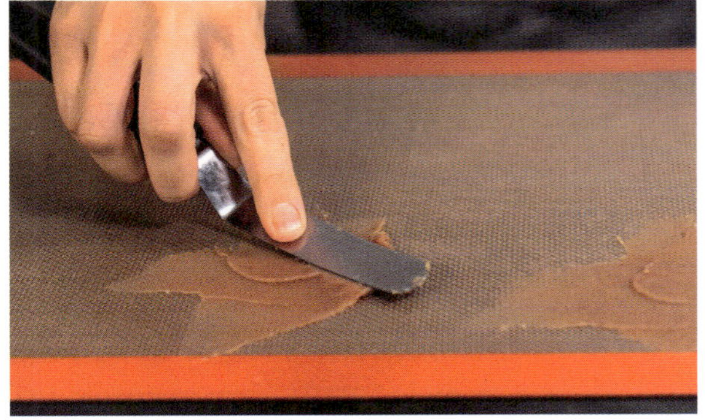

Make each chestnut tuile by spreading 2 teaspoons of the chestnut mixture into the desired shape on a baking mat

2.

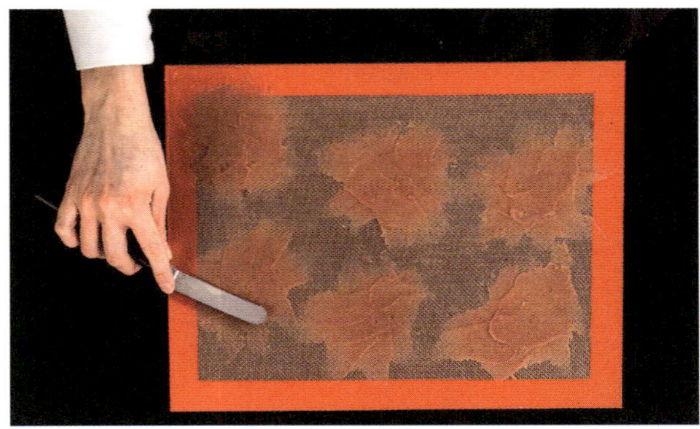

Bake at 180 °C for around 15 minutes, until evenly coloured.

3.

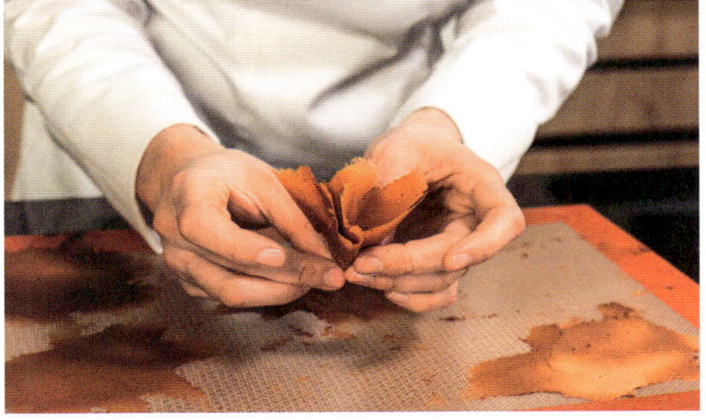

As soon as they come out of the oven, peel the tuiles off the mat and crumple them up.

4.

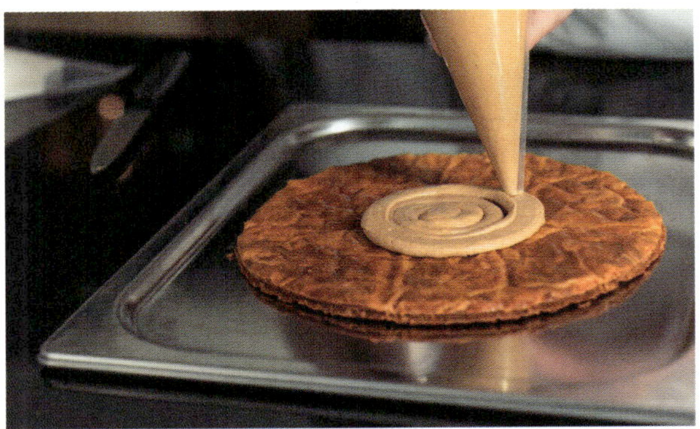

Make the chestnut ganache.

5.

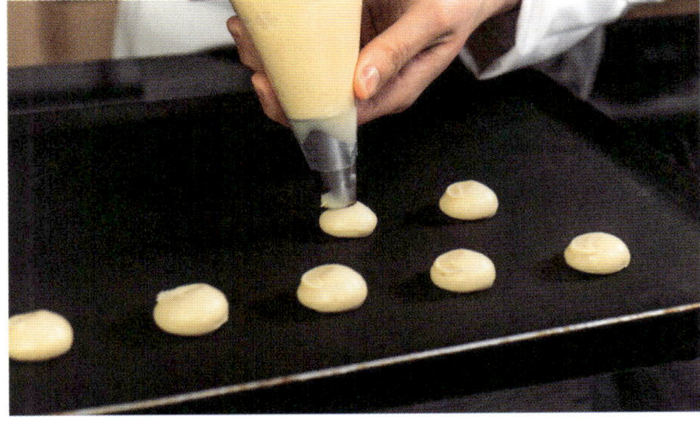

Make the choux pastry. Using a piping bag fitted with an 8-mm-diameter nozzle, pipe small choux buns onto a baking tray.

6.

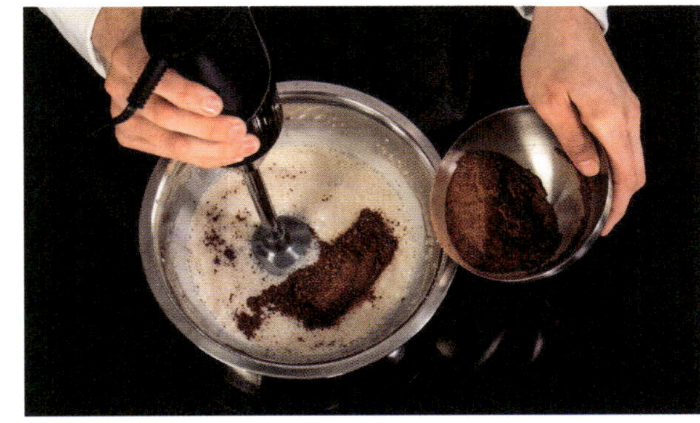

Top each choux bun with a craquelin disc. Bake at 180 °C for about 20 minutes.

7.

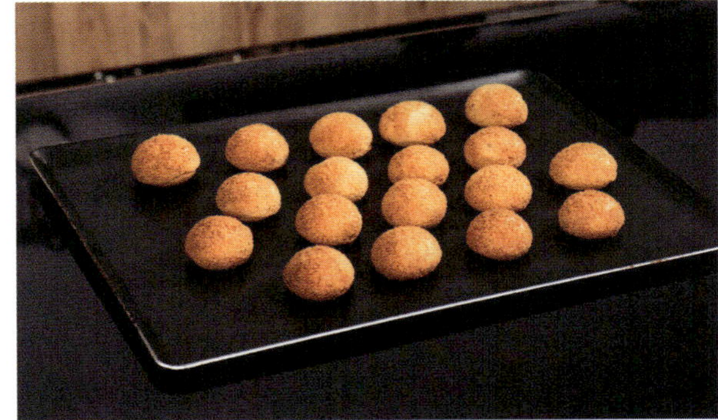

To assemble the gâteau, pipe a 1-cm-thick spiral of ganache over the pastry disc, starting at the centre and leaving 1.5 cm uncovered around the edge.

8.

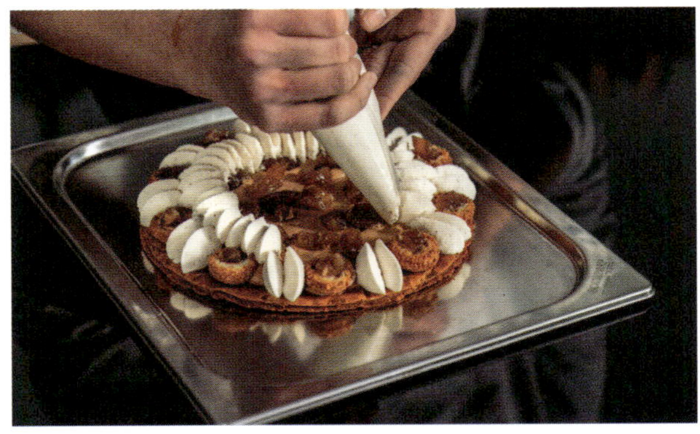

Arrange the ganache-filled choux bun bases evenly along the edge of the pastry and place chestnut pieces in the centre. Use a whisk to whip the chestnut Chantilly cream, then pipe petals of cream over the gâteau using a Saint-Honoré nozzle.

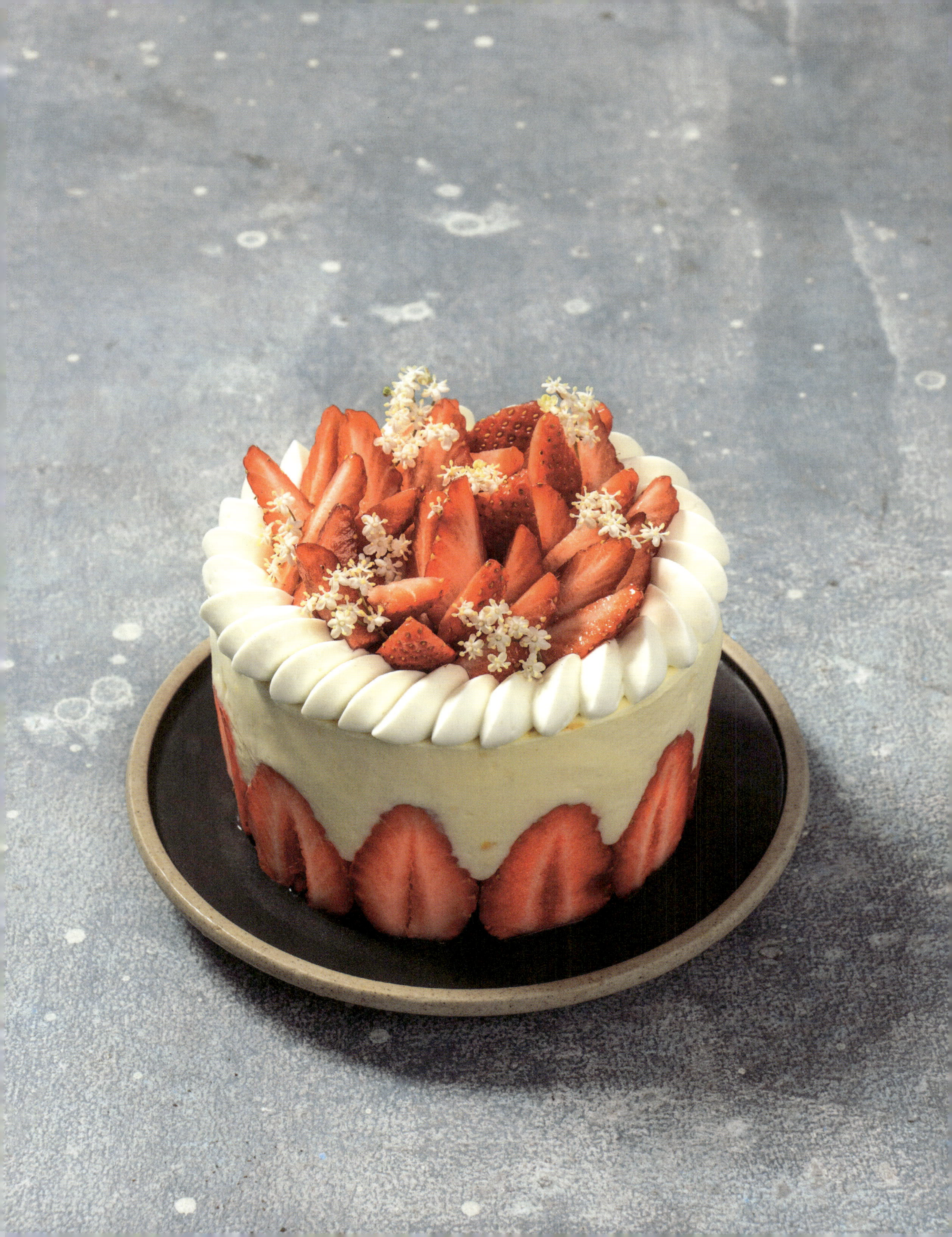

Makes 1 fraisier to serve 6

Preparation	Resting	Cooking
2 hours	3 hours	10 minutes + 4 hours

Fraisier

Pain de Gênes sponge

160 g almond paste

157 g eggs

30 g T55 (plain) flour

2 g baking powder

50 g unsalted butter, melted

7 g rum

Mixed berry syrup

60 g strawberries

60 g raspberries

60 g blueberries

60 g blackcurrants

24 g light brown soft sugar

Pastry cream

1 vanilla pod

300 g milk

54 g egg yolks

60 g light brown soft sugar

30 g custard powder

12 g unsalted butter

Lime diplomat cream

1½ gelatine leaves

150 g whipping cream

350 g pastry cream

Grated zest of 1 lime

Pain de Gênes sponge Blend the almond paste with the eggs. Add the sifted flour and baking powder to the mixture, followed by the melted butter and rum. Mix until smooth. Spread the batter in a baking tray lined with baking paper to a 1-cm thickness and bake for 8 minutes at 170°C.

Mixed berry syrup Put the berries in the freezer to break down their fibres, then mix them with the sugar. Put the berries and sugar into a large bowl and cover with cling film to create an airtight seal. Cook the berries in a bain-marie over a low heat for 4 hours, then filter the released juice through muslin without pressing.

Pastry cream Split the vanilla pod and scrape the seeds into the milk in a saucepan. Bring to the boil. Mix the egg yolks with the sugar and custard powder. Add a little boiling milk to the mixture, then add it to the remainder of the milk in the saucepan. Stir briskly until the mixture comes to the boil and allow to boil for 30 seconds. Incorporate the butter. Cool quickly.

Lime diplomat cream Soak the gelatine in iced water for at least 10 minutes, then squeeze to drain. Whip the cream. Loosen the pastry cream. In a saucepan, dissolve the gelatine in a little pastry cream over a low heat, then quickly incorporate the cold pastry cream a little at a time into the hot mixture, making sure not to allow the gelatine to set. Gently fold in the whipped cream and lime zest.

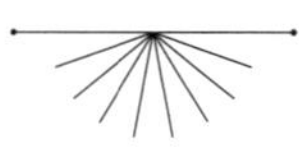

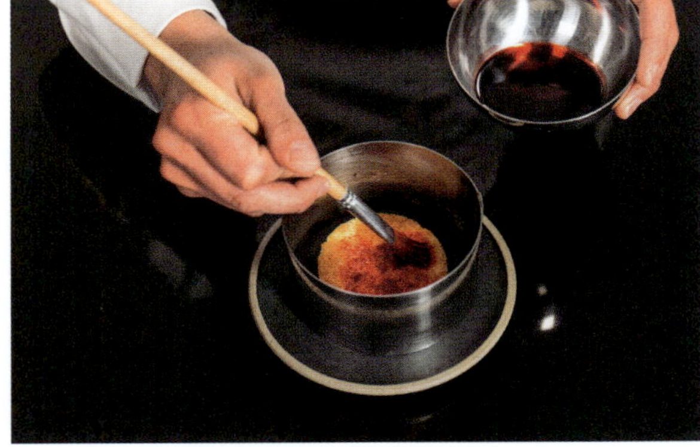

I.

To assemble the cake, place the sponge disc in the centre of a 16-cm-diameter pastry ring and brush it with the mixed berry syrup until soaked.

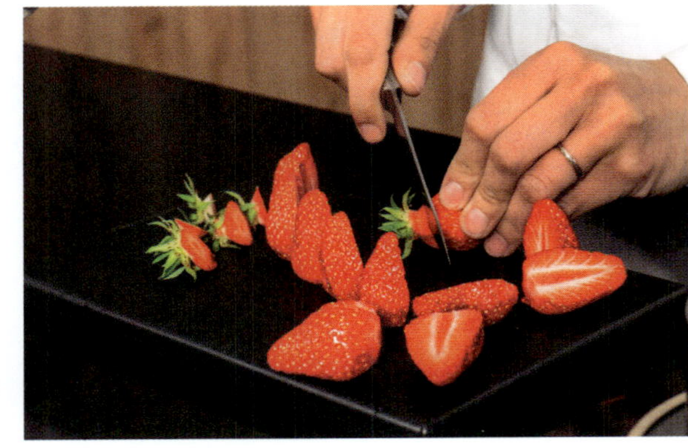

2.

Halve the strawberries.

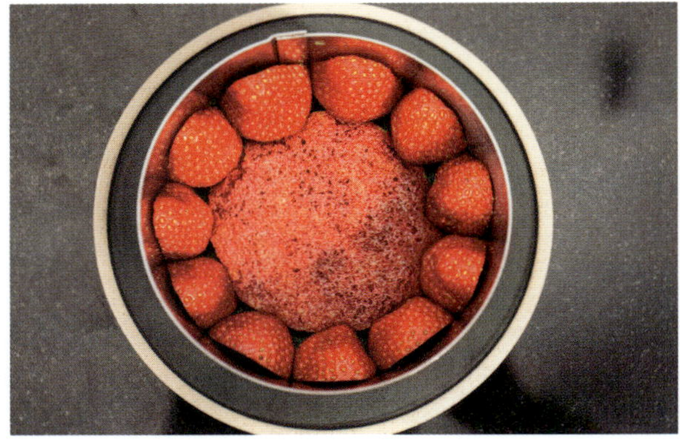

3.

Arrange the strawberries around the sides of the pastry ring.

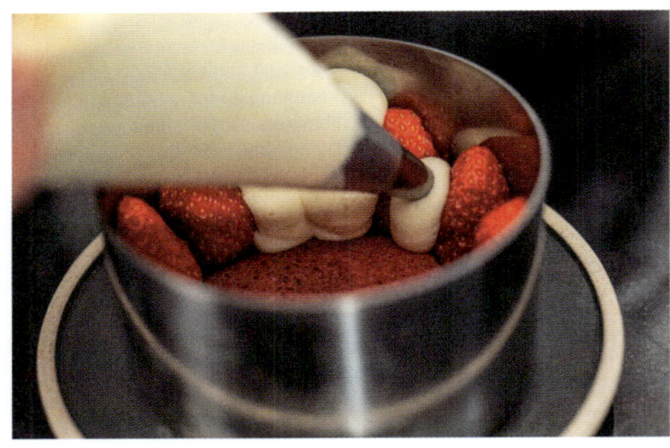

4.

Cover the strawberries with diplomat cream...

350 g fresh strawberries
3 elderflower heads
250 g whipping cream
10 g icing sugar

Assembly

Make the pain de Gênes sponge and mixed fruit syrup. Cut out a 14-cm-diameter sponge disc. Make the pastry cream and then the diplomat cream.

Place the sponge disc in the centre of a 16-cm-diameter pastry ring and brush it with the mixed berry syrup until soaked (1). Cut the strawberries (2) and arrange them around the sides of the pastry ring (3). Cover the strawberries with diplomat cream (4) and use a small palette knife to spread the cream to the rim of the ring (5). Fill the centre with strawberry halves. Cover the strawberries with diplomat cream, smooth the surface and refrigerate for 3 hours.

Lightly heat the pastry ring and carefully lift it off the cake (6). Whip the cream with the icing sugar and pipe pretty tongue shapes around the top of the cake (7). Quarter the strawberries lengthways and arrange them over the top of cake (8). Decorate with elderflowers (9) and refrigerate until ready to serve.

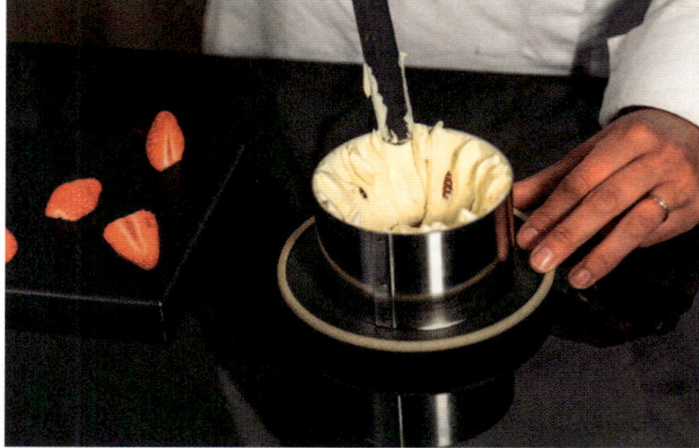

5. ...and use a small palette knife to spread the cream to the rim of the ring. Fill the centre with strawberry halves. Cover the strawberries with diplomat cream, smooth the surface and refrigerate for 3 hours.

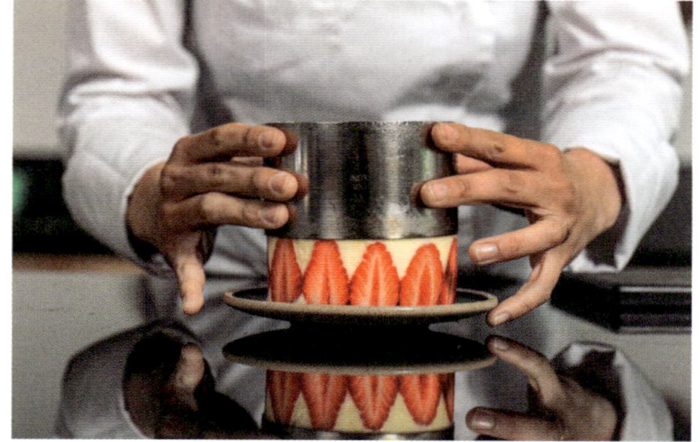

6. Lightly heat the pastry ring and carefully lift it off the cake.

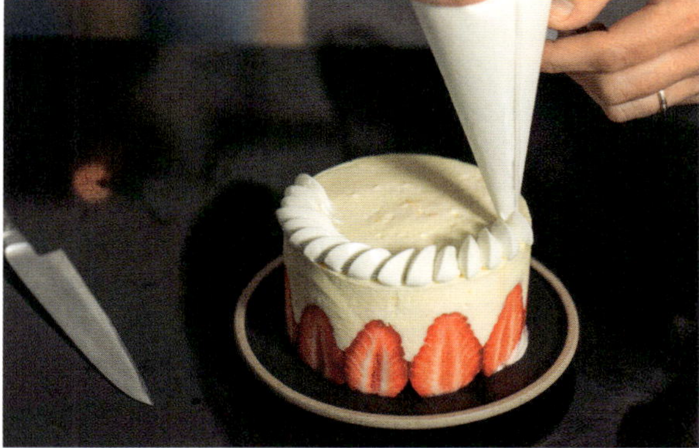

7. Whip the cream with the icing sugar and pipe pretty tongue shapes around the top of the cake.

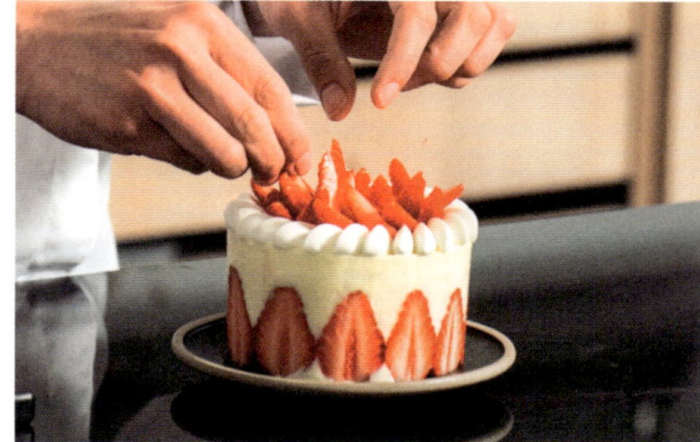

8. Quarter the strawberries lengthways and arrange them over the top of the cake.

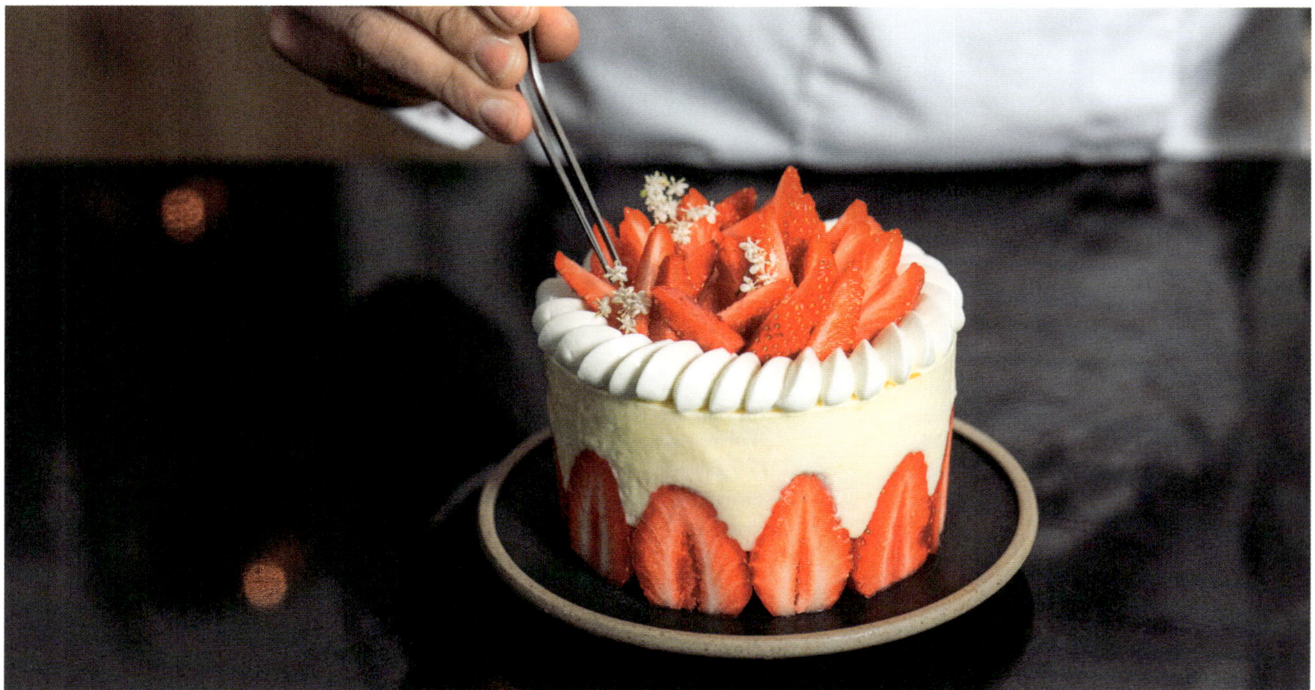

9. Decorate with elderflowers.

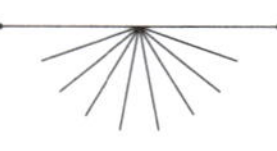

Serves 6

Preparation	Resting	Cooking
2 hours	3 hours	40 minutes

Lemon meringue tart

Sweet pastry

150 g unsalted butter, at room
  temperature
90 g icing sugar
30 g ground almonds
2.5 g salt
1 g vanilla powder
270 g T80 (stoneground white)
  flour
1 egg

Almond cream

30 g unsalted butter, at room
  temperature
30 g light brown soft sugar
30 g ground almonds
30 g egg
1 g salt

Lemon curd

½ gelatine leaf
Zest and (100 g) juice of 1 lemon
2 eggs
80 g light brown soft sugar
100 g unsalted butter

Lime meringue and decoration

150 g egg whites
150 g caster sugar
2 limes (grated zest and
  segments for decoration)
Icing sugar

Sweet pastry By hand or in a stand mixer fitted with a paddle attachment, rub the butter into the sugar, ground almonds, salt, vanilla powder and flour until the mixture resembles fine breadcrumbs. Incorporate the egg. When the pastry is smooth, refrigerate for 2 hours. Roll the pastry out to a 2.5-mm thickness and line a greased 20-cm-diameter tart ring. Bake at 160°C for about 25 minutes, until golden.

Almond cream Using a spatula, mix the butter with the sugar. Incorporate the ground almonds, egg and salt. Using a small angled palette knife, spread a thin layer of almond cream over the tart shell. Bake for 5 minutes at 170°C.

Lemon curd Soak the gelatine in very cold water and squeeze to drain. Zest the lemon with a vegetable peeler before squeezing. In a large saucepan over a low heat, bring the lemon zest and juice, eggs and sugar to a simmer. Pour the mixture through a conical sieve over the gelatine, then gradually blend in the butter using an immersion blender. Pour the mixture directly into the tart shell and allow to set in the fridge.

Lime meringue and decoration In a stand mixer, beat the egg whites to soft peaks, then gradually add the caster sugar while beating to stiff peaks. Gently fold in the lime zest. Transfer the meringue to a piping bag fitted with a Saint-Honoré nozzle and decorate the top of the tart. Dust the top with a little icing sugar and bake at 230°C for about 30 seconds, adjusting the cooking time if necessary, depending on your oven.

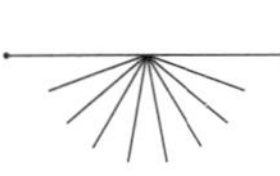

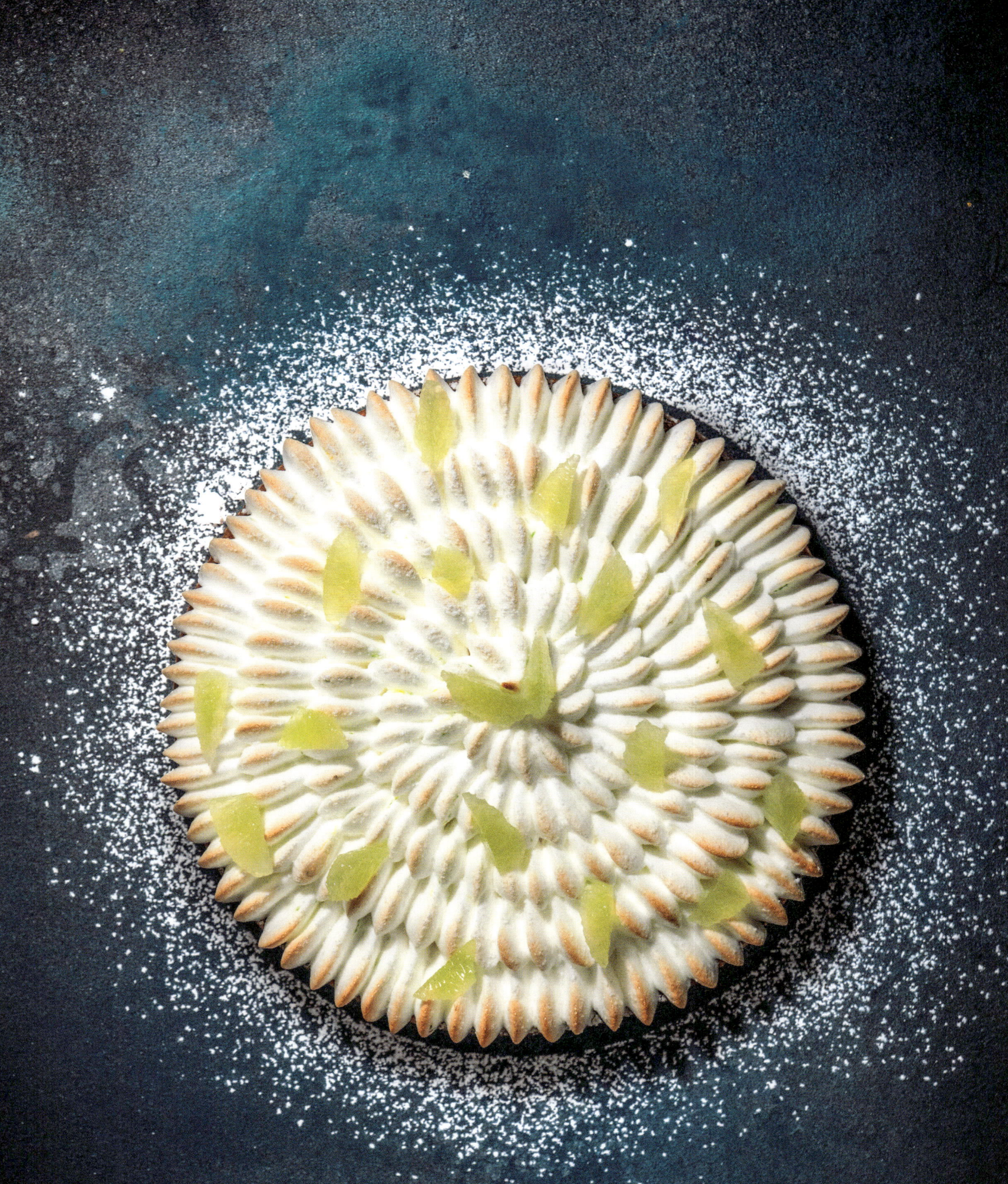

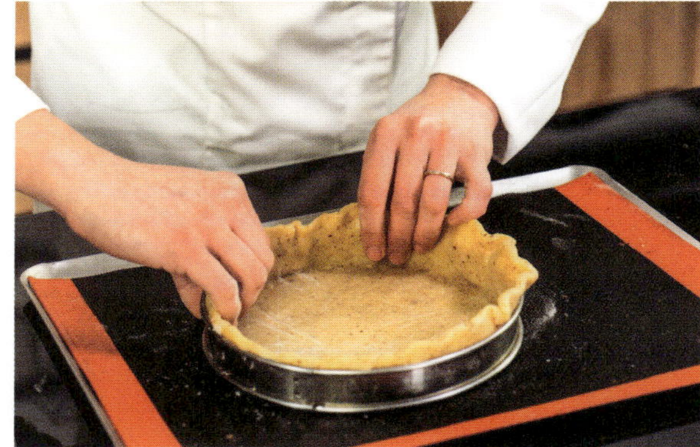

I.

Make the sweet pastry, roll out and line a tart ring.

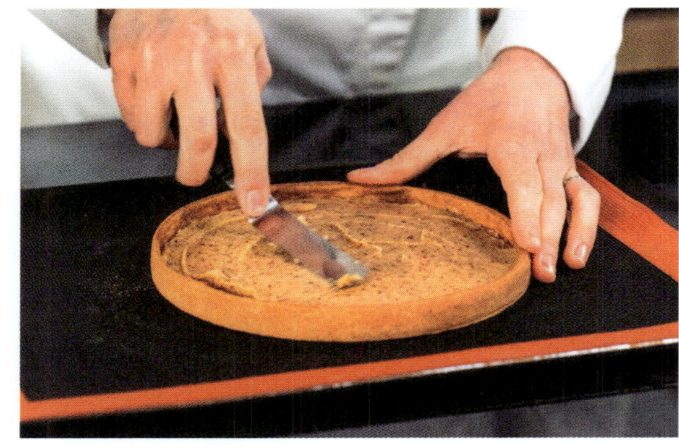

2.

Bake the tart shell. Spread almond cream inside and finish baking. Allow to cool.

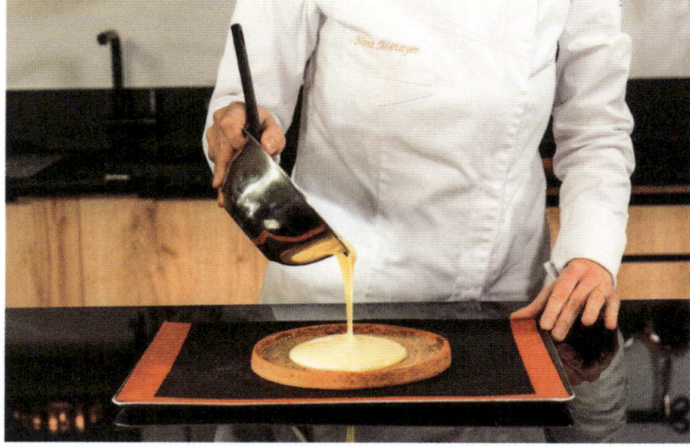

3.

Make the lemon curd and fill the tart shell. Allow it to set in the fridge for at least 1 hour.

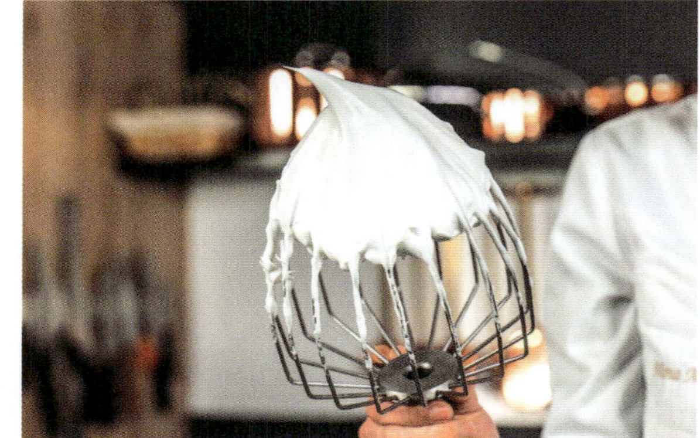

4.

Make the meringue in a stand mixer...

Assembly

Make the sweet pastry, roll out and line a tart ring (1). Bake the tart shell. Spread almond cream inside and finish baking (2). Allow the tart shell to cool.

Using a Microplane® grater, smooth the edges of the tart.

Make the lemon curd and fill the tart shell (3). Allow it to set in the fridge for at least 1 hour.

Make the meringue in a stand mixer (4) and gently fold in the lime zest (5).

Segment the limes (6).

Pipe the meringue over the tart using a Saint-Honoré nozzle (7).

Dust with icing sugar through a sieve. Bake at 230°C for a few seconds. Arrange lime segments over the tart to decorate (8).

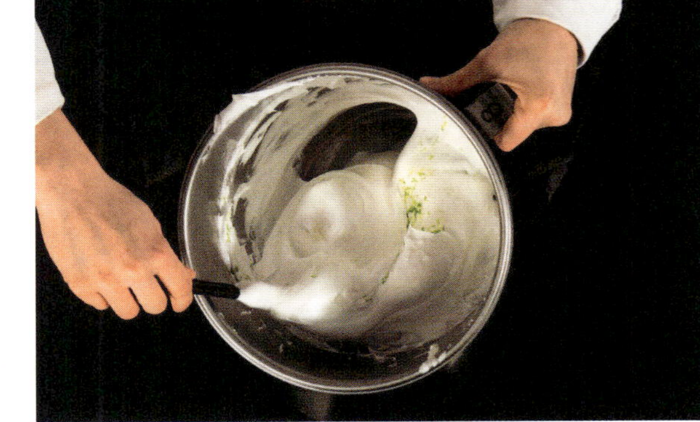

5.

...and gently fold in the lime zest.

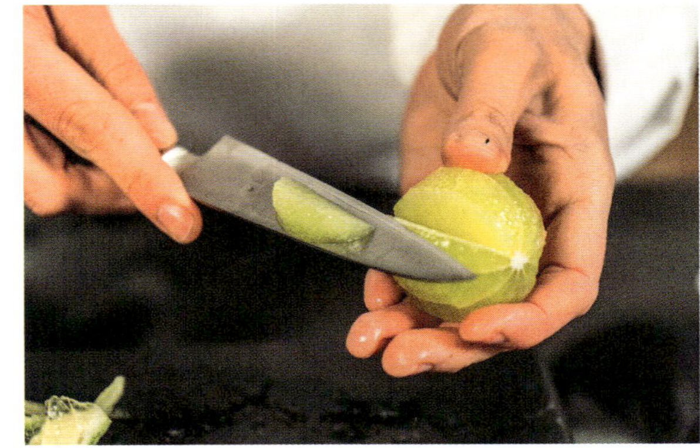

6.

Segment the limes.

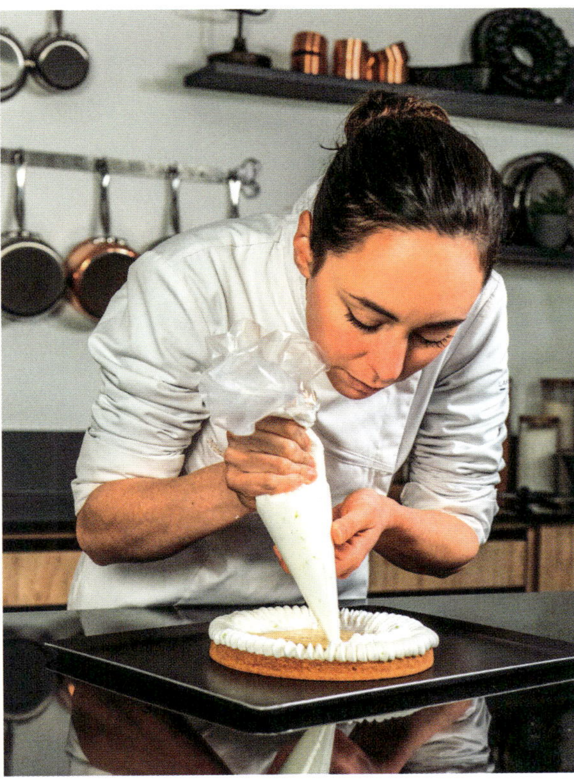

7.

Pipe the meringue over the tart using a Saint-Honoré nozzle.

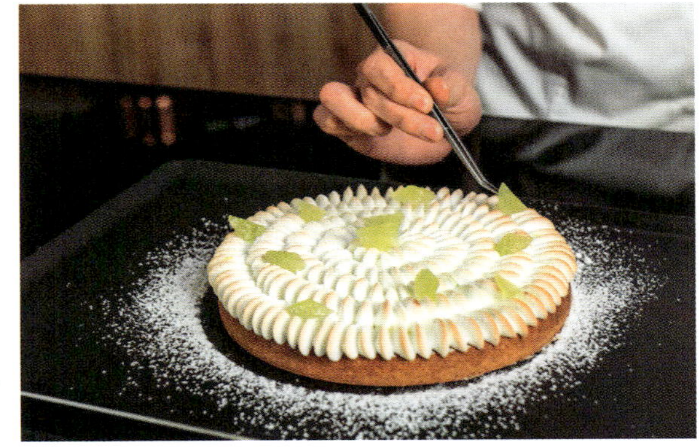

8.

Dust with icing sugar through a sieve. Bake at 230°C for a few seconds. Arrange lime segments over the tart to decorate.

'I love a lemon tart with a crisp and well-baked sweet pastry shell, a tangy lemon curd that melts in your mouth and a light meringue that isn't too sweet. A tart that is neither too sweet nor too sour, and especially one with a lovely buttery flavour!'

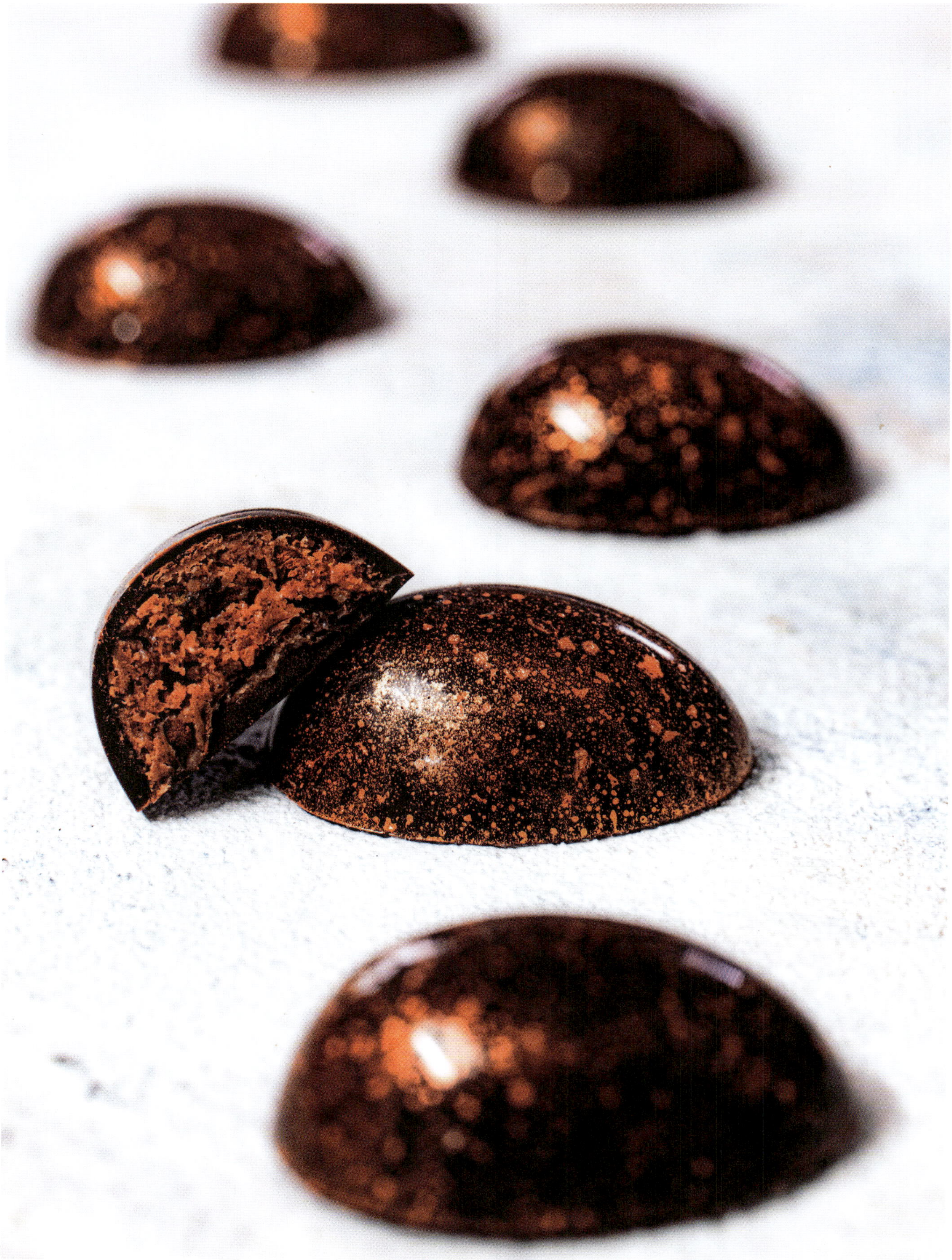

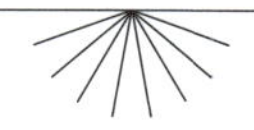

Makes 30 chocolates

Preparation
1 hour

Hardening
1 hour + overnight

Praline ganache-filled chocolates

Tempered chocolate

300 g dark chocolate
    couverture (72% cocoa)

Praline ganache

100 g milk chocolate
    couverture (39% cocoa)
200 g home-made praline
37 g feuillantine

Decoration

50 g kirsch
5 g edible bronze powder

Tempered chocolate Melt the chocolate in a bain-marie, making sure that the temperature is no higher than 55°C. Transfer it to a marble work surface until it cools to 28°C. Then lightly reheat the chocolate to 31°C in a bain-marie.

Praline ganache Melt the chocolate in a bain-marie and add the praline and feuillantine. Mix until combined. Transfer to a piping bag and set aside at room temperature.

Decoration Mix the two ingredients well.

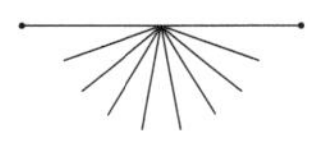

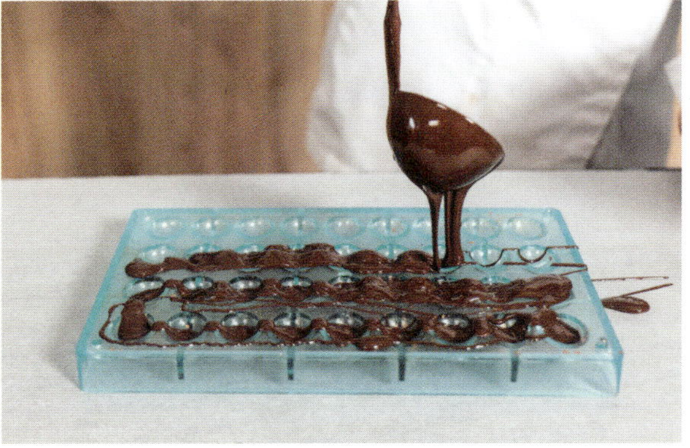

1.

Using a toothbrush, splash the chocolate mould cavities with the bronze mixture. Pour tempered chocolate into the cavities.

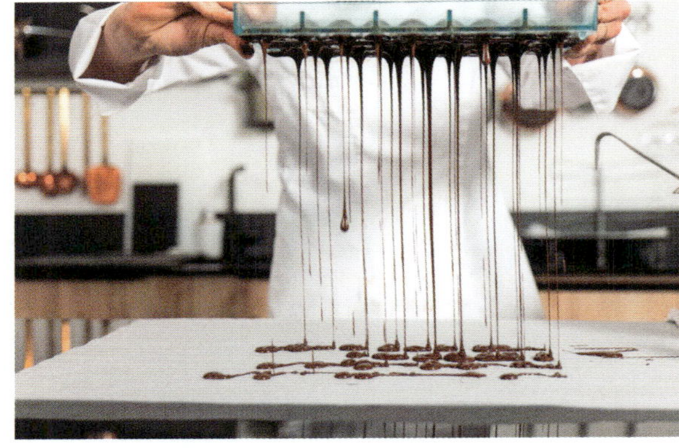

2.

Turn the mould upside down and tap lightly to remove the excess chocolate.

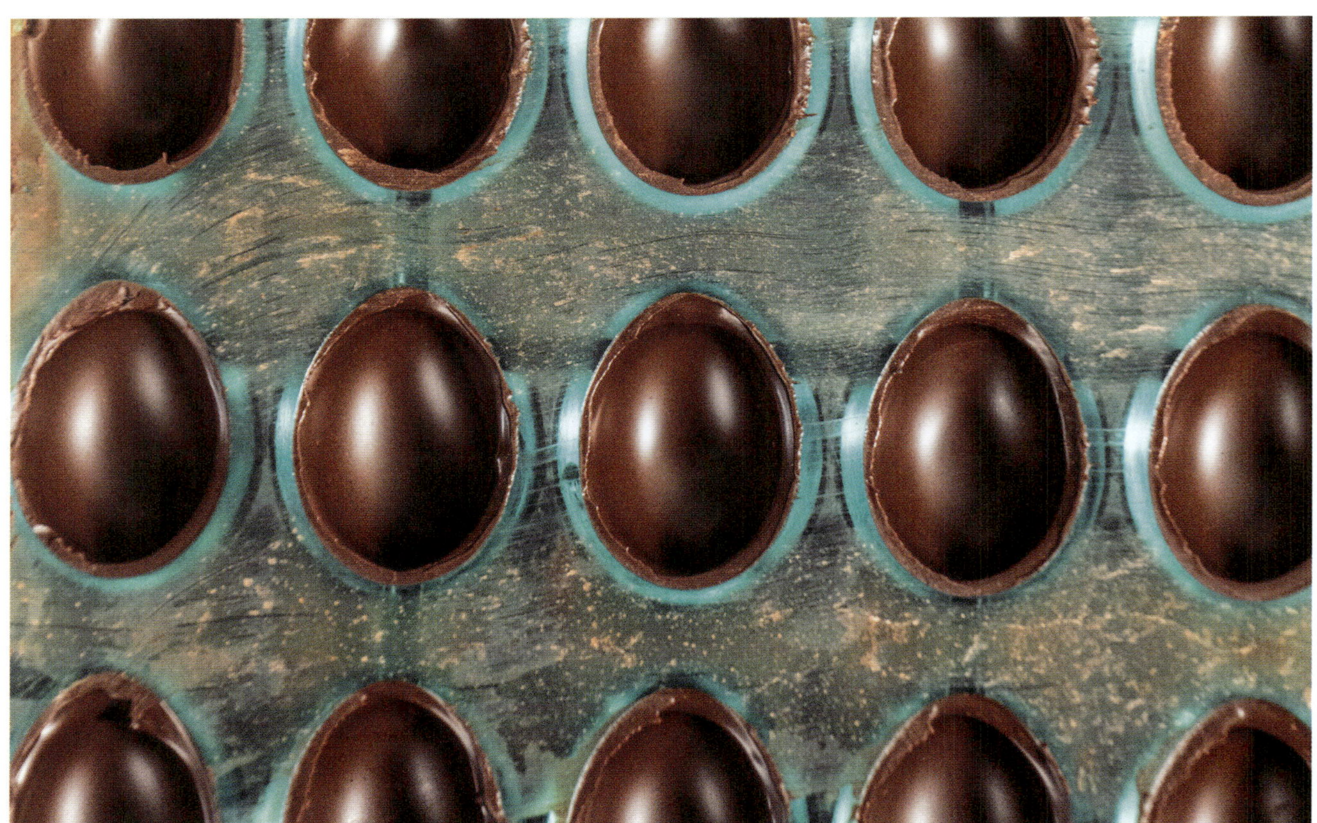

3.

Scrape off any chocolate from between the cavities. Allow the shells to harden

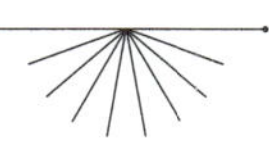

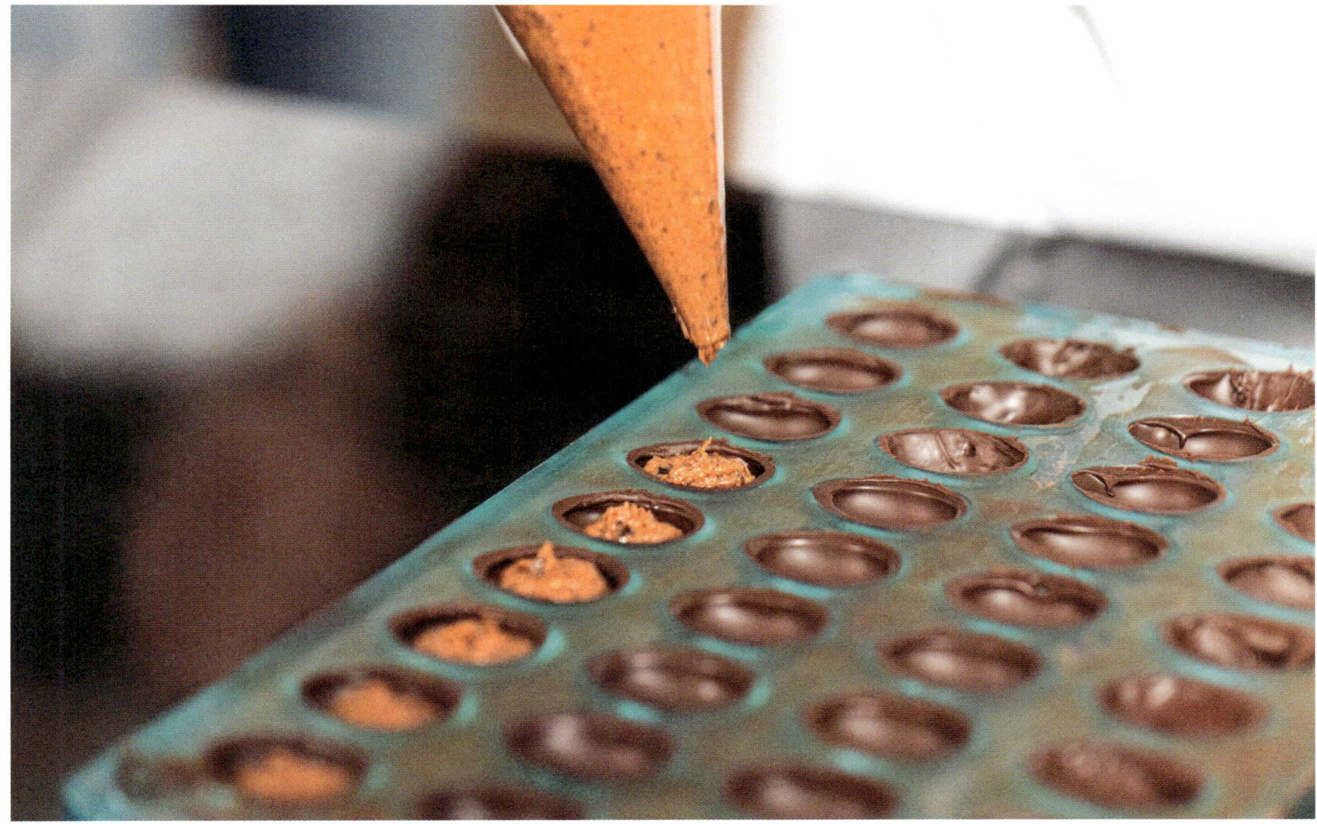

4.

Fill the shells with praline ganache.

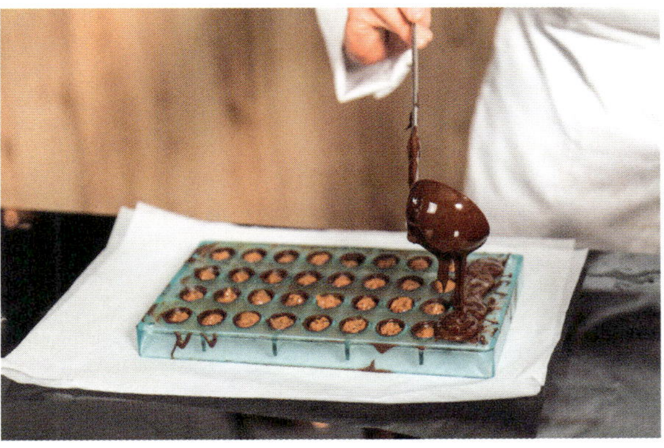

5.

Allow the filling to harden for 1 hour in the fridge, then cap the shells with tempered chocolate.

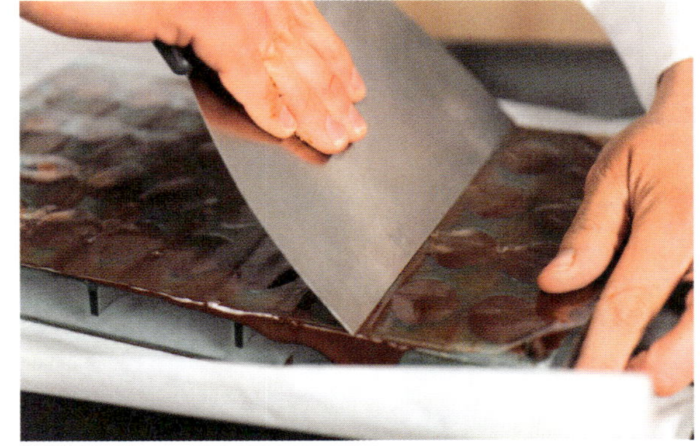

6.

Cover the mould with cling film and scrape off the excess chocolate. Allow the chocolate to harden overnight at room temperature, then turn them out of the mould.

Serves 6	Preparation	Cooking
	3 hours	10 minutes

Solitaire

Caramel sauce

50 g whipping cream
2 g loose-leaf Earl Grey tea
120 g caster sugar
1 vanilla pod
80 g unsalted butter, cold
2 g fleur de sel

Hazelnut sponge

62 g icing sugar
62 g ground almonds
62 g ground hazelnuts
5 egg whites
62 g caster sugar
25 g unsalted butter, melted
Grated zest of 1 lime

Feuillantine

100 g hazelnut praline
25 g dark chocolate
50 g feuillantine
2 g fleur de sel

Chocolate mousse

67 g milk
67 g whipping cream
2 g loose-leaf Earl Grey tea
2 egg yolks
42 g caster sugar
165 g dark chocolate
337 g whipped cream

Caramel sauce In a saucepan, bring the cream to the boil, add the tea and allow to steep for 3 minutes. Strain the cream through a conical sieve, then weigh and top up if needed to make up its original weight. Make a dry caramel with the sugar and add the cream reheated with the vanilla to stop the cooking process. Cook until the temperature reaches 106°C, then stop the cooking process by adding the cold butter and salt. Mix until smooth. Allow to thicken in the fridge.

Hazelnut sponge Sift the icing sugar and the ground nuts. In a stand mixer, beat the egg whites to soft peaks, then gradually add the caster sugar while beating to stiff peaks. Gently fold in the ground nuts and icing sugar mixture and then incorporate the melted butter and lime zest. Spread the batter in a baking tray lined with baking paper to a 5-mm depth and bake for 8 minutes at 180°C.

Feuillantine Heat the hazelnut praline and chocolate in a bain-marie and gently fold in the feuillantine and fleur de sel.

Chocolate mousse In a saucepan, bring the cream to the boil, add the tea and allow to steep for 3 minutes. Strain the cream through a conical sieve, weigh it and top up if necessary. Mix the egg yolks with the sugar. Add the hot tea-infused milk and cream mixture to the egg yolk and sugar mixture. Whisk to combine, then return the mixture to the saucepan. Cook until the temperature reaches 82°C and the crème anglaise is thick enough to coat a spoon. Then add it to the dark chocolate, previously melted in a bain-marie. Mix with a silicone spatula to combine, then blend until smooth.

Gently fold in the whipped cream.

Use the mousse immediately.

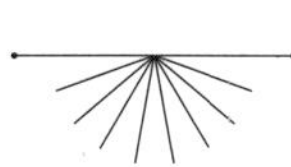

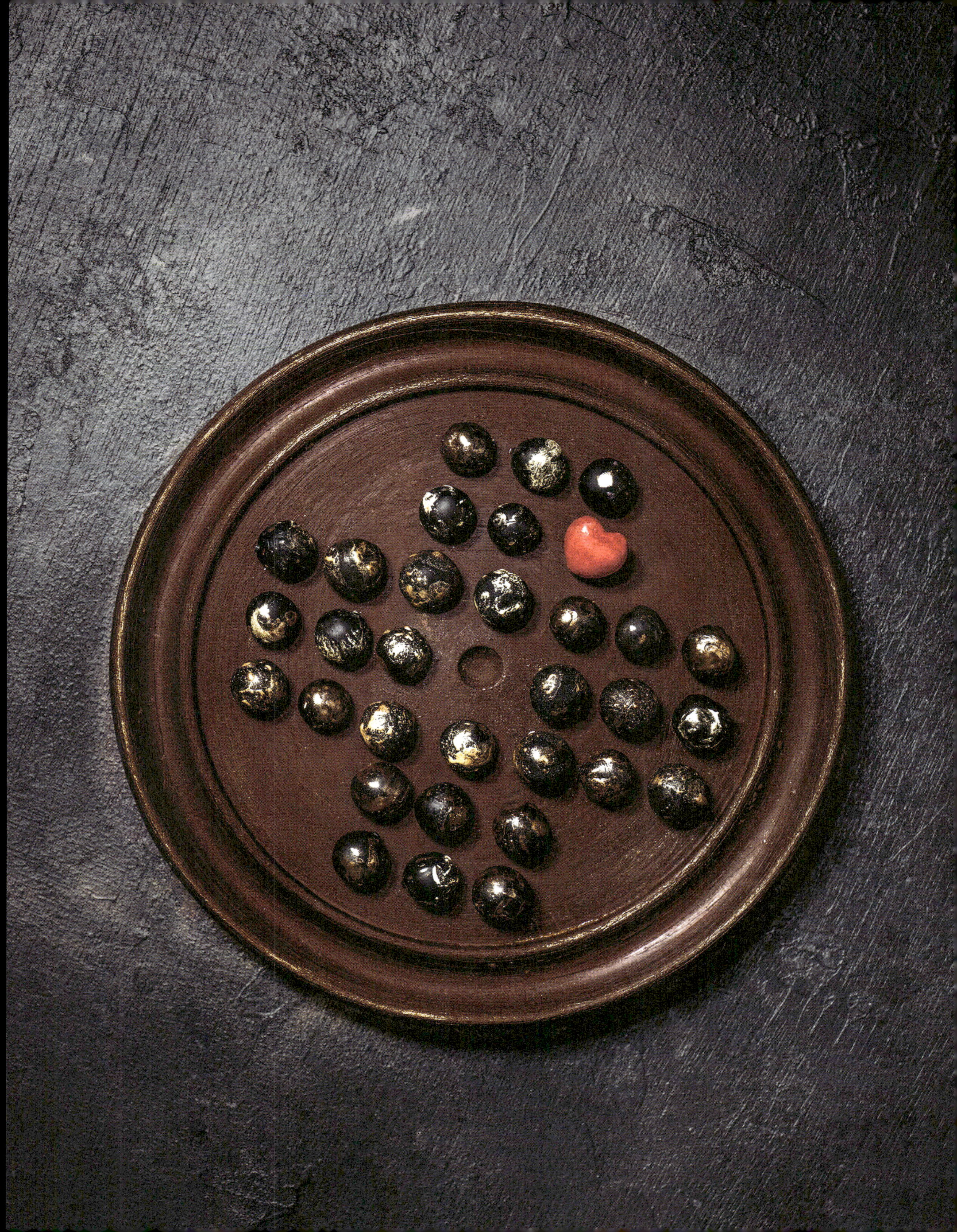

Chocolate crémeux

125 g milk

125 g whipping cream

2 egg yolks

12 g light brown soft sugar

117 g dark chocolate couverture

0.5 g salt

Dark chocolate coating

140 g dark chocolate

85 g cocoa butter

2.5 g grape seed oil

Red coating

35 g white chocolate couverture

25 g cocoa butter

1 g red fat-soluble food colouring

Assembly

100 g dark chocolate

Edible gold glitter

Chocolate crémeux In a saucepan, bring the milk and cream to the boil. Whisk the egg yolks with the sugar until thick and pale. Carefully add part of the cream and milk mixture to the blanched egg yolks. Mix until smooth. Return the mixture to the saucepan and cook until the temperature reaches 85°C. Add the custard to the dark chocolate a third or quarter at a time, add the salt and mix with a silicone spatula until combined. Then blend with an immersion blender until very thick and smooth.

Dark chocolate coating Melt all the ingredients together in a bain-marie and blend until smooth.

Red coating Melt the cocoa butter and chocolate in a bain-marie, add the colouring and blend until smooth.

Assembly Make the caramel and allow it to thicken in the fridge. For the insert, make the hazelnut sponge and cut out an 18-cm-diameter disc.

Make the feuillantine and spread it over the hazelnut sponge (1). Allow it to harden in the fridge. Transfer the caramel to a piping bag.

Once the feuillantine has hardened, turn the sponge disc over and pipe the caramel in a spiral to cover (2). Freeze the insert.

Using a brush, coat the mould with dark chocolate (3). Make the mousse (4), then pipe it into the mould, making sure to fill every nook and cranny (5). Position the feuillantine, sponge and caramel insert inside the mould (6). Cover it with mousse. Smooth the surface. Allow the board to harden in the freezer. Make the chocolate crémeux and fill silicone marble moulds. Freeze. Make the dark chocolate coating. Remove the crémeux marbles from the moulds and dip them into the dark chocolate coating. Dip the heart in the red coating. Decorate the balls with gold glitter (7).

'To make the solitaire mould, I simply used a real solitaire game board and made a mould from it using food-safe silicone. I also moulded the game marbles to obtain marbles of the correct size.'

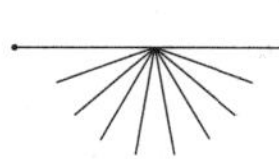

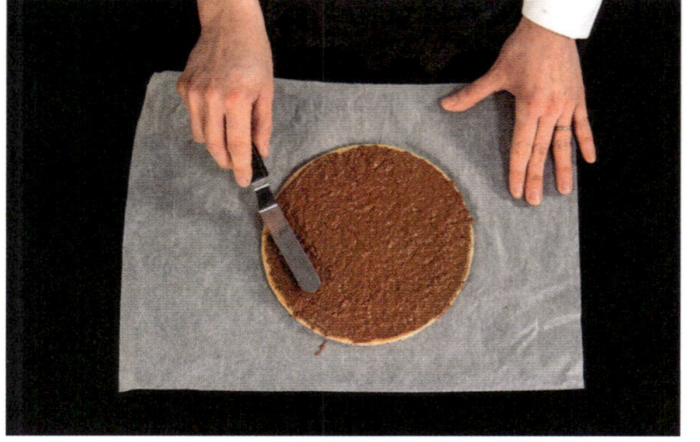

1.

To make the insert, spread the feuillantine over the hazelnut sponge cut into an 18-cm diameter disc, then allow it to harden in the fridge.

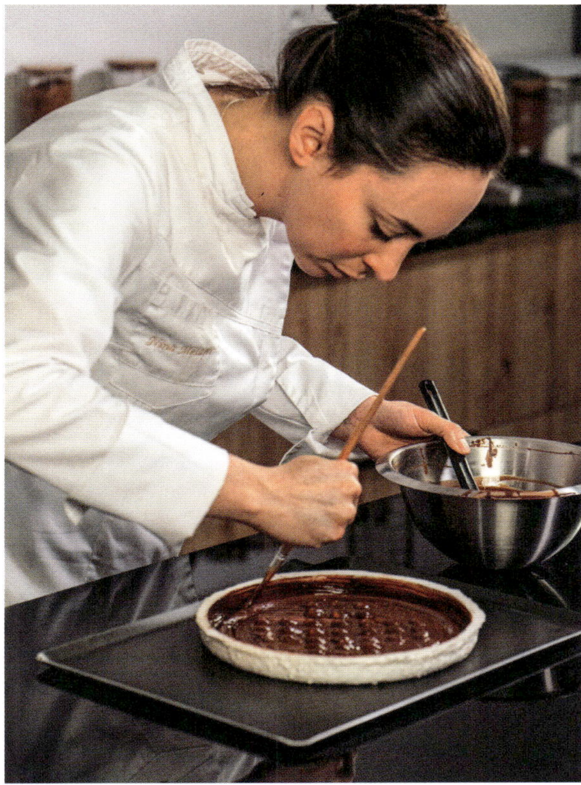

2.

Once the feuillantine has hardened, turn the sponge over, pipe the caramel in a spiral to cover and freeze the insert.

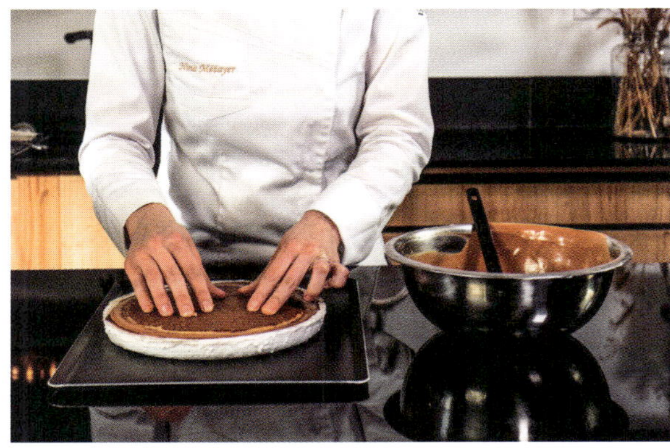

3.

For the board, brush the mould with tempered chocolate to coat.

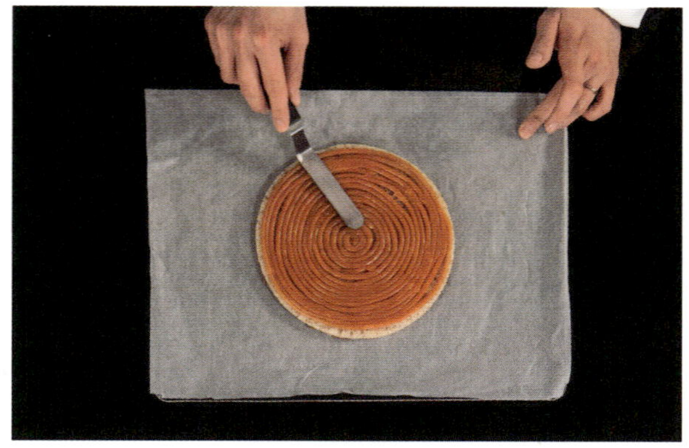

4.

Make the mousse.

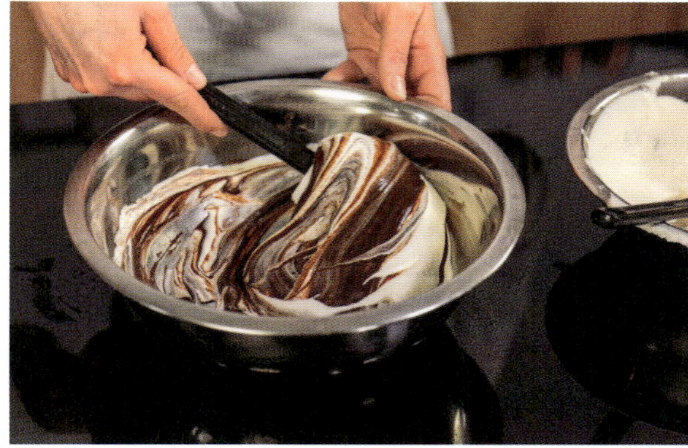

5.

Carefully pipe the mousse in the mould.

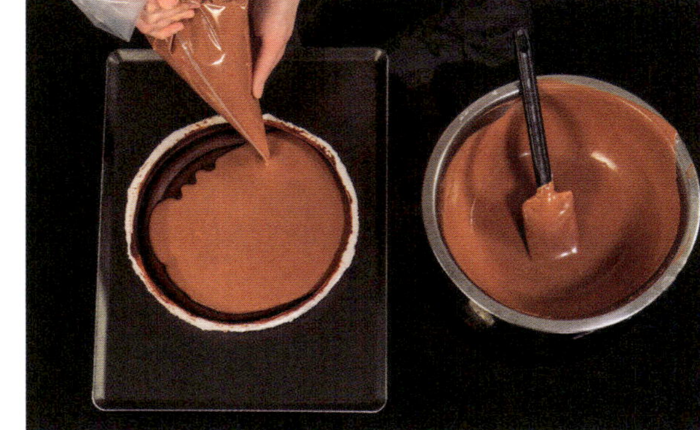

6.

Position the feuillantine, biscuit and caramel insert inside the mould and cover with mousse. Smooth and allow the board to harden in the freezer.

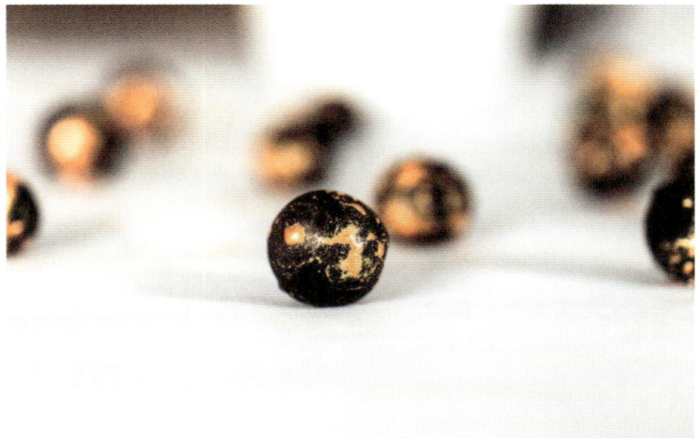

7.

To make the marbles fill the moulds with chocolate crémeux and freeze. Remove the marbles from the moulds and dip them in the dark chocolate coating. Decorate with gold glitter.

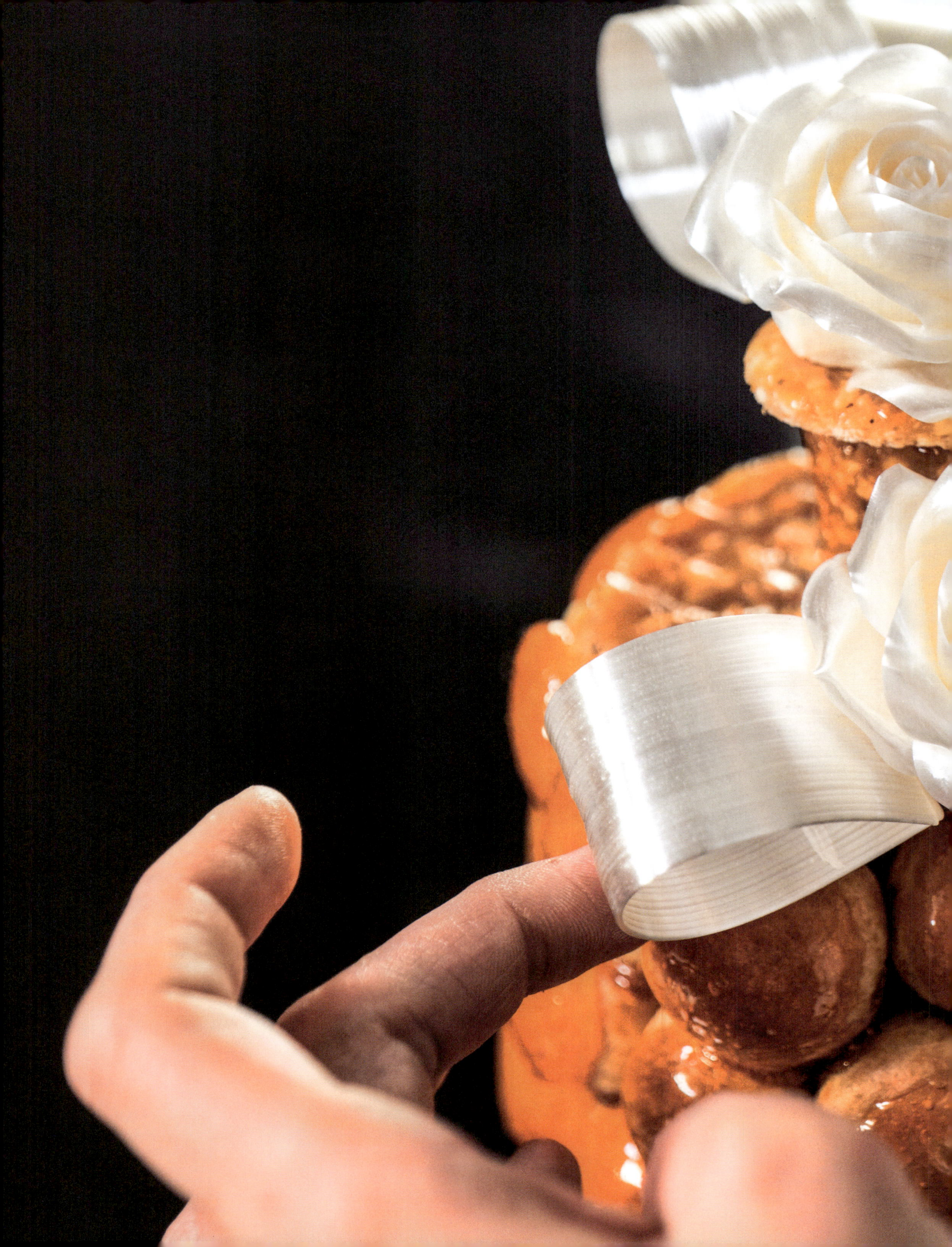

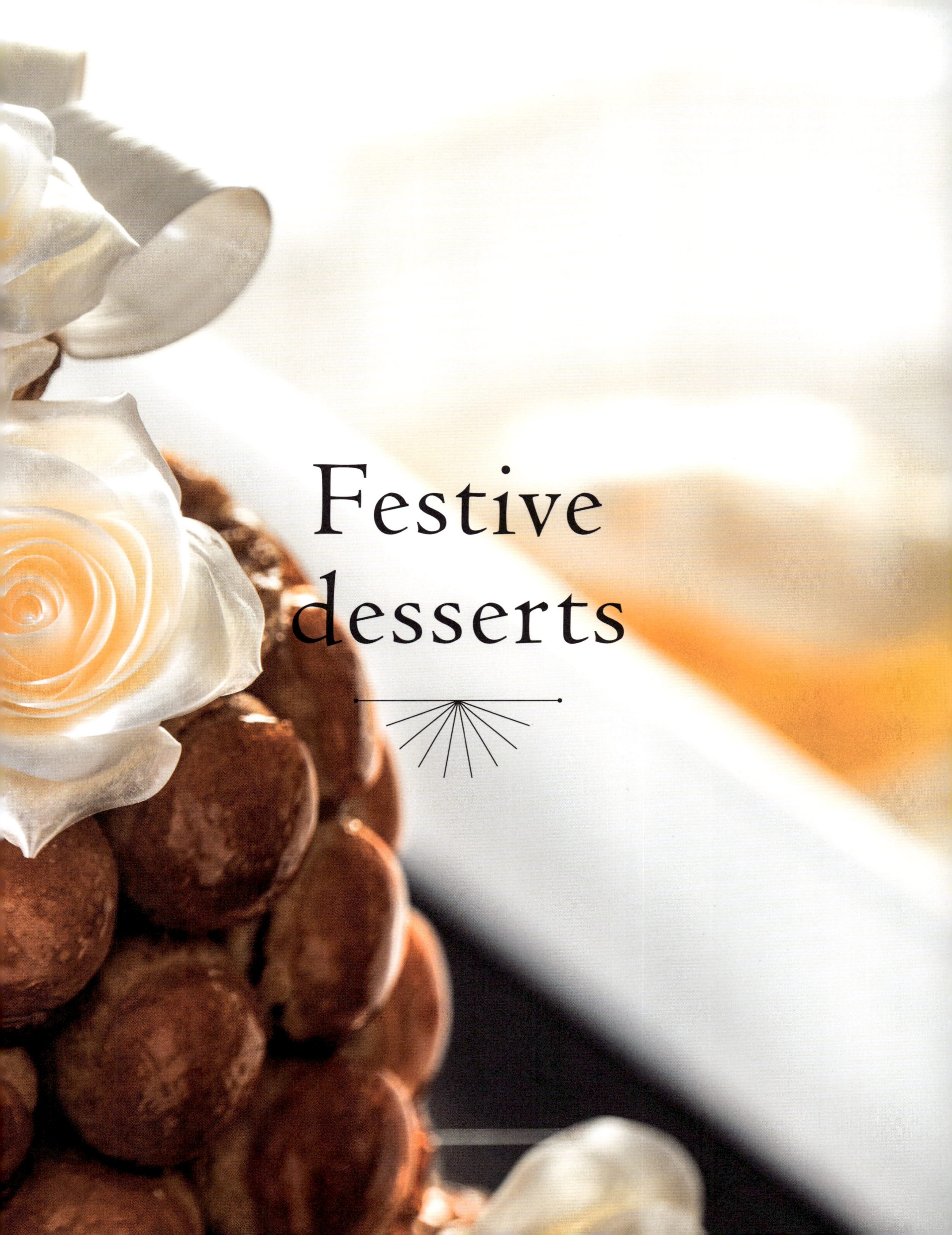

Festive desserts

Serves 6

Preparation
5 hours 30 minutes

Resting
12 hours

Cooking
30 minutes

Cigarette russe yule log

Whipped bergamot ganache

160 g bergamot purée

150 g whipping cream (1)

20 g gelatine mass

(3 g gelatine powder

   and 17 g cold water)

120 g white chocolate

250 g whipping cream (2)

1.2 g fresh bergamot zest

Hazelnut sponge

60 g ground almonds

60 g ground hazelnuts

60 g icing sugar

5 egg whites

60 g caster sugar

25 g unsalted butter, melted

Feuillantine

200 g hazelnut praline

50 g milk chocolate

100 g feuillantine

2 g fleur de sel

Filo tubes

70 g unsalted butter

3 g salt

110 g filo pastry

20 g light brown soft sugar

Whipped bergamot ganache The day before, put the cream (1) and bergamot purée into a saucepan and bring to the boil. Remove from the heat and add the gelatine mass, then pour the mixture over the white chocolate and whisk to combine. Incorporate the cream (2) and zest. Blend with an immersion blender until smooth. Allow the ganache to set in the fridge overnight before use.

Hazelnut sponge Sift the icing sugar and the ground nuts. In a stand mixer, beat the egg whites to soft peaks, then gradually add the caster sugar while beating to stiff peaks. Gently fold in the ground nuts and icing sugar mixture and then incorporate the melted butter. Spread the batter in a thin layer, lightly deflating it, over a black non-stick baking cloth and bake for 8 minutes at 180°C.

Feuillantine Heat the hazelnut praline and chocolate in a bain-marie and gently fold in the feuillantine and fleur de sel.

Filo tubes Melt the butter and add the salt. Brush the individual filo pastry sheets with melted butter (1) and sprinkle with sugar (2). Wrap each sheet around a rod (3), then bake for 12 minutes at 160°C (4).

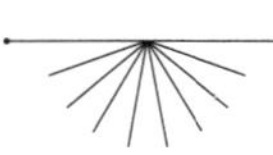

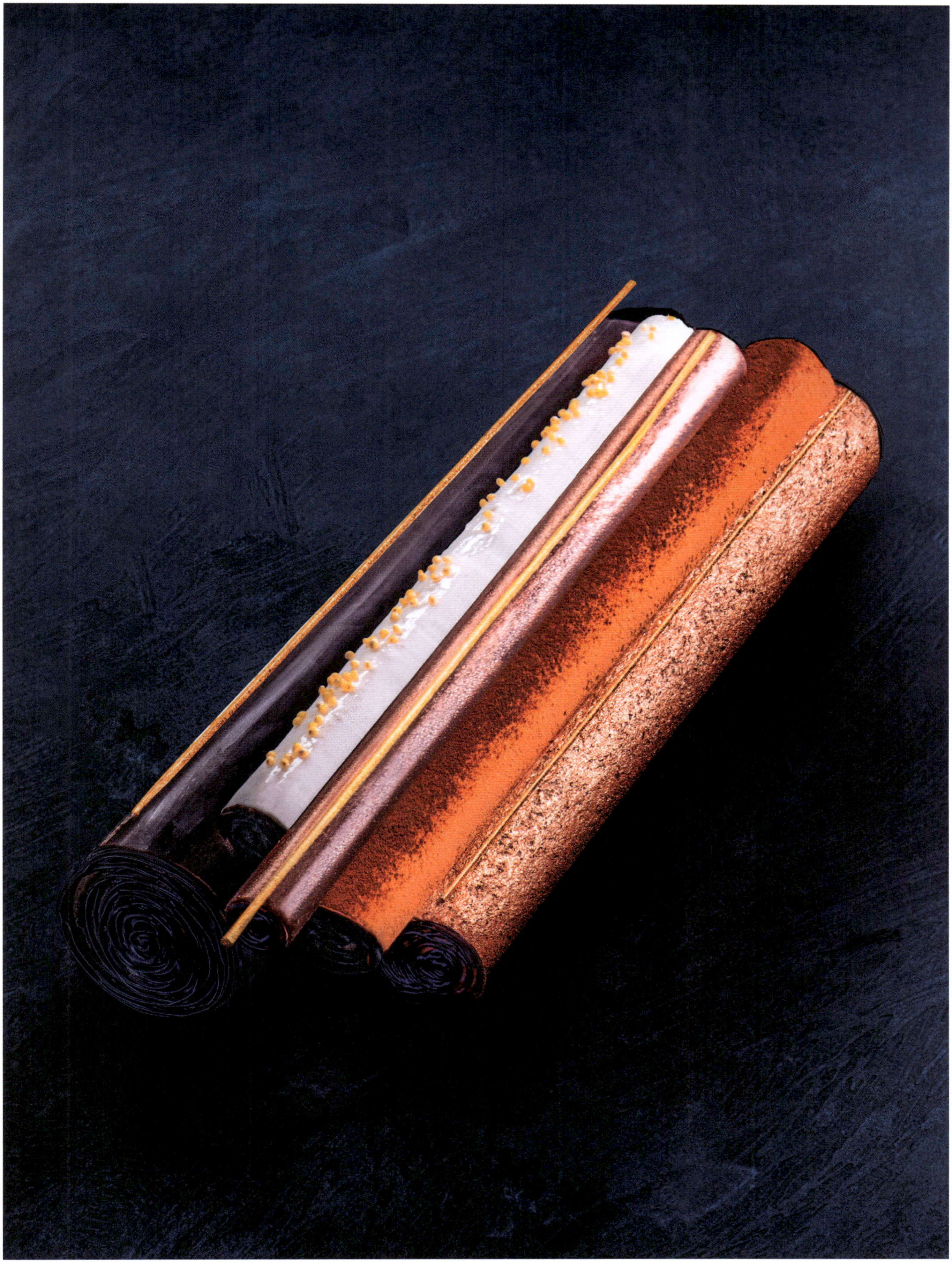

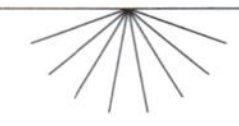

Praline filling

150 g hazelnut praline

100 g hazelnut paste

Hazelnut crémeux

125 g milk

125 g whipping cream

2 egg yolks

15 g gelatine mass

(2 g gelatine powder

    and 3 g cold water)

125 g gianduja milk chocolate

125 g milk chocolate

50 g praline

Hazelnut mousse

65 g milk

65 g whipping cream

2.5 egg yolks

30 g caster sugar

220 g milk chocolate

70 g praline

337 g whipped cream

1 g salt

Dark chocolate flocking

100 g dark chocolate couverture

    (72% cocoa)

75 g cocoa butter

Bronze coating

90 g kirsch

15 g edible bronze glitter

Gold coating

90 g kirsch

15 g edible gold glitter

Finish

Almond paste

Praline filling Mix the hazelnut praline and paste, then transfer to a piping bag and pipe the filo tubes full of praline.

Hazelnut crémeux In a saucepan, bring the milk and cream to the boil. Carefully add the hot mixture to the egg yolks and stir to combine. Return the mixture to the saucepan and cook until the temperature reaches 82°C, stirring constantly with a spatula. Incorporate the gelatine mass, then strain through a conical sieve into the melted gianduja and milk chocolate. Blend until smooth, then add the praline. Allow to set in the fridge at 4°C.

Hazelnut mousse In a saucepan, bring the milk and cream to the boil. Beat the egg yolks with the sugar until thick and pale, then add the hot mixture, stir to combine and return to the saucepan. Cook until the temperature reaches 82°C, then add the mixture to the melted milk chocolate. Whisk the mousse before blending in the praline and salt. Once the mixture has cooled to 35°C, gently fold in the whipped cream.

Dark chocolate flocking Melt the chocolate and cocoa butter in a bain-marie.

Bronze coating Mix the two ingredients together.

Gold coating Mix the two ingredients together.

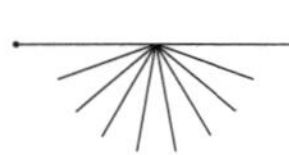

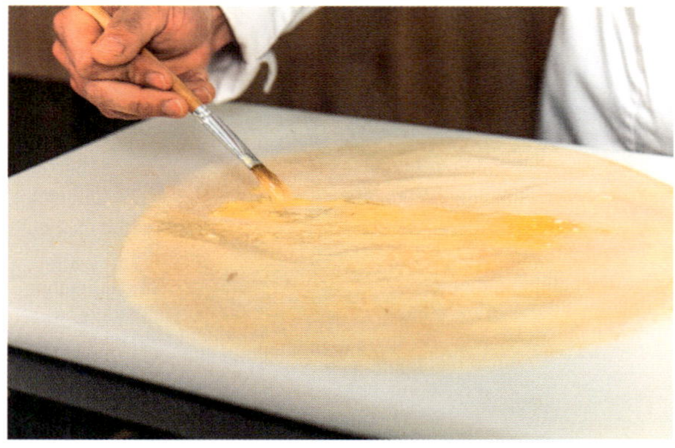

1.

For the filo insert, brush the filo sheets with melted butter.

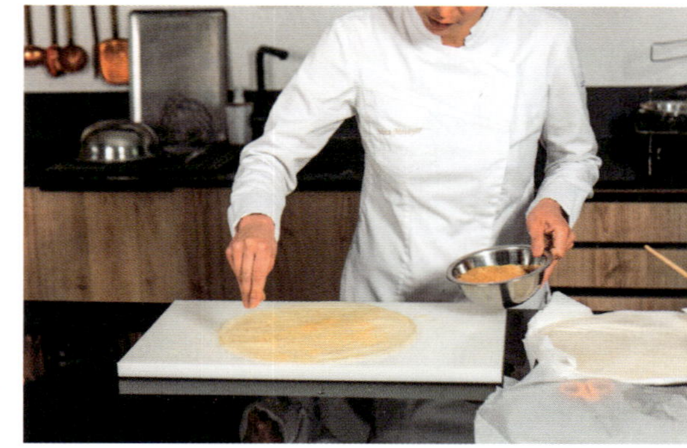

2.

Sprinkle with sugar.

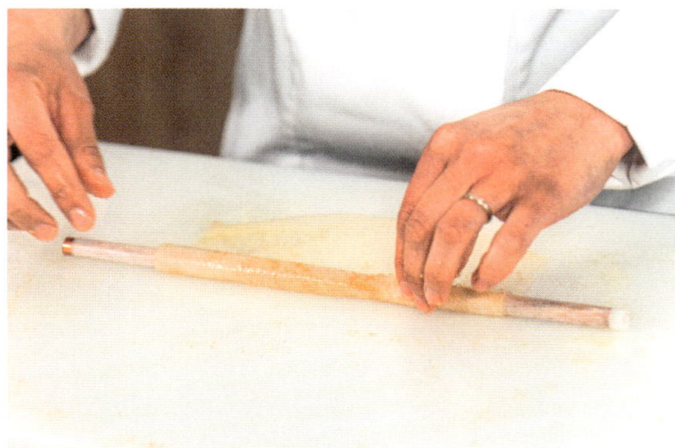

3.

Wrap each sheet around a rod.

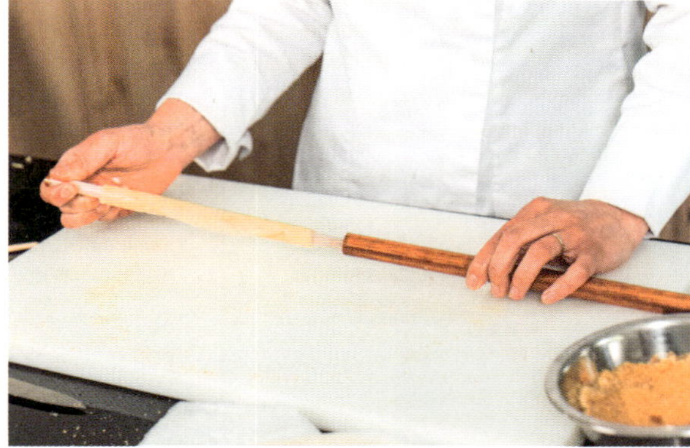

4.

Bake for 12 minutes at 160°C.

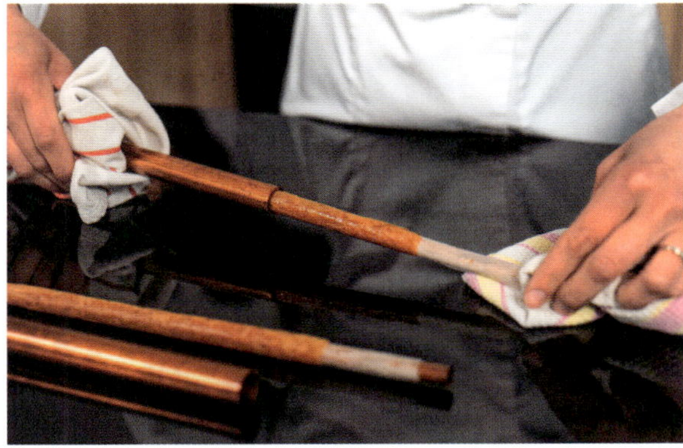

5.

Remove the rods from the pastry tubes.

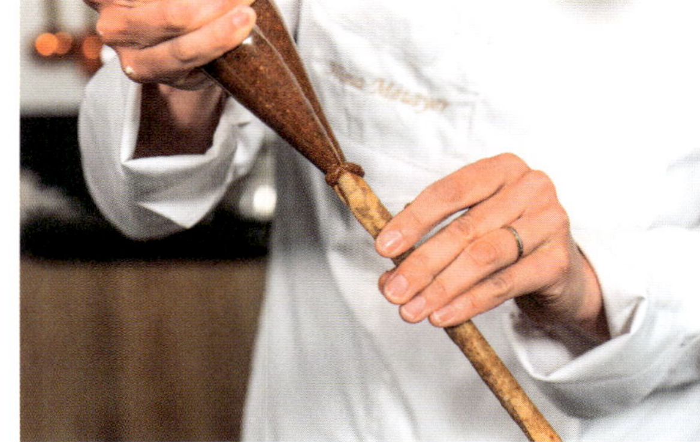

6.

Pipe the tubes full of praline.

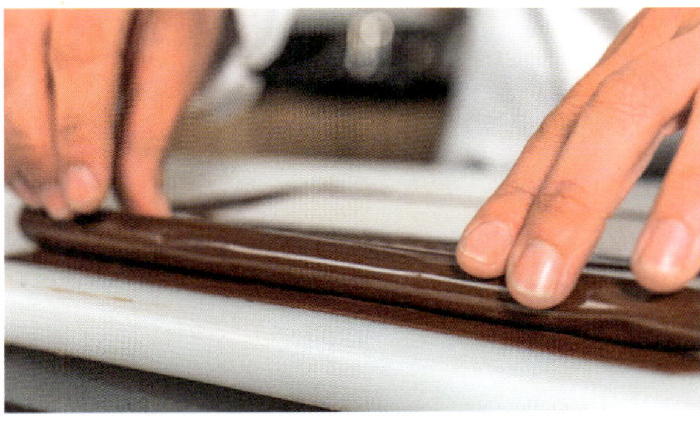

7.

Cut 6 x 20-cm strips of guitar paper and spread them with a thin and even layer of tempered dark chocolate.

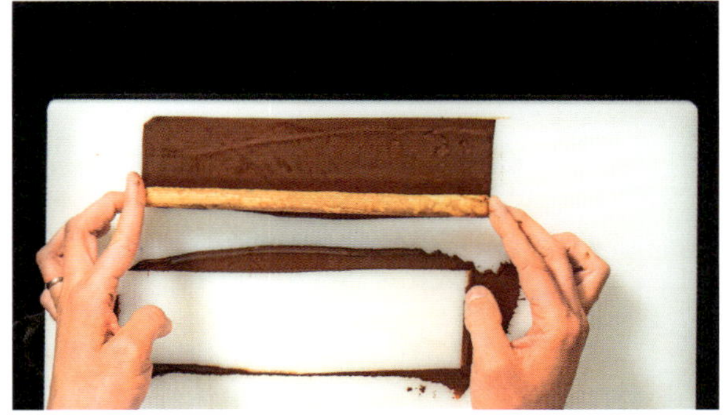

8.

Quickly wrap the filo tubes with the chocolate on the guitar paper.

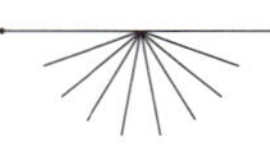

Assembly and finishing

Cylinder 1: hazelnut mousse / praline-filled filo insert / chocolate coating

For the insert, pipe the filo pastry tube full of praline (6). Cut 6 × 20-cm strips of guitar paper and spread them with a thin and even layer of tempered dark chocolate (7). Quickly roll a chocolate sheet around the filo pastry tube (8) and refrigerate at 4°C for a few minutes. Seal the end of the tube with almond paste. Remove the guitar paper and set aside in a dry place.

Use an acetate sheet to make a 4.5-cm-diameter tube, wrap the bottom end of the tube in cling film and stand it upright in a bucket. Pipe hazelnut mousse into the acetate tube and position the filo insert in the middle, taking care not to create any air bubbles, then pipe mousse into the tube to the top of the insert. Place in the freezer.

Cut an acetate sheet into a 21 × 17-cm rectangle, spread it with a thin and even layer of tempered dark chocolate and immediately wrap it around the mousse cylinder. Allow the chocolate to harden in the fridge at 4°C for a few minutes, then remove the acetate.

Cylinder 2: sponge / feuillantine / whipped bergamot ganache / praline-filled filo insert / spray gun filled with bronze coating

To make the insert, follow the instructions given for cylinder 1.

Fill a 2.7-cm-diameter tube with whipped bergamot ganache and position the filo insert centred inside the ganache. The tube should be filled horizontally, with both ends open. The consistency of the whipped ganache will keep it from leaking out. Quickly place the tube in the freezer. Then trim the frozen ganache cylinder to a length of 22 cm and set aside in the freezer.

Make the hazelnut sponge, spread the feuillantine very thinly on the smoothest side, then roll it around the 2.7-cm-diameter whipped bergamot ganache cylinder. Allow the cylinder to harden in the freezer, then trim to a length of 23 cm. Spray with the bronze coating and set aside in the freezer.

Cylinder 3: hazelnut mousse exterior / hazelnut crémeux insert / dark chocolate flocking / cocoa powder

Make a 1.5-cm-diameter tube out of an acetate sheet. Lightly loosen the hazelnut crémeux and fill the tube. Stand the tube upright in the freezer and allow it to harden. Then remove the acetate, trim the cylinder to a length of 22 cm and set aside in the refrigerator.

Make a 2.7-cm-diameter tube and wrap it in cling film, making sure to fold the cling film tightly over one end. Stand the tube upright in a bucket and fill it with hazelnut mousse. Position the hazelnut crémeux insert inside the mousse, taking care not to create any air bubbles. Allow the cylinder to harden in a blast chiller and set aside in the freezer. Trim the cylinder to a length of 20 cm. Spray the cylinder with dark chocolate flocking and dust with cocoa.

Cylinder 4: whipped bergamot ganache / neutral glaze

Fill a 2-cm-diameter tube with whipped bergamot ganache. Quickly place the tube in the freezer. Then trim the frozen ganache cylinder to a length of 22 cm and set aside in the freezer.

Melt some neutral glaze and spray it over the cylinder, then top with a few crispy grains.

Cylinder 5: hazelnut crémeux / chocolate coating / spray gun filled with bronze coating

To make the hazelnut crémeux cylinder, follow the instructions given for cylinder 3. Wrap the cylinder in chocolate according to the instructions for cylinder 1. Then spray with the bronze coating.

For the golden chocolate sticks
Temper the chocolate, then spread the chocolate over a sheet of guitar paper and make threads by scraping with the thinnest side of a decorating comb. Spray the threads with gold coating. Set aside in a container in the fridge at 4°C.

For the cylinder ends
Temper the chocolate. Pipe chocolate discs on a baking mat with the following sizes:

♦ 4.5 cm in diameter

♦ 4 cm in diameter

♦ 2.7 cm in diameter

♦ 2 cm in diameter

♦ 1.5 cm in diameter

Using a paper piping bag, pipe 2 spirals of the required size to fit each cylinder.

Assembly
Attach the corresponding chocolate discs to the ends of each cylinder.

Stack all the components to create the yule log, arranging the thickest cylinders at the base and the others as desired.

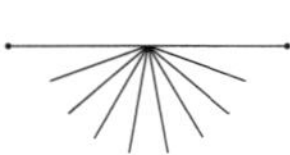

Makes 1 log to serve 8

Preparation	Cooking	Resting
2 hours	30 minutes	10 hours

Triangular yule log

Dark chocolate crémeux

375 g whipping cream
375 g milk
100 g egg yolks
75 g light brown soft sugar
300 g dark chocolate (66% cocoa)

Chocolate mousse

160 g dark chocolate (66% cocoa)
120 g milk chocolate (35% cocoa)
506 g whipping cream (1)
100 g milk
100 g whipping cream (2)
5 egg yolks

Chocolate shortbread

220 g unsalted butter, softened
180 g light brown soft sugar
70 g caster sugar
260 g T55 (plain) flour
80 g cocoa powder
4 g fleur de sel

Cocoa sponge

20 g milk
66 g unsalted butter
16 g T55 flour
16 g cocoa powder
46 g hazelnut paste
2 eggs
5 egg yolks
6 egg whites
53 g caster sugar

Triangle decoration

250 g dark chocolate (72% cocoa)
10 g edible bronze glitter
20 g kirsch

Dark chocolate crémeux In a saucepan, bring the cream and milk to the boil. Mix the sugar with the egg yolks and stir in a little of the boiling liquid. Return the mixture to the pan and cook over a low heat, stirring constantly, until the temperature reaches 82°C. Add the mixture to the dark chocolate a third at a time and mix without aerating. Blend until smooth with an immersion blender.

Chocolate mousse Melt both chocolates together in a bain-marie. In a stand mixer fitted with a wire whisk, whip the cream (1). In a saucepan, heat the milk and cream (2), then whisk the hot liquid into the egg yolks, then return the mixture to the saucepan and cook until the temperature reaches 82°C. Then add it to the melted chocolate, incorporating with a spatula until thick and smooth, and fold in the whipped cream. Use immediately.

Chocolate shortbread Using a spatula, mix the butter with both sugars, then incorporate the sifted flour and cocoa and finish with the fleur de sel. Using a rolling pin with thickness rings, roll out the pastry to a 4-mm thickness. Rest the pastry in the fridge for 30 minutes.

Cocoa sponge Put the milk and butter into a saucepan and bring to the boil. Remove from the heat and add the sifted flour and cocoa in one go. Mix well with a spatula, then add the hazelnut paste and allow the batter to dry out a little over the heat.

Transfer to a container.

Gradually add the whole eggs and yolks, incorporating with a spatula.

Preheat the oven to 200°C.

Beat the egg whites to soft peaks, then gradually add the sugar while beating to stiff peaks.

Mix a little beaten egg white into the batter, then gently fold in the remainder. Using an angled palette knife, carefully spread a thin and even layer of batter on a baking mat with raised edges. Bake at 200°C for 3 minutes. Allow to cool on a rack.

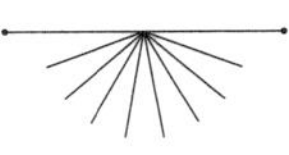

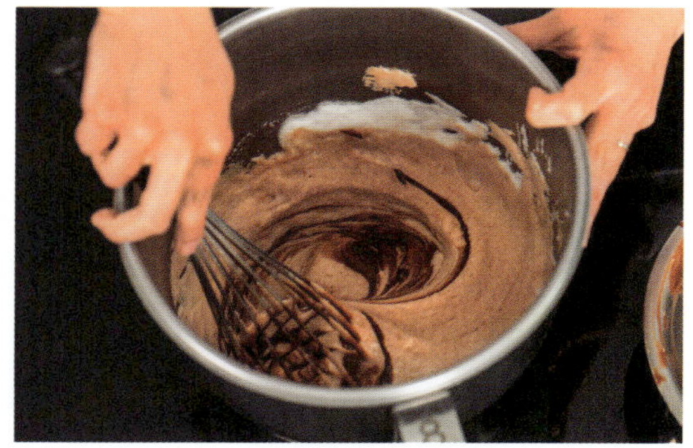

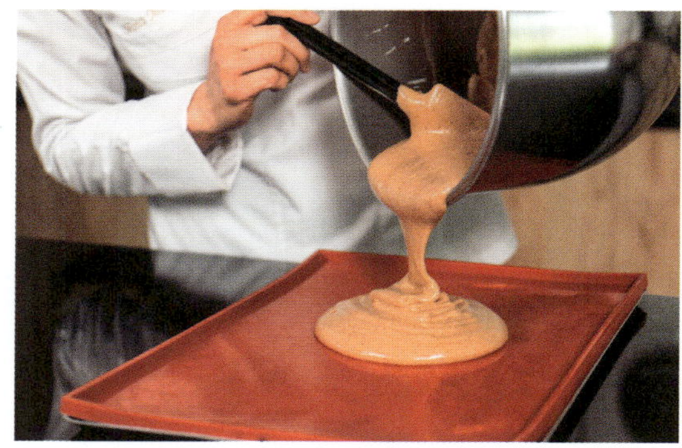

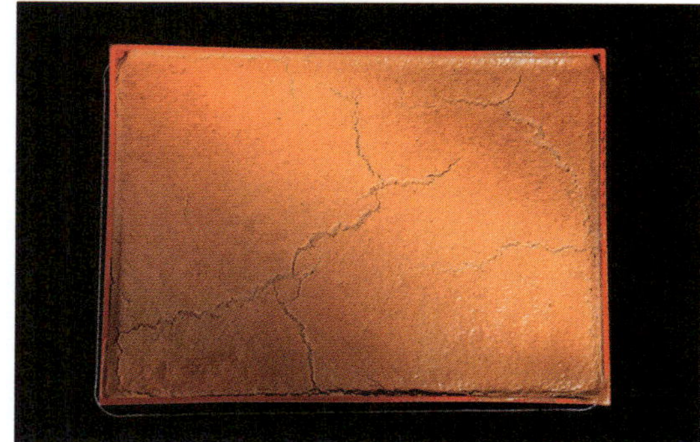

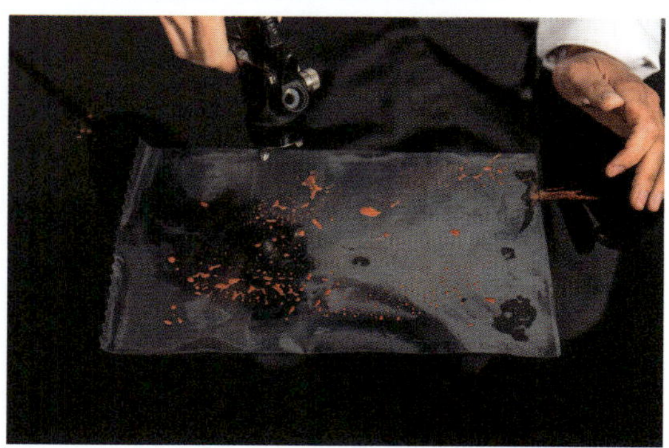

Assembly

Prepare the triangular yule log mould by lightly greasing the inside walls and lining it with a sheet of guitar paper. Make the chocolate crémeux and partially fill a triangular log mould and allow to harden in the freezer for about 1 hour 30 minutes. Repeat the operation to make 4 triangular prism crémeux inserts.

Set aside a little of the crémeux in a piping bag for use to attach the decorations.

Grease the mould again and line with another sheet of guitar paper.

Make the chocolate mousse and partially fill with the mould. Using a small palette knife, spread the mousse over the sides of the mould. Position the first crémeux insert inside the mould and cover with a little mousse, then place another insert on top of the first and pointing in the opposite direction. Spread more chocolate mousse over the sides of the inserts and position the last two inserts on either side of the middle one, pointing downwards, resulting in four triangles inside the large triangle when the log is cut. Cover everything with chocolate mousse and smooth the surface.

Allow to harden in the freezer for 4 hours.

Make the chocolate shortbread.

Allow it to harden in the fridge for 1 hour. Make the cocoa sponge, then transfer it to a rack to cool. Cut the chocolate shortbread to fit the base of the yule log, then bake for 25 minutes at 155°C.

Make the chocolate decorations.

Cut an acetate sheet into a rectangle slightly smaller than the size of the top two sides of the yule log. Spray a random pattern of bronze coating over the sheet.

Temper the chocolate.

Spread the chocolate thinly over the coating on the acetate sheet. Transfer the acetate sheet to a clean pastry board. Allow the chocolate to harden slightly. Carefully cut the chocolate sheet into triangles to fit each side of the yule log. Place them between two trays and allow to harden in the fridge.

Remove the yule log from the mould and position it on the cooled shortbread base. Cut out rectangles from the cocoa sponge to cover both upper sides of the yule log and carefully attach them. Using a very small amount of chocolate crémeux, attach the chocolate triangles to the sponge.

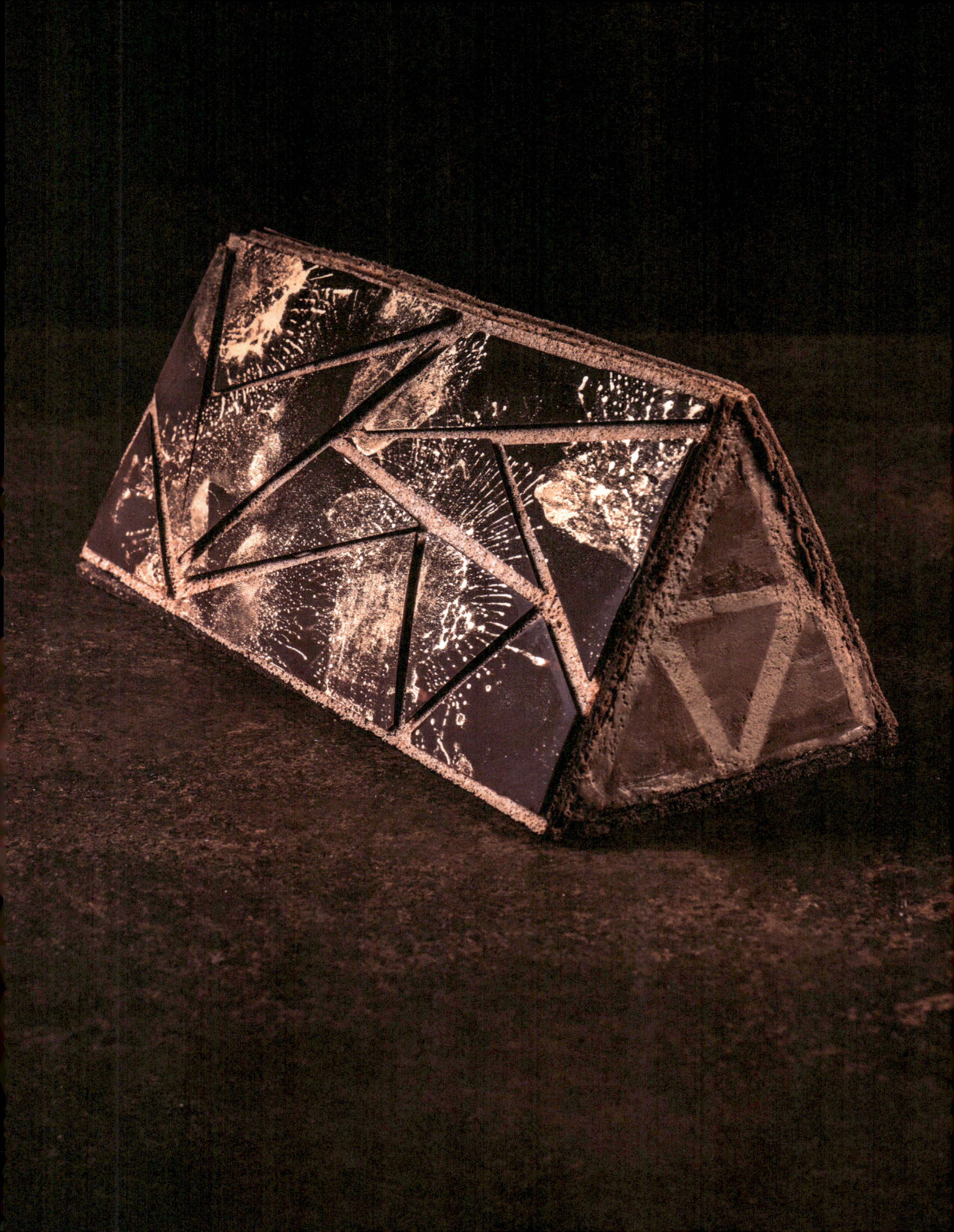

Makes 1 galette to serve 8

Preparation	Resting	Cooking
4 hours	2½ days	2 hours 10 minutes

Notre-Dame galette

Inverse puff pastry

Beurre manié

338 g unsalted butter

150 g einkorn flour

Dough

282 g T80 (stoneground white)
   flour

127 g water

90 g unsalted butter

12 g salt

4 g white vinegar

Cinnamon pastry cream

55 g light brown soft sugar

10 g cinnamon sticks

180 g milk

88 g whipping cream

1 egg

2.5 g T55 (plain) flour

15 g custard powder

8 g unsalted butter

Almond cream

60 g ground almonds

1 g ground cinnamon

60 g unsalted butter, at room
   temperature

60 g light brown soft sugar

1 egg

Beurre manié and dough The day before, mix the butter with the flour and roll out to an even thickness. Mix all the ingredients together to make the dough, then roll it out to an even thickness and place it over the beurre manié. Rest the assembled pastry in the fridge for at least 6 hours. Perform a double turn by rolling out the pastry to a 5-mm thickness and folding it over twice to make 4 stacked layers (double turn). Rest the pastry again for at least 6 hours at 4°C. Repeat the operation to perform a total of 3 double turns. Roll out the puff pastry to a 3.5-mm thickness and lift the sheet off the work surface to relax it well.

Cinnamon pastry cream Make a light dry caramel with the sugar, add the cinnamon sticks and finish cooking the caramel. Deglaze with the warm milk and cream mixture. Allow to steep for 15 minutes. Strain the caramel sauce through a conical strainer and weigh out 320 g, topping up with milk if necessary. Bring to the boil. Mix the egg with the flour and custard powder, then add the boiling caramel sauce. Return the mixture to the saucepan and bring to the boil for 1 minute. Incorporate the butter and cool quickly in a blast chiller.

Almond cream Roast the ground almonds with half the ground cinnamon at 140°C for 40 minutes. In a mixer fitted with a paddle attachment, mix the butter, sugar and remaining cinnamon, then incorporate the egg and ground almonds.

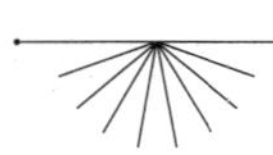

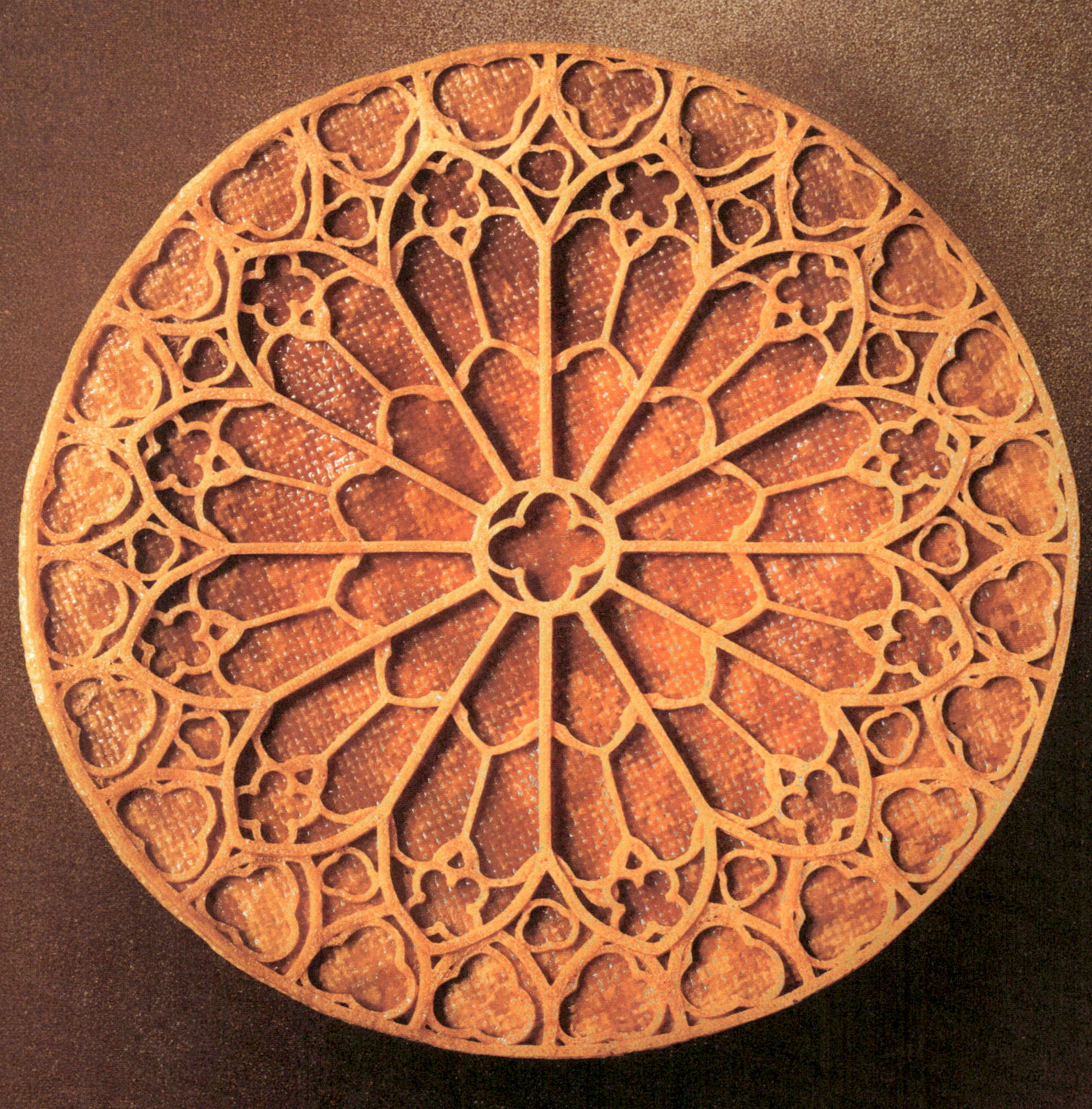

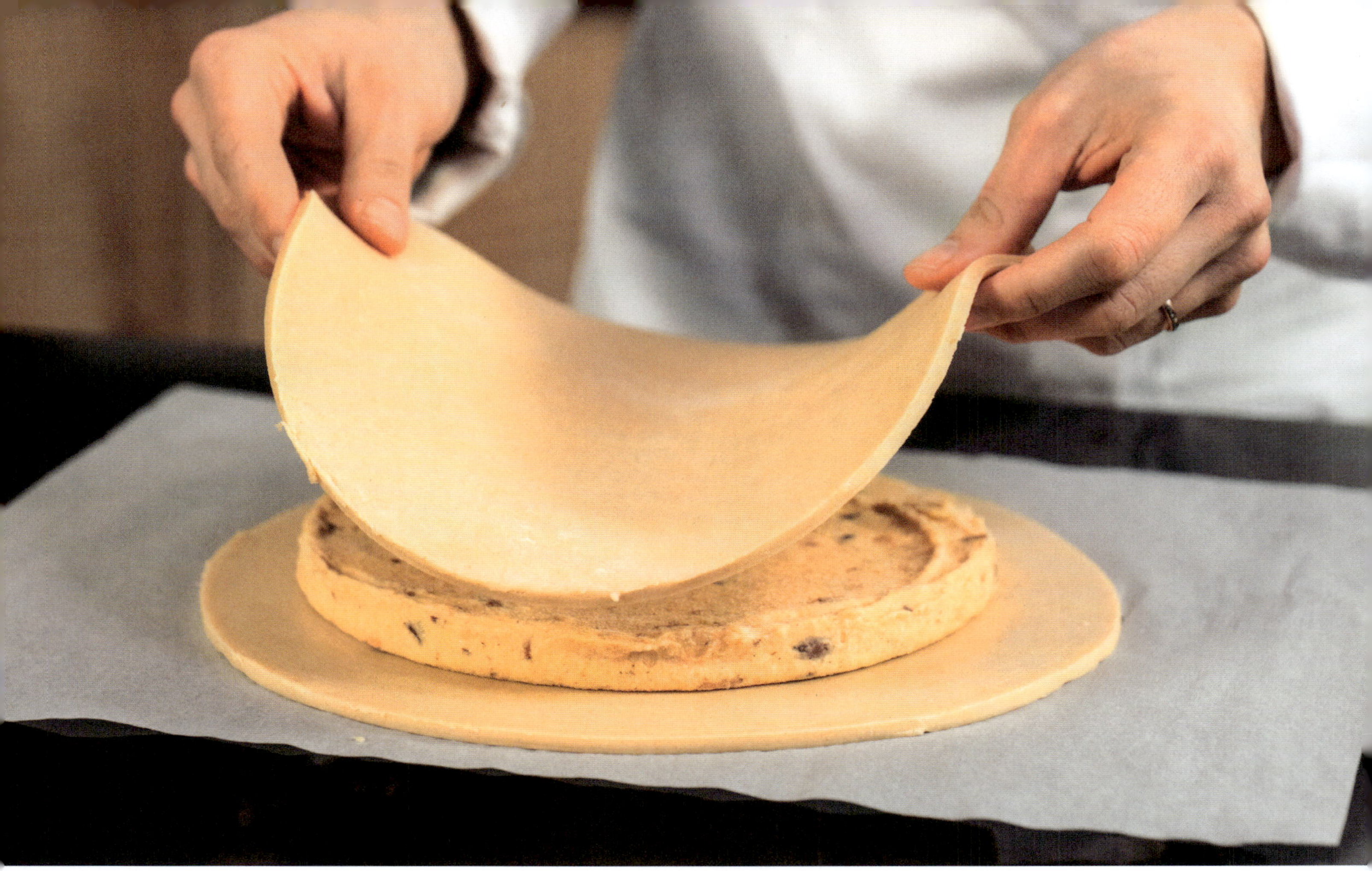

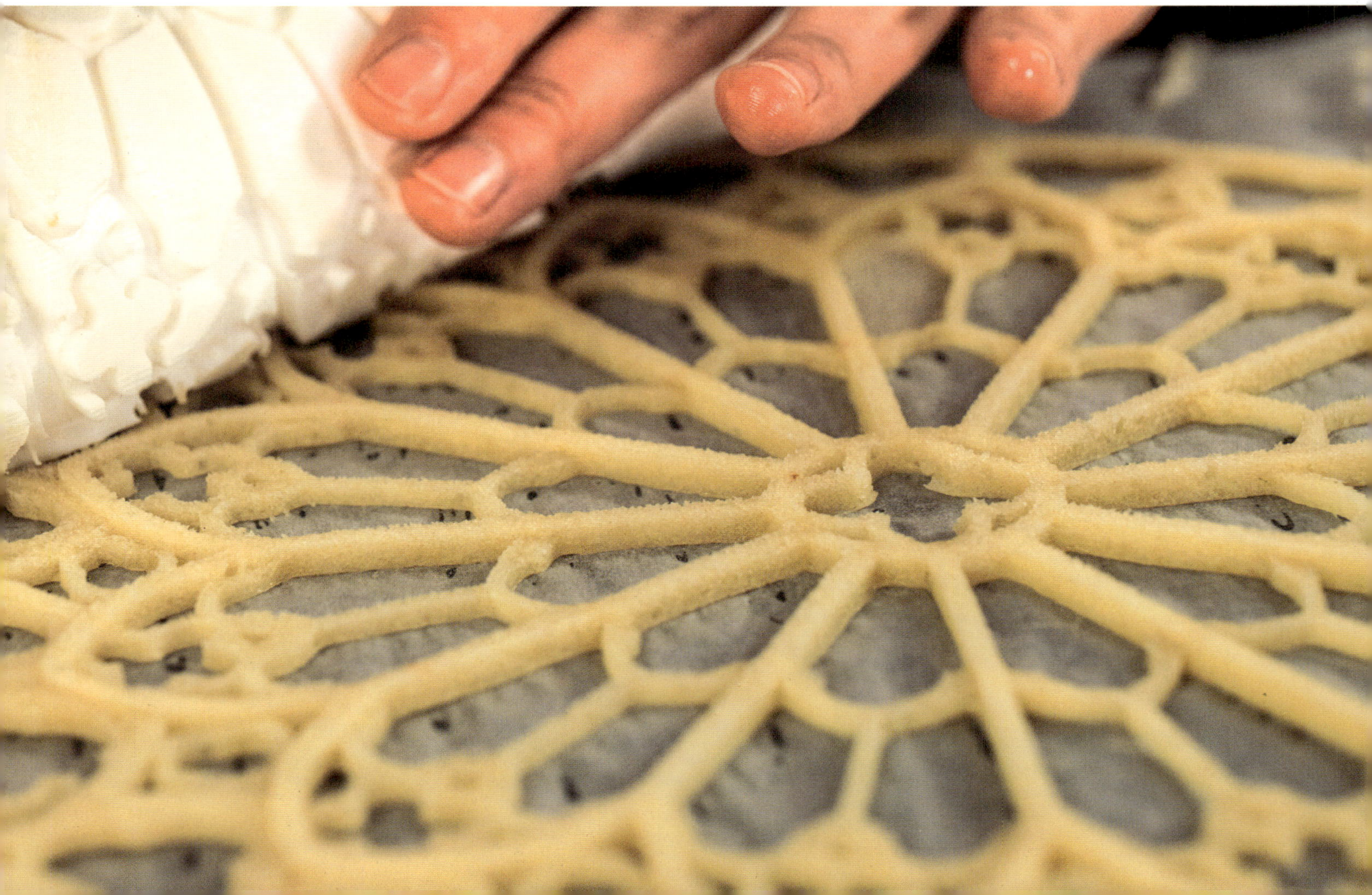

Frangipane

210 g almond cream

180 g pastry cream

9 g custard powder

0.5 g salt

30 g roasted and chopped
    almonds

Tuile

20 g unsalted butter

20 g caster sugar

20 g T55 flour

1 egg white

Syrup

100 g caster sugar

75 g water

Frangipane Mix together the almond cream, pastry cream, baking powder and salt. Spread the roasted and chopped almonds inside a 20-cm-diameter tart ring, then fill the ring with 350 g of frangipane (1), then smooth the surface, lift off the ring and freeze (2).

Tuile The day before, melt the butter, then mix it with the sugar, sifted flour and egg white. Rest the batter in the fridge at 4°C for 24 hours, then use at room temperature.

On the day, grease the rose window silicone mould well with cooking spray and spread the batter into the mould (3). Bake at 160°C for 4 minutes (4). Allow it to cool down. Turn the mould over and carefully lift it off the tuile (5). Finish baking the tuile at 155°C for 15 minutes (6).

Assembly

Make the puff pastry.

Roll out the pastry to a 2.5-mm thickness and chill until well relaxed. Cut out a 24-cm-diameter disc for the base and a 26-cm-diameter disc for the top (7). Use a knife to make a small notch in the bottom side of each disc. Allow the pastry discs to rest for 12 hours at 4°C. Take out the 24-cm disc and moisten the edges with water (8), then position the frangipane insert in the centre (9). Carefully cover the insert with the 26-cm disc, turning it so that the notch on the top disc is 90 degrees from the notch on the bottom disc (10). Press out any air before sealing the edges tightly (11). Rest the galette at 4°C before brushing with egg wash. Then freeze it for 4 hours before returning it to the fridge at 4°C for 6 hours.

Preheat the oven to 180°C.

Place the galette on a baking tray lined with baking paper. Brush with egg wash again. Bake at 180°C for 15 minutes, then at 160°C for a further 35 minutes. Check for doneness and adjust the cooking time if necessary.

Syrup In a saucepan, cook the water and sugar over a low heat to make a syrup. Finish baking the tuile at 155°C for about 15 minutes, until golden brown. When the galette comes out of the oven, brush it with syrup, place the tuile on top and bake for a further 5 minutes.

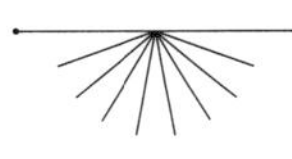

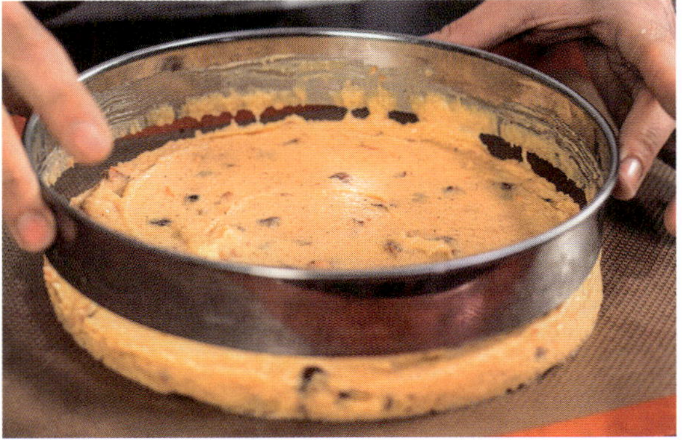

1.

To make the frangipane insert, spread the roasted and chopped almonds inside a 20-cm-diameter tart ring, then fill the ring with 350 g of frangipane...

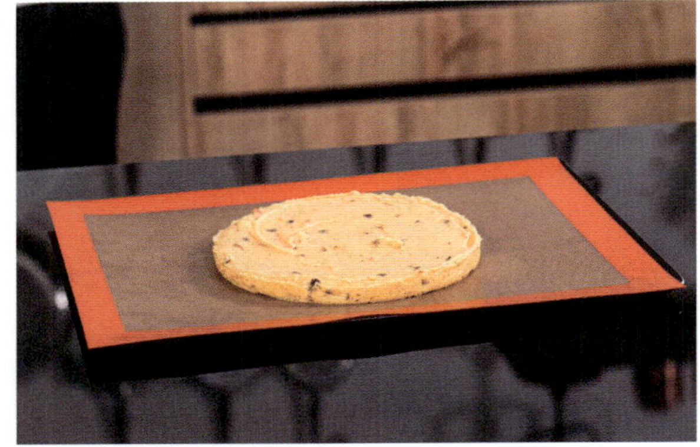

2.

...smooth the surface, remove the ring and freeze.

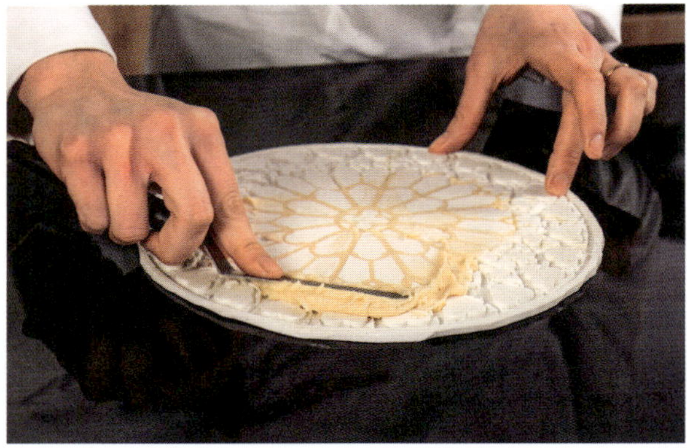

3.

To make the rose window tuile, grease the silicone mould with cooking spray and spread the mixture into the mould.

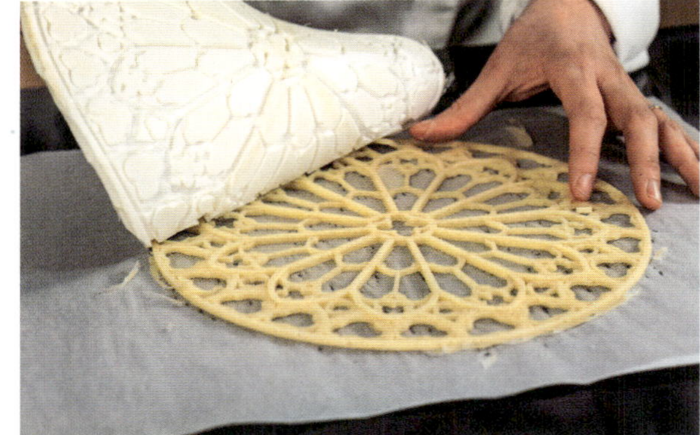

4.

Bake at 160°C for 4 minutes.

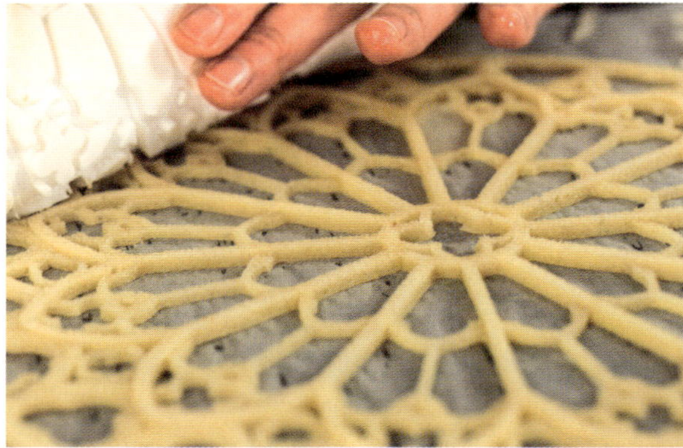

5.

Allow it to cool down. Turn the mould over and carefully lift it off the tuile.

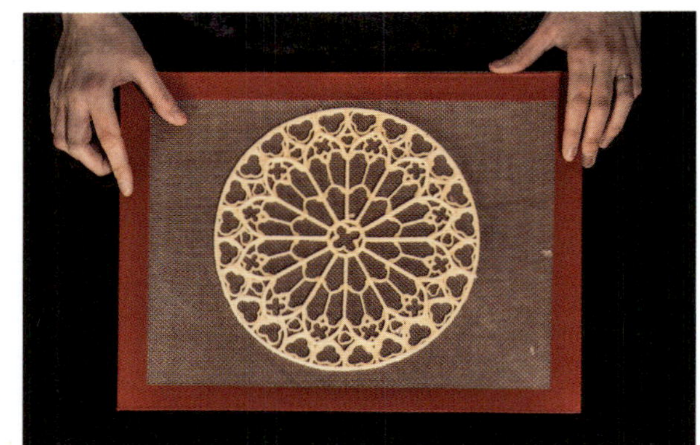

6.

Finish baking the tuile at 155°C for 15 minutes.

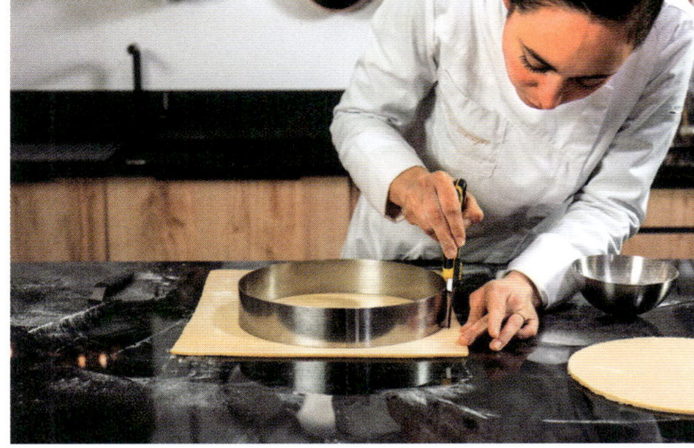

7. To assemble the galette, cut out a 24-cm diameter puff pastry disc for the base and a 26-cm-diameter disc for the top.

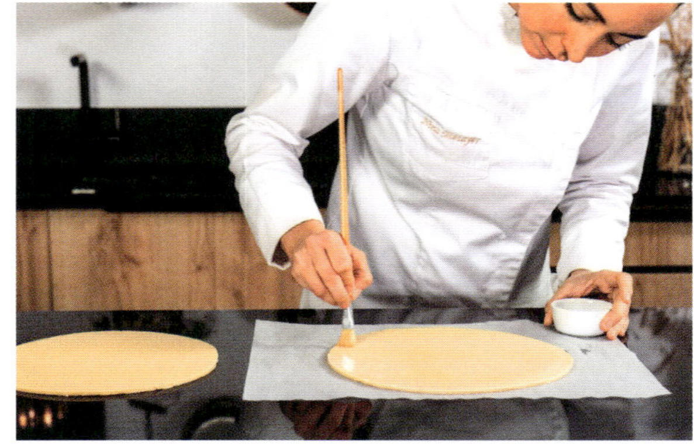

8. Brush the edges of the 24-cm disc with water to moisten.

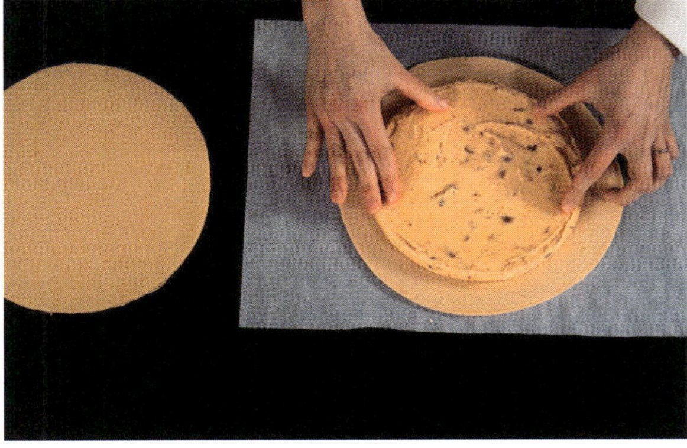

9. Position the frangipane insert in the centre.

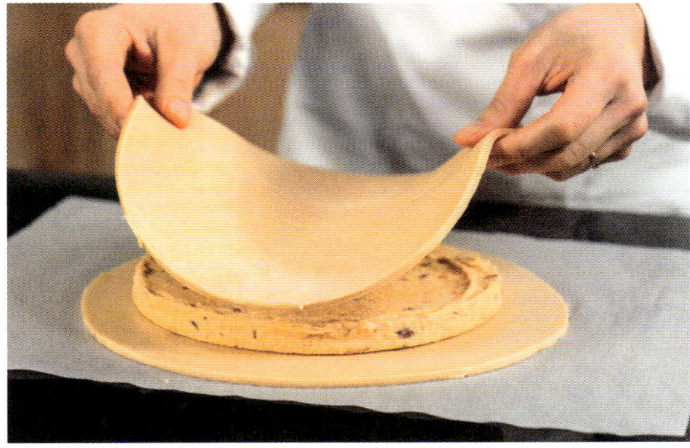

10. Carefully cover the insert with the 26-cm disc, turning it so that the notch on the top disc is 90 degrees from the notch on the bottom disc.

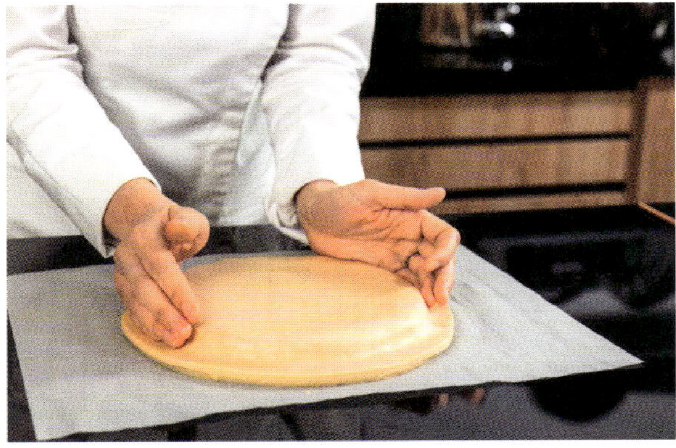

11. Press out any air before sealing the edges tightly.

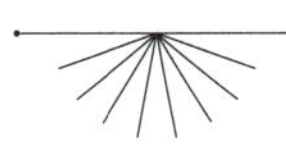

Makes 1 egg

Preparation
2 hours 30 minutes

Cooking
40 minutes

Budding Easter egg

Tempered chocolate

700 g dark chocolate
couverture (72% cocoa)

Caramelised hazelnuts

80 g roasted hazelnuts
15 g water
60 g caster sugar
5 g unsalted butter
2 g fleur de sel

Caramelised pecan nuts

40 g caster sugar
20 g water
80 g pecan nuts
5 g unsalted butter
2 g salt

Crispy feuillantine

45 g dark chocolate
couverture (72% cocoa)
120 g almond and hazelnut
praline
60 g feuillantine
1 g fleur de sel

Flocking

100 g cocoa butter
100 g dark chocolate
couverture (72% cocoa)
2.5 g edible bronze glitter

Tempered chocolate Temper the chocolate using the temperature curve method: melt the chocolate at 55°C, cool over an ice bath to 28°C and reheat to 30–31°C in a bain-marie. Use a silicone mould to make the base for the egg (see p. 214). Shape the petals using thermoformed petal moulds (1–2). Mould the two egg halves (3). Allow the pieces to harden at 16°C and remove from the moulds. Heat the bottom of a saucepan and carefully smooth the edges of the petals on it (4).

Caramelised hazelnuts Roast the hazelnuts at 140°C for 40 minutes. Make a syrup with the water and sugar, add the hazelnuts and cook over a low heat until they caramelise. Then mix in the butter and fleur de sel. Transfer the caramelised nuts to a container and separate them.

Caramelised pecan nuts Make a syrup with the water and sugar, add the pecans and cook over a low heat until they caramelise. Then mix in the butter and salt. Transfer the caramelised nuts to a container and separate them (5).

Crispy feuillantine Melt the chocolate in a bain-marie and add the praline, feuillantine and fleur de sel. Mix until combined. Set aside.

Flocking Melt the cocoa butter and chocolate in a bain-marie and blend. Use at 40°C.

Assembly Fill one half of the egg with caramelised hazelnuts and pecans and crispy feuillantine, as well as praline-filled bonbons if desired (6). Heat the other side of the egg (7) on the bottom of a hot saucepan and attach it to the filled half (8). Remove the base from the mould. Using a paper piping bag filled with tempered chocolate, attach the egg to the base (9–10). Attach the petals one at a time by piping with tempered chocolate (11–12) and a cooling spray. Spray the budding egg with the flocking. Apply bronze glitter with a brush.

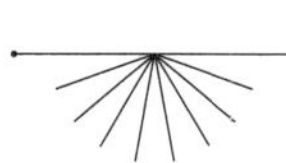

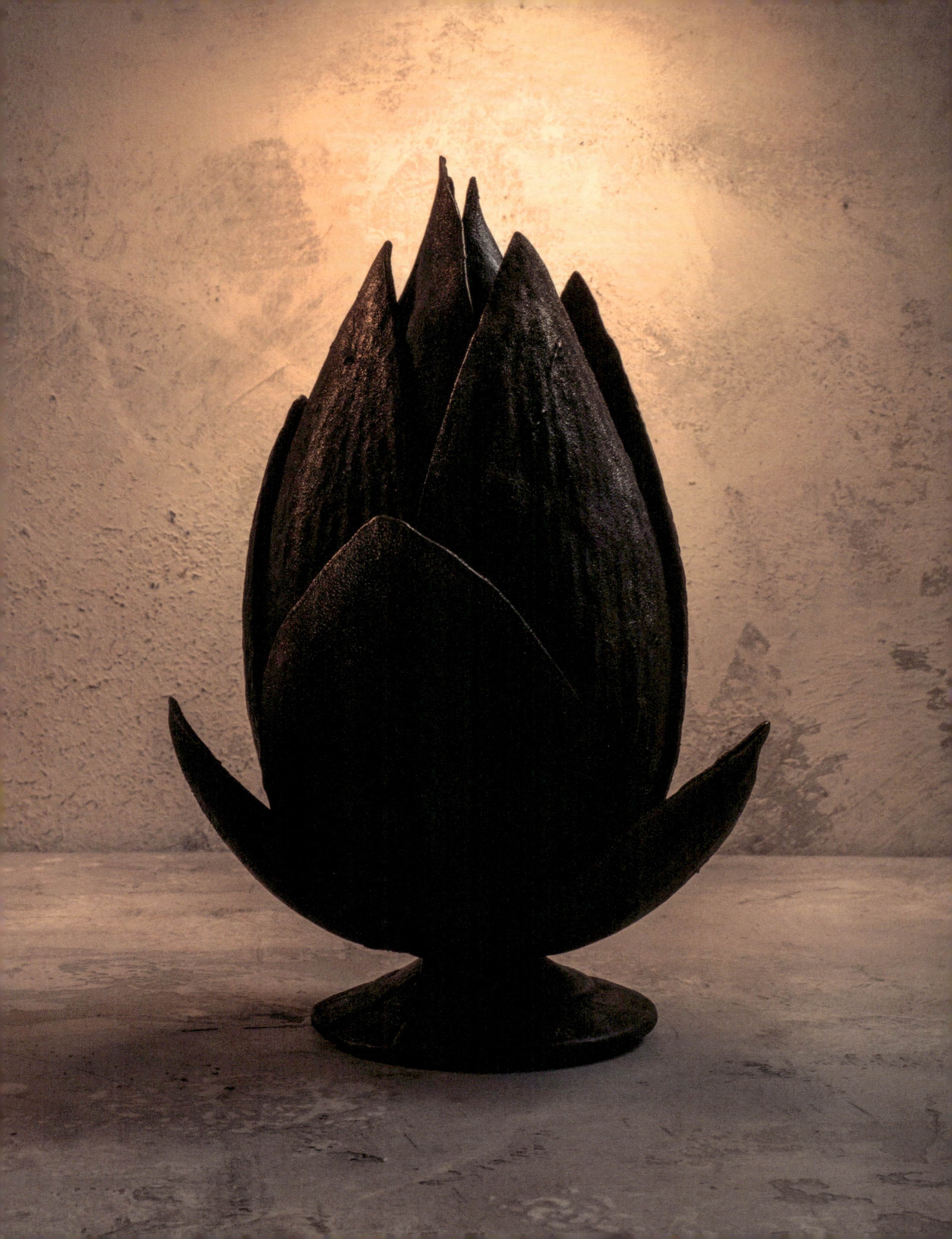

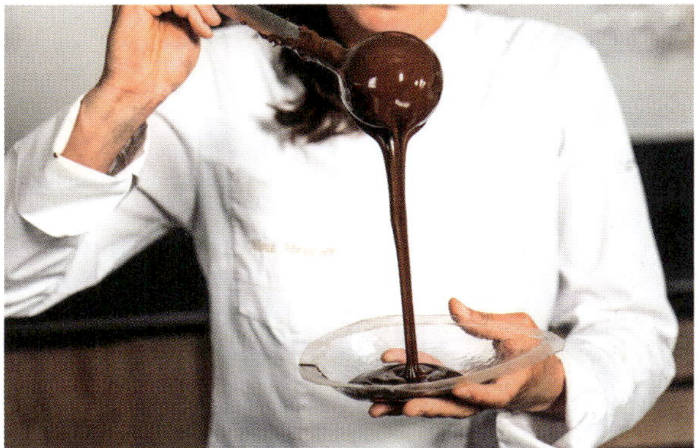

1.

Shape the petals...

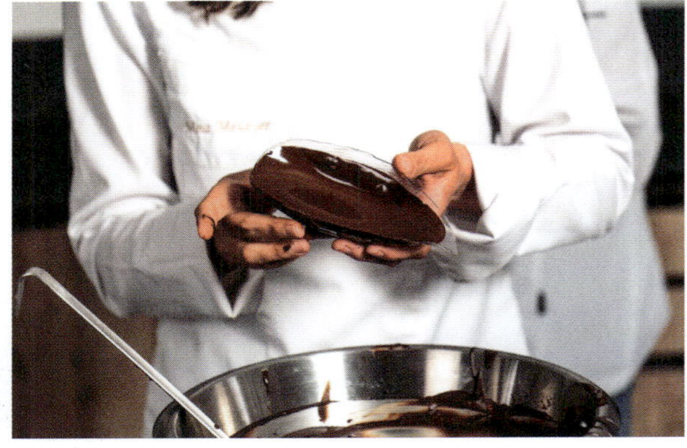

2.

...in thermoformed petal moulds.

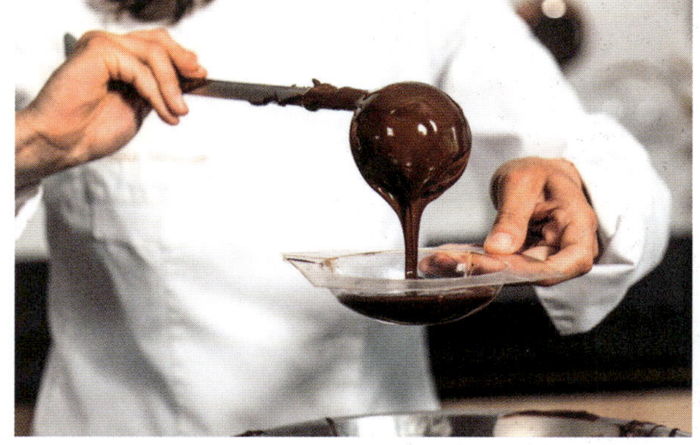

3.

Mould the two egg halves.

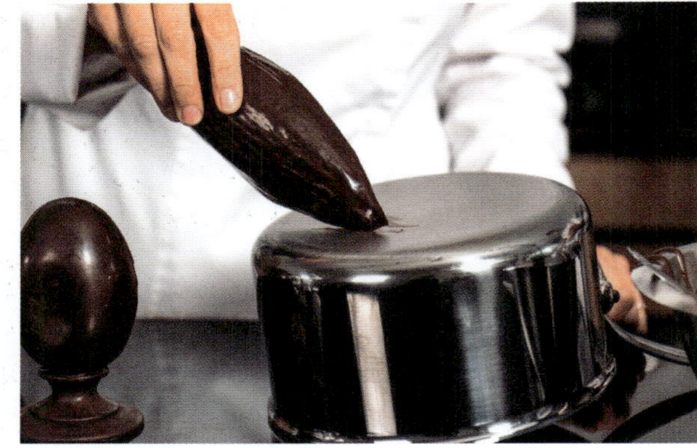

4.

Heat the bottom of a saucepan and carefully smooth the edges of the petals on it.

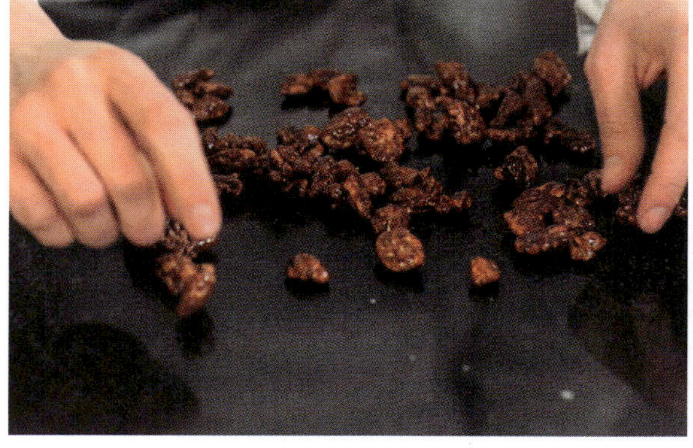

5.

Caramelise the pecans and separate them. Do the same with the hazelnuts.

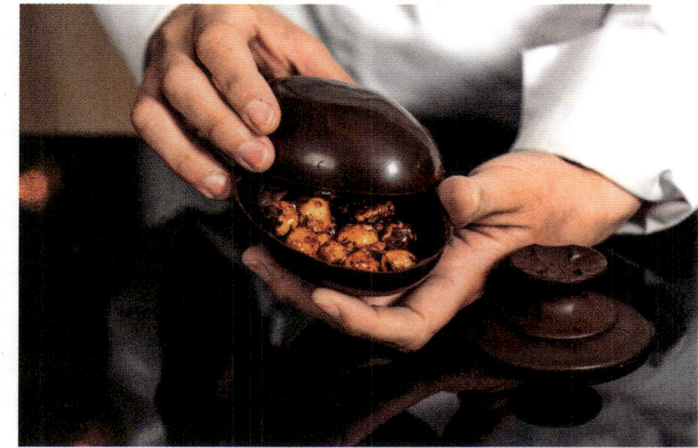

6.

Fill one half of the egg with caramelised hazelnuts and pecans and crispy feuillantine.

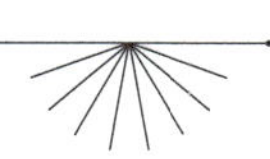

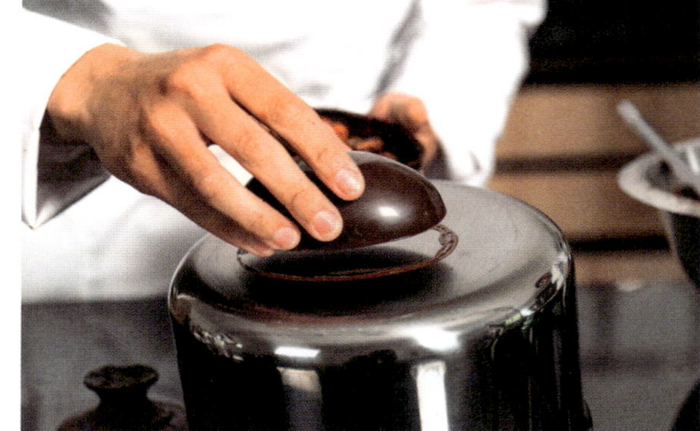

7.

Heat the other side of the egg on the bottom of a hot saucepan...

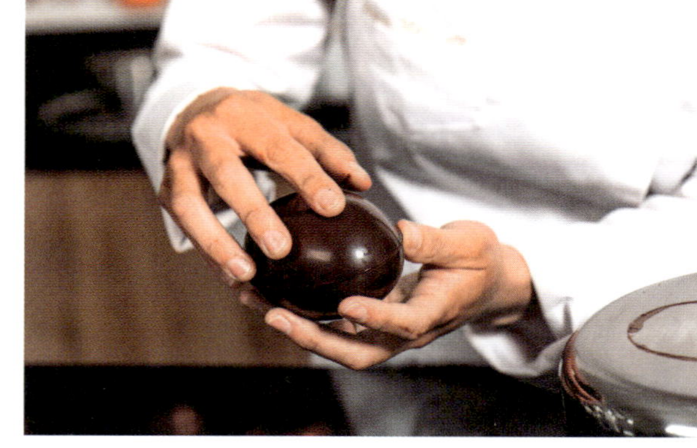

8.

... and attach it to the filled half.

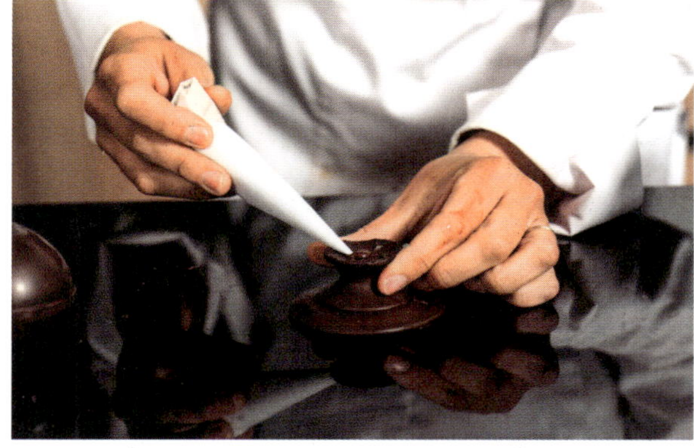

9.

Using a paper piping bag filled with tempered chocolate...

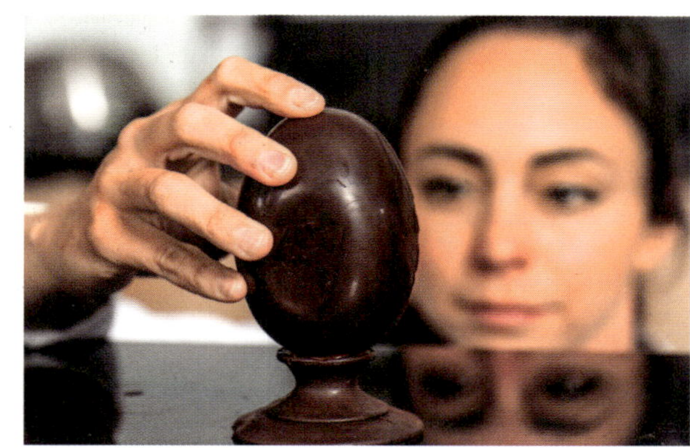

10.

...attach the egg to the base.

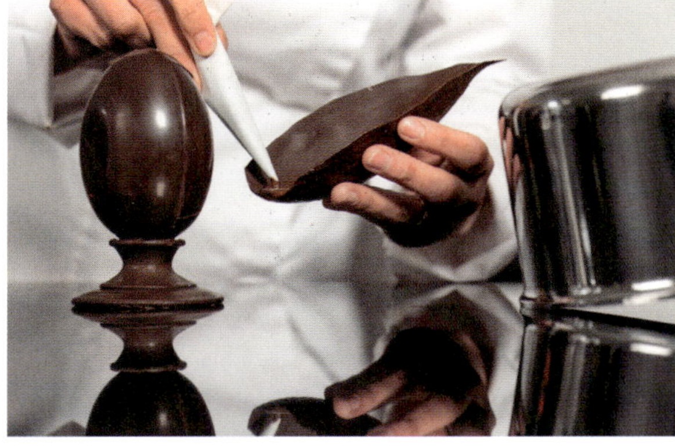

11.

Using a paper piping bag filled with tempered chocolate...

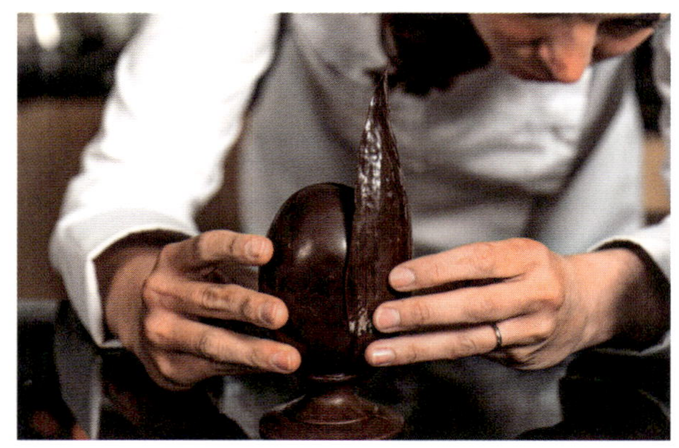

12.

...attach the petals one by one.

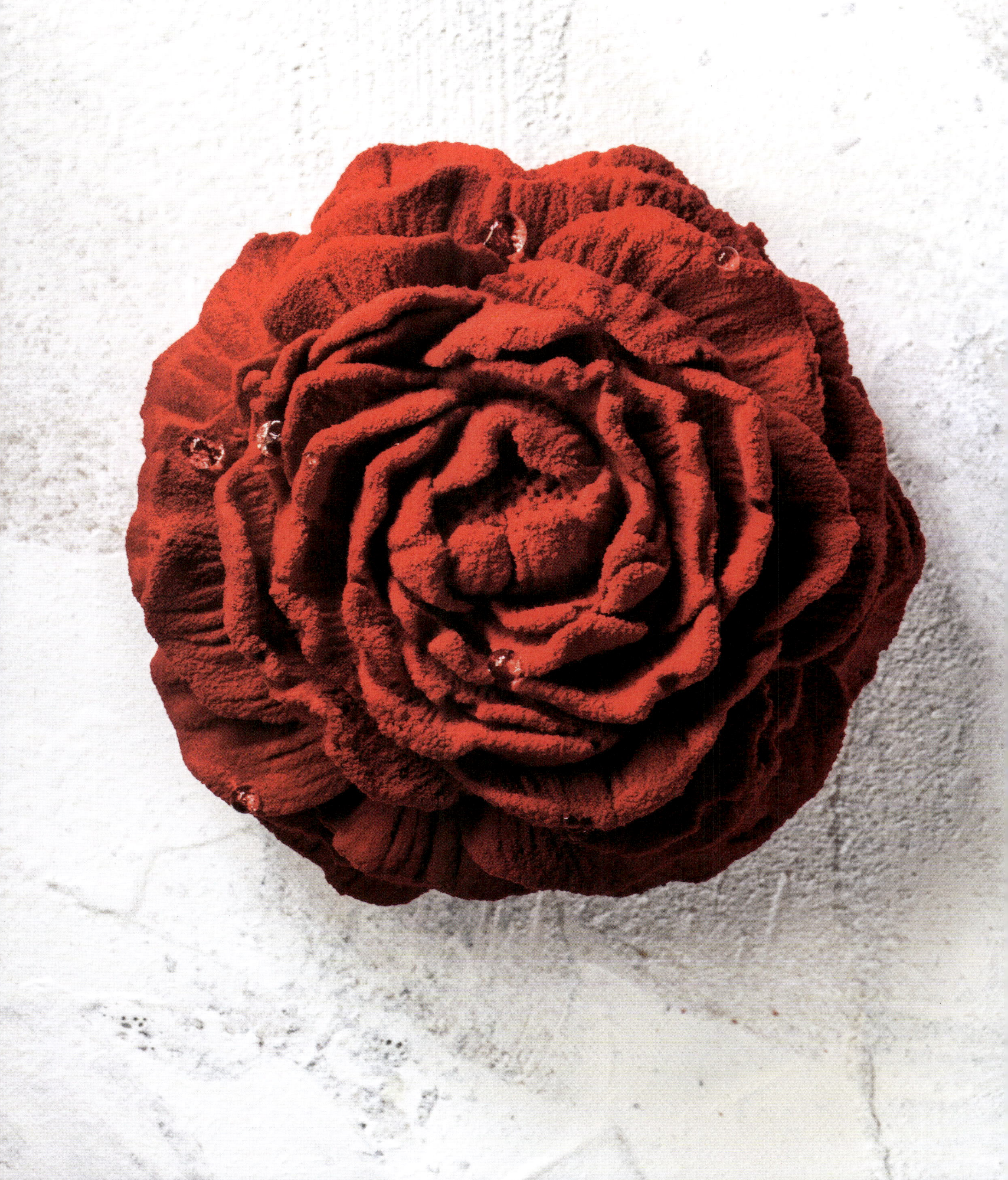

Makes 3 flowers to serve
2 people

Preparation
2 hours 30 minutes

Resting
31 hours

Cooking
3 hours 24 minutes

Saint Valentine's flower

Whipped tea ganache

300 g whipping cream (1)
10 g loose-leaf black tea with
   cornflower petals
1 g salt
20 g gelatine mass
(3 g gelatine powder
   and 17 g cold water)
111 g white chocolate
200 g whipping cream (2)

Lemon sponge

64 g unsalted butter
2 eggs
100 g light brown soft sugar
0.5 g salt
63 g whipping cream
1.5 g grated lemon zest
119 g T55 (plain) flour
3 g baking powder

Blackcurrant syrup

200 g fresh blackcurrants
20 g light brown soft sugar

Jellied blackcurrant syrup

100 g water
50 g blackcurrant syrup
20 g gelatine mass
(3 g gelatine powder
   and 17 g cold water)
30 g lemon juice

Whipped tea ganache The day before, bring the cream (1) to the boil, add the tea, cover and allow to steep for 5 minutes. Strain the infused cream through a conical sieve, then weigh and top up if needed to make up its original weight. Reheat the cream over a low heat. Remove from the heat and add the gelatine mass and salt. Add the mixture to the white chocolate and mix with a spatula. Add the cold cream (2). Using an immersion blender, blend the ganache. Allow to cool for 24 hours at 4°C before use.

Lemon sponge Make beurre noisette with the butter. Mix the eggs with the sugar and salt, then incorporate the cream, zest, flour and baking powder. Finish with the beurre noisette. Mix with a whisk. Put the batter into a baking tray and bake for 7 minutes at 180°C. Using biscuit cutters, cut out two 5-cm-diameter sponge discs and two 4-cm-diameter discs for each insert.

Blackcurrant syrup Freeze the blackcurrants to break down their fibres. Mix the blackcurrants with the sugar in a bowl, cover in cling film and cook in a bain-marie for 3 hours. Strain the syrup through a conical sieve without pressing on the berries.

Jellied blackcurrant syrup In a saucepan, heat the water and blackcurrant syrup over a low heat, then add the gelatine mass and lemon juice. Soak the lemon sponge with the jellied syrup.

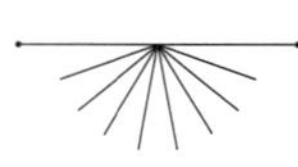

Blackcurrant confit

375 g blackcurrants, puréed

40 g caster sugar

8 g pectin NH

13 g gelatine mass

(2 g gelatine powder

   and 11 g cold water)

9 g lemon juice

10 g blackcurrant syrup

200 g fresh blackcurrants

2 g grated lemon zest

Vanilla shortbread

120 g unsalted butter, at room

   temperature

140 g T55 flour

35 g light brown soft sugar

1 vanilla pod

2 g salt

60 g ground almonds

Red flocking

100 g cocoa butter

80 g white chocolate

2 g natural red fat-soluble food

   colouring

Blackcurrant confit In a saucepan, heat the puréed blackcurrants over a low heat to 40°C. Mix the sugar with the pectin and stir into the warm purée. Bring to the boil for 1 minute, then add the gelatine mass, blackcurrant syrup and lemon juice, followed by the zest. Blend and allow to cool to 4°C. Blend again. Spread the confit over the sponge discs. Scatter over with fresh blackcurrants.

Vanilla shortbread Mix the butter with the flour, sugar, scraped-out vanilla seeds and salt, then incorporate the ground almonds. Roll out the pastry between two baking mats to a 2.5-mm thickness. Allow to firm up in the fridge, then cut out 5-cm-diameter discs. Place the shortbread discs on a baking mat and bake at 160°C for 17 minutes.

Melt the chocolate and cocoa butter, dissolve the food colouring and use a spray gun to spray the flocking over the dessert after coming out of the freezer.

Assembly

Spread the blackcurrant confit over the syrup-soaked lemon sponge discs and scatter over with fresh blackcurrants. To make the insert, stack both 4-cm-diameter sponge discs on top of both 5-cm-diameter ones. Place in the freezer at -20°C to harden.

In a stand mixer fitted with a wire whisk, whip the ganache.

Pipe the whipped ganache into a flower mould and press it down well using a small angled palette knife to prevent any air bubbles forming inside.

Place the sponge insert in the centre, cover with whipped ganache and smooth the surface. Freeze at -20°C for 3 hours.

Carefully remove the flower from the mould. Spray the flower and place it on a vanilla shortbread disc. Refrigerate at 4°C for 4 hours before serving.

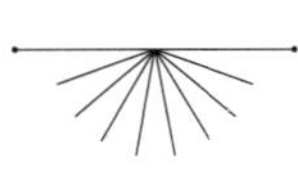

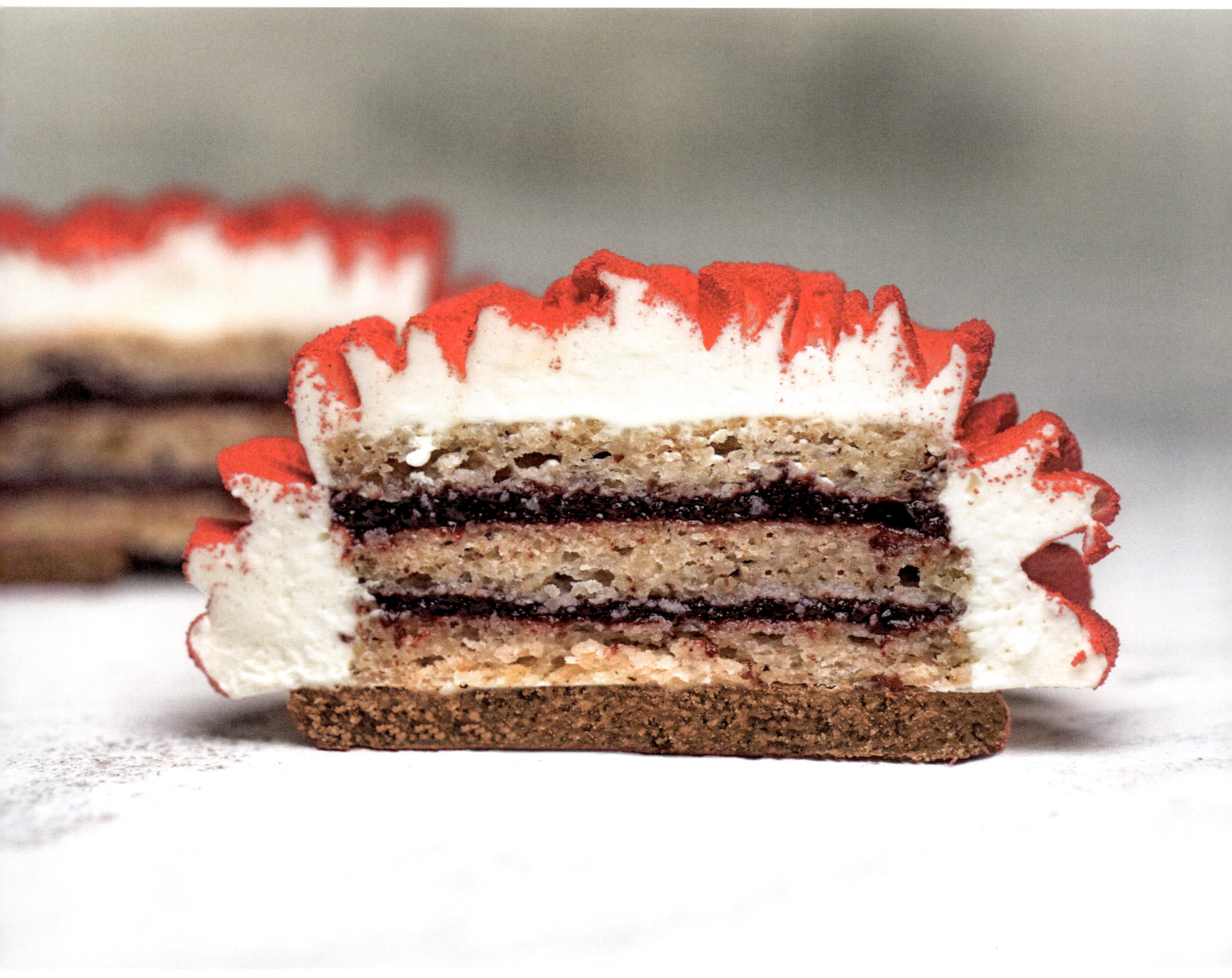

Serves 2	Preparation 50 minutes	Cooking 35 minutes	Resting At least 2 hours

You + Me

Chocolate shortbread

110 g unsalted butter, softened

125 g light brown soft sugar

130 g T80 (stoneground white
    flour)

40 g cocoa powder

2 g fleur de sel

**Reconstituted chocolate
shortbread**

85 g dark chocolate
    couverture (72% cocoa)

200 g chocolate shortbread

55 g feuillantine

1 g fleur de sel

Hazelnut ganache (insert)

125 g full-fat milk

75 g whipping cream

75 g hazelnut paste

75 g gianduja milk chocolate

0.5 g salt

7 g Kalios thyme-infused olive oil

Lemon jelly (insert)

90 g lemon juice

25 g lime juice

50 g light brown soft sugar

1 g pectin

12 g gelatine mass

(2 g gelatine powder
    and 10 g cold water)

Chocolate shortbread Rub the butter into the sugar, flour, cocoa and fleur de sel to form a dough, then break it up into crumbs. Bake the shortbread at 150°C for 35 minutes, then crumble it again.

Reconstituted chocolate shortbread Melt the chocolate in a bain-marie and gently mix in the cooked chocolate shortbread, feuillantine and fleur de sel. Using the home-made insert moulds, shape 30 g of reconstituted shortbread to fit each one (1).

Hazelnut ganache Bring the milk and cream to the boil and add the mixture a little at a time to the hazelnut paste, gianduja, salt and oil. Add 25 g of the ganache to each insert mould (to make your own moulds, see p. 214).

Lemon jelly Squeeze lemons and limes and measure out the juice. Mix together the sugar and pectin. In a saucepan, bring the juice to the boil. Add the sugar and pectin mixture and boil for 2 minutes, stirring constantly. Check the consistency. Add the gelatine mass and stir to dissolve. Transfer the mixture to a tray and cool quickly. Once cooled, blend the jelly, then pour 15 g over the hazelnut ganache in the moulds. Allow to set in the freezer.

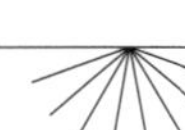

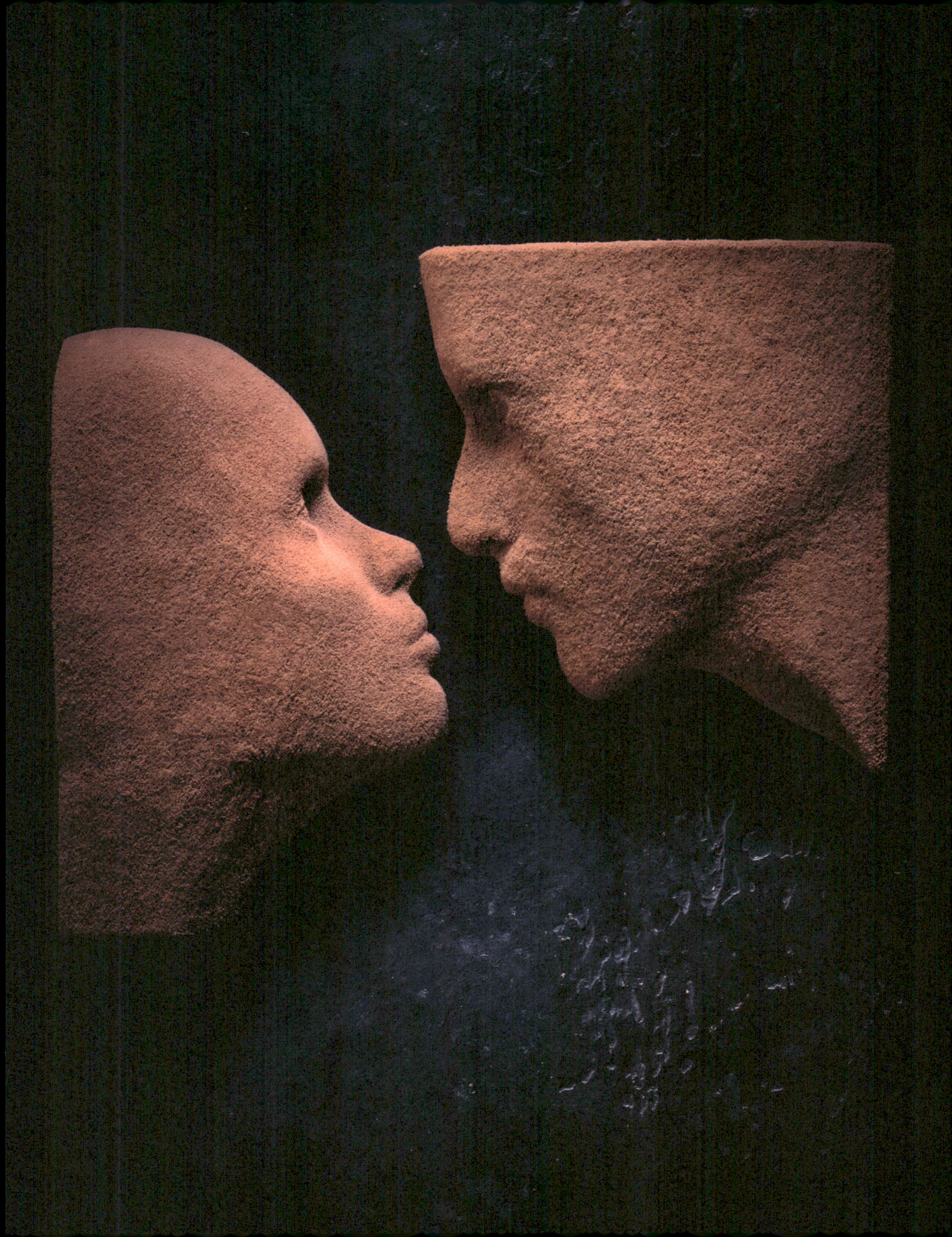

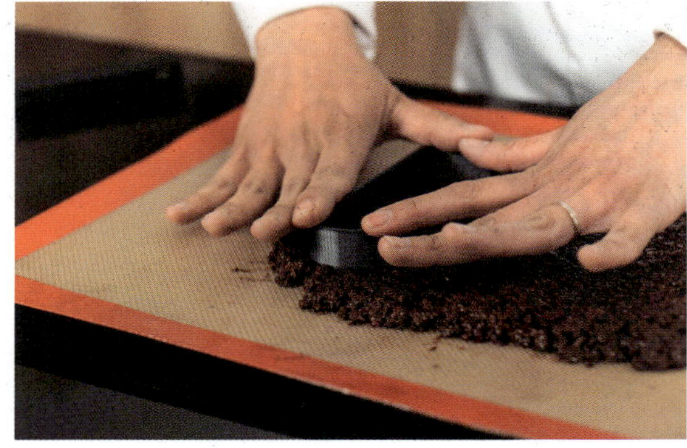

Make the reconstituted chocolate shortbread and press 30 g in each insert mould to shape.

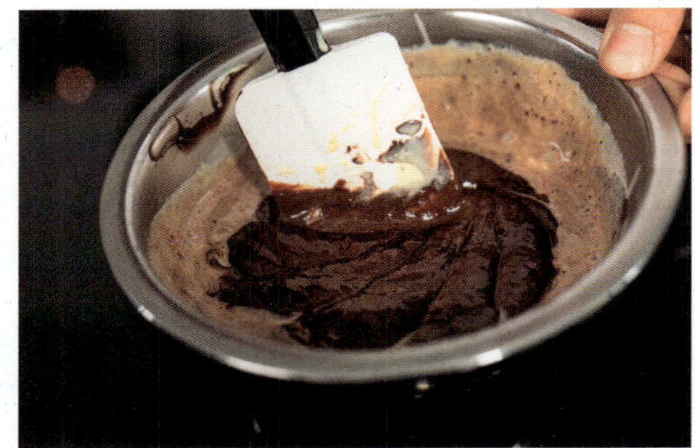

To make the dark chocolate mousse, make a crème anglaise and mix it into the melted chocolate.

Dark chocolate mousse

33 g full-fat milk

33 g whipping cream

10 g egg yolk

60 g dark chocolate couverture

165 g whipped cream

4 g Kalios thyme-infused olive oil

Black flocking

125 g cocoa butter

87 g dark chocolate (72% cocoa)

Dark chocolate mousse In a saucepan, bring the milk and cream to the boil over a low heat. Add the mixture to the egg yolk and mix. Then return the mixture to another saucepan. Cook until the temperature reaches 82°C and the crème anglaise is thick enough to coat a spoon. Then mix it into the previously melted chocolate (2). Blend in the thyme-infused oil until smooth (3). Once the mixture has cooled to 35°C, fold in the whipped cream (4). Use immediately (5).

Black flocking Melt the two ingredients together in a bain-marie and blend.

Assembly

Make the hazelnut ganache and lemon confit insert. Freeze.

Make the reconstituted chocolate shortbread and press into the insert moulds.

Make the mousse, transfer to a piping bag and partially fill the face moulds (6). Lightly press the inserts into the mousse and add a little mousse (7), then place the reconstituted chocolate shortbread on top of the inserts. Smooth the surface (8).

Allow everything to harden in the freezer.

Remove the faces from the moulds and spray with the hot flocking mixture.

Refrigerate at 4°C for at least 2 hours before serving.

'You can also make this entremets using 8-cm-diameter and 2.5-cm-deep tart rings.'

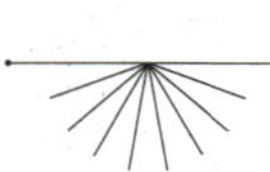

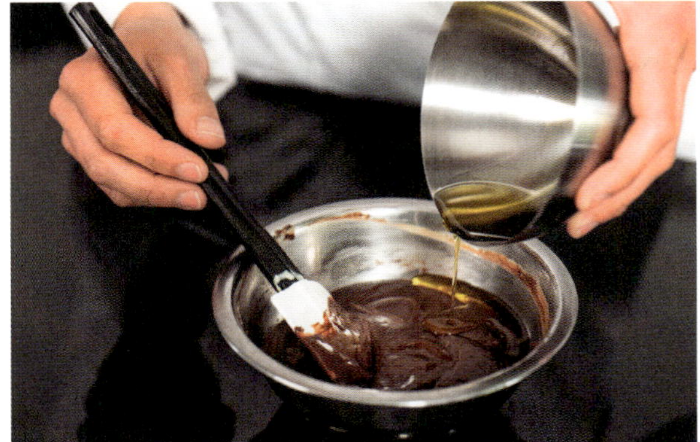

3.

Blend with the thyme-infused oil until smooth.

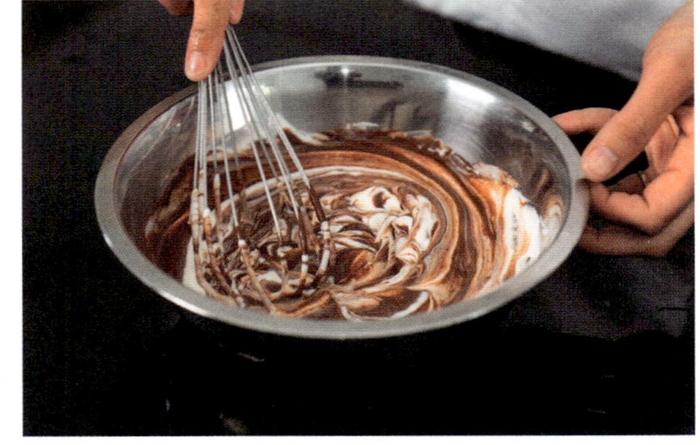

4.

When the mixture cools to 35°C, fold in the whipped cream.

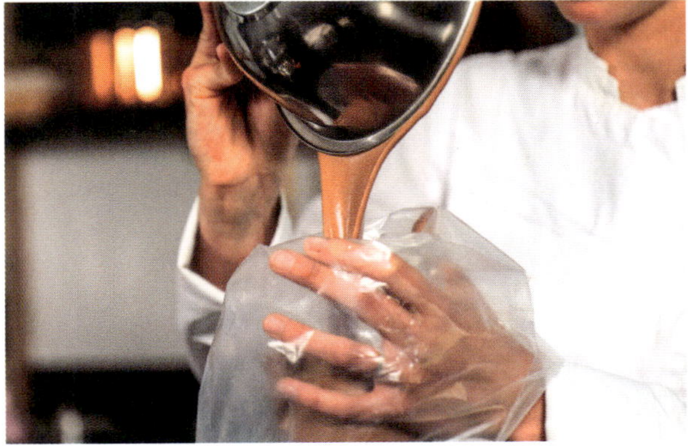

5.

Use immediately.

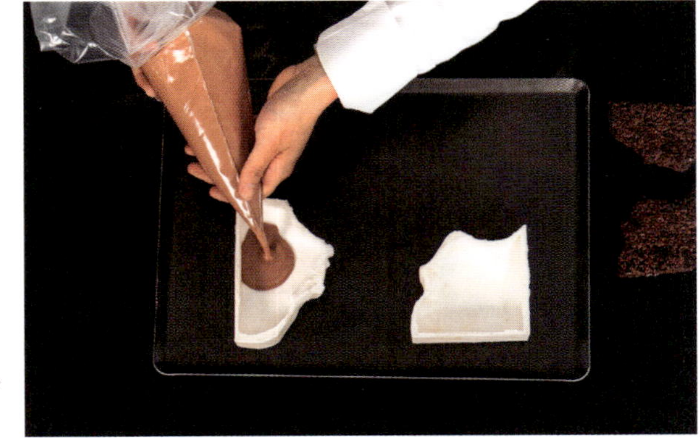

6.

To assemble, pipe mousse into the face moulds.

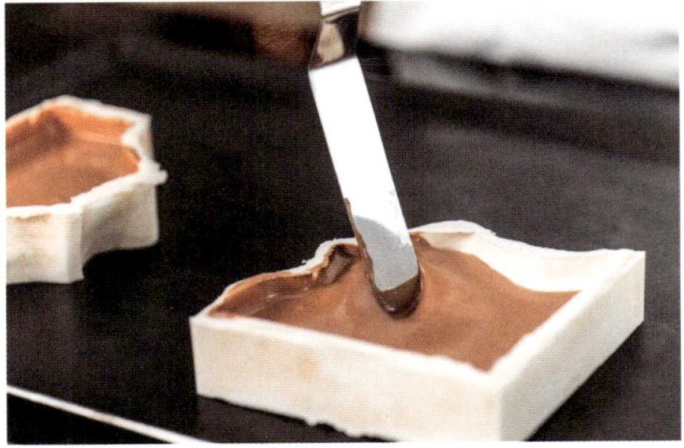

7.

Lightly press in the hazelnut ganache and lemon jelly insert and cover with a little mousse.

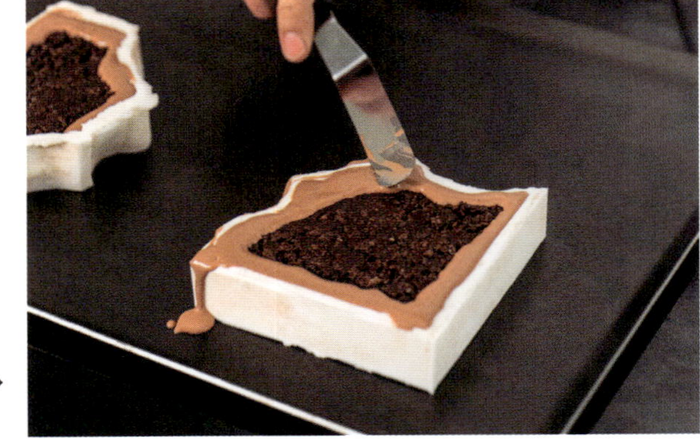

8.

Place the reconstituted chocolate shortbread on top and smooth the surface.

Serves 12

Preparation
6 hours

Resting
10 minutes

Cooking
1 hour 30 minutes

Croquembouche wedding cake

Pastry cream
500 g full-fat milk
300 g whipping cream
2 vanilla pods
4 eggs
80 g light brown soft sugar
75 g custard powder
23 g T55 (plain) flour
28 g unsalted butter

Nougatine
660 g chopped almonds
750 g glucose syrup
1110 g fondant icing
90 g unsalted butter

Pastry cream In a saucepan, bring the milk and cream to the boil, add the split vanilla pods and scraped-out seeds. Cover and allow to steep for 10 minutes. Beat the eggs with the sugar until thick and pale, then add the cream and flour and mix well. Strain the cream and milk mixture through a conical sieve, return to the saucepan and bring back to the boil. Stir half the hot milk and cream mixture into the blanched eggs, then return everything to the saucepan, bring to the boil and cook for 3 minutes over a low heat, mixing constantly with a whisk. Remove from the heat and add the butter. Transfer the pastry cream to a deep baking tray lined with cling film and cool quickly. When the pastry cream is very cold, loosen it with a whisk.

Nougatine Preheat the oven to 150°C. Roast the chopped almonds in the oven for about 50 minutes at 140°C, until golden brown. In a saucepan, cook the fondant icing with the glucose to a caramel colour, then stir in the hot, chopped roasted almonds. Mix, then add the butter. Mix until combined. Allow the nougatine to cool slightly before working with it. Using a rolling pin, spread the mixture in a thin and even layer over a baking mat. Cut out 4 nougatine discs: one 18 cm in diameter, one 16 cm in diameter and two 12 cm in diameter. Then cut out a series of 2.5-cm-diameter discs. Using a large kitchen knife, cut out large strips of nougatine, then roll them around entremets rings to make rings for assembling the cake.

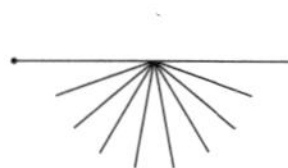

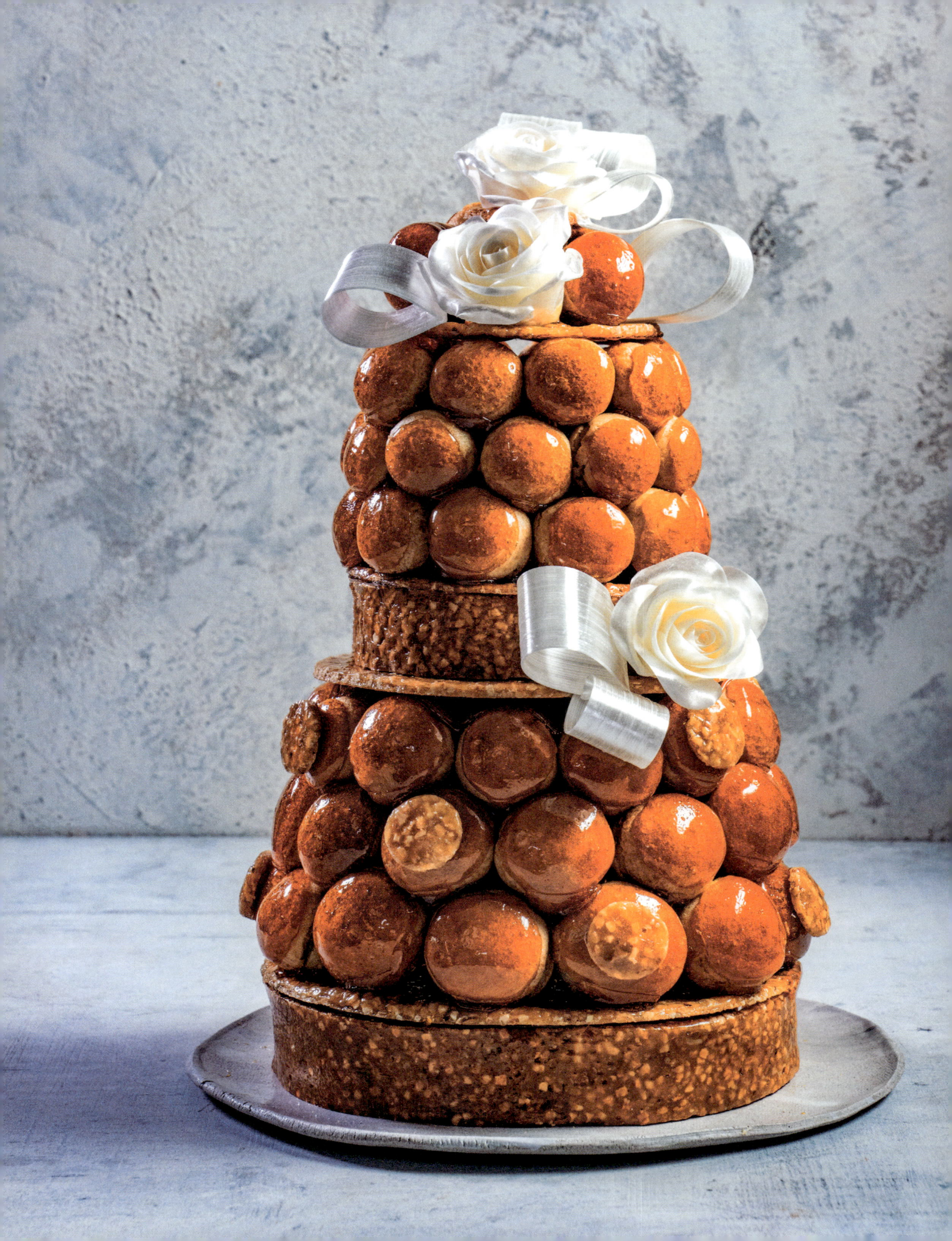

Choux buns
125 g milk
125 g water
5 g salt
2.5 g caster sugar
110 g unsalted butter
140 g T55 flour
225 g eggs

Caramel
90 g water
450 g caster sugar
110 g glucose

Pulled sugar
500 g caster sugar
174 g water
25 g glucose syrup
1 g cream of tartar

Choux buns Preheat the oven to 180°C.

Put the milk, water, salt, sugar and butter into a saucepan and bring to the boil. Then add all the flour in one go, mix briskly and allow the pastry to dry out for about 2 minutes. Using a spatula, incorporate the eggs a little at a time.

Transfer the pastry to a piping bag fitted with a 10-mm plain nozzle and pipe the choux buns directly onto a baking tray. Bake at 180°C for about 35 minutes. Take care not to open the oven during this time as the choux buns could collapse and not rise again.

Using a pastry bag fitted with a 6-mm-diameter nozzle, pipe the choux buns full of pastry cream through the bottom.

Caramel In a saucepan, cook all the ingredients over a medium heat to a nice caramel colour. Dip the profiteroles one at a time into the caramel. After glazing, use the caramel as a glue to assemble the profiteroles on the nougatine rings and discs.

Pulled sugar In a saucepan, cook all the ingredients over high heat until the temperature reaches 170°C. Transfer the sugar mass to a baking mat and allow to cool until it has the texture of a malleable paste. Wearing gloves to avoid burns, work the sugar until it has a satin gloss (1) by pulling and folding it over as it gradually cools. Make the ribbons (2). Make sure to keep the sugar at the ideal temperature for working. Make 4 small sugar mass sausages and join them together side by side. Pull them to twice their length, then fold them over and repeat the operation 4 times, stretching them further each time. Allow the pulled sugar to cool and then cut into strips. Lightly reheat them to give them shape. Make the roses (3). Shape the centre of the rose, followed by the petals, and gradually attach the petals (4). Set aside the sugar decorations in a dry place until ready to use.

Assembly
Make the nougatine. Make the pulled sugar decorations.

Make the profiteroles by piping the choux buns full of pastry cream and glaze them by dipping in caramel (5). Position the nougatine base on the serving plate. Dip each profiterole in caramel before attaching it to the nougatine and each other (6). After arranging the profiteroles in a number of rows, glue on a nougatine disc with caramel, then top with a ring and another disc. Assemble a few more rows of profiteroles, then finish with a nougatine disc and a few more profiteroles (7).

Decorate the cake by gluing a few small nougatine discs onto some of the profiteroles, then carefully position and attach the pulled sugar decorations with melted sugar or caramel (8).

Place the cake in the fridge at 4°C. However, take care not to assemble the cake too early because the moisture in the fridge will cause the caramel to melt.

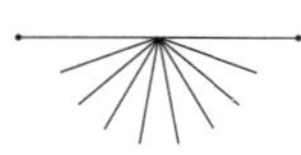

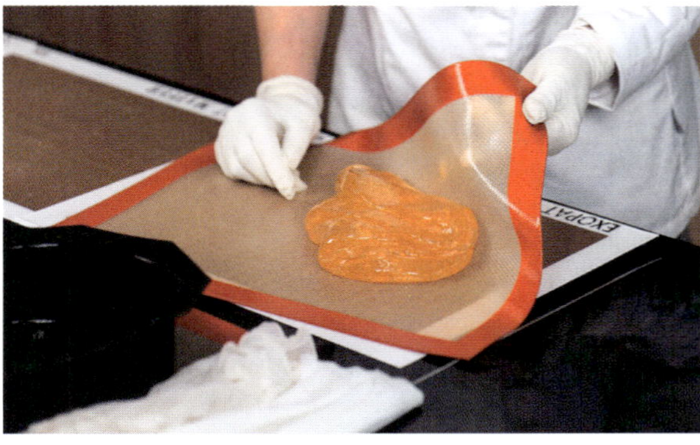

1.

Make the pulled sugar. Allow it to cool on a baking mat until it has the texture of malleable dough, then work the sugar until it has a satin gloss by pulling and folding it over as it gradually cools.

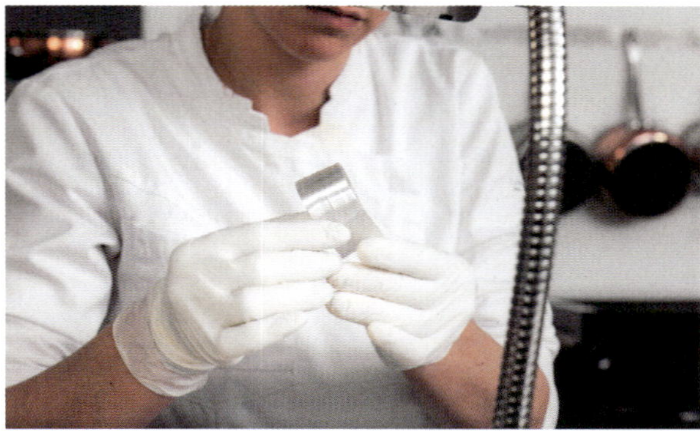

2.

Make the ribbons.

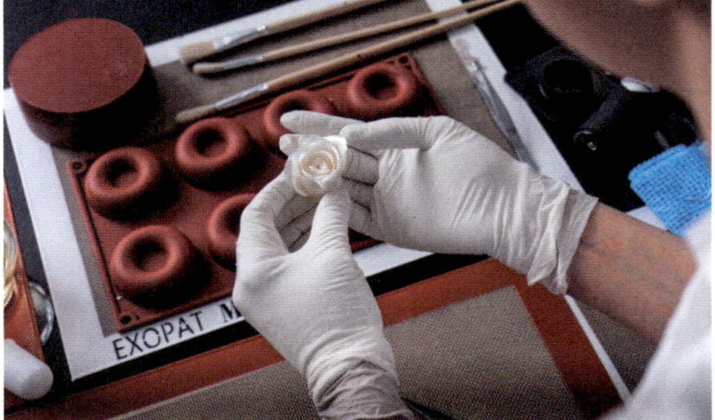

3.

Make roses.

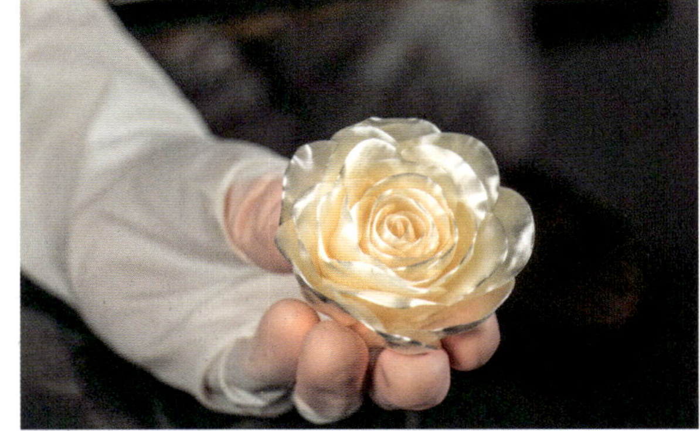

4.

Shape the centre of the rose, followed by the petals, and gradually attach the petals.

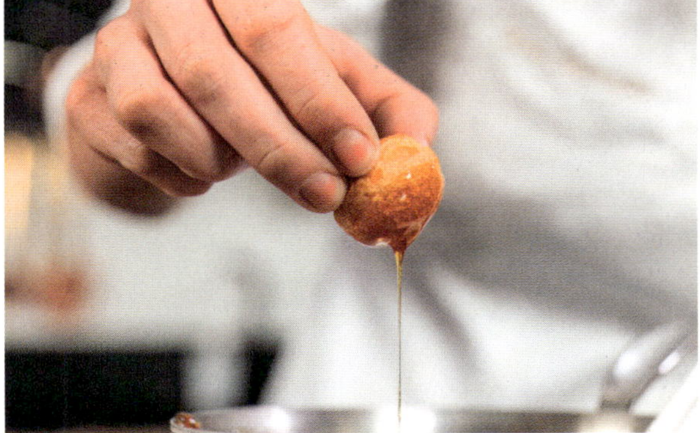

5.

Make the choux buns, pipe them full of pastry cream and glaze the profiteroles by dipping in caramel.

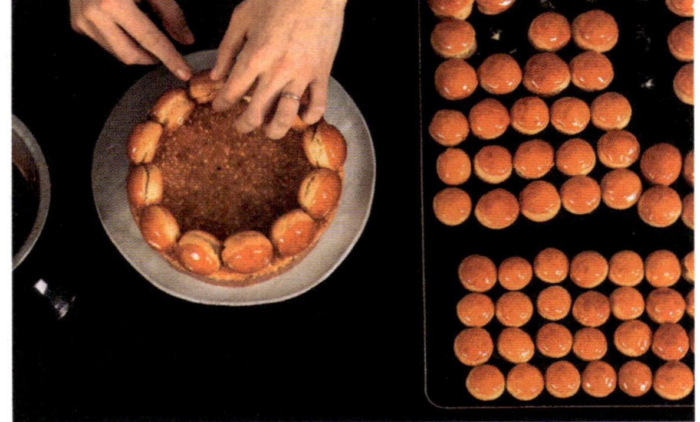

6.

To assemble, dip the profiteroles one at a time in the caramel and attach them to the nougatine base.

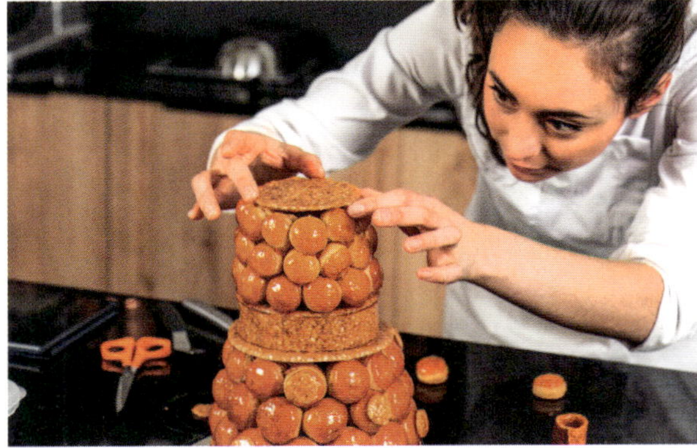

7.

After arranging the profiteroles in a number of rows, glue on a nougatine disc with caramel, then top with a ring and another disc. Add a few more rows of profiteroles before finishing with a nougatine disc and a few more profiteroles.

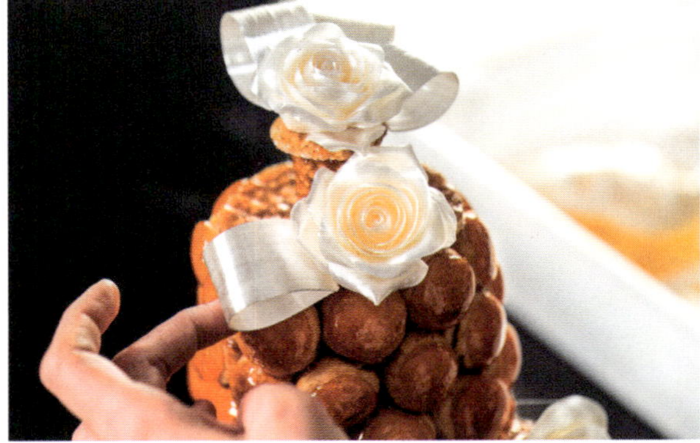

8.

Decorate by gluing a few small nougatine discs onto some of the profiteroles, then carefully attach the pulled sugar decorations.

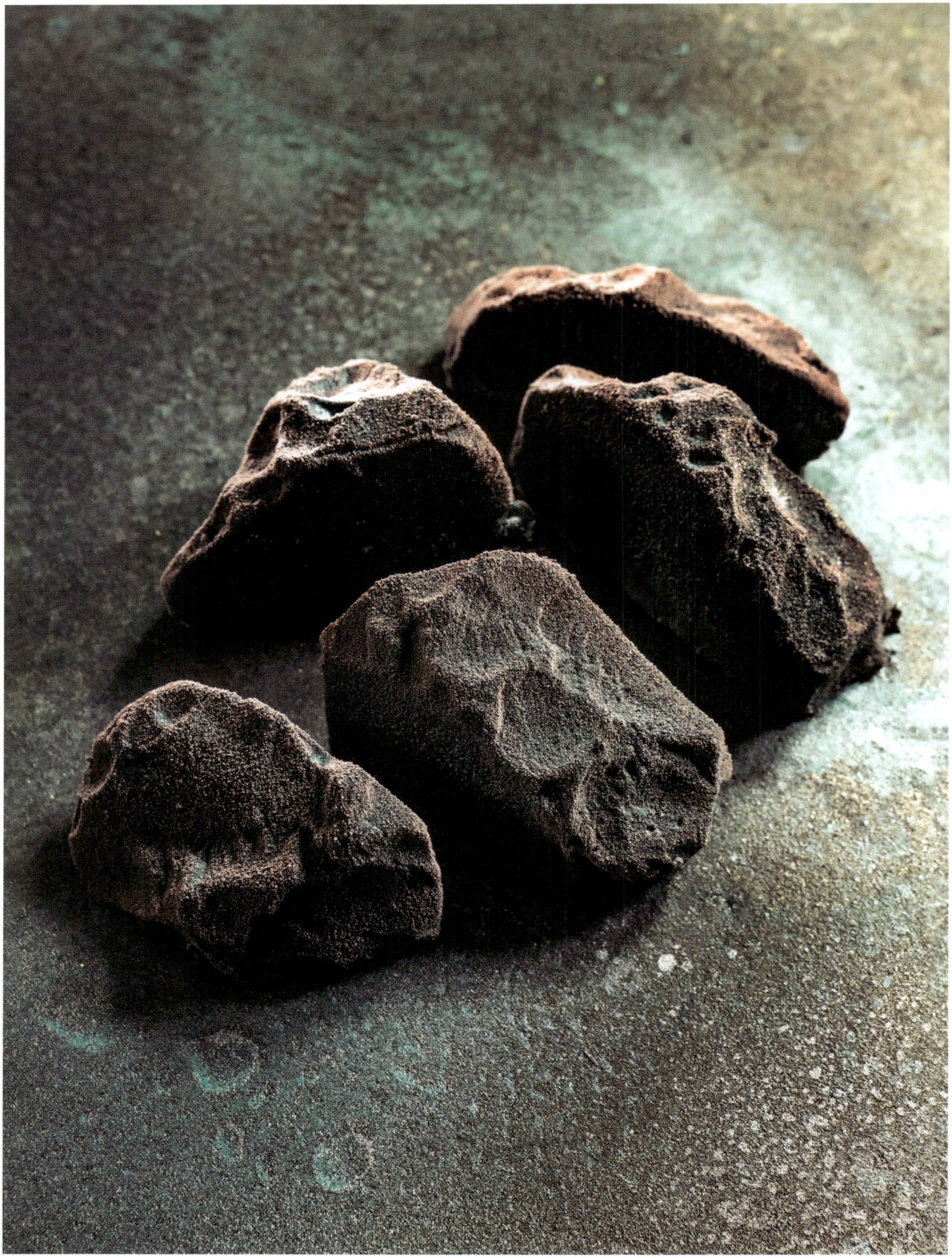

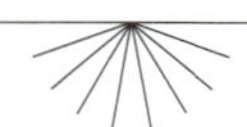

Serves 6

Preparation	Resting	Cooking
2 hours	12 hours 10 minutes	1 hour 35 minutes

Rocks

Whipped coffee ganache

10 g coffee beans
300 g whipping cream (1)
5 g instant coffee
1 g salt
15 g gelatine mass
(2 g gelatine powder
   and 13 g cold water)
150 g gianduja milk chocolate
250 g whipping cream (2)

Hazelnut and cocoa nib praline

125 g hazelnuts
62 g caster sugar
20 g water
35 g grape seed oil
2.5 g fleur de sel
50 g cocoa nibs

Spiced shortbread

77 g unsalted butter, softened
77 g muscovado sugar
1 g salt
1 g ground nutmeg
1 g tonka bean
30 g egg
110 g T55 (plain) flour
2.5 g baking powder

Whipped coffee ganache Crush the coffee beans. Put the cream and crushed coffee beans into a saucepan and bring to the boil, then cover and allow to steep for 10 minutes. Strain the cream through a conical sieve, then weigh and top up if needed to make up its original weight. Add the instant coffee and salt. Reheat the mixture, add the gelatine mass and add it a little at a time to the chopped gianduja, mixing until smooth and thick. Add the remaining cold liquid cream (2) and blend until smooth. Refrigerate at 4°C for 12 hours.

Hazelnut and cocoa nib praline Roast the hazelnuts at 140°C for 40 minutes. In a saucepan, cook the sugar and water to a caramel over a low heat and transfer to a baking mat. Put the hazelnuts, cooled caramel and oil into a blender and blend to a smooth liquid, then add the fleur de sel and cocoa nibs, blend for a further 30 seconds and transfer to a container.

Spiced shortbread Rub the butter into the sugar and add the salt, nutmeg and tonka bean. Incorporate the egg, followed by the flour and baking powder. Crumble the shortbread onto a baking mat and bake at 150°C for 35 minutes. Using a knife, chop the shortbread into small clumps (1).

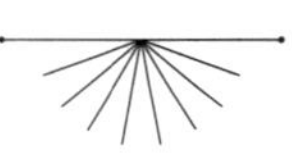

Reconstituted spiced shortbread
85 g almonds
135 g white chocolate
250 g spiced shortbread
85 g feuillantine
2.5 g fleur de sel

Blue-black flocking
80 g cocoa butter
80 g white chocolate
2 g blue fat-soluble food
  colouring
1 g charcoal food colouring

Gold coating
100 g kirsch
10 g edible gold powder

Reconstituted spiced shortbread Roast the almonds for 20 minutes at 150°C and then crush them.

Blue-black flocking Melt the white chocolate in a bain-marie. Gently fold the spiced shortbread, crushed almonds, feuillantine and fleur de sel into the melted white chocolate (2–3).

Melt the cocoa butter and white chocolate in a bain-marie. Add the food colourings and blend to combine.

Gold coating Mix the two ingredients together.

Assembly
Using a whisk, whip the ganache until soft (4).

To make the rocks, pipe some ganache into the bottom of the home-made silicone moulds (see p. 214). Using a small palette knife, spread the ganache all over the inside of each mould (5).

Pipe praline into the centre of the rock (6) and cover it with reconstituted shortbread, then fill the mould to the top with ganache and smooth the surface (7).

Allow everything to harden in the freezer. Make the blue-black flocking.

Remove the rocks from the moulds and transfer to a tray, then spray on the flocking flock. Apply the gold coating to create an ombré effect.

'You can make this dessert using individual silicone entremets moulds in any shape you like, although they should be deep enough to easily accommodate the reconstituted shortbread and praline centre. The crunch of the shortbread and praline is what makes this dessert so deliciously indulgent.'

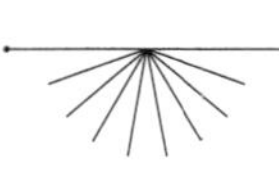

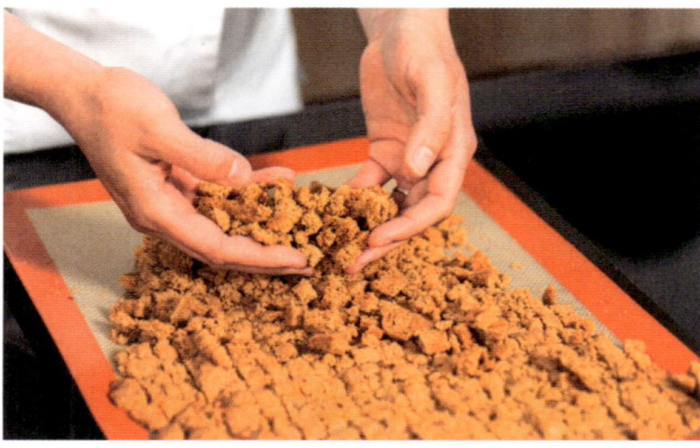

1.

Make the spiced shortbread. Chop the shortbread with a knife into small clumps.

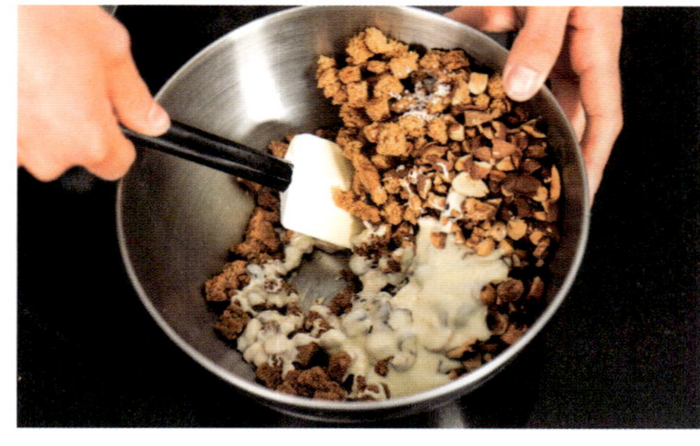

2.

To make the reconstituted shortbread, gently fold the spiced shortbread, chopped almonds, feuillantine and fleur de sel into the melted white chocolate.

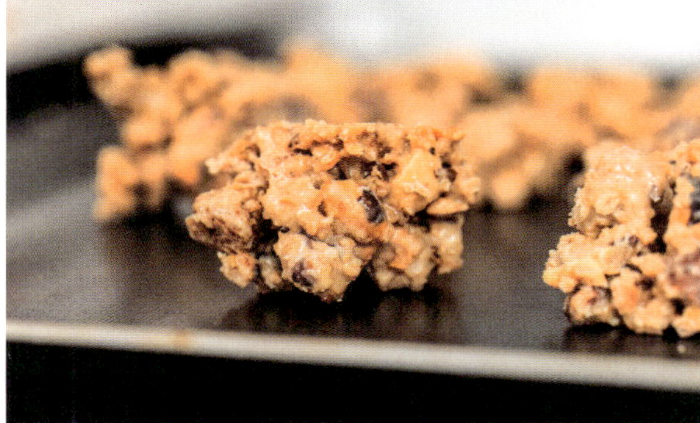

3.

The finished reconstituted shortbread.

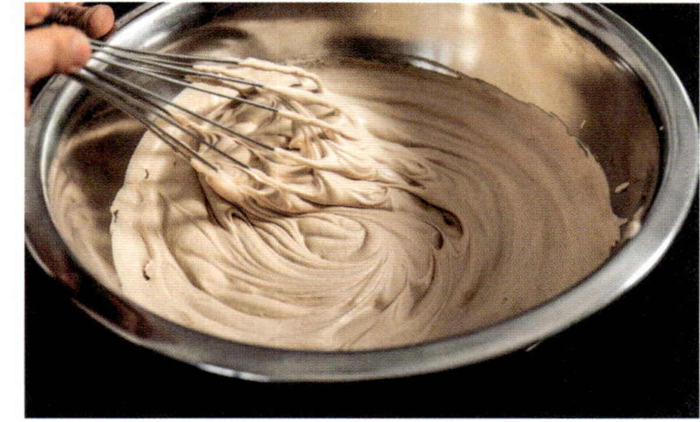

4.

Using a whisk, whip the ganache until soft.

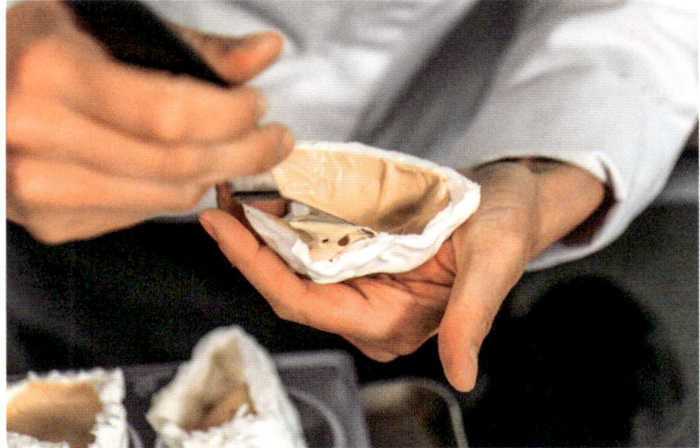

5.

To assemble the rocks, pipe some ganache into the bottom of the silicone moulds. Using a small palette knife, spread the ganache all over the inside of each mould.

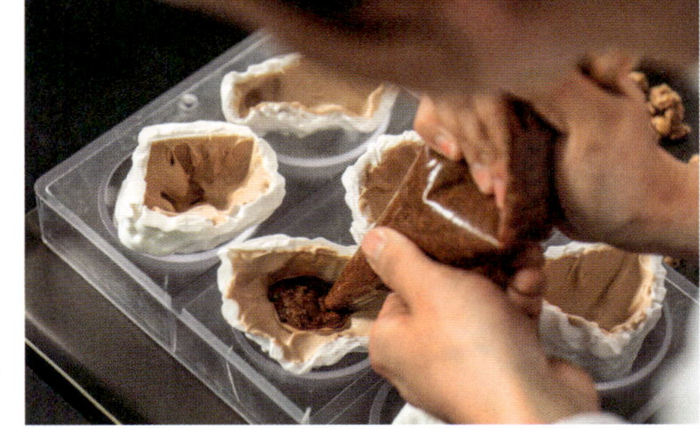

6.

Pipe praline into the centre of the rock.

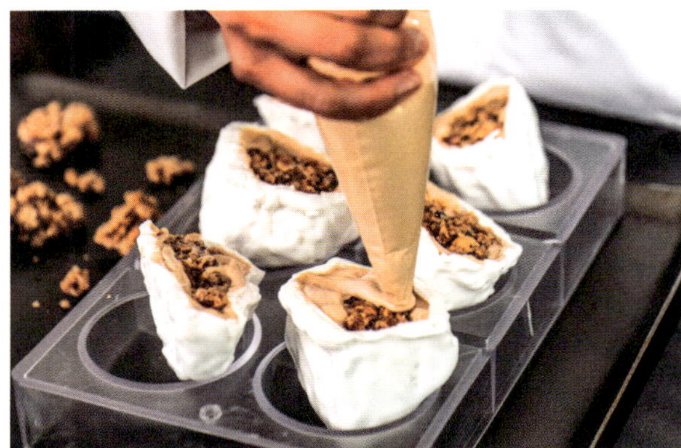

7.

Cover with reconstituted shortbread, then fill to the top with ganache and smooth the surface.

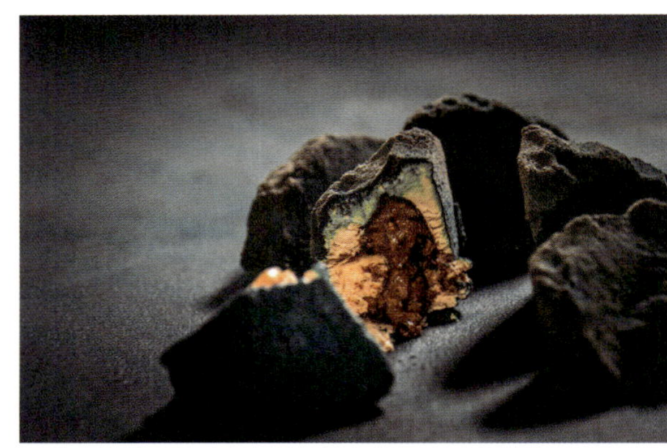

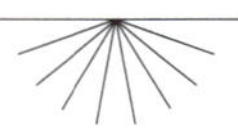

Makes 2 lace balls to share

Preparation
4 hours

Cooking
5 hours

Lace ball

Meringue lace
5 g vegetable oil
100 g icing sugar
100 g egg whites
100 g caster sugar

Rice crumble
75 g unsalted butter, at room
  temperature
75 g light brown soft sugar
50 g cornflour
40 g rice flour
40 g ground almonds
1 g fleur de sel

Crispy puffed rice
30 g almonds
100 g white chocolate
20 g puffed rice
2 g fleur de sel
150 g rice crumble

Fir honey madeleine sponge
100 g eggs
35 g muscovado sugar
60 g fir honey
100 g rice flour
4 g baking powder
1 g salt
90 g unsalted butter, melted

Meringue lace Grease two 7-cm-diameter stainless steel hemisphere moulds by brushing with vegetable oil and line with cling film. Sift the icing sugar. Beat the egg whites to soft peaks, then gradually add the caster sugar while beating to stiff peaks. Gently fold in the icing sugar. Using the smallest plain piping nozzle possible, pipe a pretty lace pattern inside the moulds (1). Pipe a circle at the bottom of one of the moulds to serve as a base for assembling the dessert.

Dry out the meringue in the oven at 60°C for 4 hours. Then very carefully remove the lace shells from the moulds. Set them aside in an airtight container with a moisture absorber until ready to use.

Rice crumble By hand or in a stand mixer fitted with a paddle attachment, cream the butter with the sugar, then incorporate the remaining ingredients.

Crumble the pastry onto a baking mat and bake at 170°C for 15 minutes. Then crumble it again while still hot.

Crispy puffed rice Roast the almonds in the oven at 140°C for 40 minutes, then coarsely chop.

Melt the white chocolate in a bain-marie. Mix all the ingredients together. Partially fill one of two 5-cm-diameter hemisphere moulds with the crispy puffed rice mixture. Allow to harden in the freezer.

Fir honey madeleine sponge Using an immersion blender, whisk the eggs with the sugar. Soften the honey in the microwave and add it to the egg mixture, then blend in the flour, baking powder and salt and finish with the melted butter. Spread the batter to a 1-cm thickness in a baking tray lined with a baking mat.

Bake at 180°C for 7 minutes.

Allow to cool on to a rack.

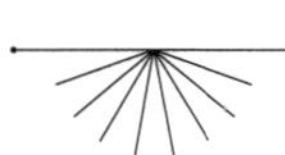

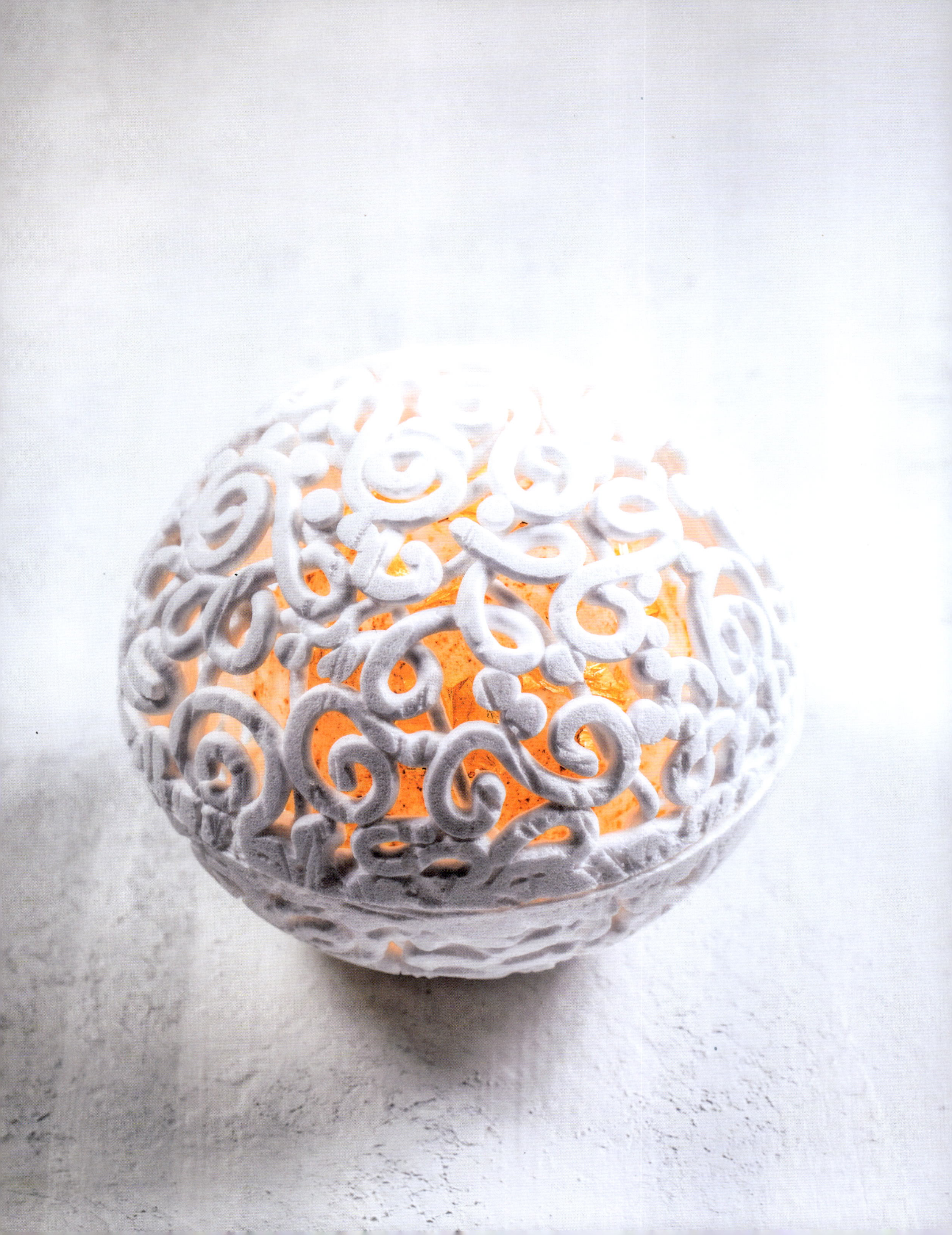

Honey bavarois

99 g milk

37 g fir honey

30 g egg yolks

18 g gelatine mass

(3 g gelatine powder

   and 15 g cold water)

120 g soft-whipped cream

Lemon jelly

90 g lemon juice

25 g lime juice

50 g light brown soft sugar

1 g pectin 325NH95

12 g gelatine mass

(2 g gelatine powder

   and 10 g cold water)

For decoration

150 g whipping cream

8 g icing sugar

1 sheet edible gold leaf

2 g edible gold glitter

Honey bavarois Make a crème anglaise with the milk, honey and egg yolks. Mix with the gelatine mass until smooth. Set aside in a large bowl in the fridge. Loosen the bavarois, using an immersion blender if necessary.

Fold in the soft-whipped cream.

Lemon jelly Squeeze the lemons and limes and measure out the juice. Mix together the sugar and pectin. In a saucepan, bring the juice to the boil. Add the sugar and pectin mixture and boil for 2 minutes, stirring constantly. Add the gelatine mass and stir to dissolve. Transfer the mixture to a tray and cool quickly. Once cooled, blend the jelly.

Assembly

Make the meringue lace and dry it out.

Make the rice crumble and then the crispy puffed rice. Partially fill one of two greased 5-cm-diameter hemisphere moulds with the crispy puffed rice (2). Spread it up the sides of the mould and make a well in the centre. Allow to harden in the freezer. Bake the sponge and cut out 2 discs, one with a diameter of 4 cm and the other of 3 cm.

Make the lemon jelly. Make the bavaroise.

Pipe a large dot of bavarois in the centre of the crispy puffed rice, then add 20 g of lemon jelly. Cover with one of the sponge discs (3). Pipe bavarois to the top of the mould and smooth around the disc (4).

Pipe a large dot of bavarois in the other mould and spread up the sides to cover.

Add 20 g of lemon jelly, cover with bavarois and top with a sponge disc (5). Smooth around the disc with bavarois, close the moulds to make a sphere and allow to harden in the freezer (6).

To unmould the sphere, apply a little heat to the mould.

Make the Chantilly cream by whipping the cream with the icing sugar. Cover the sphere with the cream, then apply gold glitter and scatter over with pieces of gold leaf.

Remove the meringue lace from the moulds. Position the side with the circular base on a plate and glue it in place with a small dot of glucose or honey.

Cut out a small sponge disc, place it at the bottom and glue the sphere onto it. Place the top half of the lace ball over the bottom and glue it closed with a small dot of glucose.

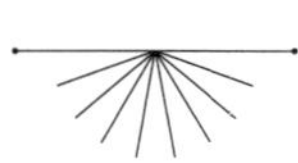

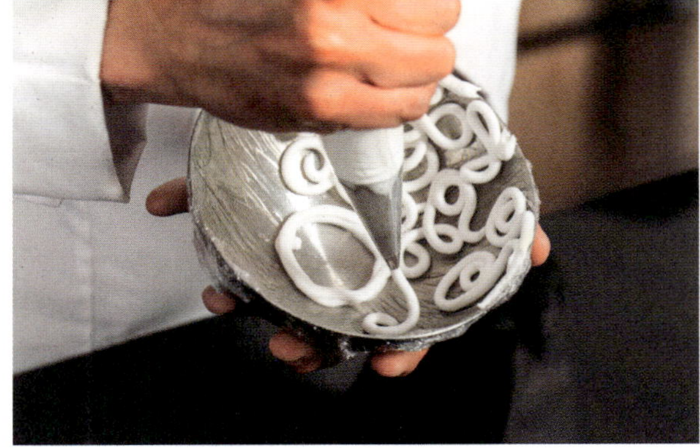

1. *Make the lace meringue: using the smallest plain piping nozzle possible, pipe a pretty lace pattern inside greased 7-cm-diameter hemisphere moulds lined with cling film.*

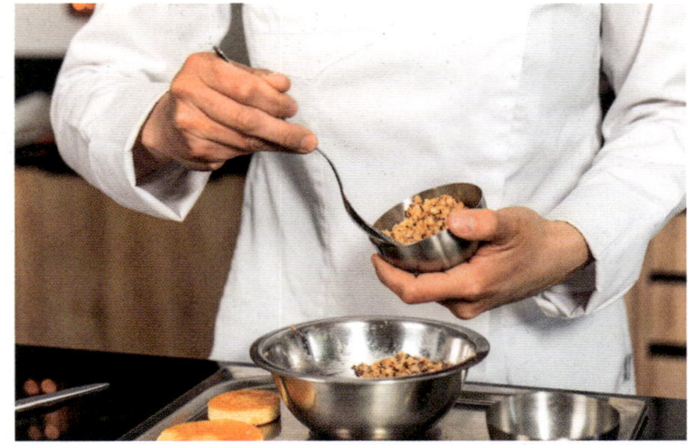

2. *Make the crispy puffed rice and partially fill one of the greased 5-cm-diameter hemisphere moulds, spreading up the sides and making a well. Allow to harden in the freezer.*

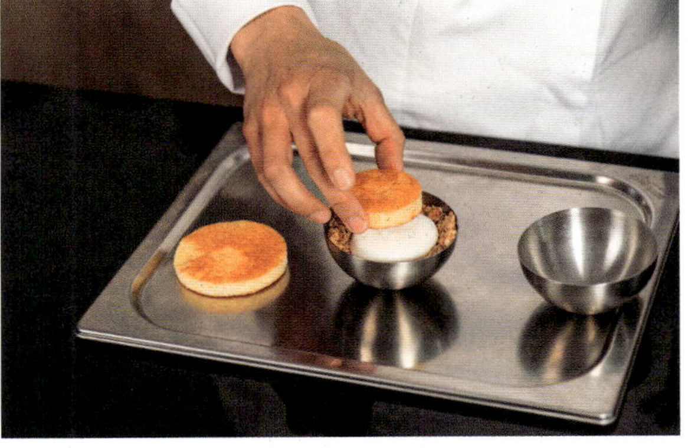

3. *Pipe a large dot of bavarois in the centre of the crispy puffed rice, add 20 g of lemon jelly and cover with a sponge disc. Smooth around the disc with bavarois.*

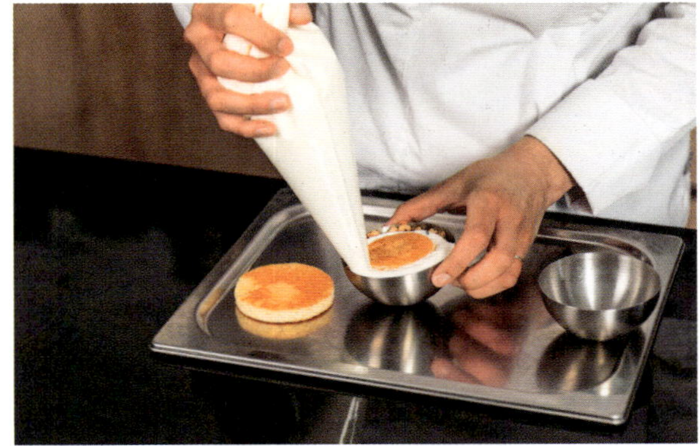

4. *Pipe bavarois into the second mould, add 20 g of lemon jelly and cover with bavarois. Place a sponge disc on top.*

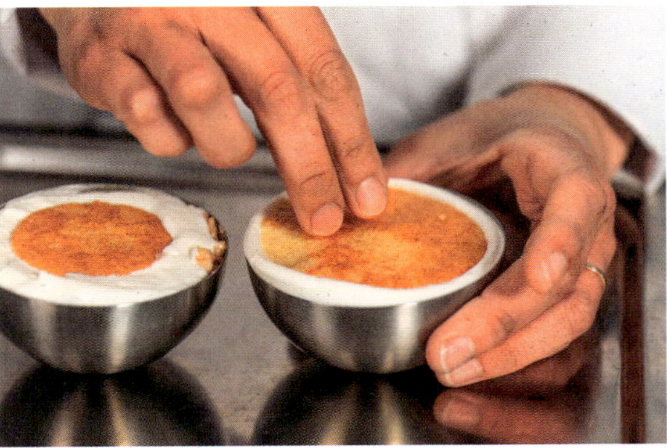

5. *Smooth around the disc with bavarois, close the moulds to make a sphere and allow to harden in the freezer.*

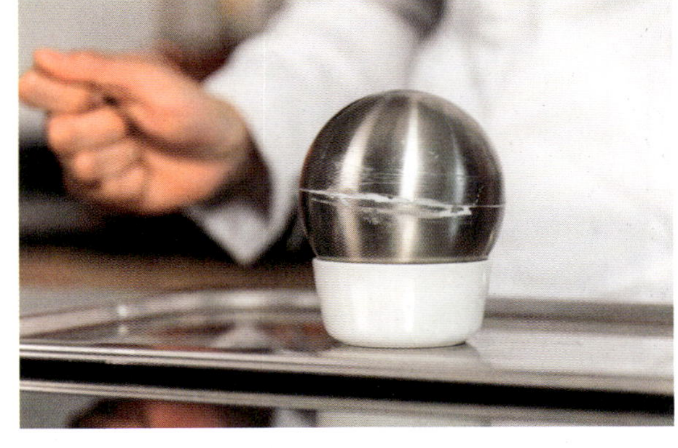

6.

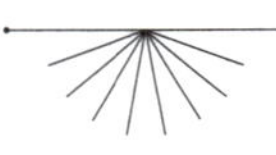

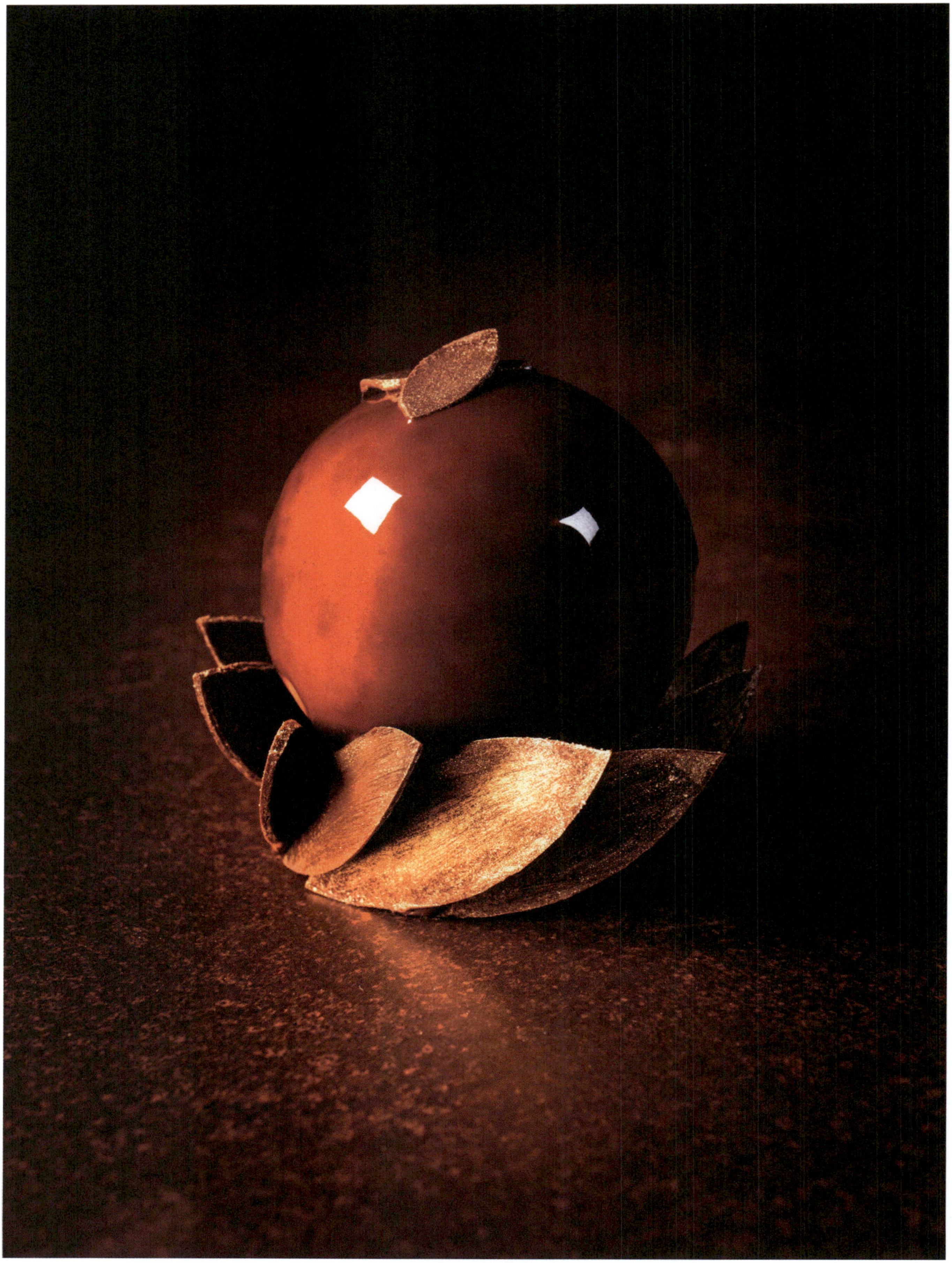

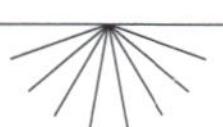

Serves 8

Preparation
3 hours 30 minutes

Cooking
43 minutes

Resting
7 hours

Caesar ball

Chocolate and fleur de sel shortbread
110 g unsalted butter, softened
125 g light brown soft sugar
130 g T80 (stoneground white) flour
40 g cocoa powder
2 g fleur de sel

Reconstituted chocolate shortbread
170 g dark chocolate couverture (66% cocoa)
310 g chocolate shortbread
110 g feuillantine
1 g fleur de sel

Chocolate sponge
120 g unsalted butter
4 egg whites
120 g caster sugar
120 g dark chocolate
30 g roasted ground almonds
50 g T55 (plain) flour
10 g potato starch

Chocolate feuillantine
100 g almond praline
25 g dark chocolate (70% cocoa)
50 g feuillantine
1 g fleur de sel

Chocolate crémeux
125 g milk
125 g whipping cream
3 egg yolks
25 g caster sugar
100 g dark chocolate

Chocolate and fleur de sel shortbread Rub the butter into the sugar, flour, cocoa and fleur de sel to form a dough, then break it up into crumbs. Bake the shortbread at 150°C for 35 minutes, then crumble it again.

Reconstituted chocolate shortbread Melt the chocolate and gently mix in the cooked chocolate shortbread, feuillantine and fleur de sel. Using a biscuit cutter, cut out 4.5-cm-diameter and 8-mm-thick discs. Allow them to harden in the fridge.

Chocolate sponge Make beurre noisette with the butter. Beat the egg whites with the sugar. Pour the beurre noisette over the chocolate and add the ground almonds, flour and potato starch, previously sifted together. Gently fold in the beaten egg whites. Spread the batter thinly over a baking mat. Bake at 180°C for about 8 minutes.

Chocolate feuillantine Melt the almond praline and chocolate in a bain-marie and gently fold in the feuillantine and fleur de sel. Spread a thin layer of the mixture, taking care to crush the feuillantine flakes as little as possible. Using biscuit cutters, cut out discs with a diameter of 2.5 cm and 3.5 cm. Allow them to harden in the fridge.

Chocolate crémeux In a saucepan, bring the milk and cream to the boil. Mix the egg yolks with the sugar and add the boiling liquid. Stir and return the mixture to the saucepan, then cook until the temperature reaches 82°C and it is thick enough to coat a spoon, stirring constantly with a spatula. Add to the chocolate a third at a time. Whisk until thick and smooth, then blend and allow to firm up in the fridge at 4°C. Fill 3-cm-diameter moulds with the crémeux and add a small sponge disc topped with a feuillantine disc.

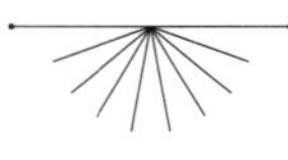

Crème anglaise

125 g whipping cream
125 g milk
2 egg yolks
25 g caster sugar

Chocolate mousse

150 g crème anglaise
155 g dark chocolate
    couverture (66% cocoa)
225 g whipped cream

Chocolate decorations

200 g dark chocolate
5 g edible gold shimmer dust

Black glaze

320 g caster sugar
135 g water
120 g glucose syrup
35 g acacia honey
235 g whipping cream
100 g cocoa powder
150 g gelatine mass
(21 g gelatine powder
    and 129 g cold water)

Crème anglaise In a saucepan, bring the milk and cream to the boil. Pour the hot liquid over the egg yolks and sugar, previously beaten until thick and pale, then stir and return the mixture to the saucepan. Cook until the temperature reaches 82°C.

Chocolate mousse Pour the crème anglaise over the chocolate and whisk until smooth and thick. Allow to cool to 25°C, then gently fold in the whipped cream. Use immediately. Partially fill the bottom half of a 6-cm-diameter sphere mould with chocolate mousse, then add a large sponge disc covered with a feuillantine disc. Pipe a small dot of chocolate mousse, then add the chocolate insert. Cover with chocolate mousse and close with the top half of the sphere moulds. Freeze.

Chocolate decorations Temper the chocolate. Cut out 3-cm-wide strips of acetate. Spread the chocolate over the strips (1–2). Using a 3.5-cm-diameter biscuit cutter, cut out leaf shapes (3). Allow the chocolate to harden before lifting it off the acetate, then gently brush the leaves with gold glitter.

Black glaze Cook the sugar and water in a saucepan to a syrup at 120°C. Put the glucose and honey into another saucepan and bring to the boil. Add the syrup to the cream, followed by the cocoa. Bring everything to the boil and add the gelatine mass. Blend and refrigerate.

I recommend making a large batch of glaze and freezing it so that you can use it for your next cakes.

Assembly

Start by making the shortbread, followed by the sponge.

Then make the feuillantine. Cut the sponge and the feuillantine into discs, make the crémeux and then create the inserts. Allow them to harden in the fridge. Remove the inserts from the moulds.

Make the mousse and assemble the balls. Freeze. Temper the chocolate, make the decorations and then make the glaze (5). Make the reconstituted shortbread and cut out the discs.

Remove a ball from its mould and glaze it (6-7), then place it on a reconstituted shortbread disc and decorate with chocolate leaves.

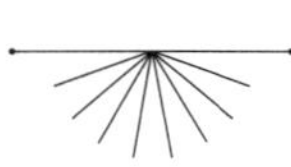

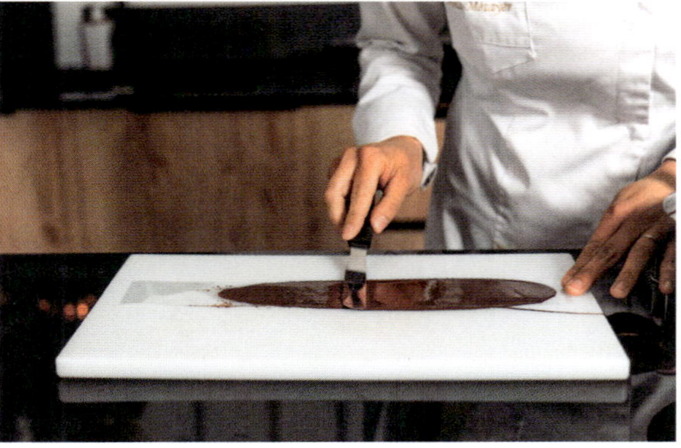

1.

To make the chocolate decorations, temper the chocolate. Cut out 3-cm-wide strips of acetate and spread them with the chocolate.

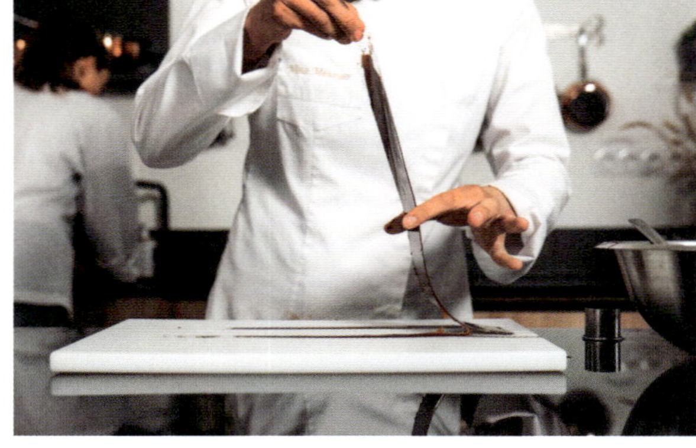

2.

The chocolate should be even.

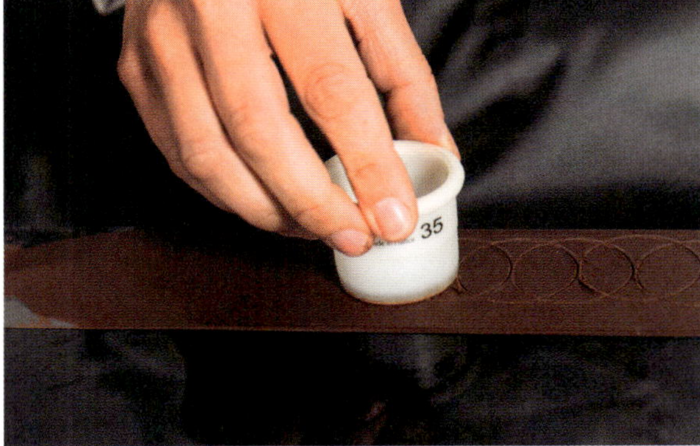

3.

Using a 3.5-cm-diameter biscuit cutter, cut out leaf shapes.

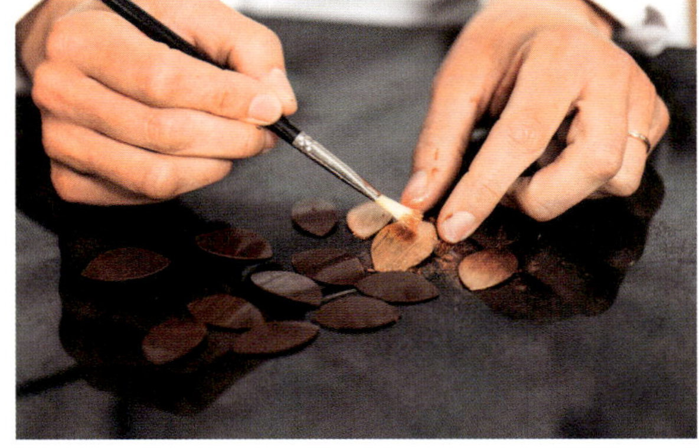

4.

Allow the chocolate to harden before lifting it off the acetate, then gently brush the leaves with gold glitter.

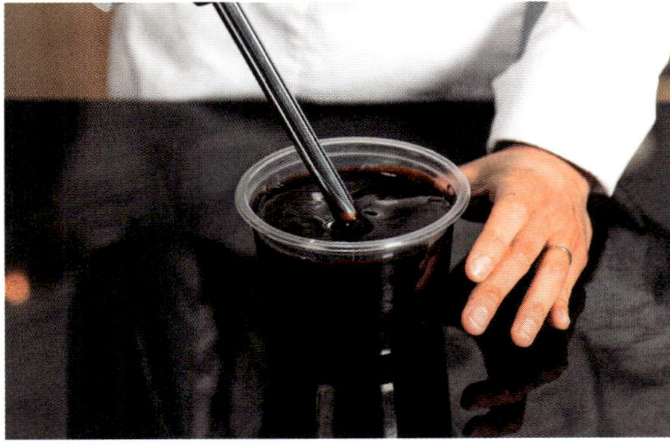

5.

Make the glaze.

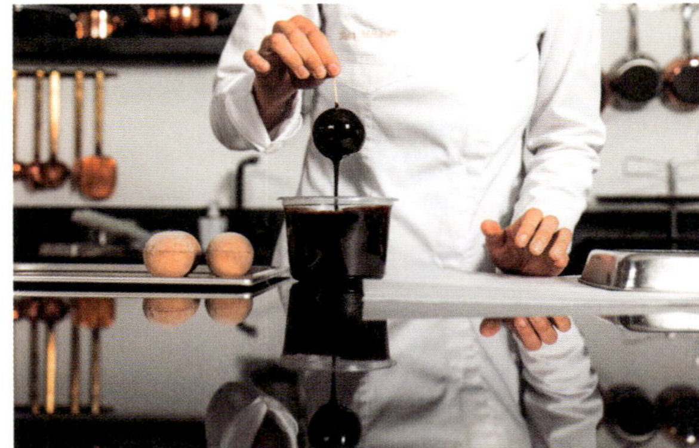

6.

Remove the sphere from the mould...

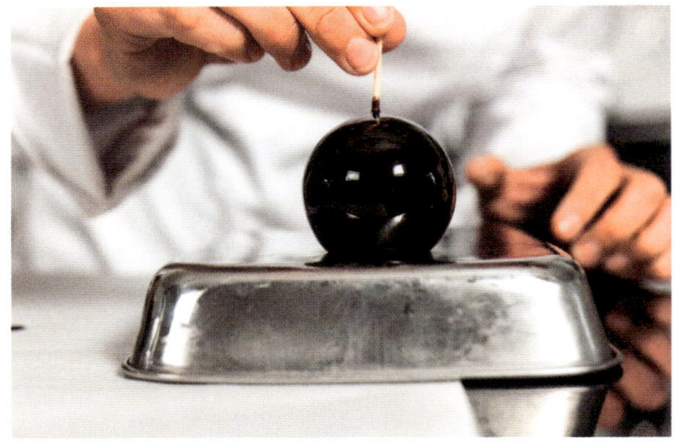

7.

...and glaze it.

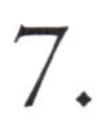
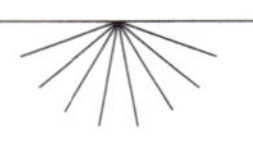

Serves 6

Preparation	Resting	Cooking
2 hours	3 hours	20 minutes

Praline wafer

Crispy insert
Filo puff pastry

150 g unsalted butter

2 g salt

7 sheets filo pastry

75 g light brown soft sugar

Feuillantine

100 g hazelnut praline

25 g dark chocolate couverture

50 g feuillantine

2 g fleur de sel

Hazelnut sponge

45 g icing sugar

45 g ground almonds

45 g ground hazelnuts

100 g egg whites

45 g sugar

17 g unsalted butter, melted

Insert chocolate coating

150 g dark chocolate

Praline bavarois

188 g whipping cream

125 g milk

30 g egg yolks

5 g light brown soft sugar

2.5 g vanilla extract

75 g praline

27 g gelatine mass

(4 g gelatine powder
  and 23 g cold water)

Filo pastry layer Melt the butter with the salt. Brush the first filo pastry sheet with the butter, then sprinkle lightly with the sugar and cover with another filo pastry sheet. Repeat the operation with the remaining sheets.

Feuillantine Heat the hazelnut praline and chocolate in a bain-marie and gently fold in the feuillantine and fleur de sel.

Hazelnut sponge Sift the icing sugar and ground nuts. Using a whisk, beat the egg whites to soft peaks, then gradually add the sugar while beating to stiff peaks. Gently fold in the ground nuts and icing sugar mixture and then incorporate the melted butter. Spread the batter to a 4-mm thickness in a baking tray lined with baking paper and bake for 8 minutes at 180°C.

Insert chocolate coating Temper the chocolate by heating it to 55°C, cooling it to 28°C and then lightly reheating it to 31°C for use.

Praline bavarois In a stand mixer fitted with a wire whisk, whip the cream. Set aside in the fridge. Bring the milk to the boil and pour into the egg yolk beaten with the sugar, then stir in the vanilla extract, return the mixture to the saucepan and cook until the temperature reaches 82°C. Remove the custard from the heat, add the gelatine mass and mix with the praline. Allow it to cool in the fridge, stirring regularly. Gently fold in the whipped cream.

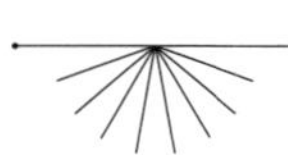

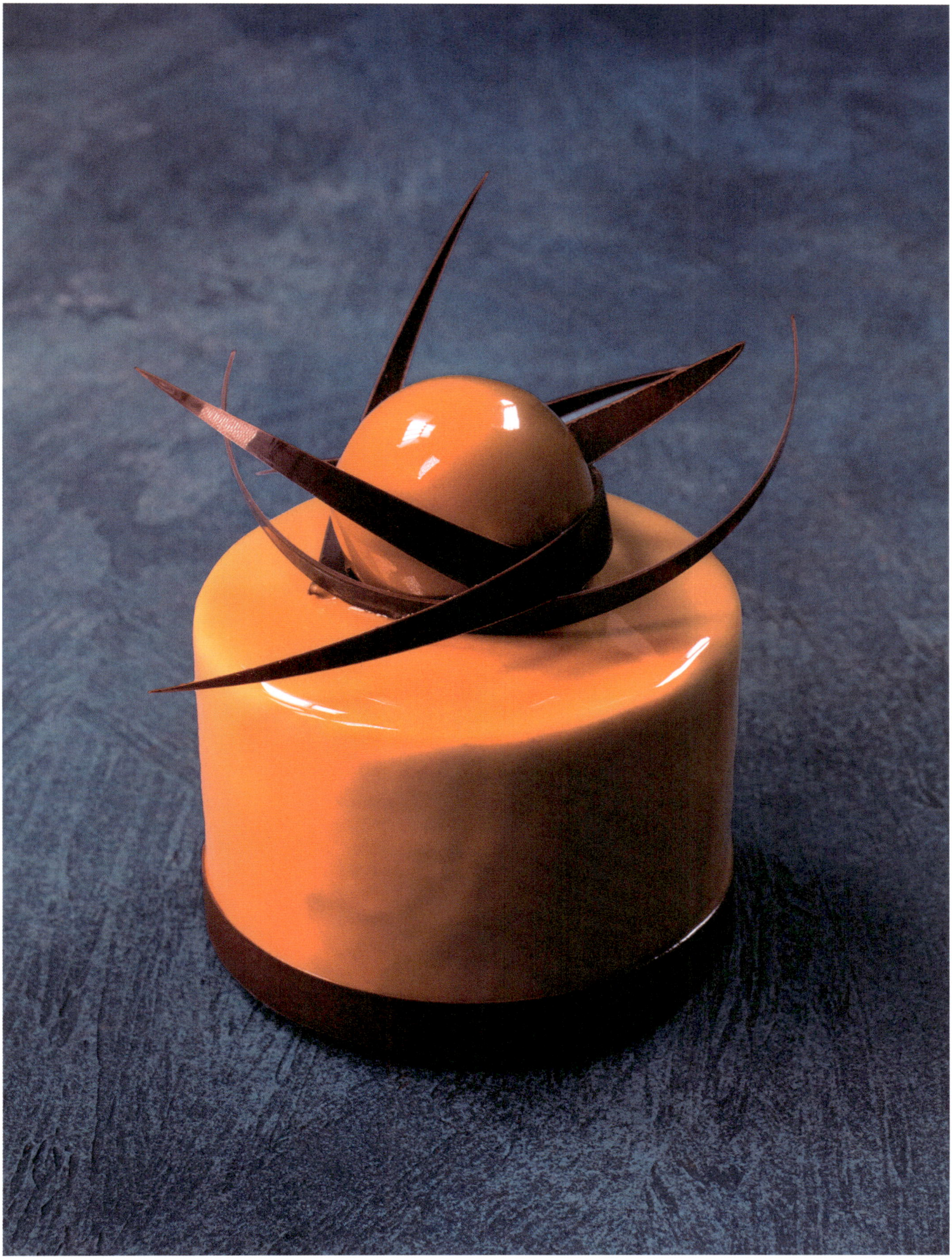

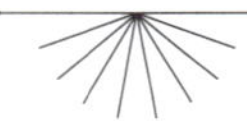

Praline sauce
87 g praline
100 g hazelnut paste
1 g fleur de sel

Chocolate coating
90 g dark chocolate
40 g cocoa butter

Caramel glaze
250 g sugar
300 g whipping cream
60 g gelatine mass
(9 g gelatine powder
    and 51 g cold water)

For decoration
200 g dark chocolate

Praline sauce Mix all the ingredients and transfer to a piping bag.

Chocolate coating Melt the chocolate and cocoa butter in a bain-marie.

Caramel glaze Make a dry caramel with the icing sugar and add the hot cream to stop the cooking process. Remove from the heat and stir in the gelatine mass. Allow it to cool before use.

Assembly

Make the crispy inserts: filo puff pastry, sponge and feuillantine.

Make the filo puff pastry. Using a biscuit cutter, cut the filo puff pastry into 4-cm-diameter discs and bake for 20 minutes in the oven at 160°C.

Carefully spread the feuillantine in a thin layer over a baking mat and cut out 4-cm-diameter discs. Allow them to harden in the freezer.

Make the hazelnut sponge and allow it to cool, then using a biscuit cutter, cut out 4-cm-diameter discs. Use a filo puff pastry disc as the base for each insert and cover it with a feuillantine disc, a second filo disc and then a second feuillantine disc. Place a third filo disc on top. Refrigerate. Cut acetate sheets into 3.5-cm-wide and 15-cm-long strips. Temper the dark chocolate for the crispy insert coating. Using a small angled palette knife, spread a thin layer of chocolate over the strips and wrap the acetate around the filo and feuillantine inserts. Allow the chocolate to harden, then place a hazelnut sponge disc on top to seal in the insert and remove the acetate. Dip the bottoms of the inserts in the chocolate and allow to harden in the fridge at 4°C.

Make the praline sauce and fill 3-cm-diameter hemisphere moulds. Freeze. Remove the moulds and attach hemispheres to make spheres. Insert a cocktail stick into the spheres and dip them in the tempered chocolate to coat. Remove the sticks, place the spheres in hemisphere moulds and allow the coating to harden in the fridge.

Make the praline bavarois. Line 6-cm-diameter and 4.5-cm-deep pastry rings with acetate. Fill the ring with 55 g of praline bavarois and position a crispy insert in the centre, level with the rim of the ring. Smooth around the insert with bavarois and place in the freezer at -20°C for at least 3 hours.

Finishing

Lif the rings off the entremets and unwrap the acetate, then cover them with the glaze warmed to about 25°C. Coat the praline sauce balls by inserting a cocktail stick and dipping them in the glaze.

Arrange a praline ball on top of each entremets, with the hole made by the stick concealed underneath.

Make the chocolate decorations.

Spread a thin layer of chocolate on an acetate sheet and score rhombus shapes about 1 cm wide and 11 cm long. Roll the strip into a ring and allow the chocolate to harden in the fridge.

Cut acetate sheets into 1-cm-wide and 26-cm-long strips. Spread a thin layer of chocolate over the strips and wrap them around the glazed entrements. Peel off the rhombus decorations and arrange them in groups of three around the praline sauce ball.

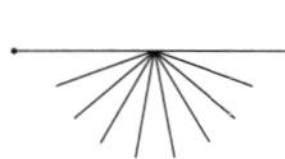

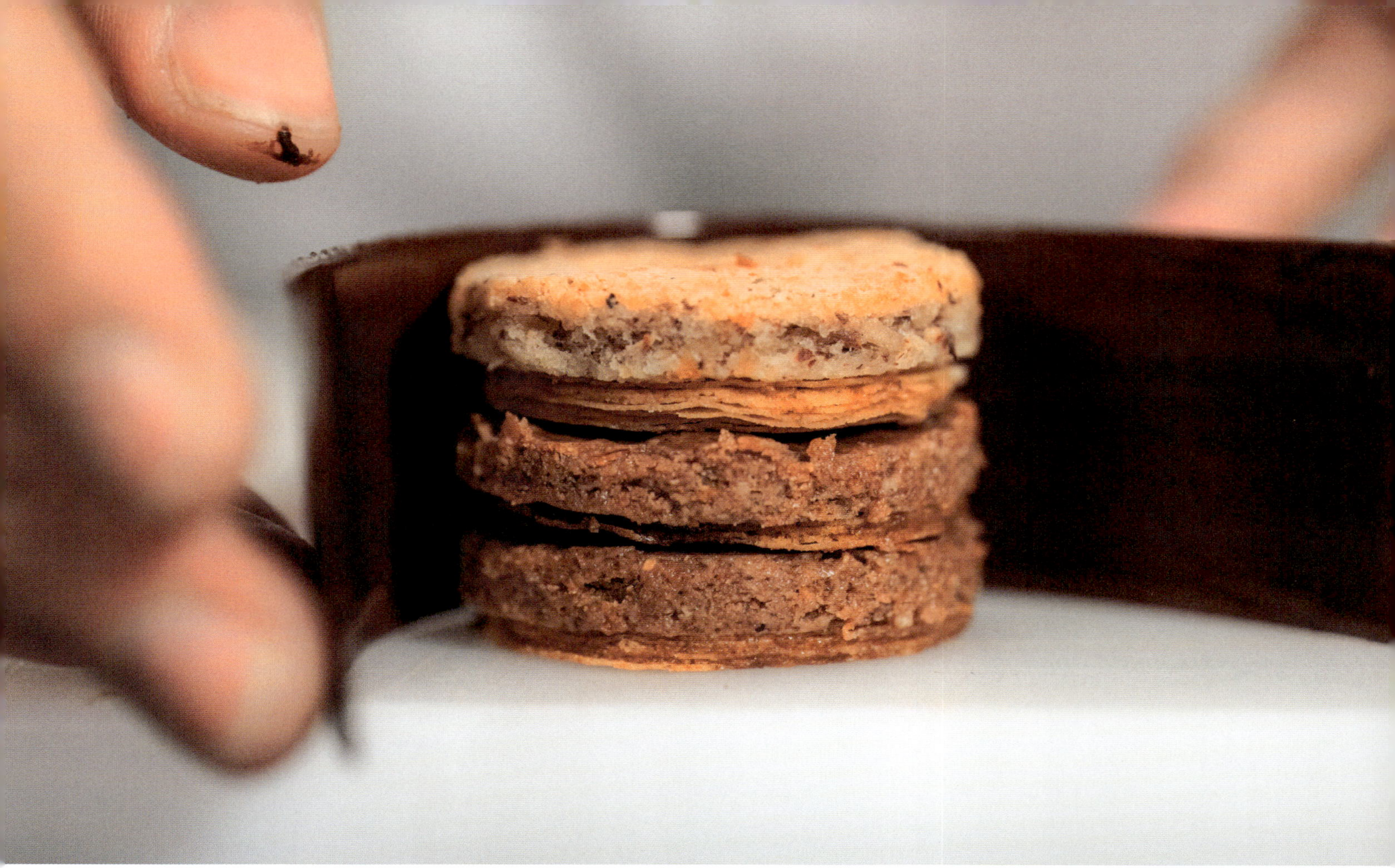

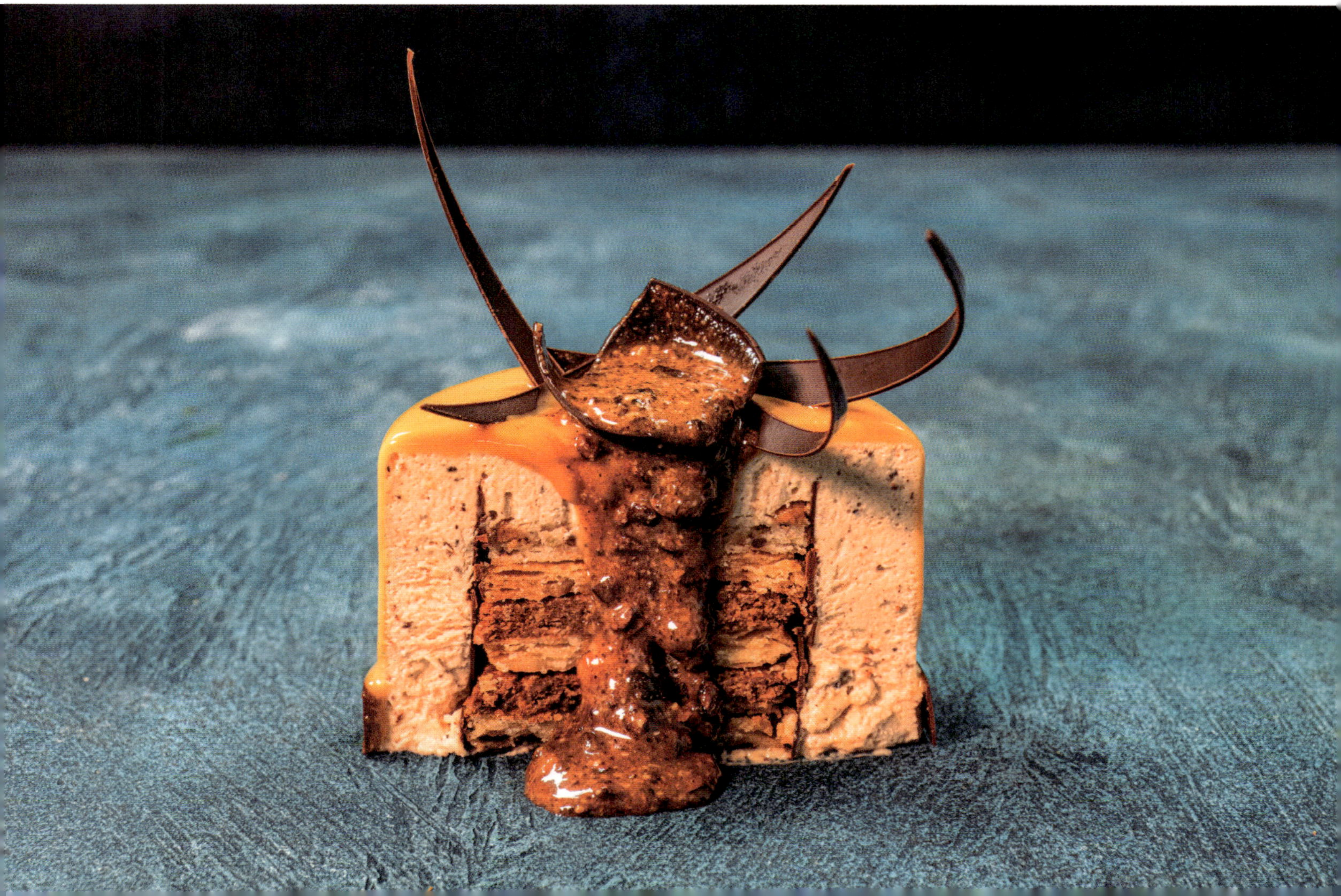

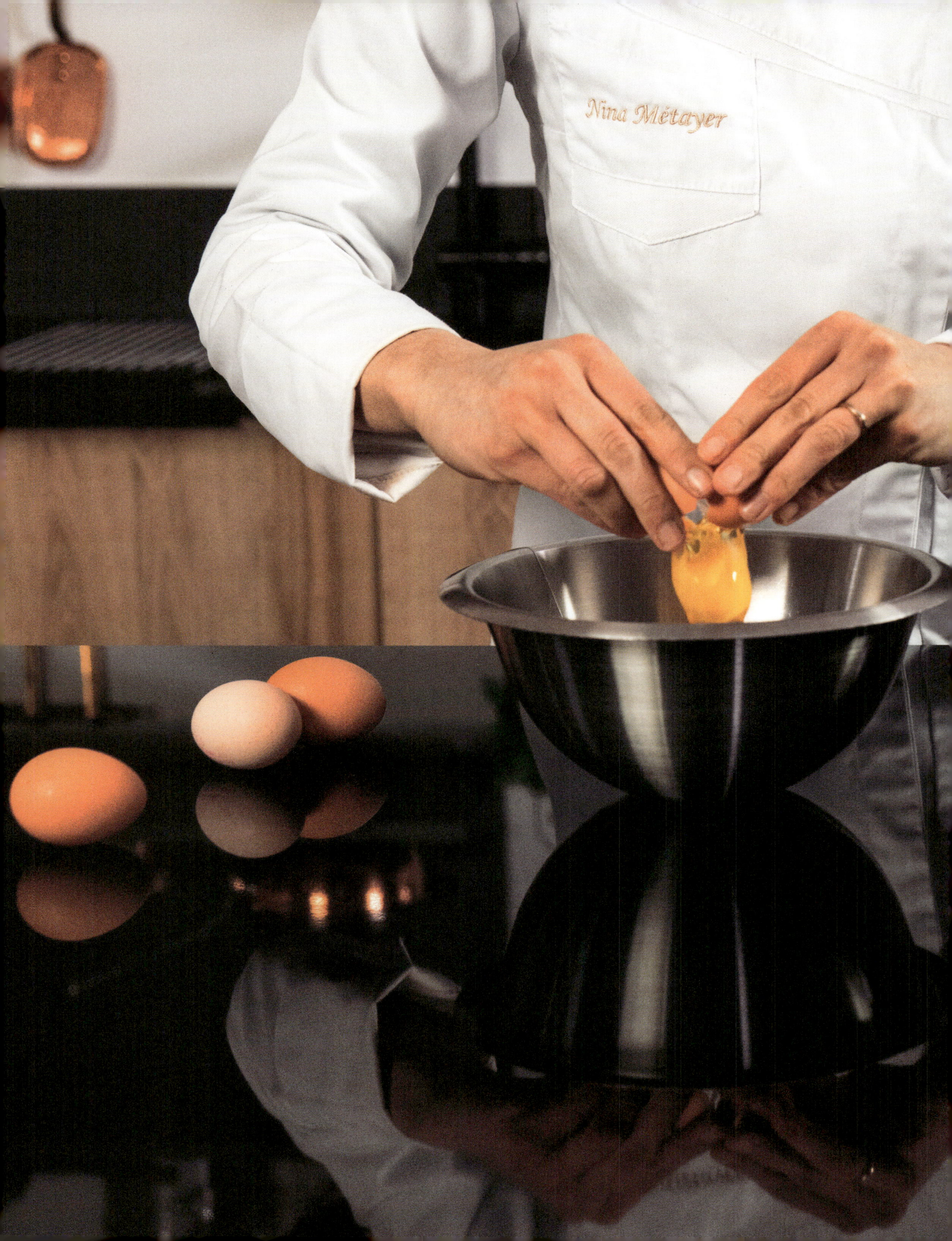

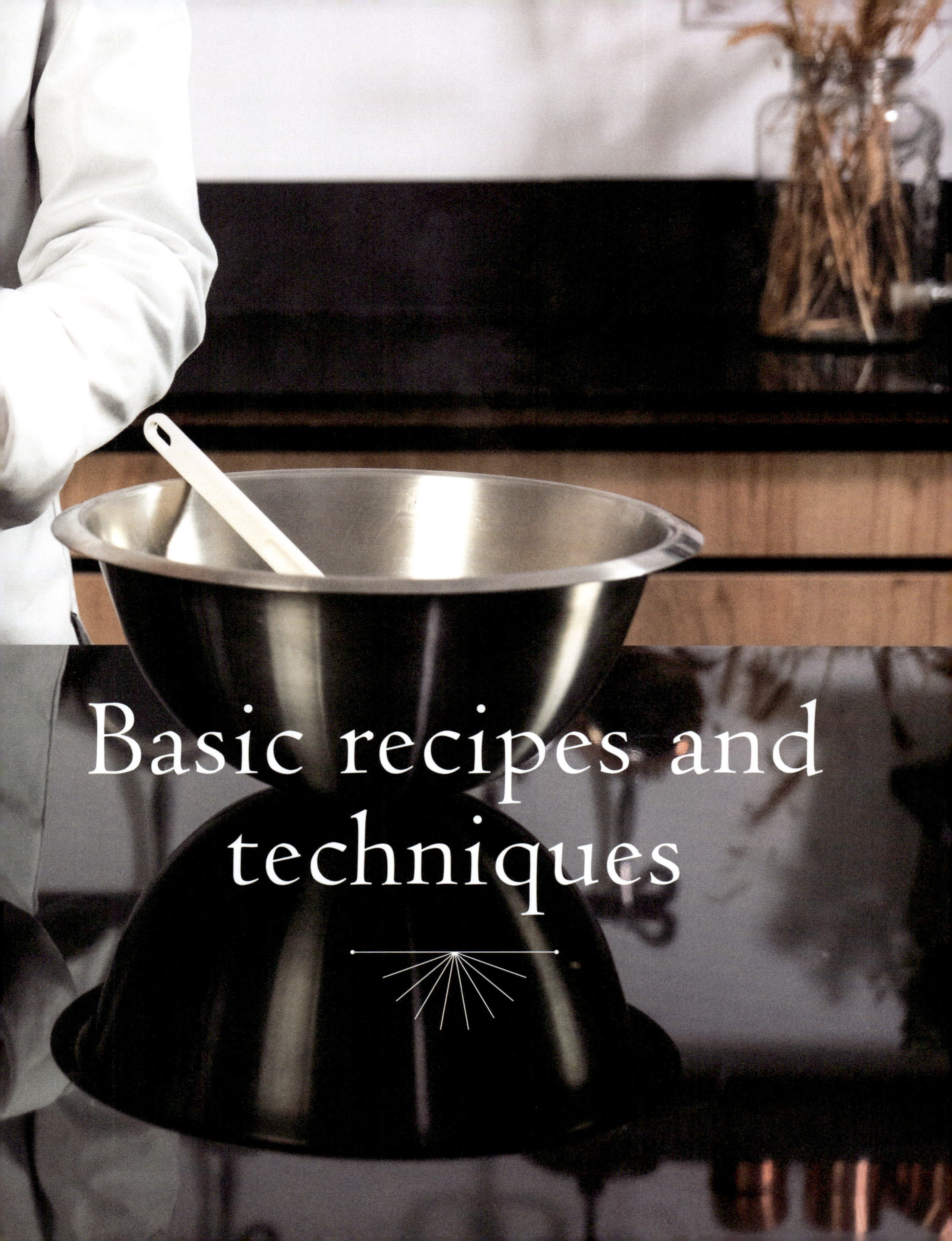

Basic recipes and techniques

Levain and milk levain

20 g water
20 g T110 (semi-wholemeal) flour
  20 g sourdough mother

Sourdough mother

To make a levain, you will need a sourdough mother, or mother culture. For this purpose, it is important to use stoneground, semi-wholemeal flour, preferably organic, so that it contains as many microorganisms as possible.

First, you need to make a mixture of flour and water, put it in a closed jam jar near a heat source and feed it regularly (1). After 48 hours, add 20 g of flour and 20 g of water; this is what is referred to as feeding, or refreshing. 24 hours later, take 40 g of sourdough mother and feed it with 20 g of flour and 20 g of water. The following day and every day after that, repeat the operation of feeding 40 g of sourdough mother with 20 g of flour and 20 g of water until small bubbles form on the surface. If your sourdough mother is having trouble starting, you can add a drop of honey (2), or soak organic apple peels (3) for at least 12 hours in the water you use to feed your sourdough (4).

When your sourdough is well established, after several weeks it will be full of bubbles, so you will need to keep feeding it every day if you use it often. In this case, keep 20 g of sourdough mother and discard the rest. Add 20 g of flour and 20 g of water and mix.

If you use it less often, you can keep it in the fridge at 4°C for up to 1 week, then refresh it (for 40 g of sourdough mother, add 20 g of flour and 20 g of water) at least once a week. After refreshing it, keep it out at room temperature for at least 4 hours before returning it to the fridge.

When you want to use it to make a levain, bring it to room temperature 48 hours beforehand and feed it twice a day (adding 20 g of flour and 20 g of water each time). Allow it to grow according to the quantity of levain you will need for your recipe. The colder your levain, the more acidic it will be. You can play with the taste of your levain by changing the flours and fermentation temperatures.

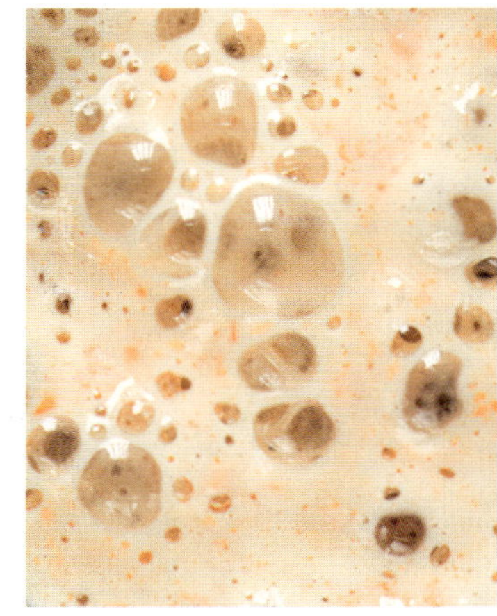

75 g sourdough mother
150 g T65 (strong white) flour
150 g full-fat milk

Milk levain

To make a milk levain, first prepare a classic sourdough mother from scratch if none is available. You then will need to take a small amount of your sourdough mother and feed it with flour and milk to produce lactic acid fermentation. I recommend using milk levain when making leavened pastries as it adds extra flavour and allows them to keep longer.

Adjust how much flour and milk, and feed your sourdough mother according to the quantity you need.

1. 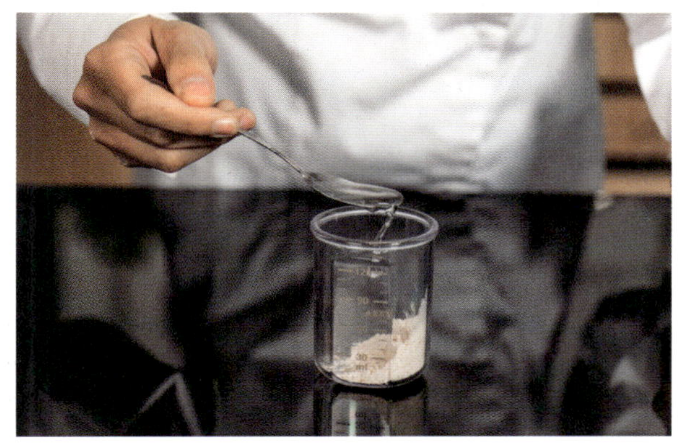

2. 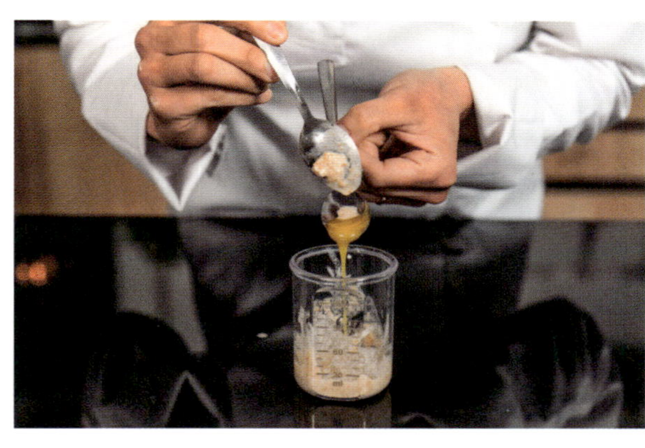

3. 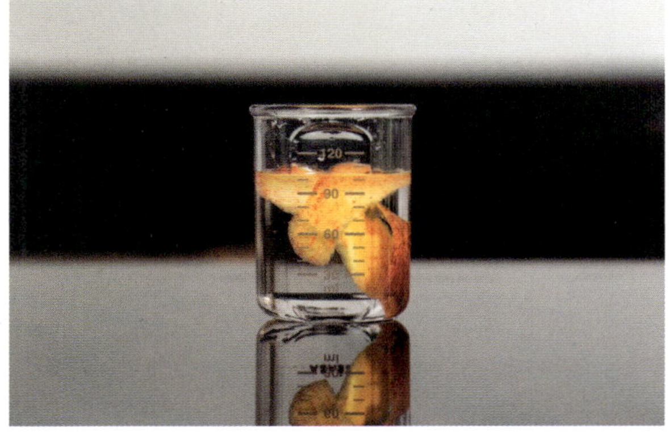

4. 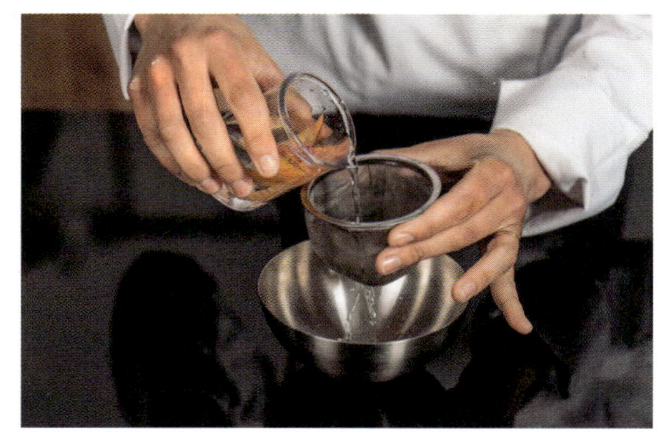

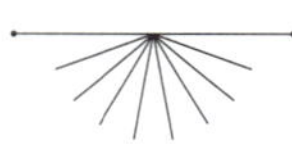

Choux pastry

125 g milk

125 g water

5 g salt

2.5 g light brown soft sugar

110 g unsalted butter

140 g T55 (plain) flour

5 eggs (225 g)

Preheat the oven to 180°C.

Prepare your baking trays; they need to be very flat and clean.

Cut the butter into small pieces. Sift the flour.

Make the panade. To do this, put the milk, water, salt, sugar and butter into a saucepan and bring to the boil (1).

Then remove from the heat and add all the flour in one go. Whisk the mixture briskly until smooth (2). Using an exoglass or wooden spatula, stir the pastry well for about 2 minutes over a low heat to dry it out well (3).

Adjust the drying time to the amount of pastry you need to make. The panade will be dry enough when a little fat starts to seep out.

Transfer the panade to a large bowl or the bowl of a stand mixer and allow to cool for 2 minutes.

Add the eggs one at a time while very gently mixing with a spatula or beating in the mixer with the paddle attachment on low speed to prevent aerating the pastry (4).

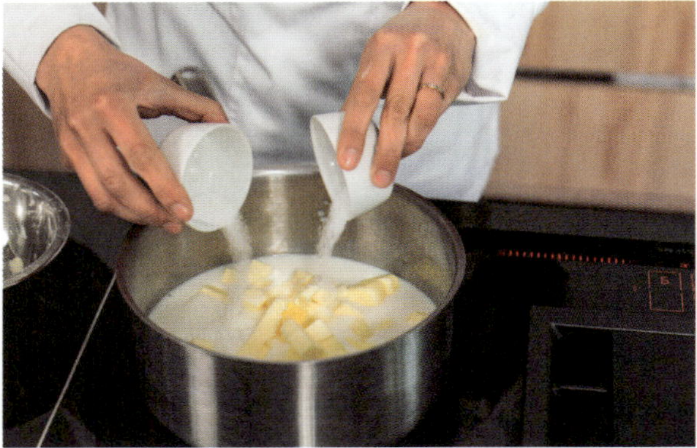

I.

Make the panade. Put the milk, water, salt, sugar and butter into a saucepan and bring to the boil.

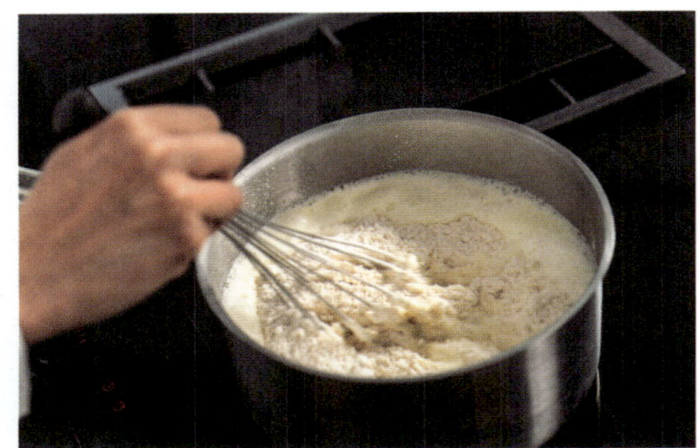

2.

Remove from the heat and add all the flour in one go. Whisk the mixture briskly until smooth.

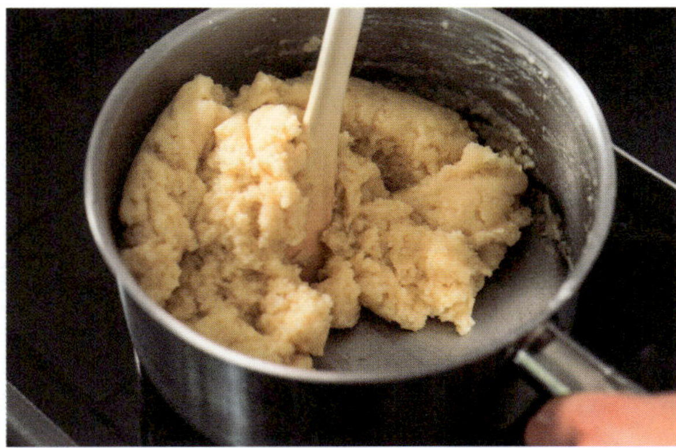

3.

Using an exoglass or wooden spatula, stir the pastry well for about 2 minutes over a low heat to dry it out well.

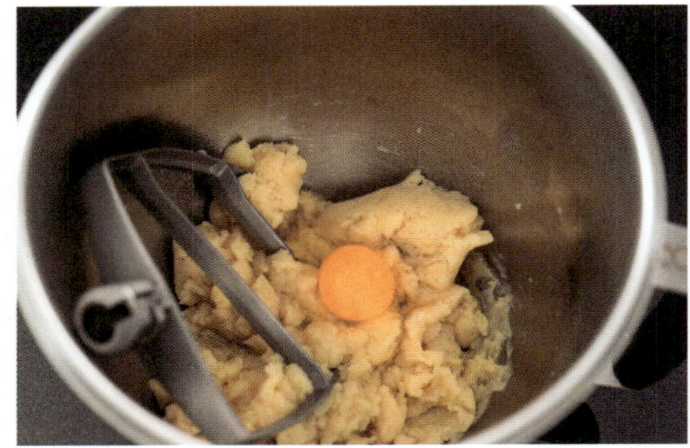

4.

Transfer the panade to a large bowl or the bowl of a stand mixer and allow to cool for 2 minutes. Add the eggs one at a time while very gently mixing with a spatula or beating in the mixer with the paddle attachment on low speed to prevent aerating the pastry.

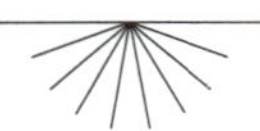

Depending on how well the panade dried out, you will need to add more or less egg. There is no exact recipe for a beautiful choux pastry.

It should have a soft consistency without being runny (5).

When you run a fingertip over the pastry, the indentation should close up very gently.

Pay attention to the temperature of the choux pastry when observing its consistency: the hotter it is, the runnier it will be as it contains a lot of butter.

You can make your choux pastry in advance and store it in the fridge in a container covered with cling film in direct contact with the pastry for up to 2 days before use. It isn't a big problem if it darkens a little, this is simply caused by oxidation.

Unbaked choux pastry freezes well. You can pipe choux buns and freeze them to use when you need them.

Choux buns

Lightly grease a baking tray with oil. Pipe the choux buns directly on the baking tray (6). For choux buns with a craquelin topping, place a craquelin disc on top of each choux bun (7).

Place the tray in the hot oven without opening the oven door for at least 15 minutes for small choux buns and 30 minutes for large ones (8).

Make sure to allow the choux buns to dry well so that they are crisp on the outside and soft inside.

Choux buns take a long time to cook, so don't hesitate to lower the oven temperature at the end if you see them turning too dark.

5.
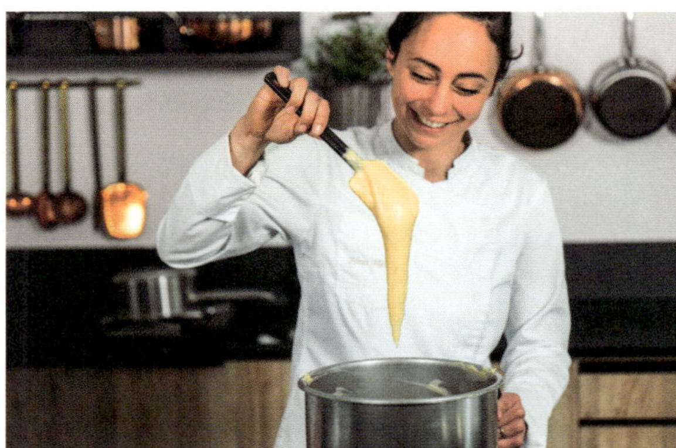

Depending on how well the panade dried out, you will need to add more or less egg. There is no exact recipe for a beautiful choux pastry. It should have a soft consistency without being runny.

6.
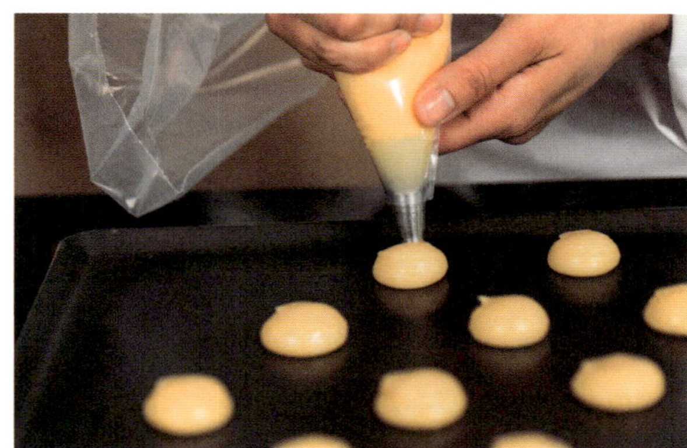

Pipe the choux buns directly on the baking tray.

7.
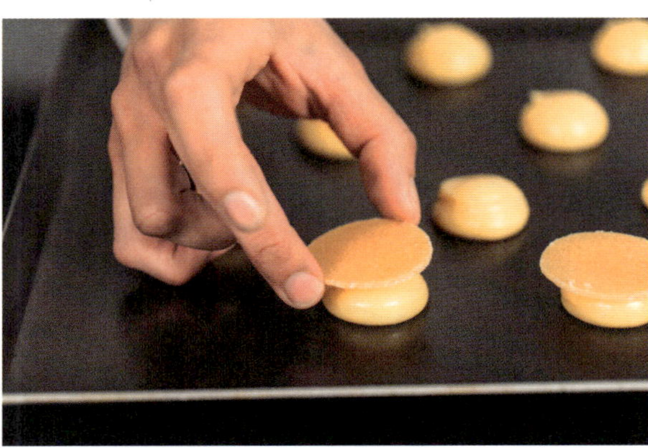

For choux buns with a craquelin topping, place a craquelin disc on top of each choux bun.

8.
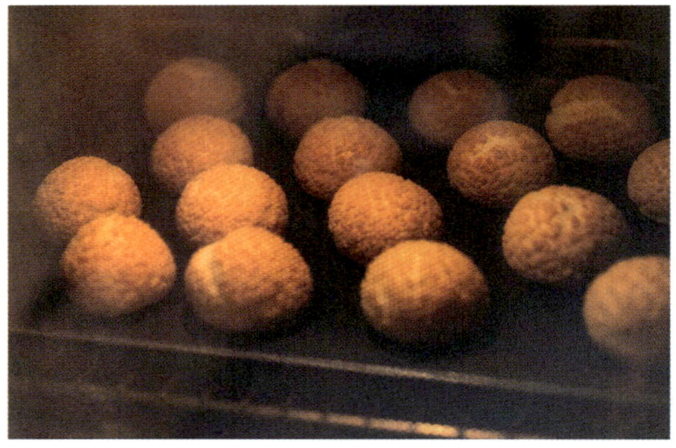

Place the tray in the hot oven without opening the oven door for at least 15 minutes for small choux buns and 30 minutes for large ones.

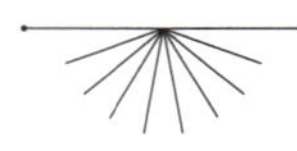

Sweet pastry

90 g icing sugar
30 g ground almonds
150 g unsalted butter, softened
2.5 g salt
1 g vanilla powder
270 g T80 (stoneground white) flour
1 medium egg (50 g)

Sift the icing sugar and ground almonds (1).

By hand or in a stand mixer fitted with a paddle attachment, rub the butter into the sugar, ground almonds, salt and vanilla powder (2), then add the flour (3).

Incorporate the egg (4). Mix to a smooth dough (5).

Wrap the pastry in cling film and rest it in the fridge for at least 2 hours (6).

Take the pastry out of the fridge and remove the cling film. Dust the work surface and pastry with flour. Roll out the pastry a little at a time, making sure it doesn't stick to the work surface. If the pastry is too sticky, put it back in the fridge for 10 minutes before continuing to work with it.

This pastry has several uses. To make a tart shell, roll out the pastry to a 3-mm thickness. Cut out a disc 4 cm larger than the tart ring you will be using. Grease the ring with butter and carefully line it with the pastry. Put the tart shell in the freezer for 30 minutes to firm it up. In a preheated oven at 180°C, bake the tart shell for 10 minutes, then lower the temperature to 150°C and bake for a further 25 minutes.

Allow it to cool. Using a spice grater, gently smooth the edges.

You can replace the T80 flour with T55 (plain) flour or T45 (soft white) flour. I like using T80 flour because it absorbs the butter better and shrinks less as it bakes.

'Sweet pastry is always an important component of a dessert. You need to use the right ingredients and master the cooking process to bring out all the flavours. Slow and gentle baking brings out all the flavours of the flour, almonds and butter. The pastry must be evenly coloured and cooked through.'

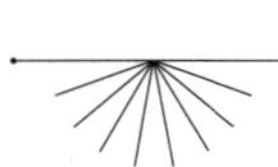

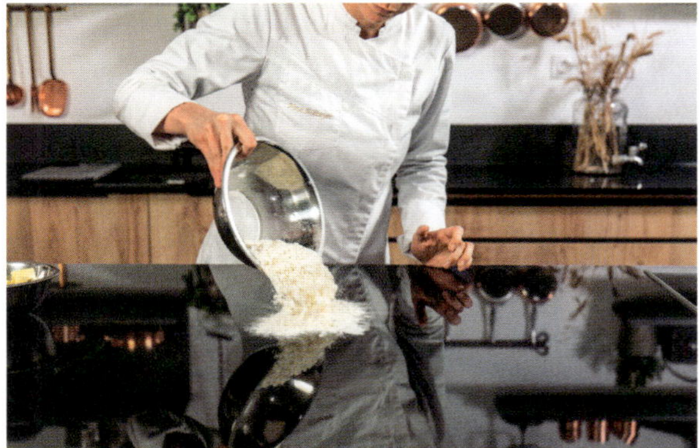

1.

Sift the icing sugar and ground almonds.

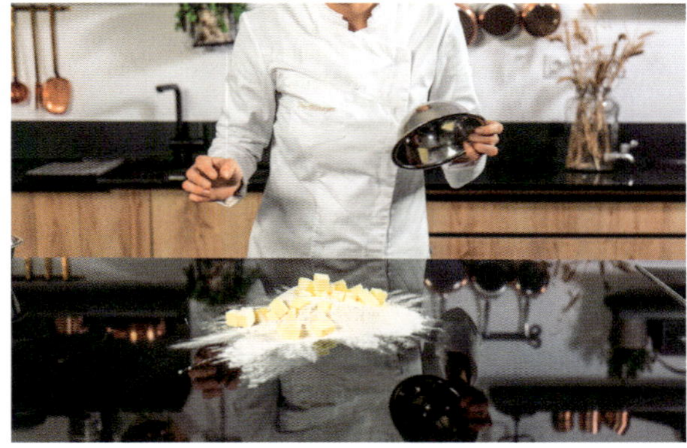

2.

By hand or in a stand mixer fitted with a paddle attachment, rub the butter into the sugar, ground almonds, salt and vanilla powder.

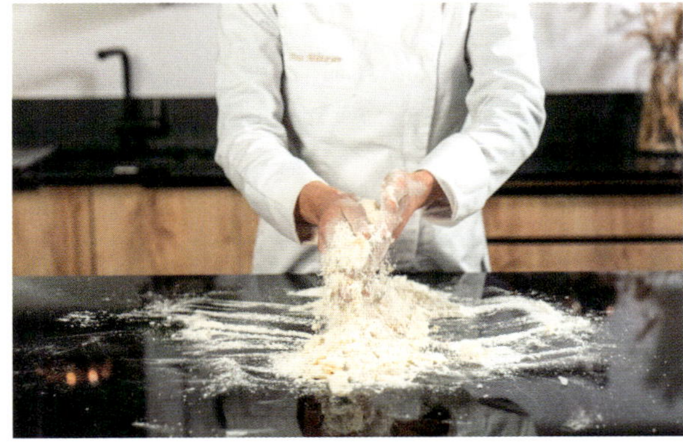

3.

Add the flour.

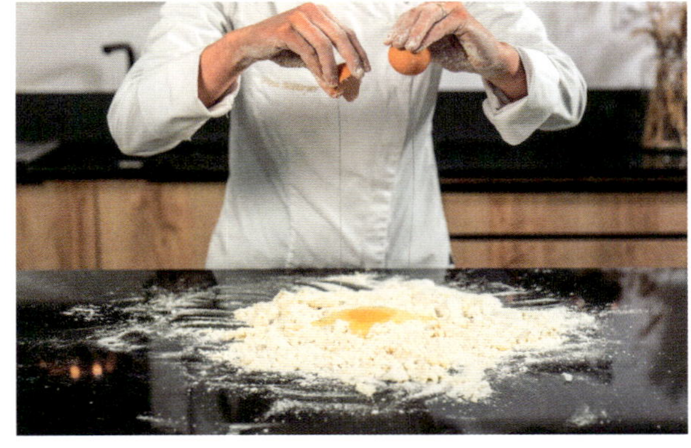

4.

Incorporate the egg.

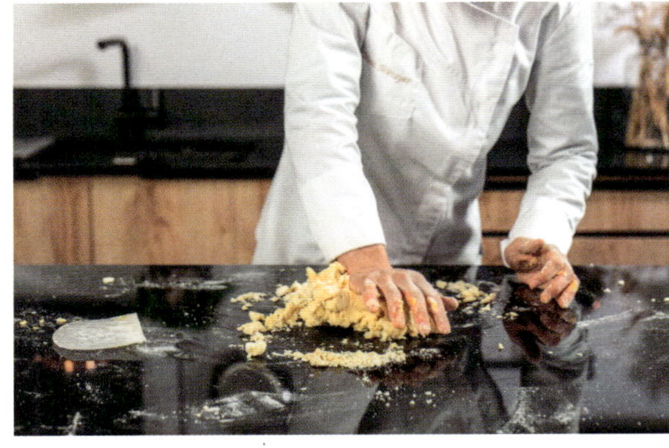

5.

Mix to a smooth dough.

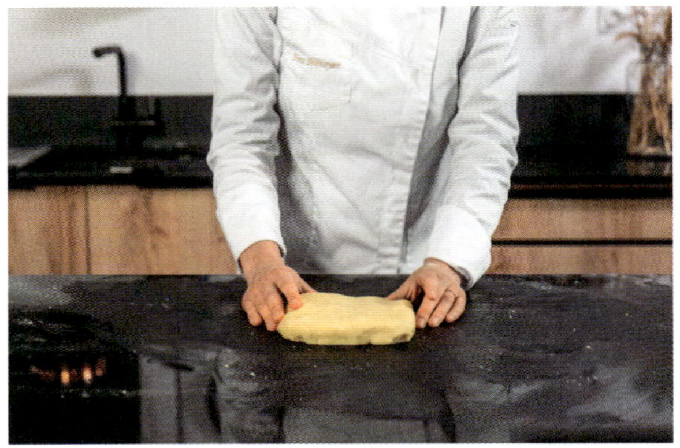

6.

Wrap the pastry in cling film and rest it in the fridge for at least 2 hours.

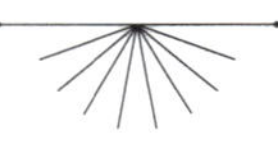

Hazelnut sponge

62 g icing sugar
62 g ground almonds
62 g ground hazelnuts
25 g unsalted butter
5 egg whites
62 g caster sugar

Preheat the oven to 180°C.

Sift together the icing sugar and ground nuts (1). Melt the butter.

In a stand mixer fitted with a wire whisk, beat the egg whites to soft peaks, then incorporate the caster sugar in a thin stream. Then beat for a further 30 seconds (2).

Note: the meringue should still be soft and not too stiff.

Gently fold in the ground nut and icing sugar mixture (3), then mix in the melted butter (4). Make sure that the batter is very smooth.

You can add the grated zest of a lemon or other citrus fruit at this point if you would like to flavour the sponge.

Spread the batter to a 5-mm thickness in a baking tray lined with baking paper and bake for 8 minutes at 180°C (5).

Adjust the cooking time according to the oven you use. The sponge should be a light golden colour (6).

Immediately transfer the sponge to a rack or cold baking tray.

You can set aside the sponge in the fridge or freezer tray lined with cling film until ready to use.

"I love this sponge; it's so delicious and can be used to make so many different desserts. I like to flavour it with citrus zest or orange blossom, and I can replace the ground hazelnuts with grated coconut or ground pistachios.'

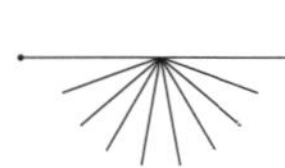

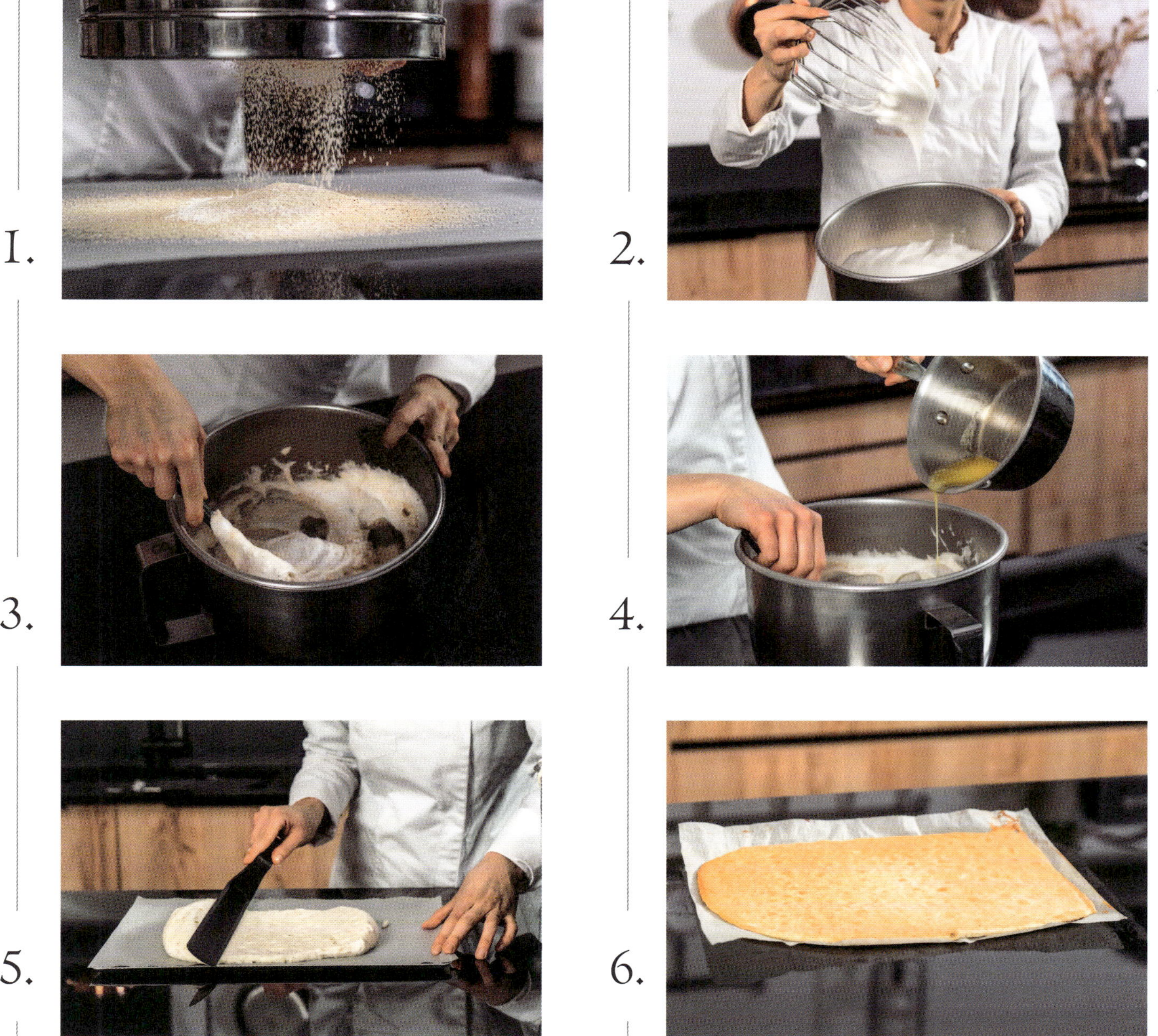

1.
2.
3.
4.
5.
6.

Inverse puff pastry

Beurre manié
338 g unsalted butter
150 g einkorn flour

Dough
282 g T80 (stoneground white) flour
127 g water
90 g unsalted butter
12 g salt
4 g white vinegar

The day before, make the beurre manié by mixing the butter and flour (1), then roll it out to an even thickness (2–3).

Make the dough by mixing all the ingredients, then roll it out to an even thickness and place it over the beurre manié (4). Rest the assembled pastry in the fridge for at least 6 hours (5).

Roll out the beurre manié and dough combination (6) to a thickness of 5 mm, then fold it over with the dough on the outside, then over again to perform a double turn. The result should be 4 stacked layers of pastry (7).

Rest the pastry for 2 hours in the fridge, then place the pastry on the work surface with the folded ends on the right and left (8). Then roll out the pastry again to 5-mm thickness and perform a second double turn (9). Rest the pastry in the fridge for 2 hours.

Repeat the operation to perform a third double turn (10). Rest the pastry for 6 hours in the fridge.

Roll out the pastry to the desired thickness, depending on the intended use. Make sure to relax the puff pastry well before cutting it out.

You can freeze your raw puff pastry and take it out whenever you need it.

To keep track of your progress, you can mark the number of turns made as you go by indenting the pastry with your fingers (11).

' I quite like using inverse puff pastry; I find it very good, plus it's easier to work with than regular puff pastry. This recipe uses flours that are different from the ones normally used; they contain more of the grain, which means that they are less strong and, therefore, the pastry shrinks less as it bakes. But it also keeps better because the flours better absorb the water and fat. And on top of all that, the pastry tastes really good! If you don't have these flours, you can use your usual flours to make this recipe, but I recommend T55 (plain) flour rather than T45 (soft white) flour.'

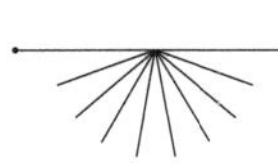

I.

The day before, make the beurre manié by mixing the butter with the einkorn flour.

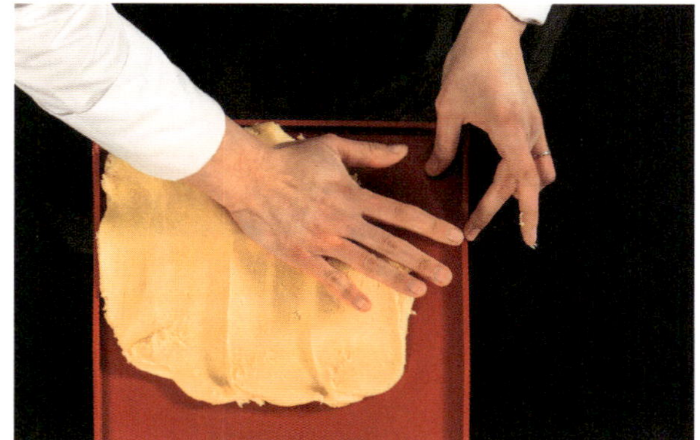

2.

Roll it out to an even thickness.

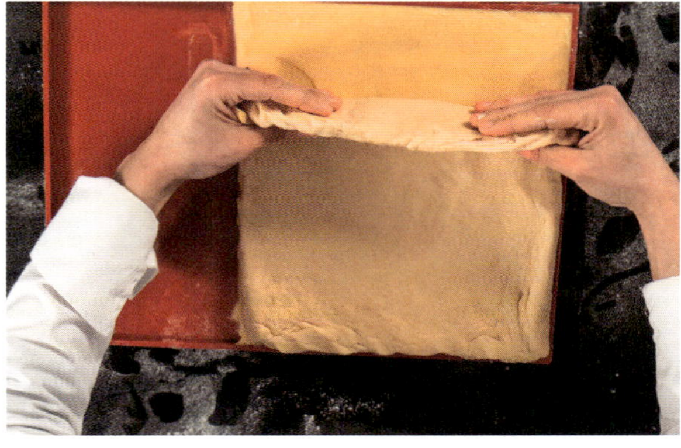

3.

Like this.

4.

Make the dough by mixing all the ingredients, then roll it out to an even thickness and place it over the beurre manié.

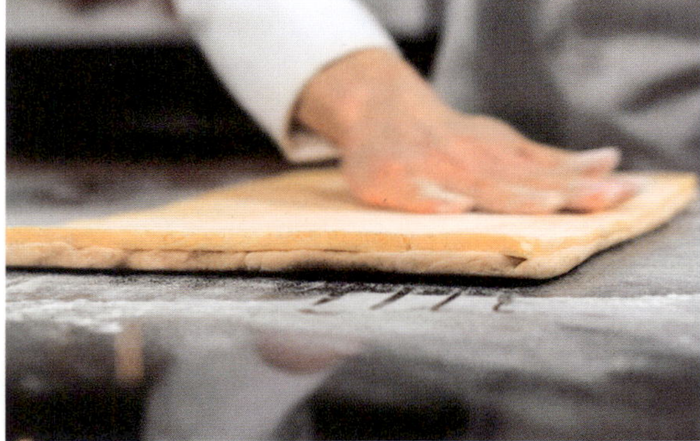

5.

Rest the assembled pastry in the fridge for at least 6 hours.

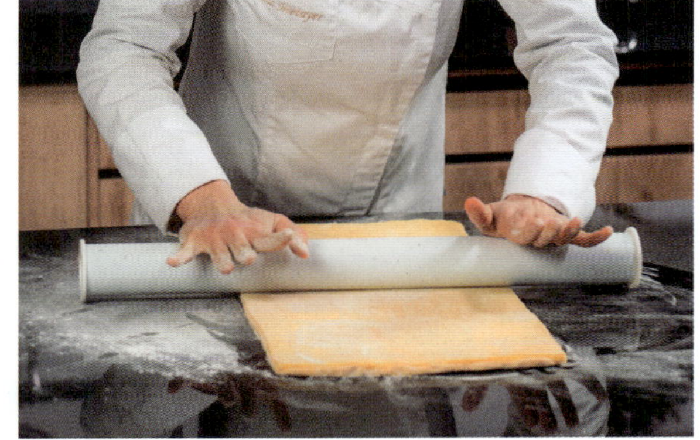

6.

Roll out the beurre manié and dough combination to a thickness of 5 mm.

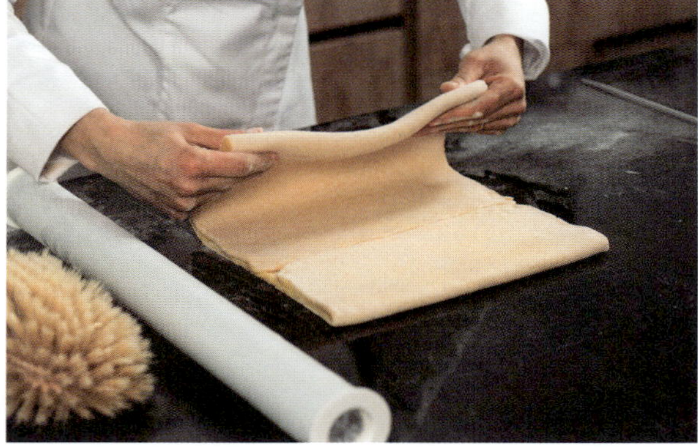

7.

Fold the pastry over, then fold it over again with the dough on the outside to perform a double turn. The result should be 4 stacked layers of pastry.

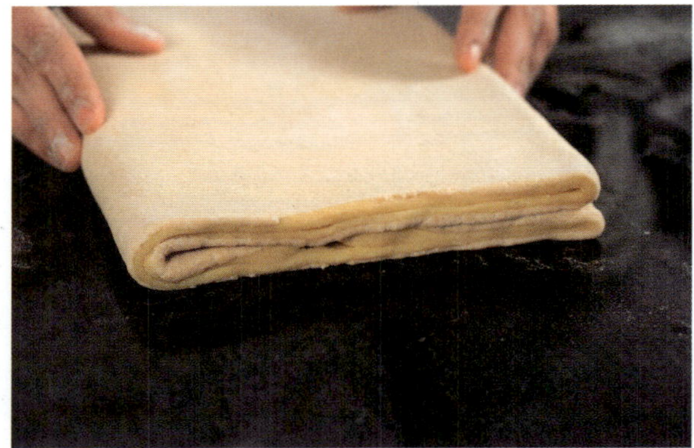

8.

Rest the pastry in the fridge for 2 hours, then place the pastry on the work surface with the folded ends on the right and left.

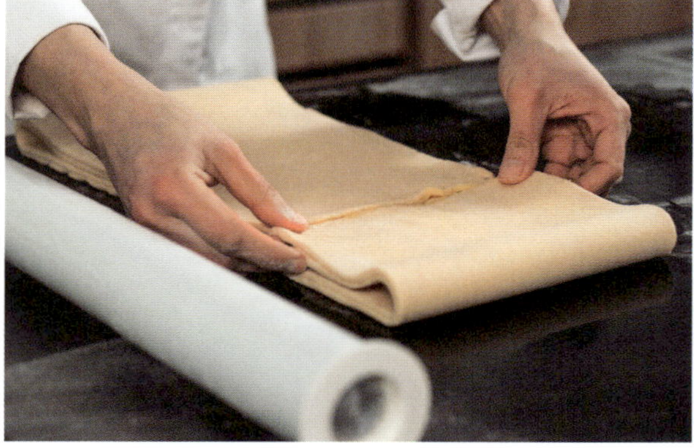

9.

Roll out the pastry to a 5-mm thickness and perform a second double turn. Rest the pastry in the fridge for 2 hours.

'The secret to good puff pastry is its temperature when you work with it. You need patience above all. Put the pastry back in the fridge if it heats up too much, or wait a while before working with it if it feels too cold.'

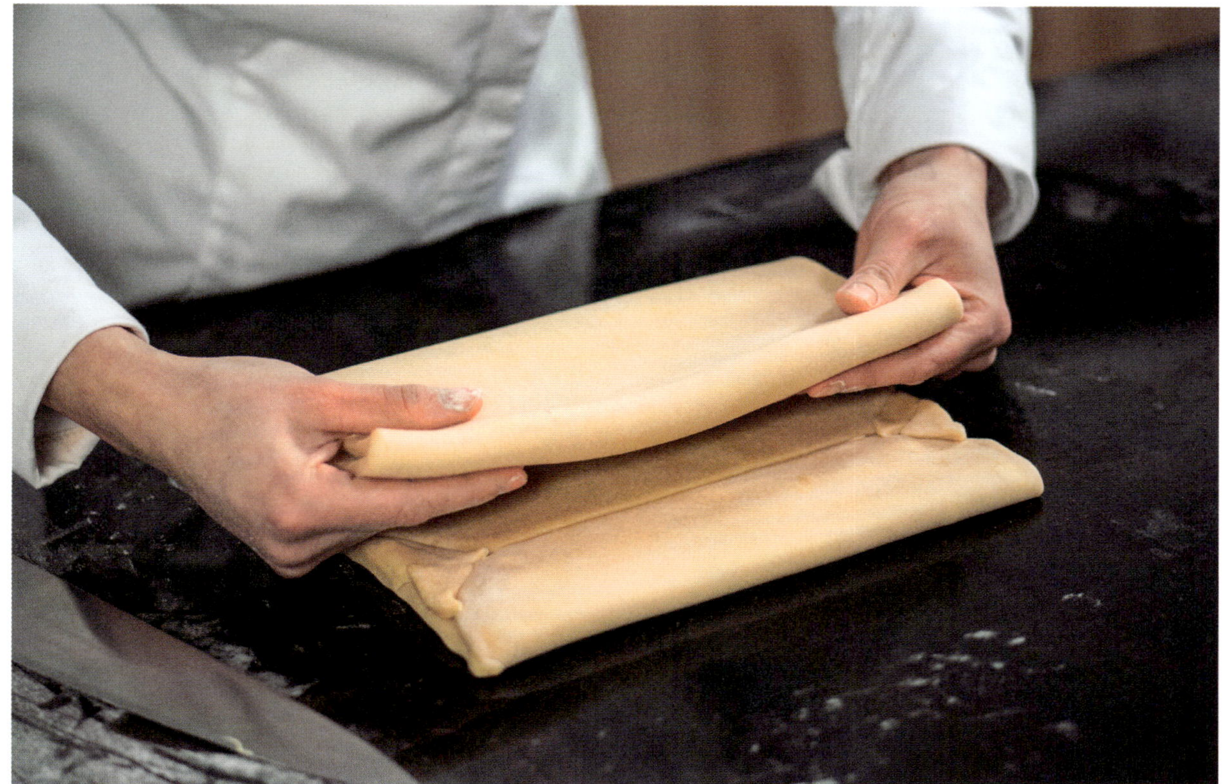

10.

Repeat the operation to perform a third double turn. Rest the pastry in the fridge for 6 hours.

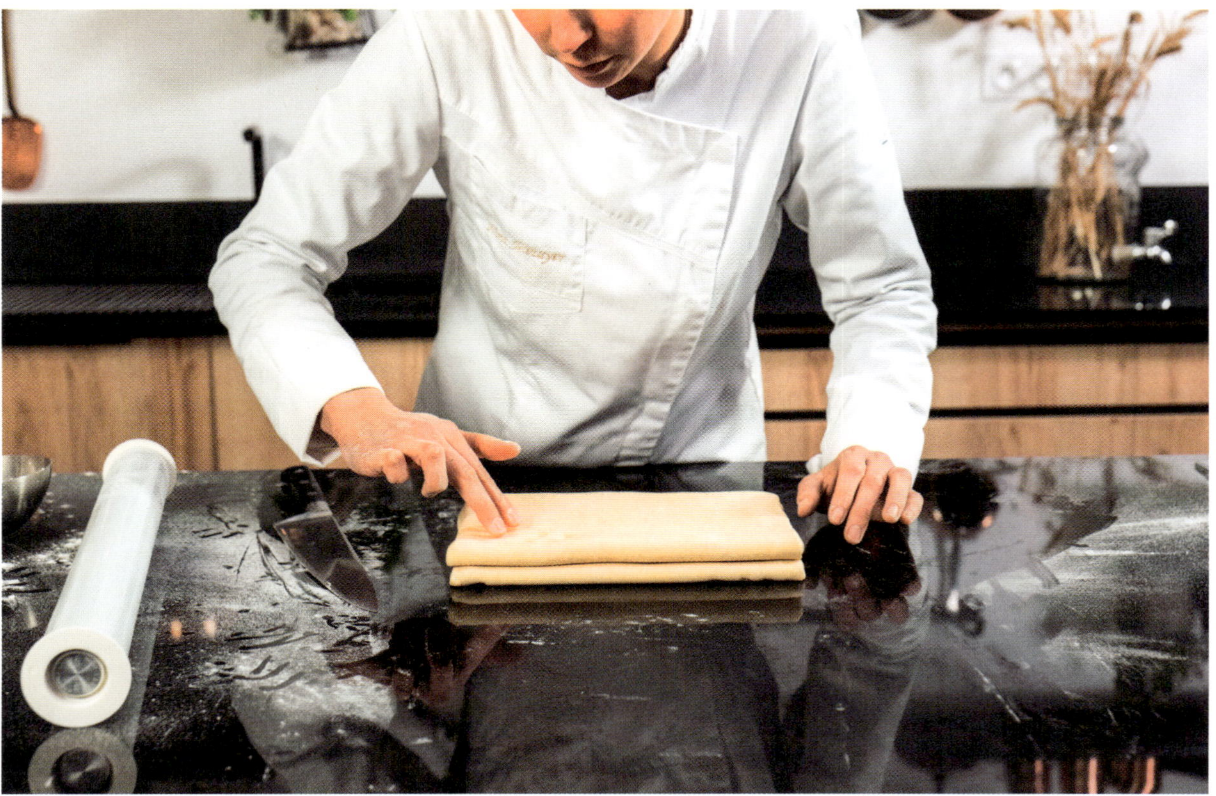

11.

To keep track, you can mark the number of turns made as you go by indenting the pastry with your fingers.

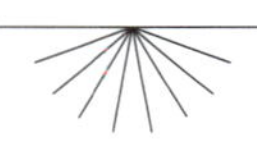

Pastry cream

280 g full-fat milk
140 g whipping cream
1 vanilla pod
70 g light brown soft sugar
35 g cornflour
10 g T55 (plain) flour
2 eggs
15 g unsalted butter

Put the milk and cream into a large saucepan and add the split vanilla pod and scraped out seeds (1). Heat the mixture to 50°C. Once it begins to steam, cover the saucepan with cling film and allow the vanilla to steep for at least 20 minutes.

Line a deep metal tray with cling film and place it in the freezer.

In a large bowl, mix the sugar, cornflour and flour, then add the eggs and mix briskly (2). Cut the butter into small pieces.

Bring the vanilla-infused mixture to the boil over a high heat and add it to the egg mixture. Whisk the mixture well and return it to the saucepan. Cook the pastry cream over a medium heat, stirring constantly. Then bring it to the boil for about 30 seconds (3).

Remove it from the heat and mix in the butter until smooth (4–5).

Remove the tray from the freezer and fill it with the pastry cream (6). Cover the pastry cream with cling film and allow it to cool quickly in the fridge.

Before use, remove the vanilla pod from the pastry cream, transfer it to a large bowl and loosen with a whisk.

You can't freeze pastry cream, but you can keep it in the fridge for up to 3 days after the day it was made.

'You can flavour your pastry cream in countless ways: citrus zest, spices, orange blossom, pistachio paste, etc. If you have a little left over, use any pastry trimmings and fruit to make tartlets to have with coffee.'

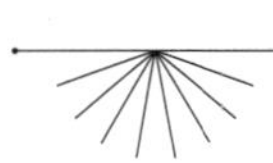

1.

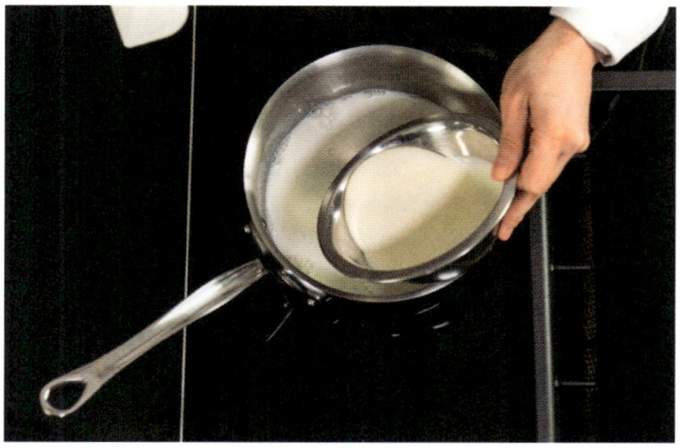

2.

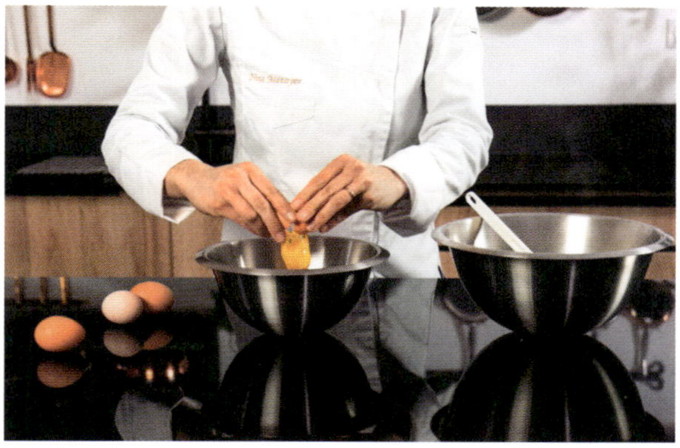

3.

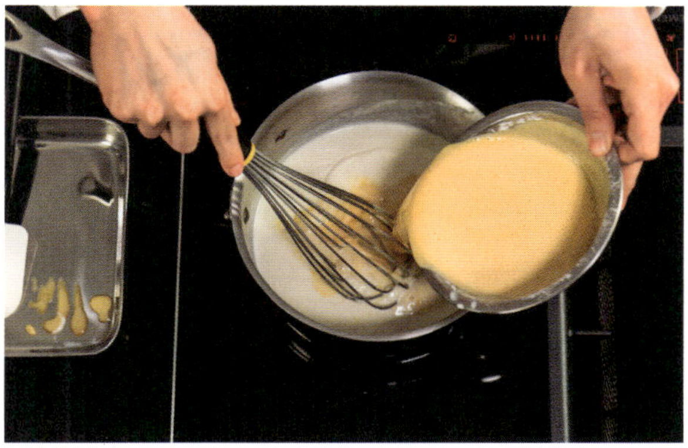

4.

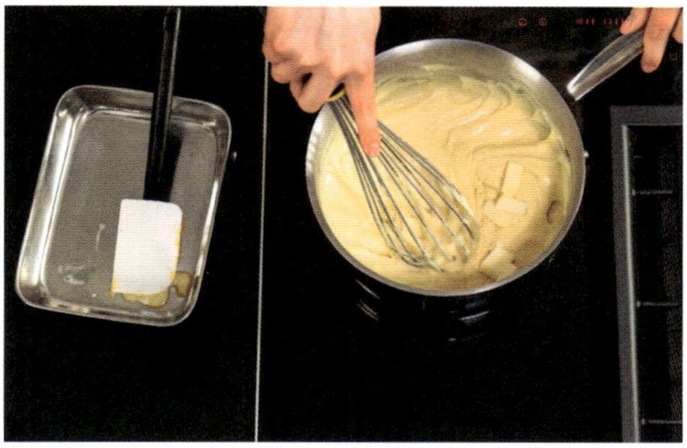

5.

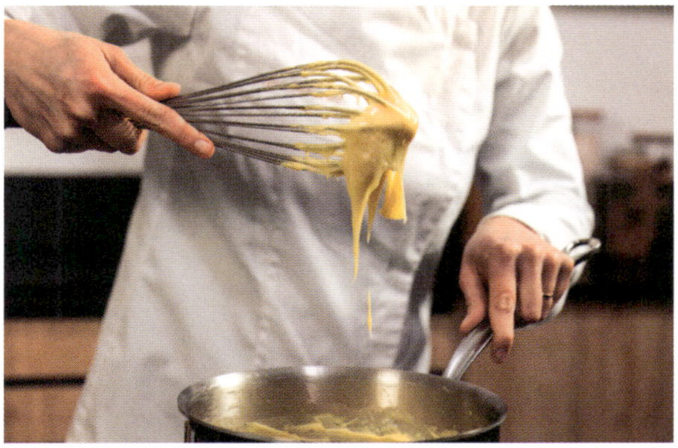

6.

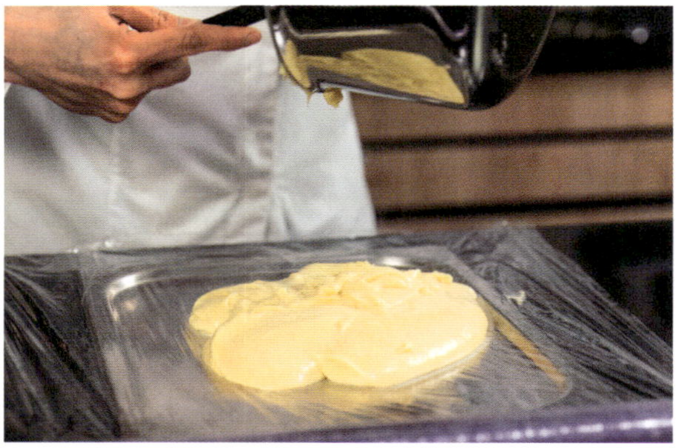

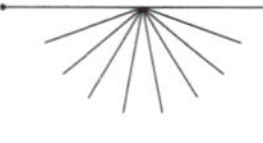

Praline

250 g hazelnuts
124 g caster sugar
40 g water
70 g grape seed oil
4 g fleur de sel
100 g cocoa nibs

Roast the hazelnuts in the oven at 140°C for 40 minutes. In a saucepan over a low heat, cook the sugar and water to a caramel (1) and transfer to a baking mat (2).

Blend the hazelnuts, cooled caramel (3) and oil (4) to a liquid consistency. Add the fleur de sel and cocoa nibs, blend for a further 30 seconds (5) and transfer to a container (6).

You can make praline with any nut or nuts of your choice.

You can replace the hazelnuts and cocoa nibs in this recipe with roasted peanuts or almonds.

With certain nuts, I like to use hazelnuts or almonds as a base to give the praline a smoother texture and, for instance, to tone down the bitterness of walnuts.

You can also experiment with oils; I like to use olive oil for certain pralines, like almond and pine nut praline.

You can also play with the texture of your praline by adding more or less oil. The more oil you add, the runnier the praline will become.

The more you blend the nuts, the runnier and smoother your praline will also be.

I recommend making praline in large quantities (depending on the size of your blender) as it will keep for a long time in the fridge.

'I love to eat praline on toast with salted butter on Sunday mornings. I replace my usual chocolate and hazelnut spread with homemade praline, which has a much crunchier texture.'

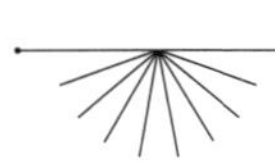

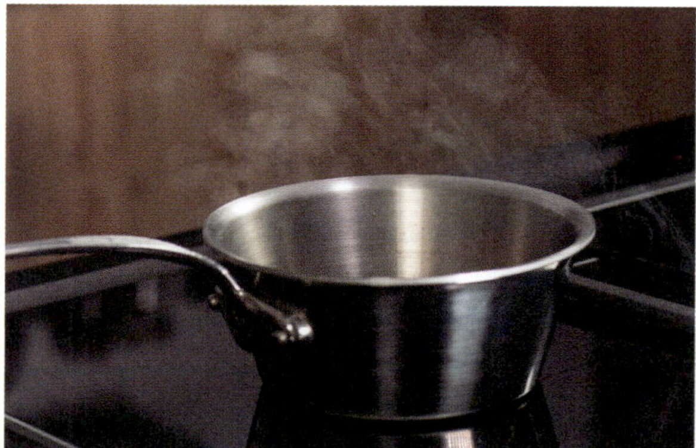

1.

In a saucepan, cook the sugar and water to a caramel over a low heat.

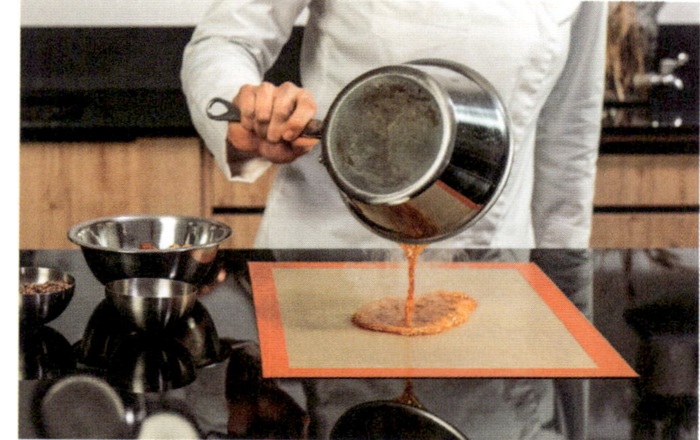

2.

Transfer the caramel to a baking mat.

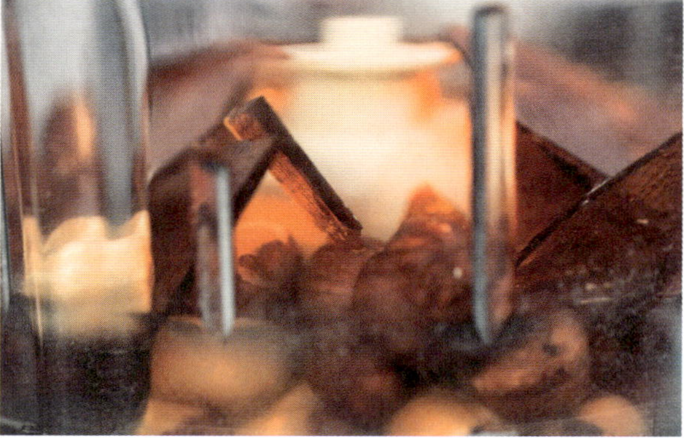

3.

Blend the roasted hazelnuts, the cooled caramel...

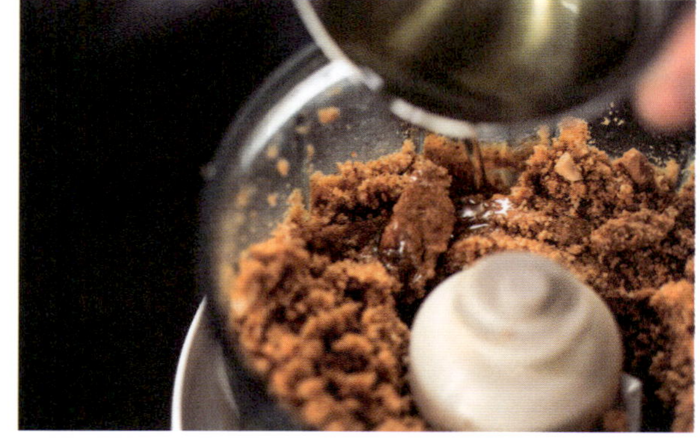

4.

...and the oil.

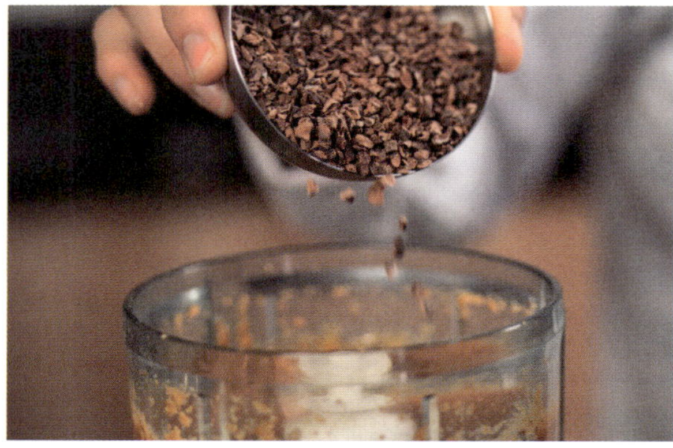

5.

Once the consistency is liquid, add the fleur de sel and cocoa nibs and blend for a further 30 seconds.

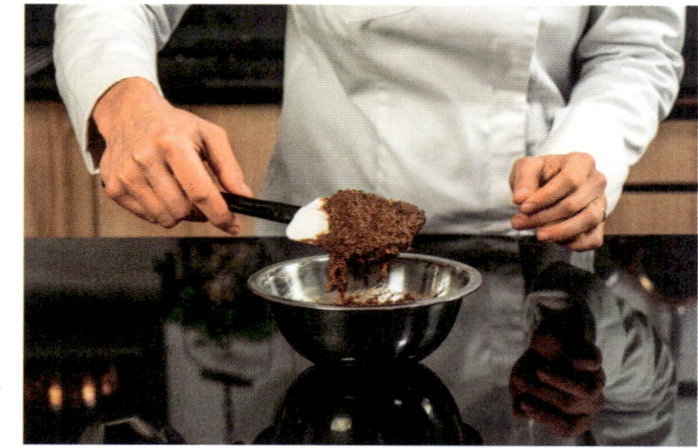

6.

Transfer to a container.

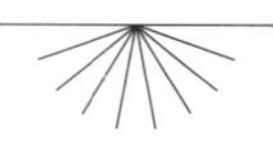

Chocolate: tempering and decorations

TEMPERING

Tempering is an important stage in preparing chocolate for use. It stabilises the cocoa butter in the chocolate to give it a glossy appearance and a good snap, as well as allowing it to be stored for longer.

The chocolate must be melted to completely destroy the cocoa butter crystals (decrystallisation).

Dark chocolate: 50–55°C

Milk chocolate: 45–50°C

White chocolate: 45°C

It then needs to be cooled to a specific temperature to allow the cocoa butter to recrystallise.

Dark chocolate: 28–29°C

Milk chocolate: 27–28°C

White chocolate: 26–27°C

The tempered chocolate then needs to be heated slightly to make it slightly fluid and easier to work with.

Dark chocolate: 31–32°C

Milk chocolate: 29–30°C

White chocolate: 28–29°C

TEMPERING CHOCOLATE INVOLVES TWO TECHNIQUES:

1. Bain-marie

Place a saucepan filled with a little water over the heat, then melt the chocolate in a heatproof bowl set over the simmering water. Stir the chocolate as it melts and check its temperature with a thermometer.

Once the chocolate is at the correct temperature, place the bowl of melted chocolate in a large bowl filled with very cold water with ice cubes for a few seconds. Then take it out immediately, place it on a cloth next to the ice bath and stir well. Repeat this cooling process as many times as necessary until the desired temperature is reached. Reheat the water in the saucepan to allow the chocolate to be brought up to its working temperature in the bain-marie.

2. Tabling

Heat the chocolate in a bain-marie until it reaches the required decrystallisation temperature (1).

If you have a marble slab or work surface, you can table the chocolate directly on it (2), otherwise I advise you to line your work surface with cling film. Pour three quarters of your chocolate onto the lined work surface.

Using a palette knife and a chocolate scraper (3), spread and scrape the chocolate until the desired temperature is reached (4). Return the chocolate to the bowl and check the temperature. If it is still too high, repeat the process with a smaller amount of chocolate. Then raise the temperature in a bain-marie.

CHOCOLATE DECORATIONS

Before you start to work with chocolate, you should make sure that you have all the necessary equipment ready and that your workstation is clean.

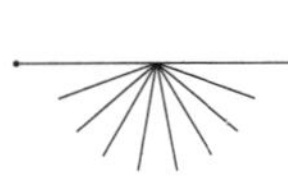

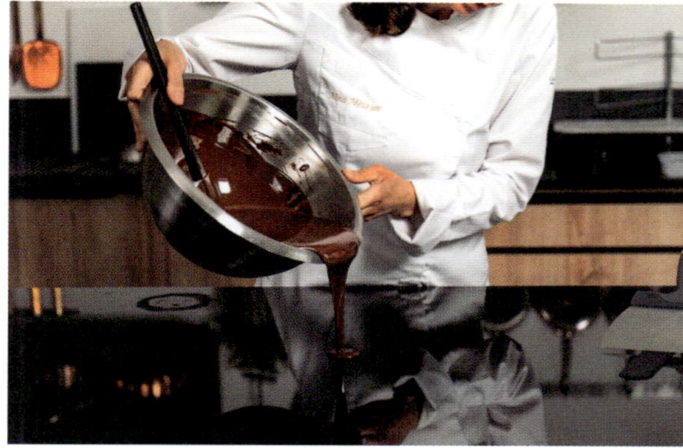

I.

Prepare the chocolate for tabling by melting it in a bain-marie to the required decrystallisation temperature.

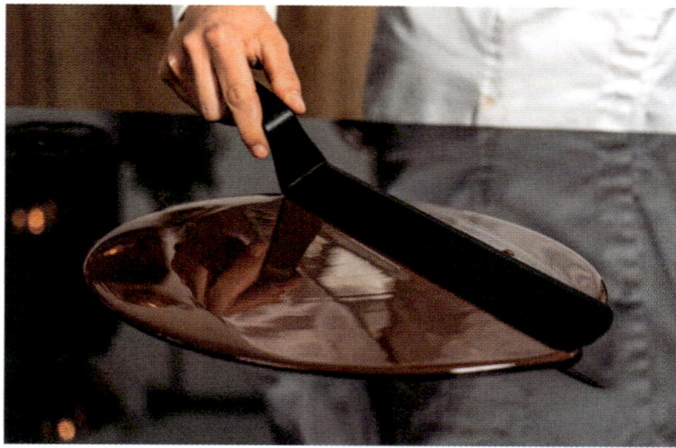

2.

Pour the melted chocolate onto the work surface.

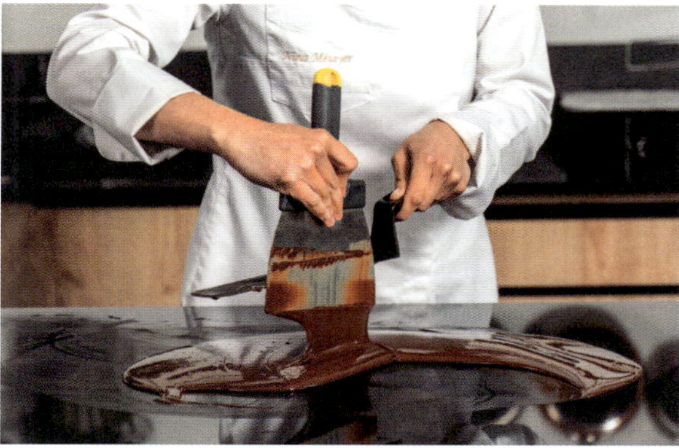

3.

Using a palette knife and chocolate scraper...

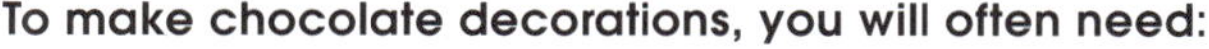

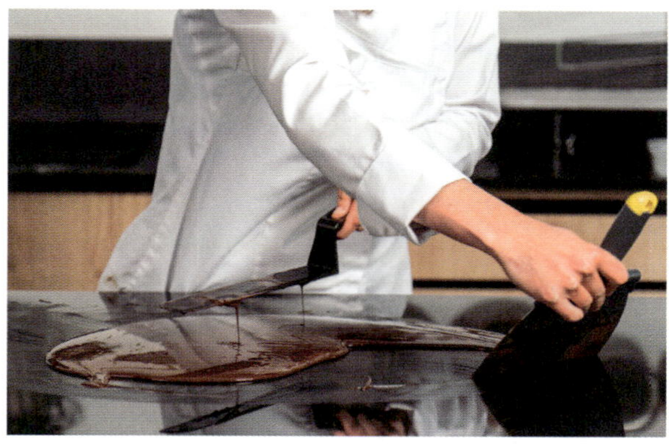

4.

...spread and scrape the chocolate to cool it to the required temperature.

To make chocolate decorations, you will often need:

- Paring knife
- Small angled palette knife
- Chopping board
- Silicone spatula
- Dough scraper
- Silicone or polycarbonate mould
- Rods
- Box cutter
- Pastry brush
- Yule log mould
- Acetate sheets or strips
- Guitar paper
- Baking paper
- Cling film

Temper the chocolate for immediate use.

Take note of the temperature of your workspace.

If it's cold, work quickly and make sure the tempered chocolate in the bowl doesn't harden.

You can use a hairdryer to regularly warm the sides of the bowl.

If the weather is hot and the chocolate takes a long time to harden, speed up the process by placing the decoration in the fridge.

I recommend making lots of decorations at the same time; you can store them for a long time in an airtight container in the fridge for future desserts.

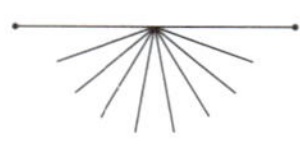

Passion fruit paper

1½ gelatine leaves
125 g water
63 g mango purée
125 g passion fruit purée
25 g caster sugar
1.5 g pectin NH325

The day before, soak the gelatine in iced water for 10 minutes, then squeeze to drain.

Put the water, mango purée and passion fruit purée into a saucepan and place over the heat. Mix the caster sugar with the pectin, add this mixture to the fruit purées and bring to the boil for 1 minute. Dissolve the gelatine in the mixture. Refrigerate for 6 hours.

On the day, preheat the oven to 250°C with non-stick trays inside, then transfer the mixture to the very hot trays (1–2). Bake for 3 hours at 85°C with the oven in fan mode, then cut out 5–6-cm-diameter discs (3), detach them from the tray and crumple them up (4). Store them in an airtight container with a moisture absorber.

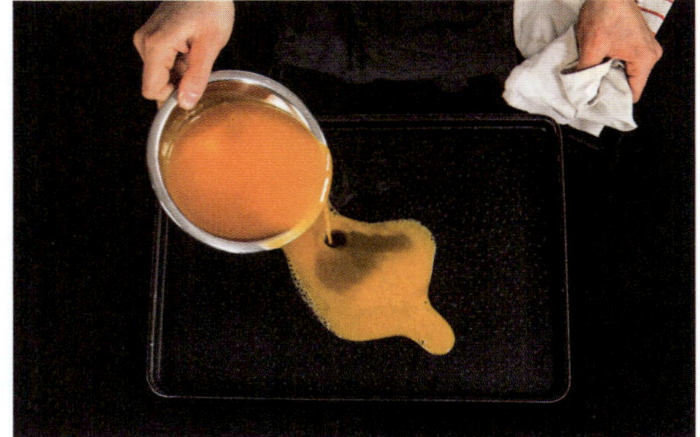

1.

2.

'You can also replace the mango and passion fruit purée with a red berry purée. In summer, I freeze any overripe fruit I have and purée it till it's very smooth so I can make decorations.'

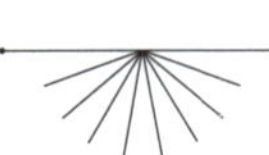

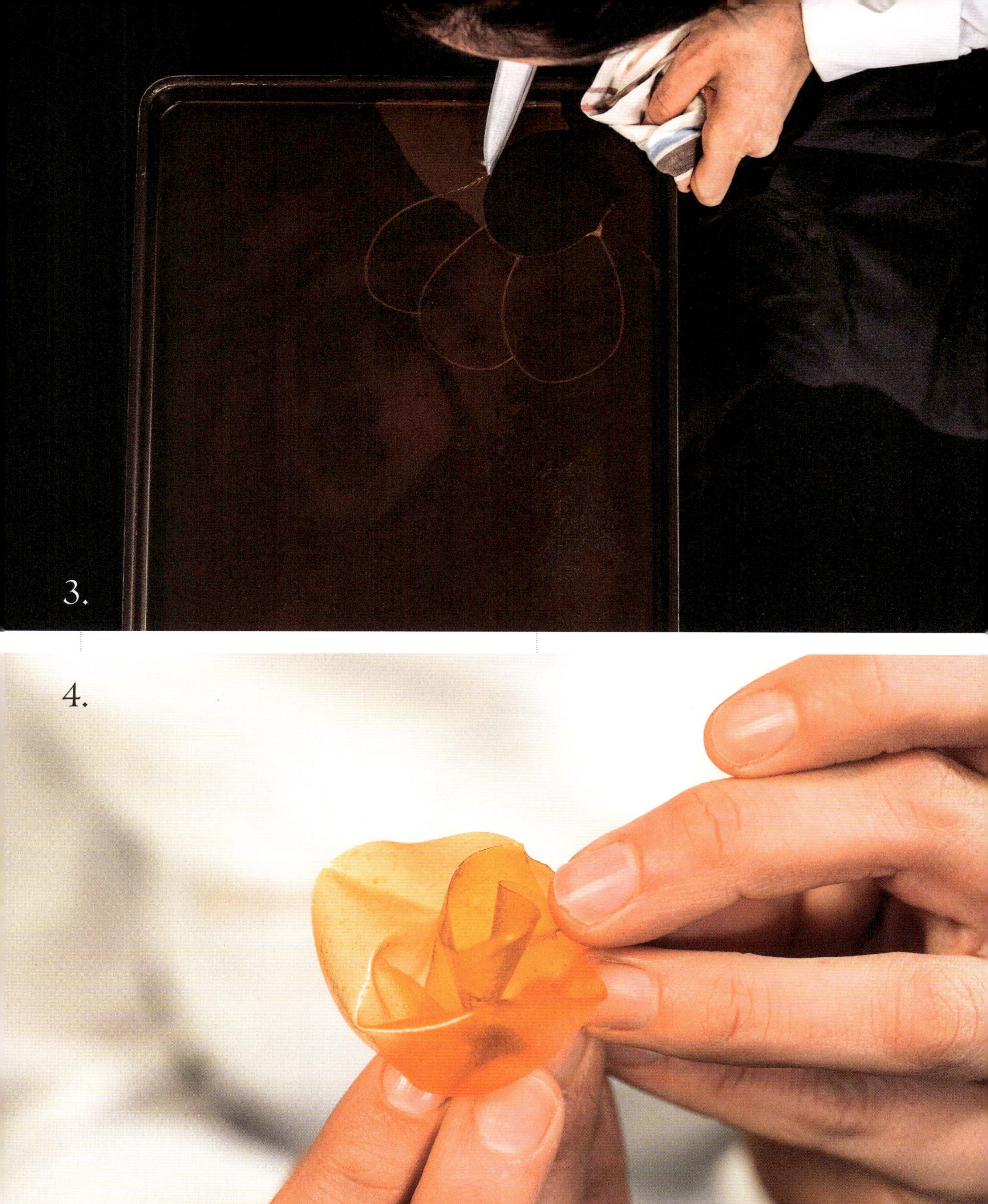
3.
4.

Silicone mould

100 g food-grade silicone
10 g silicone catalyst

You can very easily make moulds out of food-grade silicone at home and create your own shapes for cakes and decorations.

You can find food-grade silicone in baking supplies shops, craft supplies shops and on the Internet.

You can make your mould template from all sorts of materials; I like to sculpt in chocolate (1–2) and plaster. You can also sculpt or mould wax, or simply use an everyday object.

I advise you to securely fasten the object to be moulded using double-sided tape or to glue it on a base or at the bottom of a suitably sized box.

If using a box, make sure it's well suited to the size of the object so that you don't use too much silicone. Ideally, the silicone should only be 3 mm thick. You can also make your own cardboard box, but make sure all the folds and corners are taped over. Silicone is liquid before the catalyst is added to set it, so watch out for leaks.

Grease or oil the object for moulding (3).

Before working with silicone, protect your work surface with a baking mat or cling film. Use a spoon to mix the silicone and catalyst at room temperature in a container, then pour the silicone over the object to cover it. Allow it to set for at least 8 hours at room temperature (4). You can speed up the setting process by gently heating the silicone with a hairdryer.

After 8 hours, carefully remove the silicone mould from the object and wash it. You can use it straight away (5).

Depending on the shape of the piece for which the mould is to be used, you may need to make a cut into the mould to enable it to be removed. Use a box cutter for this purpose. By carefully making a cut into one of the sides, you will be able to open and close the mould whenever you need to use it for a particular dessert.

Your food-grade silicone mould can be used for both freezing and baking.

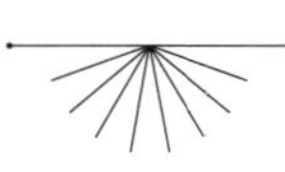

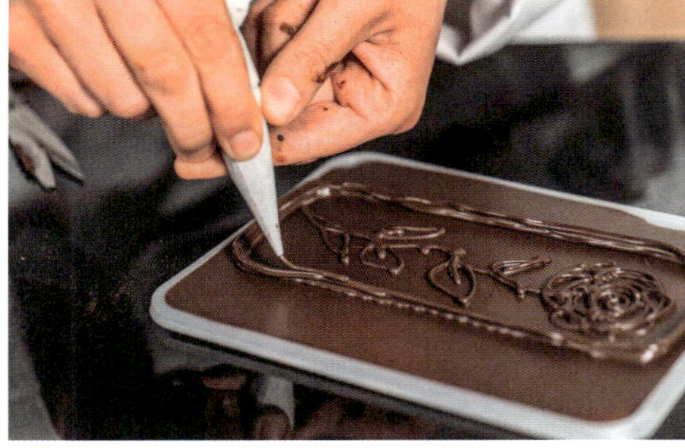

1.

You can make your mould template from all sorts of materials, such as chocolate in this case. Make the design for your template in chocolate, and give it a border that will serve as the edge of your mould.

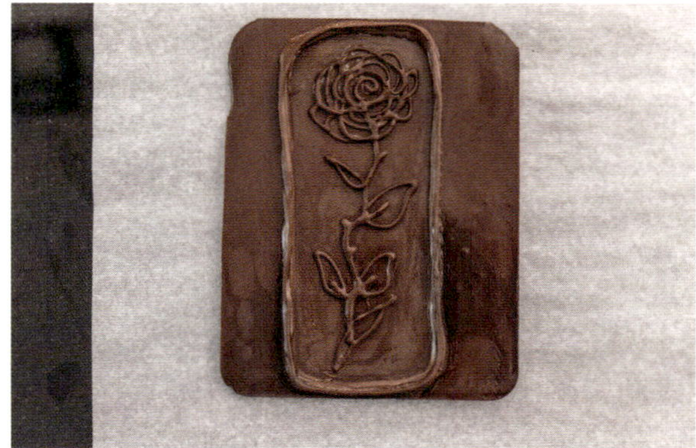

2.

The finished template.

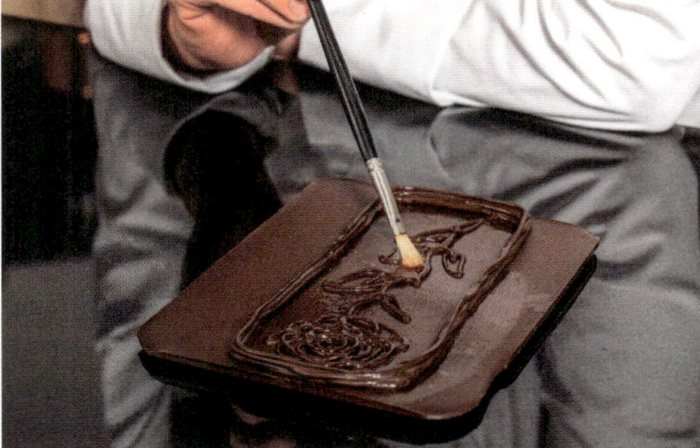

3.

Grease the template.

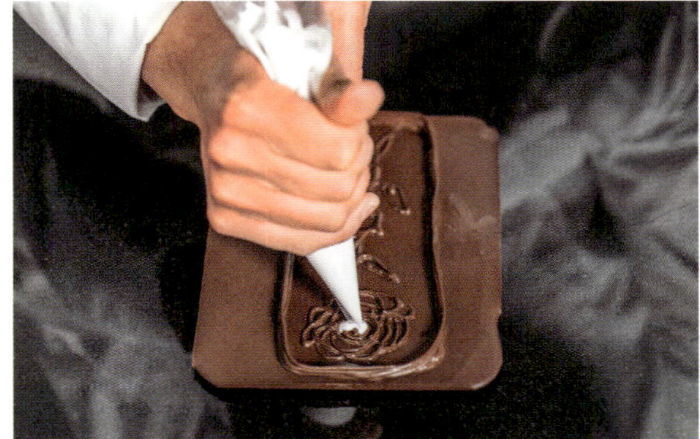

4.

Mix the silicone and catalyst at room temperature and apply the silicone to the template to completely cover the shape. Allow the silicone to set for at least 8 hours at room temperature, then carefully remove the mould from the template.

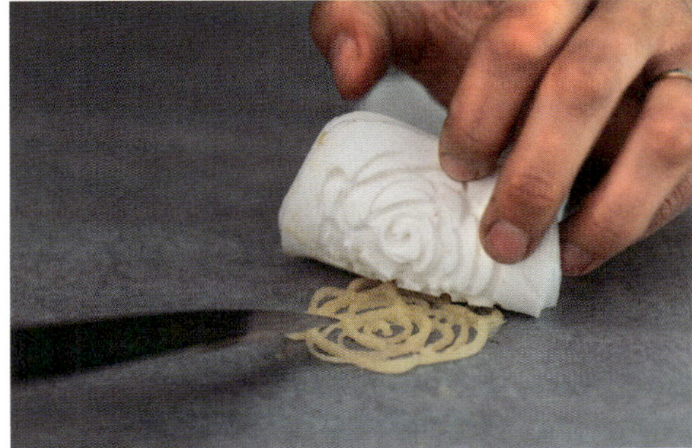

5.

Wash the mould to make it ready for use, in this case for use with pâte à cigarette.

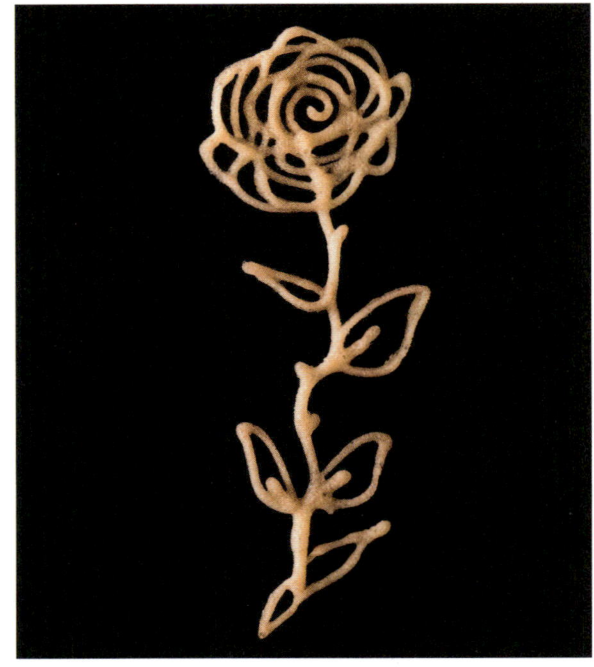

6.

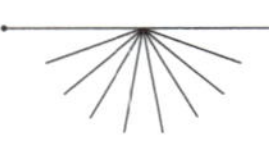

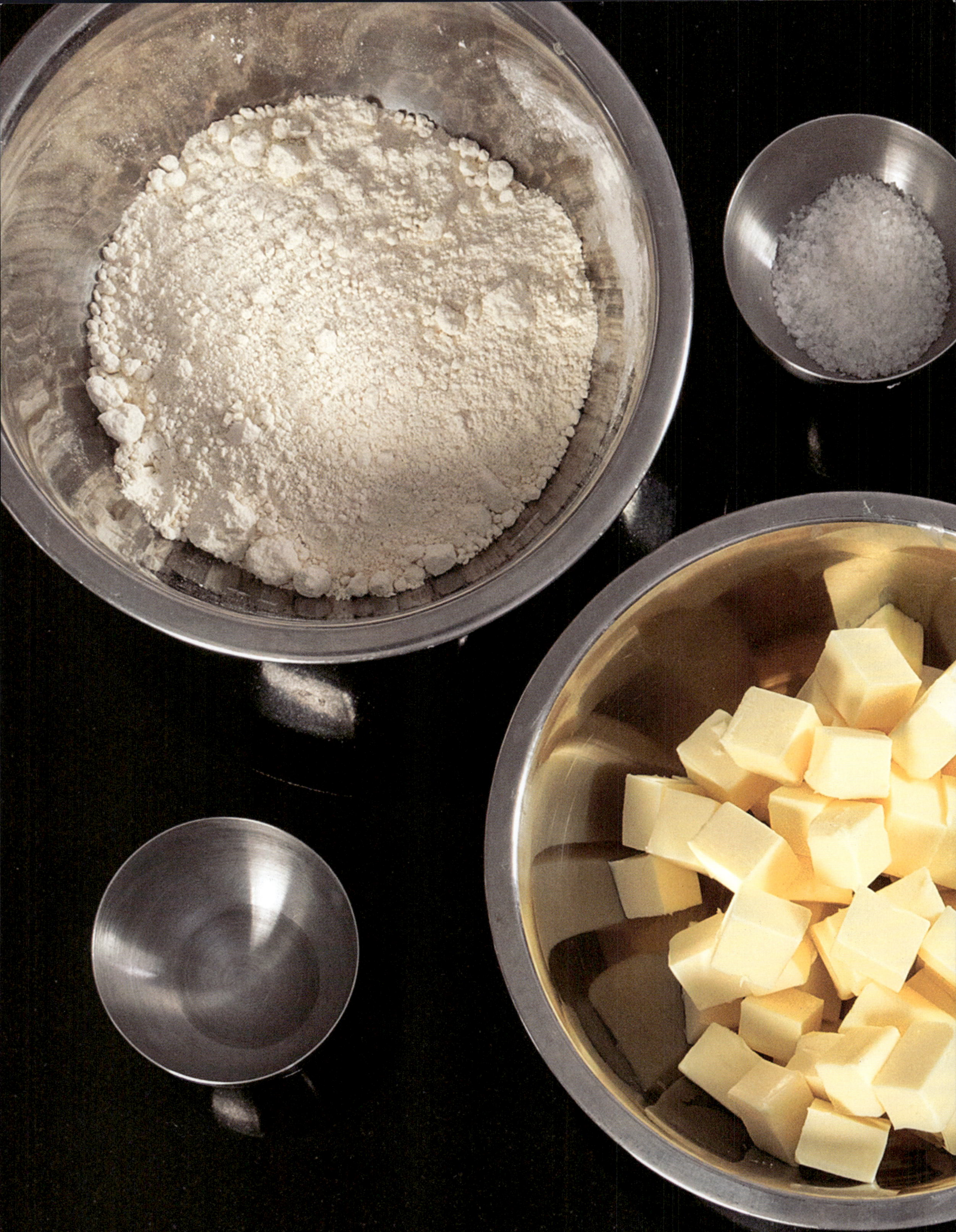

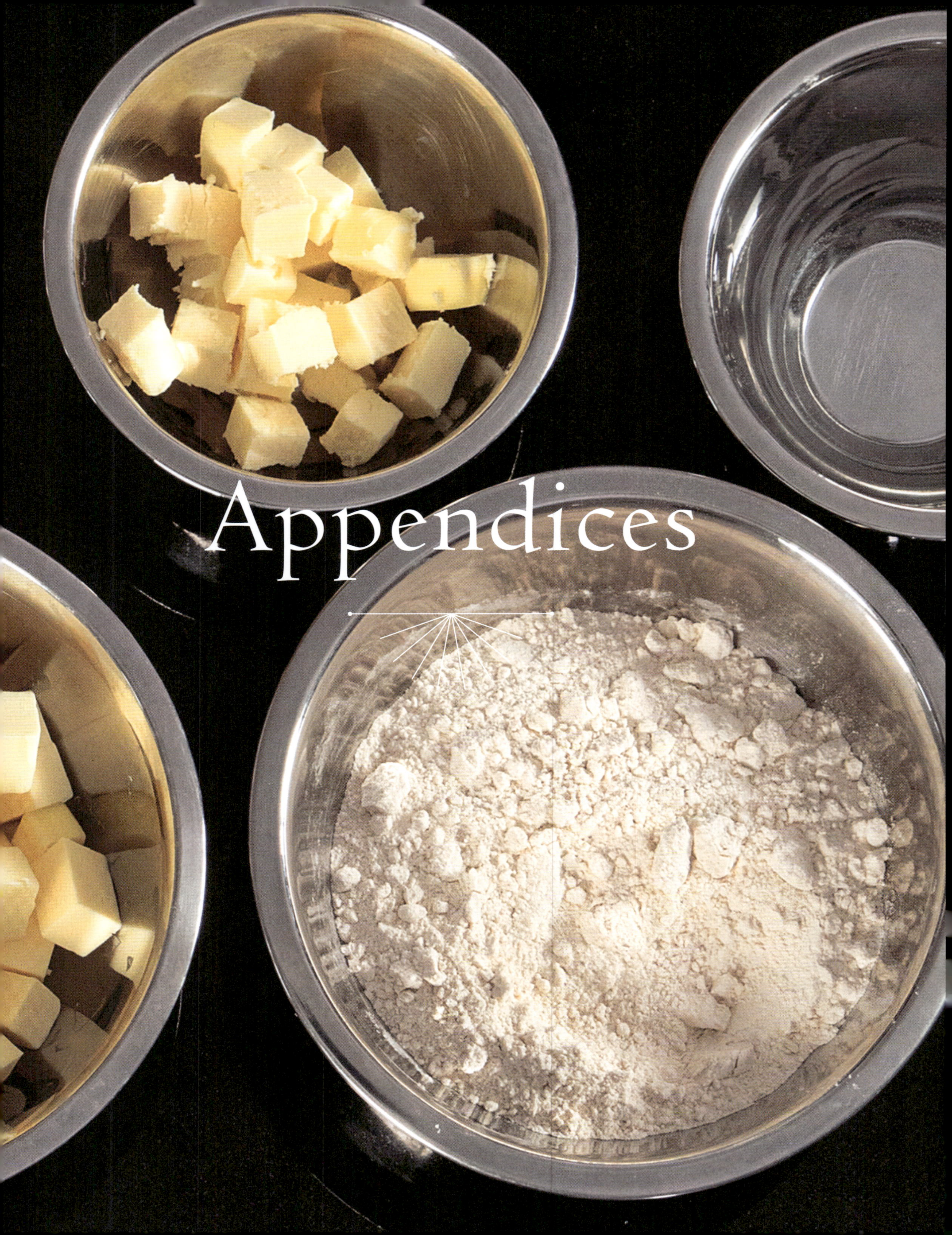
Appendices

Recipe index

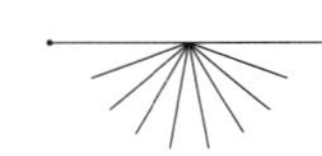

Recipe index (aphabetical)

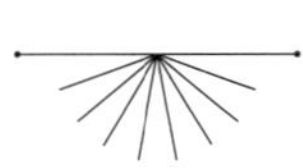

Acknowledgements

I have so much to say! Much more than just a book, these pages as I see them are a snapshot of my life, of wonderful years at the service of fine food. It's a story of sharing, of love, of effort. A shared memory of encounters, of men and women without whom nothing would have been possible. Therefore, it is with heartfelt emotion that I acknowledge them and their contributions.

Thank you Mathieu, my love, my friend, my partner, my colleague, my photographer, my videographer and my soulmate! Thank you for pushing me further every day and for supporting me through the difficult times. Thank you for nourishing our lives with passion and new projects every day, so that tomorrow will be even more beautiful than yesterday. I love you; I'm so proud of you; bravo for this book!

To my parents, my supporters from the very first day until the completion of this book, thank you for allowing me to fulfil myself, for being there every day, and for your passion, generosity and commitment to our happiness. I'm very lucky to have you, mum and dad, and to have inherited your affection, your watchful eye and your taste for the good things in life!

To my incredible team! My thanks to Océane, Chloé, Paul, Célestin and Géromine, and to your delicate hands and smiling hearts, for this shared journey that has brought us to where we are today. Thank you for being yourselves. Thank you for your high standards, your willingness, your unfailing commitment, and for all the positive energy you put into your daily drive for excellence.

To my children, Anastasia and Adèle, my rays of light who accompany me in my passion. To the grown-ups you will become and who will one day understand these lines, thank you for being such sweet little girls and for your zest for life. You give me strength.

To darling nana Laurence, who shows them so much love every day. Thank you for your presence and the attention you gave your granddaughters throughout the writing of this book.

Thanks to Pandora and Paloma, my brilliant, talented and generous sisters who never lose touch, even at the other side of the world.

Thanks to everyone who has accompanied us on the journeys that are our projects and our lives. To Camille, Thibault (Cabinet Soyer & Soyer), Stéphane, Ari, Louise, Luca and Konstantin, for embarking on the Délicatisserie adventure, whether for a few days or a few months. Thanks to our families and friends, and to our partners Bernard, Laurien, Jocelyne, Lucien; there is a part of each and every one of you in this book. Thanks to all of you for demonstrating your love in so many ways, for holding my daughters in your arms between takes, for being there in both hard times and good, and for being in our lives.

Thank you to my publisher La Martinière; to Agathe and Laure for your proofreading and advice; to Sarah for your food styling and your good taste; to Laurence for the beautiful layout; thank you all for contributing so much to this book.

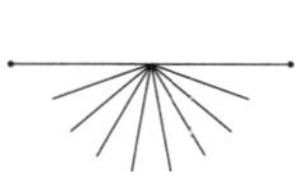

Thank you to my bosses and chefs, to my mentors, to everyone who has passed on their knowledge to me and who have enabled me to grow with kindness; I owe the happiness that I've found in my craft to you. In the order in which you appeared in my story, I thank Denis Baron, Yannick Alléno, Camille Lesecq, Amandine Chaignot, Jean-François Piège and Philippe Urraca.

Thank you to my partners, to the men and women who lead the different companies. Your materials, equipment, supplies, products, utensils and decorative elements enabled me to give this book the high standard I had intended it to have.

Thanks go to Lafont for their French know-how in workwear, for the pretty linen jackets that I wear every day and throughout the pages of the book.

I thank Charentes-Poitou PDO butter from my region, which has the taste of the love of goodness and elevates my baking, as well as my puff pastries.

My thanks to Moulins Virons for their excellent French flours, and for still reaching out to me even in the midst of lockdown.

Thanks to Siemens, one of the very first supporters of this project, for their precision ovens, induction hob with integrated ventilation system and all the kitchen appliances that aren't always shown in the photos.

I thank Matfer, leading French manufacturer of innovative and precise pastry-making equipment at the service of artisan bakers, and the wonderful people who run it.

Thanks go to Mauviel, whose cookware that you can see throughout these pages is as beautiful as it is precision-made.

My thanks to Schmidt Paris 15 for fitting out my beautiful, functional kitchen, which is as pleasing to look at as it is to use.

Thanks to Ferme des Peltier, supplier of quality produce from Normandy.

My thanks to Délice & Création, who are committed to sourcing French food products.

Thanks to all my suppliers, artisans, farmers and producers in general who are committed to the quality food, flavour and respect for people and nature.

Thanks to Alexandra, Christophe, Laurent, Clarisse, Françoise, Joseph, Cédric, Alexandra, Alexandre, Guillaume, Cyril, Blandine, Cerise, Marine, Valérie, Jason, Émilie, Patricia, Manon…

My thanks go to the institutions, associations, professional groups and all the professionals who support these wonderful initiatives for helping me progress and for doing so much good work.

My thanks also go to anyone I haven't mentioned; you know who you are. It's so difficult to remember at times, and I'm so afraid that I'll forget! Please know that I'm thinking of you and that you have my gratitude, thank you very much.

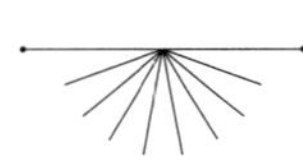

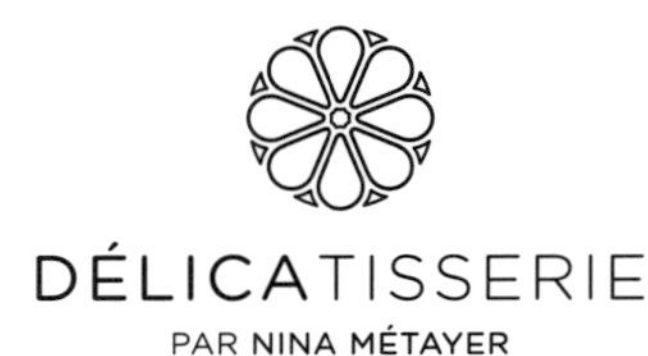

See you soon!

Now that this chapter is closed, we can start others together. I hope to have the pleasure of meeting you at a trade fair, an event or a food festival, or perhaps one day, when you enjoy cakes from Délicatisserie. This is the continuation of my pastry-making adventure, a place where I can show you my world and offer you my new creations that change with the seasons.

It's easy to contact me:

ninametayer.com, delicatisserie.com, YouTube, Instagram, Facebook, LinkedIn, TikTok.

I want you to know that I see and read all your communications, and that it's always a great pleasure for me to receive your feedback, photos and messages.
I often reserve my answers for face-to-face meetings, but each of your words brightens up the day for me and my teams, so keep them coming.

Thank you very much for reading this book. And long live traditional skills!

Best wishes,

Nina

———

Published in 2026 by Grub Street
4 Rainham Close
London
SW11 6SS

Email: food@grubstreet.co.uk
Web: www.grubstreet.co.uk
X: @grub_street
Facebook: Grub Street Publishing
Instagram: @grubstreet_books

ISBN 978-1-911714-44-6

A CIP catalogue for this book is available from the British Library.
Published originally in French as *La Délicate Pâtisserie* Nina Metayer
Copyright © 2021 Éditions de La Martinière
Editorial Director: Laure Aline
Editor: Agathe Masson

Printed and bound by Finidr, Czechia.